INFORMATION SYSTEMS AND GLOBAL DIVERSITY

Information Systems and Global Diversity

CHRISANTHI AVGEROU

OXFORD
UNIVERSITY PRESS

OXFORD
UNIVERSITY PRESS

Great Clarendon Street, Oxford OX2 6DP

Oxford University Press is a department of the University of Oxford.
It furthers the University's objective of excellence in research, scholarship,
and education by publishing worldwide in

Oxford New York

Auckland Bangkok Buenos Aires Cape Town Chennai
Dar es Salaam Delhi Hong Kong Istanbul Karachi Kolkata
Kuala Lumpur Madrid Melbourne Mexico City Mumbai Nairobi
São Paulo Shanghai Singapore Taipei Tokyo Toronto

with an associated company in Berlin

Published in the United States
by Oxford University Press Inc., New York

British Library Cataloguing in Publication Data
Data available

Library of Congress Cataloging in Publication Data

Avgerou, Chrisanthi.
Information systems and Global Diversity / Chrisanthi Avgerou.
p. cm.
Includes bibliographical references.
1. Information technology—Social aspects—Cross-cultural studies.
2. Organizational change—Cross-cultural studies.   I. Title.
HM851 A93 2001   303.48′33—dc21   2001046493

ISBN 0–19–924077–9

1 3 5 7 9 10 8 6 4 2

Typeset by Newgen Imaging Systems (P) Ltd., Chennai, India
Printed in Great Britain
on acid-free paper by
Biddles Ltd., *www.biddles.co.uk*

To the memory of my mother
Angeliki Economou-Avgerou

Enthusiastically modern, she taught me
how modernity can take human proportions with
large doses of affection and common sense

Preface

This is one of those books that has been written over a long period of time. My curiosity for its core subject, the way the exploitation of the potential of information technologies takes different courses in different social contexts, was triggered in the mid-1980s while I was studying the practices of systems development in social security organizations in four European countries. At that time I was impressed with the differences manifested in the computerization efforts pursued in similar organizations of different countries. Although all four organizations were engaged in developing very similar applications through quite similar professional systems development practices, the motives and background against which the development processes were deployed, and the consequences of innovation projects in their socio-organizational context differed substantially.

Since then I have had the opportunity to hear numerous stories demonstrating the 'way the IS development is shaped by local social factors' from students participating in the graduate seminars on 'IT in Developing Countries' at the London School of Economics. Invariably those seminars involved over a dozen nationalities, and many students had considerable professional experience from a cross section of industries and public sector institutions. It is not, therefore, surprising that discussions on IT innovation exposed variation. What is surprising is how little supporting theory the seminar discussions could find in the information systems literature to make sense of the variation revealed in the stories of the students' experience. In fact, I noticed that the information systems literature had an insidious influence on the seminars' discourse. Like a deforming lens, it made students see the images they were familiar with in a particular shape, to express roles and titles in particular terms, and to judge them by particular 'success' criteria. The variety of actors and interests they were familiar with—big and small business proprietors, administrators, government appointees or politicians, workers or civil servants—were all transformed to managers in pursuance of competitive advantage. No wonder few 'successful' outcomes could be seen in such caricatures.

In addition to the students of my seminars, many other people helped me to shape and refine the ideas I discuss in this book. First, I am indebted to those who made the case studies that form the empirical backbone of the book possible, both by providing valuable information themselves and by opening access to the data resources of the organizations I studied: Horacio Guevara, Gustavo Mohar Betancourt, Carlos Hentschel, José Alfredo Pérez Aguilar, Aris Sissouras, Nikos Varelidis, G. Hiotis, Paul Matsiras, I. de Zegher, Olymbia Stylianou, Alexandros Michaelides. Also I feel indebted to the many people who contributed to the tracing of the history of events that constitute these case studies and the understanding of their context by formal interviews, informal discussions, demonstrations, group brainstorming, or by providing me with relevant documentation. I cannot name them all here, but I owe them sincere thanks for the time they gave me, invariably out of very busy work schedules, and for sharing with me their personal interpretations of the ICT innovation of their experience.

I am particularly grateful to the fellow researchers who helped me to make sense of and interpret the case studies data. Natalia Volkow, with her passion for the history and culture of her country, Mexico, answered an endless stream of questions about the case of Pemex. Phyvos Chysohos helped me to make sense of the flexible specialization case in Cyprus and challenged me with his belief that that experiment shouldn't be seen as a 'failure', even when all the officials we interviewed were keen to leave it behind and move to a new policy. The researchers in the 'DUR project' of the LSE, Elias Mossialos, Paul Matsiras, Nancy Pouloudi, Rogerio Barbosa, Tony Cornford, Angeliki Poulymenakou, and Shakir Merali helped me enter a totally new and particularly challenging area of ICT innovation.

I would like to thank several other people. Four years ago Alexandros Kyrtsis read the draft of the first thirty pages and suggested, subtly, that I should start again and try to do better. I have not had the chance to benefit from his advice since, but his influence at the beginning of my journey of the writing of this book had a long-lasting effect. I am grateful to my colleagues at the LSE Frank Land, Tony Cornford, Shirin Madon, Edgar Whitley, Susan Scott, and Mike Cushman who read draft chapters and provided valuable critical comments. Also I wish to thank David Musson and Sarah Dobson at Oxford University Press for their support and guidance, and Lynn Childress for the much needed editorial improvements of my typescript.

Finally, a great thank you to my daughter Margarita, who so easily learnt to live with a mother who could disappear to her books and computer at any time of any day or night. I understood at some point that she had no sense of the institution of 'working hours'; she was surprised to realize that there are people who work for specific periods of the day, and specific days of the week. But, this may not have been the wrong example for a woman-to-be in the information age. I just hope that she will also maintain the wonderful cheerfulness and resoursefulness for 'fun' that made all the difference at those very frequent occasions that my writing was slow and poor.

C.A.

Contents

Introduction

That information and communication technologies are deeply implicated in changes occurring in all kinds of human organizations is one of the least controversial statements. Either through well considered, deliberate, and planned actions or through improvisations, and incremental, often ad hoc, 'emergent' action, the implementation of technology-based information systems is understood to be associated with changes in work processes, the structure, and often the mission of organizations. The change that results from a single information systems project may be negligible, but overall there seems to be little doubt that information and communication technologies (ICT) are associated with profound change in the way material products are designed and constructed, services are delivered, wealth is created, and social relations are formed.

A prominent research stream in information systems and management has elaborated the dynamic alignment of ICT innovation and organizational reform. Several competing theoretical propositions have been made as to how organizational and technological characteristics match each other and through what processes technology innovation and organization reshaping takes place (Huber 1990; Scott Morton 1991; Ciborra and Lanzara 1994; Orlikowski et al. 1996). There have also been many suggestions as to what kind of new technology/organizational forms are fit for contemporary economic conditions (Drucker 1988; Applegate 1994; Ciborra 1996; Lucas 1996; Dutton 1999). Despite some concern that on certain occasions ICT-mediated ways of organizational functioning are rejected (DeSanctis and Fulk 1999), this vibrant stream of research contributes a powerful message that with ICT organizations are being reshaped to form a new socio-economic context.

Yet, on closer examination these confident views of ICT and organizational change are based on a limited selection of organizations found in contemporary societies and hide many uncertainties.[1] Research on information systems innovation has studied only a narrow range of organizations, and an even narrower range of aspects of change. By far the largest research effort has been dedicated to professionally managed business organizations in a free market context. If we take a global perspective and if we include organizations other than professionally managed competitive business companies, the overall picture, blurred and fragmented for lack of systematic research, seems to be quite different. Without considering the diversity of organizations, many of the current theoretical generalizations about ICT innovation and organizational change are misleading.

Although ICT has been heralded for its capacity to open new socio-economic prospects for all and worldwide efforts have been made to introduce it in all societies

---

[1] See e.g. the anxiety expressed in the literature on information systems failures (Sauer 1999).

and all types of organizations,[2] the positive dynamics of ICT innovation and organizational change are found in only a few parts of the world (Palvia and Palvia 1996). In stark contrast to the literature mentioned above, the accounts on ICT innovation in developing countries suggest slow and tortuous processes with ambiguous outcomes (Odedra-Straub 1996; Avgerou and Walsham 2000; Sahay 2000), and there is almost no information about ICT in the sweeping organizational reform taking place in the so-called economies of transition of Eastern Europe.

Moreover, understanding of the way ICT is implicated in the reform of sectors other than the professionally managed competitive organizations, sectors such as the public sector and small family-owned enterprises, whether in industrialized or developing countries, is partial and much more limited. In the shadow of the rhetoric about e-government and the information society, there are indications of chronic difficulties in utilizing computer technology in public sector reform (Heeks 1999; Margetts 1999; Peled 2000) and in the struggle of small firms—on which many economies depend—to face global competition (Lind 2000; Volkow 2000).

In most countries professionally managed business organizations coexist with a variety of other types of organizations, such as family-run enterprises, state-controlled organizations, voluntary organizations, partnerships of business and public service agencies. Throughout the 1980s and 1990s, economic organizations and public service institutions alike were confronted with 'liberalization policies', that is, change from state-governed to market-governed status. Protectionist policies were lifted or weakened and organizations everywhere were faced with the vastness of the world market. For many, this meant a change of fundamental mission, such as from producing to create wealth for the nation, or for the family, to becoming profitable under global competition. It meant also a change of values, such as from adhering to traditional local meanings to becoming 'modern', measuring local performance against international standards. Such changes, rarely acknowledged in the literature of information systems and management studies,[3] are significant for the way the potential of ICT is perceived and exploited in contemporary societies. And while many of the theoretical issues that information systems research has raised through its limited focus on market-driven professionally managed organizations are perhaps of universal validity—such as the analyses of the various ways change is enacted, or the nature of ICT-mediated work—the uneven capacity of organizations in different regions and diverse sectors to exploit ICT is poorly understood.

The research on information systems introduced in the health care sector can, at this point, demonstrate the variety of issues that emerge in settings different from that of the business organization[4] (see e.g. Bloomfield, Cooper, and Rea 1992; Louw 1996;

---

[2] See e.g. the way ICT and socio-economic development is discussed by international development institutions such as the World Bank, the Canadian International Development Agency, and the Commonwealth Secretariat (Labelle 1995; Talero and Gaudette 1995; Valantin 1996; Qureshi 1998).

[3] For an exception, see Mitev's study (1996) of the implementation of a new computer-based reservation system in the French railways in relation to the European transport liberalization policy.

[4] ICTs in the health sector, and to a lesser extent the education sector, have been researched mostly in specialist fields, such as health informatics or computer-assisted learning. Such research only marginally

Bloomfield et al. 1997; Louw 1999; Braa et al. 2000; Dunker 2000; Klecun-Dabrowska and Cornford 2000). Such publications highlight a variety of context-specific dimensions of ICT innovation and organizational change. They examine, for example, how ICT affects issues of judgement and accountability of different professional groups—doctors, nurses, and managers. They are also concerned with the emergence of context-specific organizational forms, captured in concepts such as 'internal market' or 'managed care'. Invariably information systems research in health care organizations is more explicitly associated with the societal context, as for example the political dilemmas in maintaining the national health services of welfare states in Europe and the socio-economic conditions of developing countries striving to put in place modern information health care services.

The aim of this book is to contribute to the opening of the research perspective of information systems and organizational change in order to accommodate meanings and concerns manifested in the diverse organizational contexts into which ICT is entering. The hypothesis on organizational diversity at the outset of this research is based on pragmatic observations in the course of over twenty years of my research and practice in different countries, and has been reinforced by reading of contemporary social theory. The significance of addressing organizational diversity needs to be understood in relation to the contemporary pervasive discourse of globalization. Both of these points—organizational diversity and globalization—require clarification in this introductory note.

ON DIVERSITY

With a pragmatic attitude towards diversity, the starting point of the research presented in this book is simply the acknowledgement of the existence of different organizational settings. No assumption is made about a general pattern of organizational performance and ICT innovation resulting from imperatives such as market, technology, or even ethical objectives, such as employee 'emancipation'. It is just noticed that in almost all societies we find variations of hierarchical Weberian bureaucracies that do not respond well to modern management rationalization interventions. We find small enterprises that show no tendency to grow towards more sizeable and formally managed firms, or to link formally onto industrial networks thought to be capable of competing in modern economies. Also we find complex fields, such as health care and education, where a mix of organizations—small or large, professional and science or craft-based, competitively or politically driven—coexist.

This research is intended to understand organizations and their efforts to appropriate ICT to their own circumstances. The position taken is that organizations not adhering to the models of mainstream organizational theory and unorthodox in

addresses issues of technology implementation and organizational change. Nevertheless, there has been information systems research in hospitals and health care institutions, particularly in countries, as in the UK, in which the health sector has been undergoing transformation intervention intended to introduce a market logic.

terms of management principles may be suitable entities for collective human action within the society that sustains them. But even if there is common agreement that the structure and work processes of an organization are ineffective and unsatisfactory for all concerned—as is the case of many organizations in developing countries—action for change has to make sense in the socio-economic context of that society and organization.[5] Reform and ICT innovation interventions following predetermined principles of organizing behaviour may well be ineffective, frustrating rather than improving the capacity of the organization concerned to enact roles legitimate in their socio-economic context.

A cursory look at the literature provides plenty of evidence supporting this position. Businesses which do not comply with the 'rational' view of efficient organization may be successful economically. Within the context of globalization, various cases that diverge from the principles assumed to be necessary for effective business organizing, such as the Taiwanese small business firms embedded in networks of close family ties and government influence or the Korean mix of state and corporate governance, have proved economically effective (Hobday 1995; Castells 1998). In areas where local, state, and market organizations have not developed their own capacity to deliver the goods and services of a modern society, interventions which followed predetermined general models and principles of structure and process have often led to poor results and controversial side effects. The history of 'modernization' in the developing world is littered with initiatives that had almost the opposite effects from what was intended.[6]

Inasmuch as a vast number of organizations around the world have been unable to use ICT effectively for their purposes, the research presented here is aimed at understanding the nature of the problems involved, thus contributing towards a theoretical conception of the diversity of globalization that is relevant for information systems innovation.

Support for the validity of the effort to understand organizations without a preconceived typology or ideal model of how they should be organized and how they should use technology is found in the literature of several fields engaged in the critique of modernity. Several authors challenging modernity and its institutions have drawn attention to organizations which are atypical, and indeed problematic, in relation to the conceptions preoccupying organizational theory, management, and information systems (see e.g. Clegg 1990; Escobar 1995; Burrell 1997; and Latour 1993). Their message is clear: organized human activities and uses of technology may be otherwise than those that development agencies and general management theories suggest as desirable norms. Understanding the organization that differs from the accepted norm—the other—as an autonomous social entity is the underlying concern of the theoretical exploration, the empirical studies, and the concluding discussion in this book.

However, autonomy is not taken here to mean action of a societal actor independent from its environment and the global context. The search to understand 'the

---

[5] Using Peter Checkland's terminology, action for change must be culturally feasible as well as systemically desirable (Checkland 1981).
[6] See e.g. El-Kenz 1991.

other' in its own merits and agonies inevitably takes a relativist stance, but the main effort of the research in this book is to explore the relationship of local action—or inaction—to its broader context. Diversity is a relational concept. If one concentrates on the details of particular organizations—their internal processes and features of innovation—without consideration of their interrelations with other organized social entities, the sources and significance of diversity remain hidden.

THE SIGNIFICANCE OF DIVERSITY IN GLOBALIZATION

The need to address organizational diversity and to develop understanding of the kind of changes 'organizational change' comprises around the world becomes all the more important in the context of current interest in globalization. Diversity is a common conclusion in a wide range of literature exploring phenomena of contemporary globalization, whether economic or social (see e.g. Clegg 1990; Beck 2000; and the conclusions in Foray and Freeman 1993). This research, therefore, engages in the globalization discourse, drawing from the unfolding debates and assumptions and adding a particular set of arguments regarding the processes of appropriating ICT in globalization.

Specifically, information and communication technologies are given a central role in many theoretical accounts of contemporary globalization (Rosenau 1980, 1990; Castells 1989, 1996; Harvey 1989; Giddens 1990). They are, as Archibugi and Michie put it, the 'technologies of globalization' (Archibugi and Michie 1997: 4). ICTs, it has been argued, play a significant role in the economic and social processes of what is considered to be globalization.

However, globalization does not entail a uniform global spread of the use of ICT. It is possible to have social and economic globalization heavily dependent on uneven ICT deployment, with regions or arenas of activities hyper-informatized, while others stay relatively, or almost completely devoid of ICT use. Indeed as Chapter 4 makes clear, this is what globalization is like at the beginning of the twenty-first century.

Many writers have been concerned about the potential undemocratic form of social and economic globalization due to the uneven distribution and use of ICT (see e.g. Castells 1996; Sachs 2000). Invariably, they adopt a stance that ICT is a necessity in the contemporary globalization and every effort must be made for its diffusion. This tends to create sweeping universal generalizations about the imperative of ICT use, irrespective of the social and economic circumstances of particular localities, communities, and organizations. In relation to this discourse, information systems studies of ICT innovation processes situated in the circumstances of different localities or sectors reveal missing details of the processes of globalization. To the extent that the diffusion of ICT innovation is fundamental for the socio-economic form of globalization, understanding the way this diffusion is enacted or resisted contributes knowledge to refine the over-optimistic and over-pessimistic perspectives through which globalization is presented.

Another note of clarification should be added at this point. In this book I do not consider globalization either as a self-evidently desirable target or as an undesirable turn of world affairs that should be resisted. What globalization encompasses, to whom it might be desirable, and in what sense, are considered to be open questions.[7] And while the enabling role of ICT for participation in many global processes is not denied, this book does not follow the discourse of 'necessity', which sees anything that stands in the way of technology innovation as an obstacle that is required to be overcome by investment, technical training, or by adopting social processes and relations that have elsewhere proved conducive to technology adoption. Instead, it attempts to uncover the source of the resistances and distortions. By so doing it sheds some light on a different side of the question why the technologies of globalization (and the lack of them) contribute to such a skewed globalization. It adds understanding not of how investment can be mobilized, how millions of, perhaps illiterate, users could be trained, and how economic activities should be re-engineered to rectify the uneven use of ICT, but of what values and ways of thinking and acting of others make ICT innovation a more complex issue than a plain necessity.

THEORETICAL APPROACH ·

Several strands of theory offer insights for the study of ICT innovation with the assumption of organizational diversity. In the social sciences competing theories coexist. As Walsham (1993) explains in his book on interpretive information systems studies, it is not a matter of choosing the 'correct' theory, but of following theoretical routes that assist in shedding light on interesting aspects of the question under consideration. Thus, the theoretical challenge for the information systems researcher attempting to study a question with dimensions that cross multiple disciplinary boundaries is the creation of a conceptual perspective which is relevant and appropriate for the particular question, while it does not oversimplify or hide the controversies that surround the theoretical ideas in their original field.

The stated question—how do ICT innovation and organizational change unfold in the global context—and its brief justification outlined above already suggest the casting of this research in terms of a theoretical approach with three dimensions. The first concerns the study of organizations as entities whose behaviour is not adequately described in rational economic terms, but is to a large extent socially shaped. Using Granovetter's terms (1985), this is a theoretical orientation which seeks to overcome the widespread 'under-socialized' view of organizations that gives

---

[7] From an ethical perspective, globalization, in the abstract sense of free movement of people, ideas, and economic resources across national borders may be seen as desirable by most, although by no means all, people. In its actual state, the contemporary globalization raises major ethical concerns (Hamelink 1999). Many economists concerned about the current gap between the 'poor' and the 'rich', tend to believe that globalization is the only hope for the 'poor' (see e.g. Meghnad Desai's article: <http://www.lse.ac.uk/depts/global/meghnad2.htm> visited on 24 Nov. 2000). Even if such a hope is allowed to be realized politically, there are non-economic implications and risks, such as ecological consequences of unfettered economic growth, which complicate the moral questions.

overwhelming prominence to economic rationality. The research here focuses more on the social not because the economic rationality is irrelevant, but because it aims to explore the substantive rational underpinning of non-economic action. The second aspect of the theoretical approach concerns the study of innovation as a situated process. This requires the elaboration of a concept of context which extends beyond the organization in order to encompass the influences that shape the innovation process. The third theoretical dimension stems from questioning the supremacy of a particular rationality over all else. By doing so this research takes a stance of critical theory and seeks to elaborate a way to account for the multiple rationalities involved in the context of particular innovation processes.

None of these theoretical perspectives are new in information systems research. The departure from a narrow technical/rational analysis of information systems and organizational change, the emphasis on the event in its context, as well as the critical theory perspective are all present in information systems research. However, my interest in the question of the nature of diversity presents particular requirements regarding these perspectives. The following section uses representative examples of information systems research on each of these theoretical dimensions to explain the main additional features or modifications elaborated in the theoretical investigation in this book.

Towards a Socialized Conception of Organizations Suitable to Address Diversity

That information systems innovation is not a technical/rational process within a technically/rationally behaving organizational context is documented by many studies in information systems research. It has been argued convincingly that business and ICT strategies are constructed in a messy way that involves improvisations, tinkering, drifting, and politics (Orlikowski 1996; Knights, Noble, and Willmott 1997; Ciborra 1999). Their implementation is subject to internal and external events, some predictable by analysis of the dynamics of an enterprise and its socio-economic context, some more surprising, almost random, such as 'out of the blue' advent of a new technology, or a rise of new actors in the market of suppliers, customers, and competitors. A good example of such research is Monteiro and Hepsø's case study (2000), which contains details on the way a particular technology was chosen, took shape, and spread in a Norwegian oil corporation. This study shows that the alignment of particular ICTs to business interests is not straightforwardly planned and controlled according to rational economic criteria, but shaped by negotiations, bottom-up action, improvised responses to opportunities or setbacks. In other words, alignment by power, opportunistic behaviour, and improvised action complementing rational choice.

On the assumption that information systems innovation takes place in an environment of competitive business, the aim of Monteiro and Hepsø's study, and that of much of the research which challenges the functionalistic relationship between ICT innovation and organizational performance, is to uncover how business management is actually performed. To be sure, as most studies position their cases in their wider context and trace the actions of agents involved in the innovation, many complications of the business context are manifested. Monteiro and Hepsø's study (ibid.) is concerned with a state-owned oil company, Statoil, that '(a)fter years sheltered from unbiased competition guaranteed through a broad, political coalition . . . is transforming itself into an internationally oriented, competitive enterprise'(p. 148). There are several indications that the original status of Statoil as a 'product of negotiations in Norwegian politics' (p. 150), marked its early management and the perceptions of the role of ICT, but the story told in this case is of a collective commitment to make Statoil an 'internationally competitive oil and gas producer' (p. 151). ICT, whether as a cost or a strategic opportunity, was seen to be enrolled in this uncontroversial, in this case, transformation.

This book highlights the existence of organizations which are not entirely driven by imperatives of free market competition in a global context; environments where different underlying values continue to motivate agents and different concerns restrict or provide opportunities for action. There, I argue, thinking of information systems innovation as if it were a process aligned with the processes of business management—whether technically executed or improvised—misses important concerns and in many cases frustrates action. Thus, the case study of Pemex in Chapter 5, while similar to that analysed by Monteiro and Hepsø in many respects regarding the emergent nature of decision making and action, seeks to show that the organization's history as a company inexorably linked to Mexico's national development struggles is crucial to understanding its convoluted processes of organizational change and information systems innovation. This is so partly because legal and financial imperatives of the state–company status determine particular management constraints. More importantly, the values that have motivated Pemex's actors, their aspirations and concerns, and the sources of power that have fuelled and sustained them, are different from those of actors in a free market business environment. Forcing a business management discourse in the professional practice of information systems innovation irrespective of such fundamental differences of organizational context in many cases leads to mockery. In others it leads to rejection of the information systems intervention, which is generally accounted as failure in the conventional information systems literature.

Therefore this book seeks to construct a theoretical platform that does not privilege the business and management discourse and is capable of tracing other concerns involved in particular ICT innovation and organizational change situations. To that end, it draws from the theory of institutions and the critique of rationality and argues that information systems and management practice, mutually reinforcing each other, constitute a particular rationality, which may be confronted with other locally valid rationalities, that is, other historically legitimate ways of organizing.

Analysing Context

'Situated' analyses of innovation in information systems research have primarily sought to point out that a great deal of innovation and change emerges from organizational actors' response to 'everyday contingencies, breakdowns, exceptions, opportunities, and unintended consequences' (Orlikowski 1996: 65). Such analyses, as the example of Monteiro and Hepsø's study discussed above shows, challenge the view that innovation and change has to be pre-planned by matching technologies to organizational needs and organizing action accordingly. To understand how innovation and change effectively take place from action in the particular circumstances of an organization, situated studies uncover the details of the enactment of the organizational participants' everyday practices. In this way, for example, Orlikowski (1996) studied the gradual, but significant, change in the work practices of the customer support specialists in a software company that followed the use of a technology to keep track of customer cases.

Such situated studies reveal the local dynamics of change: the way people enact their roles and what meaning these roles ascribe to a particular technology innovation; how the organizational structures and relationships enable or constrain them; what opportunities they perceive; and how, within the context of constraints and opportunities of the organization's particular setting, technology is shaped and change is enacted.

What such analyses do not show, though, is where the particular features of the organization, technology, and actor's rational behaviour stem from. The course of the particular organizing, the choice and shaping of the technology are all explained from within. This does not help in understanding why actors in different organiza tions perceive differently the constraints and opportunities of certain technologies and may engage in very different enactments of change or resistance. On the whole, without understanding the origins of the meaning of organizational action, the reader may assume that organizational actors obey some overall rational patterns of behaviour, or that they act idiosyncratically. The former continues the universalist tradition, the latter implies a paralysing relativism.

It is argued here that situated analysis needs to consider a longer history of an organization under study in order to account for the origin of the behaviours manifested in particular innovation and change incidents, and to extend the perspective of context beyond the organizational borders. Again, such an approach is already familiar in information systems research, most prominently through Pettigrew's contextualist method, which focuses on 'the event in its setting', and studies the history of emergent changes in an organization, shaped by the organization's social, economic, and political context. Pettigrew's contextualist method guides the analyst to explore what changes take place when new information and communication technologies are introduced in organizations (the content of change), and how such changes occur (the process of change) in relation to the environment within which they take place (the context of change) (Pettigrew 1985; Pettigrew et al. 1992).

Such a contextual study of a phenomenon involves a process analysis tracing the historical unfolding of events in terms of interdependencies between higher or lower levels of context, which may be at the level of the organization and at the level of the nation. Pettigrew's contextual analysis delineates a set of levels of context and strives to understand the way these levels are connected. It requires a theory of the process of change concerned, capable of explaining how this process is constrained by its context and also contributes to its shaping.

This contextualist approach has been used in several information systems research studies (Avgerou 1989; Madon 1993; Walsham 1993). For example, Madon (1993) studied the implementation of a computer system designed to support the administration of a rural development programme (CRISP) in Indian District authorities. In that study she distinguishes two layers of context. The outer context refers to government policy towards rural development planning and towards information technology, the structure of development administration, and the wider social structure of society. The inner context includes work practices and information flows at local levels of administration. Madon described the process of development, implementation, and use of the new system over a period of almost ten years and in different districts. She analysed the relations between the changing central and local administration contexts and the take up and use of the new system and demonstrated how organizational culture and the wider community culture affected the uses of technology, and how the conflict of power between central and district administration affected the local administrators' attitude towards technology.

The layered contextualist analysis is adapted in this book to address ICT innovation and organizational change as a process involving multiple socio-technical forces that may unfold across multiple contexts. For example, in the case of Pemex the story of the company's reform and ICT innovation efforts presents the influence of events taking place in many fields of actions—the oil industry, its financial transactions and political relations, and ICT professional practice—which cross the organizational, national, and international spaces. The analysis of the case considers innovation and change situated at the cross sections of multiple fields of institutionalized activities, each of which may span a variable number of geographic layers.[8]

Another point that needs clarification with regard to contextualist analysis is the distinction between content and context. Often, the content of change under study is the technical innovation, and context is the social setting within which such innovation is considered to take place. The position adopted in this book is that the relationship of the content of ICT innovation and its social context is so intertwined that, as Callon and Law (1989) have argued, a distinction between technology as content and society as context is an oversimplification. It obscures the complex processes where technology and human actors jointly take part in forming socio-technical entities (Callon and Law 1989). The content of change studied in this book is not technical innovation, but the interaction between the simultaneously co-evolving processes of ICT innovation and organizational change. As is explained in Chapter 2, this is a long-standing position in the socio-technical research tradition which considers information systems to be social systems. With such a conception of information system, the term 'information systems innovation' is used in the main chapters of the book to refer to 'ICT innovation and organizational change'.

---

[8] Also—as is explained in Chaps. 1 and 9—institutionalized activities may be disembedded from specific geographies, having been institutionalized as global forces. It is argued here that this is the case with ICT as an institutional force.

Critique of Rationality

Critical studies of information systems have a relatively long history. In the 1970s, various authors voiced concern about the instrumental reason that computers reinforced, while neglecting questions on the ends they served (Braverman 1974; Cooley 1980; Mowshowitz 1980). Since the early 1980s a stream of studies that used the critical social theory of Habermas to analyse systems development practice became visible in information systems research (Lyytinen 1986, 1992; Hirschheim, Klein, and Lyytinen 1996).

For example, Hirschheim, Klein, and Lyytinen (1996) use a classification of 'orientations'[9] of purposeful social action from Habermas's theory of communicative action to propose a framework for the intellectual trends in information systems development research. From Habermas's critical perspective, the orientation taken in information systems development may be to control—either 'instrumentally' or 'strategically'—to communicate for sense making, or to support rational argumentation. Hirschheim et al. combine this analysis with Etzioni's ideas on domains of change (Etzioni 1968), thus identifying organizational change as one area with which the social action of systems development is concerned. This analysis maps the literature on systems development and organizational change in four categories. First, those who see systems development as mechanistically resulting in particular organizational outcomes. Second, those who see systems development as having an impact on the political relations within an organization, where power relations and domination are the essence of organizational life. Third, those who see information systems as affecting the social interactions through which social actors make sense of their role in the organization. Fourth, those who see information systems as having the potential to improve the rational argumentation among organizational actors. It is in this fourth category that Habermas's analysis contributes a vision of the shaping of the technology in ways enhancing consensus decision making, democracy in the workplace, and emancipation.

However, the Habermasian perspective is based on a particular set of 'humanistic' values and assumptions about the social context.[10] It critiques the dominant rationality of modernity as instrumental and locked into repressive power relations, hence overriding the inherent human capacity of common understanding through rational argumentative speech. In many contexts the fundamental values conveyed in this critique may be shared to a sufficient degree that makes the ideal rationalization through communication feasible. However, I do not find this approach adequate for understanding the uneven processes of information systems innovation in the conditions of severe inequalities sedimented in the variety of institutions of the global context. Thus, other theoretical perspectives need to be explored in order to develop a critical conceptual basis for such analysis.

---

[9] Orientation means 'attitudes, beliefs, values, etc. governing the human intentions and goals' (Hirschheim, Klein, and Lyytinen 1996: 10).

[10] For a critique of Habermas's assumptions and, consequently, Hirschheim et al.'s framework, see Introna 1996.

In the 1990s many different analyses of information systems and organizational change drew from theories which were critical to the fundamental rationality of modernity. Giddens's views on the constitution of modern society, Foucault's analysis of power and knowledge, and Latour's and Callon's analyses of science and technology in modern society have been used by many authors to elucidate the nature of the social change process that the implementation of information systems entails (see e.g. Orlikowski and Robey 1991; Walsham 1993; Monteiro and Hanseth 1996; Introna 1997; Jones 1999). This book builds on the debate such authors have been pursuing. But, rather than following the thought of a particular critical social theorist, it discusses the critique of the rationality of modernity staged by a succession of social theorists throughout the twentieth century. It also attempts to present some critiques—albeit in a much more limited fashion—from the position of non-Western societies. My review of the debate on rationality does not end up either with a preferred critical theoretical view, or with a well-shaped synthesis of theory. In a more eclectic manner my analysis borrows concepts to express an understanding of the bias of rationality met in different information systems innovation contexts. To that end, it suggests the concept of 'organizing regimes' to refer to organizations as settings of action that involve multiple rationalities of historically derived systems of value and meaning.

STRUCTURE AND CONTENT

Part I explores the roots of organizational diversity from the following theoretical perspectives: the way organizations and ICT are socially constituted, the relationship between technology and society, globalization, and the critique of the rationality of modernity. Although, as explained above, most of the theories I draw from have been used in prior information systems studies, they may not be familiar to all information systems scholars. Thus, each chapter introduces the core theoretical ideas as well as using them to set out arguments relevant to the study of information systems innovation in conditions of diversity. Adding such a tutorial character to these chapters is not an elegant way to make theoretical arguments, but I chose this route to avoid the risk of producing a text that the readers I wish to address might find difficult to penetrate.

Chapter 1 draws on institutionalist theory, which takes social structures and long-enduring organizing processes to be historically formed and culturally sustained. From such a perspective, the way organizations are structured and governed is shaped by processes of institutionalization, that is, by internal and external social processes, such as the historical events of their formation, powerful leaders, and a variety of influences from their environment. Therefore, change entails challenging the taken-for-granted validity of established structures and processes and contesting alternative organizing options.

From this general theoretical perspective, management and ICT are seen as institutionally constituted. Chapter 1 draws from studies which argued that, far from being merely the outcome of rational knowledge, management know-how is the result of specific social processes. And rather than seeing ICT as a set of converging technologies that spread everywhere by virtue of their technical functionality, ICT is discussed here as a network of industries, professions, and widely cultivated assumptions about the value of information, computers, and telecommunications in modern society. Such a perception, I should explain, does not deny the utility of ICT in very many areas of organizational activities, but it stresses that the particular significance attributed to ICT and its pervasiveness in modern society are achieved by much more than this. This perspective also points out the close institutional link between ICT and management, a relationship which is further elaborated in the following chapters as a limitation of the capacity of information systems innovation to come to terms with organizational diversity.

Chapter 2 examines the relationship of information systems innovation and organizational context, substantiating theoretically the position outlined in this Introduction: that technology innovation is inseparable from the social processes of organizational change. It traces relevant theoretical debates in the socio-technical stream of information systems research and the multidisciplinary study of technology and society, on the whole drawing mostly from the sociology of translation of the theory of actor networks. Information systems innovation is seen as a process whereby particular actors in an organization succeed in translating their interests into the development and use of ICT applications. In this way the outcomes of information system innovation are not determined by the properties of the technology, but result from contested interests in complex networks of actors and intermediaries. Whatever structures the institutionalized ICT may inscribe, they are contested and may be rejected or modified.

But while convincingly arguing for the non-deterministic, non-homogenization thesis, the relativistic perception of the dynamics of actor networks stops short of indicating what kind of interests are implicated in contemporary information systems innovation. This is a question explored in the following two chapters.

Chapter 3 discusses diversity in relation to rationality. It reviews several critical aspects of the technical, scientific, and economic rationality that occupy a privileged position in modernity and argues that what is considered rational in the context of modernity—science and economics—is in essence ideological. Several key concepts—such as Weber's substantive rationality, Foucault's regime of truth, and Giddens's reflexivity—are drawn from this literature to form a pluralistic understanding of rational behaviour in organizations.

Chapter 4 traces the root of diversity confronting information systems innovation in the unfolding processes of globalization. It starts from the concept of globalization as the shrinking of time and distance, which directly implicates ICT. It then explores globalization as a multidimensional phenomenon comprising changes in economic, political, and cultural activities. And while the extent to which the discernible trends in each of them increase or decrease diversity across the globe may be a matter of debate, it is shown that globalization is much more multifaceted than the notion of global competitive markets to which information systems studies tend to be restricted. Taken together, the multiple facets of contemporary globalization reveal a much more variable organizational context. The extent of the variability is confirmed by a look at the current state of the global economy, which is grossly uneven. Any suggestion of homogenization is absurd when considering the widening gap between the 'poor' and the 'rich'.

The first four chapters of Part II present and discuss case studies and the final chapter draws from this empirical evidence to support a set of arguments in theoretical terms. I should explain that the case studies are not representative of marginalized organizations and societies in the contemporary global contexts. Rather, they are concerned with organizations which have been in a position to sustain organizational and information systems efforts, with varying outcomes.

In each of the Chapters 5 to 8, I first present the case stories as realistic narratives, using the language in which these stories have been constructed through interviews with their participants and documents collected from the organizations concerned. Methodological details for the case studies are described in the Appendix. Each of the four cases draws also from theoretical perspectives and commentaries in other disciplines which are relevant and appropriate to shed light on their particular contextual characteristics.

The presentation and discussion of each case highlight questions about ICT innovation—or lack of—and its organizational consequences, revealing paradoxes according to the current information systems theory and issues that have not received attention in information systems literature. Then I seek to understand these issues through the theoretical perspective developed in Part I, pointing out the way the information systems of each case are rational products of their institutional contexts.

More specifically, Chapter 5 studies the efforts of Pemex, the Mexican oil corporation to develop effective information systems over the past four decades. The information systems innovation processes are presented and discussed in association with the broader struggles for reform of Pemex. To make sense of the significance attached to information systems innovation in the organization, the difficulties faced, and controversies that arise, this case study describes the links of Pemex with its national context, the international oil industry, and the international financial and political institutions. The analysis that follows shows that the information systems innovation efforts in this company have reflected the struggle over its complex role: simultaneously an actor in a competitive market and the most significant asset for the country's socio-economic development. Information systems innovation, aligned with the managerial efforts which increasingly saw the company as a free-market-driven business organization, was often in conflict with the powerful alternative rationality of its national role.

Chapter 6 is the case study of IKA, a social security organization in Greece. IKA is a public sector institution with computer services which run as inefficiently as its bureaucracy. From the early 1980s IKA has conceived several strategies to use ICT for the modernization of the organization, but up until the end of the 1990s none of these had been implemented. To explain why IKA faced such severe difficulties in utilizing ICT, analysis of the case draws from sociological studies of the Greek public sector. These studies suggest that the modernization objectives associated with information systems innovation clashed with the historically legitimate but hidden mission of public administration in Greece as a political employer. The case study explains the annihilation of the efficiency potential of ICT by the organization's rational performance in terms of its hidden role.

Chapter 7 examines a ten-year effort to reform the furniture manufacturing sector of Cyprus according to the industrial model of flexible specialization. The reform initiative involved the setting up of information services and the development of information systems to strengthen the management of the small production firms and their consortia. Little innovation took place, though, and the whole reform experiment was abandoned in the mid-1990s. The analysis of the case examines the way the theory of flexible specialization considered information systems innovation as a prerequisite of good management. The argument that is articulated is that management and formal information processing and communication were alien and threatening to the owners of the small production firms, whose life values and entrepreneurial competencies could not be stretched to enable the promotion of export-oriented business.

The fourth case study, in Chapter 8, examines the way a category of information systems is implicated in conflicting rationalities and is subject to different implementations under different conditions of reconciling them. Specifically, it examines information systems regarding the use of medical drugs, known as drug utilization systems, although they are also referred to by other names, for instance, in the United Kingdom, as prescription systems. The significance of such systems was first recognized by the pharmaceutical industry, and was also highlighted by the World Health Organization in the 1960s. Nevertheless, in the United States and in Europe information systems that monitor drug utilization, and influence doctors' prescribing behaviour, acquired far greater significance from the 1980s and onwards, as costs of drug treatments grew and health care organizations faced the increasing problem of cost containment. By outlining what drug utilization systems have been implemented in the United States and the United Kingdom—two countries with very different health care systems and both experiencing reform pressures—this case study shows two things. First, how different information systems emerge in health care systems organized according to different principles of rationality. Second, how, even in the same country and organizational setting, information systems are confronted with different and competing substantive rationalities, in this case economic management, equitable high-quality public service, and science-based professional conduct.

The last chapter draws the main lessons from the empirical studies through the theoretical lenses proposed in Part I. It elaborates on the non-deterministic nature of ICT, explaining why it does not deliver its expected value when the organizational circumstances do not match the rationality it conveys in its current professional pattern of practice. This defies the modernizing and rationalizing role ICT is often presumed to play. Moreover, it points out that the diffusion of ICT, which is usually considered a positive indicator of modernization, may not provide the benefits generally associated with modernization. In some of the case studies, ICT is found to adapt to the organizational circumstances, without contributing to the changes that it was intended to promote—according to the formal plans of their champions. The second lesson drawn in this final chapter is about the significance of rationalities other than the economic logic that surface at the occasions of information systems innovation. Evidence from the case studies is used to substantiate the message that the current close alignment of information systems innovation with the rationality of business management limits the extent to which information systems professionals recognize and address alternative rationalities. The third lesson is an elaboration of the notion of context that is relevant to information systems innovation. It is shown how the relevant context of information systems innovation can be drawn as an intersection of the fields of multiple institutions, each with a variable geographical span: national, foreign national, international, and some disembedded from particular geographic locations.

Finally, Chapter 9 discusses the implications of these lessons for information systems research and practice. As far as research is concerned, it stresses the contribution that studying the nature of diversity of circumstances faced in information systems innovation can make towards understanding globalization. As ICT is highly implicated in globalization, researching the issues of information systems innovation in the diverse conditions of the global context exposes facets of the globalization phenomenon. As far as practice is concerned, the recognition of diversity of rationalities under the influences of multiple institutional contexts points to a professional role capable of understanding and interpreting them. This requires decoupling of information systems expertise from the currently dominant practice of management as a set of organizing principles expressing exclusively the economic rationality.

References

Applegate, L. M. (1994). 'Managing in an Information Age: Transforming the Organization for the 1990s', in R. Baskerville, S. Smithson, O. Ngwenyama, and J. I. DeGross (eds.), *Transforming Organizations with Information Technology*. Amsterdam: North-Holland, 15–94.

Archibugi, D., and Michie, J. (1997). 'Technological Globalisation and National Systems of Innovation: An Introduction', in D. Archibugi and J. Michie. *Technology, Globalisation and Economic Performance*. Cambridge: Cambridge University Press, 1–23.

Avgerou, C. (1989). 'Information Systems in Social Administration: Factors Affecting their Success'. Ph.D. thesis, Information Systems Department, London School of Economics.

——and Walsham, G. (eds.) (2000). *Information Technology in Context: Studies from the Perspective of Developing Countries*. Aldershot: Ashgate.

Beck, U. (2000). *What is Globalization?* Cambridge: Polity Press.

Bloomfield, B. P., Coombs, R., Knights, D., and Littler, D. (1997). 'Doctors as Managers: Constructing Systems and Users in the National Health Service', in B. P. Bloomfield, R. Coombs, D. Knights, and D. Littler, *Information Technology and Organizations: Strategies, Networks, and Integration*. Oxford: Oxford University Press, 112–34.

——Cooper, D. J., and Rea, D. (1992). 'Machines and Manoeuvres: Responsibility Accounting and the Construction of Hospital Information Systems'. *Accounting, Management and Information Technology*, 2(4): 197–219.

Braa J., Macome, E., da Costa, J. L., Mavimbe, J. C., Nhampossa, J. L., José, B., Manave, A., and Sitói, A. (2000). A study of the actual and potential usage of information and communication technology at district and provincial levels in Mozambique with a focus on the health sector, in S. Sahay (ed), the proceedings of the IFIP WG 9.4 conference Information Flows, Local Improvisations and Work Practices, Cape Town, 23–26 May.

Braverman, H. (1974). *Labor and Monopoly Capital*. New York: Monthly Review.

Burrell, G. (1997). *Pandemonium: Towards a Retro-Organization Theory*. London: Sage.

Callon, M., and Law, J. (1989). 'On the Construction of Sociotechnical Networks: Content and Context Revisited'. *Knowledge and Society*, 9: 57–83.

Castells, M. (1989). *The Informational City: Information Technology, Economic Restructuring and the Urban-Regional Process*. Oxford: Blackwell.

—— (1996). *The Rise of the Network Society*. Oxford: Blackwell.

—— (1998). *End of Millennium*. Oxford: Blackwell.

Checkland, P. (1981). *Systems Thinking Systems Practice*. Chichester: Wiley.

Ciborra, C. U. (1996). 'The Platform Organization: Recombining Strategies, Structures, and Surprises'. *Organization Science*, 7(2): 103–18.

—— (1999). 'A Theory of Information Systems Based on Improvisation', in W. L. Currie and B. Galliers (eds.), *Rethinking Management Information Systems*. Oxford: Oxford University Press, 136–55.

—— and Lanzara, G. F. (1994). 'Formative Contexts and Information Technology: Understanding the Dynamics of Innovation in Organizations'. *Accounting, Management and Information Technology*, 4(2): 61–86.

Clegg, S. R. (1990). *Modern Organizations: Organization Studies in the Postmodern World*. London: Sage.

Cooley, M. (1980). *Architect or Bee? The Human Price of Technology*. London: Hogarth Press.

DeSanctis, G., and Fulk, J. (1999). 'Conclusion: Research Issues and Directions', in G. DeSanctis and J. Fulk (eds.), *Shaping Organization Form: Communication, Connection, and Community*. Thousand Oaks, Calif.: Sage, 497–502.

Drucker, P. (1988). 'The Coming of the New Organization'. *Harvard Business Review*, Jan.–Feb., 45–53.

Dunker, E. (2000). 'How LINCs Were Made: Alignment and Exclusion in American Medical Informatics'. *The Information Society*, 16(3): 187–99.

Dutton, W. H. (1999). 'The Virtual Organization: Tele-access in Business and Industry', in G. DeSanctis and J. Fulk (eds.), *Shaping Organization Form: Communication, Connection, and Community*. Thousand Oaks, Calif.: Sage, 473–95.

El-Kenz, A. (1991). 'Algerian Society Today: A Phenomenological Essay on the National Consciousness', in A. El-Kenz, *Algeria: Challenge of Modernity*. London: Codesria, 7–39.

Escobar, A. (1995). *Encountering Development*. Princeton: Princeton University Press.

Etzioni, A. (1968). *The Active Society: Theory of Societal and Political Processes*. New York: Free Press.

Foray, D., and Freeman, C. (eds.) (1993). *Technology and the Wealth of Nations: The Dynamics of Constructed Advantage*. London: Pinter.

Giddens, A. (1990). *The Consequences of Modernity*. Cambridge: Polity Press.

Granovetter, M. (1985). 'Economic Action and Social Structure: The Problem of Embeddedness'. *American Journal of Sociology*, 91(3): 481–510.

Hamelink, C. J. (1999). 'The Elusive Concept of Globalisation'. *Global Dialogue: The Globalisation Phenomenon*, 1(1): 1–9.

Harvey, D. (1989). *The Condition of Postmodernity*. Oxford: Blackwell.

Heeks, R. (ed.) (1999). *Reinventing Government in the Information Age: International Practice in IT-enabled Public Sector Reform*. London: Routledge.

Hirschheim, R., Klein, H. K., and Lyytinen, K. (1996). 'Exploring the Intellectual Structures of Information Systems Development: A Social Action Theoretical Analysis'. *Accounting, Management & Information Technology*, 6(1/2): 1–63.

Hobday, M. (1995). *Innovation in East Asia: The Challenge to Japan*. Cheltenham: Edward Elgar.

Huber, G. P. (1990). 'A Theory of the Effects of Advanced Information Technologies on Organizational Design, Intelligence, and Decision Making'. *Academy of Management Review*, 15: 47–71.

Introna, L. D. (1996). 'Commentary on *Exploring the Intellectual Structures of Information Systems Development: A Social Action Theoretic Analysis* by Hirschheim, Klein and Lyytinen'. *Accounting, Management & Information Technologies*, 6(1/2): 87–97.

—— (1997). *Management, Information and Power: A Narrative of the Involved Manager*. Basingstoke: Macmillan.

Jones, M. (1999). 'Structuration Theory', in W. L. Currie and B. Galliers (eds.), *Rethinking Management Information Systems*. Oxford: Oxford University Press, 103–35.

Klecun-Dabrowska, E., and Cornford, T. (2000). 'Telehealth Acquires Meanings: Information and Communication Technologies within Health Policy'. *Information Systems Journal*, 10: 41–63.

Knights, D., Noble, F., and Willmott, H. (1997). '"We should be total slaves to the business": Aligning Information Technology Strategy—Issues and Evidence', in B. P. Bloomfield, R. Coombs, D. Knights, and D. Littler, *Information Technology and Organizations*. Oxford: Oxford University Press, 13–35.

Labelle, H. (1995). 'Telecommunications and Sustainable Development'. *Information Technology for Development*, 6: 67–72.

Latour, B. (1993). *We Have Never Been Modern*. New York: Harvester Wheatsheaf.

Lind, P. (2000). 'On the Design of Management Assistance Systems for SMEs in Developing Countries', in C. Avgerou and G. Walsham (eds.), *Information Technology in Context: Studies from the Perspective of Developing Countries*. Aldershot: Ashgate, 40–55.

Louw, G. (1996). 'Reducing the Need for Computer-Based Information Systems in Healthcare through the Use of Self-Contained Organizational Units', in W. J. Orlikowski, G. Walsham, M. Jones, and J. I. DeGross (eds.), *Information Technology and Changes in Organizational Work*. London: Chapman & Hall, 21–36.

—— (1999). 'Health Informatics: Evaluation and Evidence-Based Practice'. *Information Technology & People*, 12(3): 234–303.

Lucas, H. C. J. (1996). *The T-Form Organization: Using Technology to Design Organizations for the 21st Century*. San Francisco: Jossey-Bass.

Lyytinen, K. (1986). 'Information Systems Development as Social Action—Framework and Critical Implications'. *Department of Computer Science*. Finland, University of Jyvaskyla.

—— (1992). 'Information Systems and Critical Theory', in M. Alversson and H. Willmott (eds.), *Critical Management Studies*. London: Sage, 159–80.

Madon, S. (1993). 'Introducing Administrative Reform through the Application of Computer-Based Information Systems: A Case Study in India'. *Public Administration and Development*, 13: 37–48.

Margetts, H. (1999). *Information Technology in Government: Britain and America*. London: Routledge.

Mitev, N. (1996). Social, organisational and political aspects of information systems failure: the computerised reservation system at French railways. 4th European Conference on Information Systems, Lisbon.

Monteiro, E., and Hanseth, O. (1996). 'Social Shaping of Information Infrastructure: On Being Specific about the Technology', in W. Orlikowski, G. Walsham, M. R. Jones, and J. I. DeGross (eds.), *Information Technology and Changes in Organizational Work*. London: Chapman & Hall, 325–43.

—— and Hepsø, V. (2000). 'Seize the Day at Statoil', in C. U. Ciborra and associates (eds.), *From Control to Drift: The Dynamics of Corporate Information Infrastructures*. Oxford: Oxford University Press, 148–71.

Mowshowitz, A. (1980). 'Ethics and Cultural Integration in a Computerized World', in A. Mowshowitz, *Human Choice and Computers, 2*. Amsterdam: North-Holland, 251–70.

Odedra-Straub, M. (ed.) (1996). *Global Information Technology and Socio-economic Development*. Nashua, NH: Ivy League.

Orlikowski, W. J. (1996). 'Improvising Organizational Transformation over Time: A Situated Change Perspective'. *Information Systems Research*, 7(1): 63–92.

—— and Robey, D. (1991). 'Information Technology and the Structuring of Organizations'. *Information Systems Research*, 2(2): 143–69.

—— Walsham, G., Jones, M., and DeGross, J. I. (eds.) (1996). *Information Technology and Changes in Organizational Work*. London: Chapman & Hall.

Palvia, P. C., and Palvia, S. C. (1996). 'Understanding the Global Information Technology Environment: Representative World Issues', in P. C. Palvia, S. C. Palvia, and E. M. Roche, *Global Information Technology and Systems Management: Key Issues and Trends*. Nashua, NH: Ivy League, 3–30.

Peled, A. (2000). 'First-Class Technology—Third-Rate Bureaucracy: The Case of Israel'. *Information Technology for Development*, 9: 45–58.

Pettigrew, A. M. (1985). 'Contextualist Research and the Study of Organizational Change Processes', in E. Mumford, R. Hirschheim, G. Fitzgerald, and A. T. Wood-Harper (eds.), *Research Methods in Information Systems*. Amsterdam: North Holland, 53–78.

—— Ferlie, E., and McKee, L. (1992). *Shaping Strategic Change: The Case of the NHS*. London: Sage.

Qureshi, S. (1998). 'Fostering Civil Associations in Africa through GOVERNET: An Administrative Reform Network'. *Information Technology for Development*, 8: 121–36.

Rosenau, J. (1980). *The Study of Global Interdependence*. London: Frances Pinter.

—— (1990). *Turbulence in World Politics*. Brighton: Harvester.

Sachs, J. (2000). 'A New Map of the World'. *The Economist* (London), 24 June: 99–101.

Sahay, S. (ed.) (2000). Information Flows, Local Improvisations and Work Practices, in the proceedings of the IFIP WG 9.4 conference Information Flows, Local Improvisations and Work Practices, Cape Town, 23–26 May.

Sauer, C. (1999). 'Deciding the Future for IS Failures: Not the Choice You Might Think', in B. Galliers and W. L. Currie (eds.), *Rethinking Management Information Systems*. Oxford: Oxford University Press, 279–309.

Scott Morton, M. S. (1991). *The Corporation of the 1990's, Information Technology and Organizational Transformation*. New York: Oxford University Press.

Talero, E., and Gaudette, P. (1995). 'Harnessing Information for Development: A Proposal for a World Bank Group Vision and Strategy'. *Information Technology for Development*, 6: 145–88.

Valantin, R. (1996). 'Global Program Initiative: Information Policy Research'. *Information Technology for Development*, 7: 95–103.

Volkow, N. (2000). 'Strategic Use of Information Technology Requires Knowing How to Use Information', in C. Avgerou and G. Walsham (eds.), *Information Technology in Context: Studies from the Perspective of Developing Countries*. Aldershot: Ashgate, 56–69.

Walsham, G. (1993). *Interpreting Information Systems in Organizations*. Chichester: John Wiley.

PART I

THEORY

1

The Institutional Nature of ICT and Organizational Change

On the whole, information systems research has relied heavily of the assumption that ICT and organizations are created, shaped, and transformed by purposeful action in response to competitive market forces. Much of the information systems literature in the 1980s and 1990s emphasized the competitive pressures on organizations and sought to understand the ways management can harness the potential of ICT in order to secure a competitive position of a firm within its environment (see e.g. influential publications such as Porter and Millar 1984; Scott Morton 1991; Hammer and Champy 1993; Ciborra and Andreu 1998). The information systems field is aware that such research, comprising its 'mainstream' corpus, has major limitations, namely that it tends to be overwhelmingly concerned with the technical decisions and actions pertaining to ICT innovation and organizational change and to overemphasize the economic drivers of individuals and organizations. Indeed, information systems research has put forward alternative views, stressing that the development and use of ICT in organizations is only partly a matter of formal decision making and cannot be completely accounted for in terms of improving individuals' economic gains and organizations' market position. There are broader social dynamics involved (see e.g. Kling and Iacono 1989; Orlikowski 1992; Walsham 1993).

Here, I begin the enquiry into the social dimensions of ICT innovation and organizational change by drawing from the theory of institutions, mainly as it has been developed in the sociology of organizations[1] in the United States (see e.g. March

---

[1] It should be explained that the institutionalist perspective of organizations challenges the 'resource dependency' theory of organizational studies (Lawrence and Lorsch 1969; Pfeffer and Salancik 1978), which studies the survival and development of organizations in terms of their strategic choices in response to their competitive environment. Research adhering to the resource dependency theoretical perspective seeks to promote the decision making capacity of organizational management, and has been widely influential in business management literature. Another stream of theory that challenges the centrality attributed to rational/instrumental management action in explaining the features of organizations and the relationship between an organization and its environment is the organizational ecology theory (Hannan and Freeman 1989). This theory considers organizational populations, such as factories, financial services, and retailers rather than individual organizations. It argues that organizational forms survive or disappear according to whether they are adequately suitable for the economic, political, cultural, legal, and technological environment. In other words this perspective suggests an analogy with the Darwinian theory of natural selection for the survival and evolution of biological species. It contributes useful insights regarding the long-term formation of organizational patterns, but its explanatory capacity regarding the questions studied in this book is limited. The organizational ecology theory does not address the processes taking place internally in organizations in adequate detail to provide a convincing alternative to the emphasis given by the resource dependency type of studies to the purposeful actor of change.

and Olsen 1989; Powell and DiMaggio 1991; Scott and Meyer 1994). The American institutionalist theory of organizations[2] provides a conceptual platform to study actions stemming from the cultural and power processes embedded in them, as well as the influences of their social environment.

The concept of 'institution' has a broad sense in institutionalist theory.[3] It refers to authoritative, established, rule-like procedures in society, with a self-sustaining character. In other words, to 'those social patterns that, when chronically reproduced, owe their survival to relatively self-activating social processes' (Jepperson 1991: 145).[4] Institutions are 'taken-for-granted' standardized sequences of activity in their environment. People tend to believe that there is a functional rationale for their existence and purpose and that they are historically justified, and therefore their validity is not challenged.

A common view formed under the influence of institutionalist theory is that innovation is first adopted and diffused partly for its technical merits (Zucker 1983), and partly under the influence of powerful actors (Granovetter and McGuire 1998). Subsequently, through socio-cultural processes an innovation becomes accepted as a social fact and is maintained because of its acquired legitimacy, quite often irrespective of whether it produces its promised technical benefits, and no longer having to rely continuously on powerful personalities. There is therefore a tendency in institutionalist studies to address non-technical aspects mainly as factors leading to stability, inhibiting innovation and change, and often as sources of resistance to change. Also, institutional forces tend to be associated with the spread of uniform organizational features through imitation, coercion, or standard practices, and not to be thought as a way to account for diversity.

This is a limited view of institutional processes though, considering them as contributors to the perpetuation of an organizational situation rather than to innovation. And it has been challenged in recent institutionalist studies. A few notable

---

[2] Contemporary literature on institutionalist theory has used the term 'new institutionalism', to refer to the stream of research on the nature and significance of institutions that emerged after the 1960s. The term is meant to distinguish these recent theoretical efforts from earlier, cruder—although fundamental—attempts to conceptualize influences from the broader environment on organizations, by such gurus of social theory as Parsons and Selznick. While this distinction was important to make at the time the proponents of institutionalist ideas were seeking to attract attention and mark the novelty of their ideas, it is less important now that these ideas have gained their position in organizational theory, and indeed the prefix 'new' tends to be omitted in more recent publications.

[3] Many authors in information systems use the term 'institution' to refer to social entities in the environment of an organization that exert influence and regulation on them, such as the various policy making and administration entities of national or international government (King et al. 1994). Other 'institutional' studies are concerned with the 'internal structure, culture, history and dynamics of an organized cooperative effort in order to understand how it changes' (Bransson and Olsen 1998: 30). However, the significance of the institutionalist perspective is that it provides insights on the links between the internal social processes in an organization and those taking place in its environment. In this book the concept of institution is used in its general sense that accounts for both micro-level and macro-level social patterns.

[4] Among the examples of 'institutions' suggested by Jepperson (1991) are presidency, academic tenure, wage labour, the formal organization. Some of them are found in a few societies only, while others, such as the formal organization, constitute established features of all modern societies.

publications in information systems have argued that institutional forces from the environment of an organization as well as from its internal culture play a significant role in innovation (King et al. 1994; Swanson and Ramiller 1997). Also, research by organization theorists has shown that, in the contemporary conditions of globalization, organizations are subject to influences from multiple institutional fields, and the overall effects are likely to be diversity rather than uniformity of organizational behaviour and structure (Westney 1993). Thus, an understanding of the institutional character of ICT innovation and organizational change requires a critical discussion of the institutionalist theses of organizational theory which continue to be an active subject to research and debate.

ORGANIZATIONS AS INSTITUTIONS

The concentration and structuring of people's work activities in formally organized social units is one of the most significant institutional elements in modern society. The formal organization of work is to such an extent established today that productive activities delivered without a formal organizational basis, such as homework, even in the modern form of telework, lack adequate legitimacy and are only marginal within the Western countries' economies.

Organizations differ enormously in terms of structure of work tasks, control mechanisms, reward systems, and ownership. Nevertheless, organizations in modern industrialized societies are identifiable as distinctive social entities by a number of elements. They hold specific values related to their *raison d'être*, part of their commonly accepted mission, for example, market values for business organizations, educational values for schools, political values for government organizations. They involve professional roles, which determine valid action for their individual members. They involve structures of authority, which determine certain ways of power distribution as valid and others as inappropriate. They are subject to legislation and supervisory authorities determining the scope and rules of acceptable organizational output.

The institutional character of formal organizations lies in the sustenance and perpetuation of organizational aspects, such as structure, decision making, and work practices, by unconsciously taking-for-granted the way these aspects are. This unconscious element of organizational collectives, institutionalist theorists argue, tends to make alternatives unthinkable. Participants of organizations share common understandings about what is appropriate and meaningful behaviour (Zucker 1983). Actions follow rule-like patterns, 'norms' that are embedded in formal structures and are not tied to particular actors or situations. In this way, work practices in organizations, although socially defined, come to be seen as being 'objective', part of the 'external' world, rather than as being subjective understandings and actions (Zucker 1983, 1991).

Thus, the core argument in the institutionalist theory of organizations is that formal structures and processes are maintained not because they, necessarily, constitute efficient ways of carrying out complex activities, but because they are sustained by powerful 'myths', that is, by shared assumptions about their functionality and necessity (Meyer and Rowan 1991). In modern societies such myths are 'rationalized', impersonal prescriptions, through which certain practices are taken-for-granted as efficient, without evaluation of their outcomes. For example, professional roles carry a strong element of rational myth, as they legitimize individuals' activities on the basis of acquired expertise, without necessarily evaluating the results of their actions.

The most prevalent type of formal organization in the twentieth century was the large hierarchical bureaucracy. Zucker (1983) traced the history of the establishment of the bureaucratic organizational form in the United States by examining industrial records of the early twentieth century. Formally organized manufacturing enterprises emerged in the late eighteenth century, but they spread very slowly until the beginning of the twentieth century. In the 1920s, under the influence of F. W. Taylor's principles of scientific management, organizations in the United States introduced specialization of wage-paid work, which is defined impersonally in order to be repeatable by others in the same position. It involved centralized planning, design of distinct operations of production, and detailed instruction and control of workers' performance. Several technical/rational factors have been identified in the development of this type of organization of production in American manufacturing, such as technological changes, the large proportion of unskilled, often illiterate, immigrant workforce, and the demand for standardized products after the First World War. But there were also significant political factors which contributed to the establishment of modern professionally managed bureaucratic organizations in the United States, such as an influential group of industrial engineers and a state ideology that emphasized efficiency and economic rationalization (Lash and Urry 1987). Furthermore, this formal organization of work was strengthened by legislation, which prohibited homework in manufacturing because it could lead to social problems such as child labour and worker exploitation. The history of that period suggests that there was resistance from existing institutional structures. Formal hierarchically structured organizations were established more widely at first in the newer cities, where less discontinuity from established structures was implied (Zucker 1983).

Subsequently, the large-scale hierarchical organization became a stable and ubiquitous way of concentrating and structuring all kinds of economic as well as political activities, such as social services and even social movements. The diffusion and stability of the formal organization not only in the United States but in all industrialized countries occurred despite widely acknowledged limitations. A number of remedies to the gross inefficiencies of the professionally managed bureaucratic form have been worked out, and the structuring of collective activities in formally organized hierarchical concentrations has become a dominant feature of modern society.

The formal organization, reinforced by other social institutions, developed specific social structures that became key features of Western industrial societies. One such structure which combines institutional features of the formal organization with legal and financial institutions is the industrial corporation. It refers to professionally governed formal organizations, legally recognized as autonomous social units, 'owned' by shareholders, and financed through financial markets. The corporate organization form is understood as a type of 'socialized property,[5] whereby firms are owned by many individuals, who, in turn, usually own pieces of many firms (Roy 1990, 1997). In explaining the emergence and subsequent institutionalization of the corporation, Roy highlights the power relationships embedded in the social institutions in the United States in the early twentieth century. The favourable institutional conditions involved a network of interested parties, such as investors, bankers, workers, lawyers, and politicians. Also, the state played a significant role, not only in its capacity as legislator of property law, but by directly creating and endowing with resources large professionally managed organizations. Roy's message is that the rise of large corporations was neither inevitable nor 'natural'. They were not developed by decisions on the basis of their efficiency advantages in the face of technological development,[6] but they were historically contingent, a product of the social circumstances of the United States. Indeed, Roy's account points out a number of contingencies, of circumstances and events. Had they not occurred, the history of the corporation could have been very different.

Another institutional structure that acquired significance for modern economies is the industrial mode of mass production known as Fordism. The Fordist industrial organization is based on assembly line techniques operated with semi-skilled labour. It involves the separation of ownership and control of production in large corporations and hierarchical management of distinctive divisions of work. Moreover, it relies on a system of state regulatory functions and collective labour bargaining. Thus, Fordism is understood to involve a virtuous circle of economic growth, which comprises mass production, rising productivity based on economies of scale, rising incomes linked to productivity, increased mass demand due to rising wages, increased profits based on full utilization of capacity, and increased investment in improved mass production equipment and techniques (Jessop 1991). Fordism is associated with a particular societal context that involves consumption of standardized commodities in nuclear family households, and the mediation of the bureaucratic state to provide social welfare services—such as education, health, and a range of social security benefits—to regulate the collective bargaining and manage conflict between capital and labour.

The industrial mode of mass production was challenged in the 1970s when stagnation of mass consumerism, and demand for non-standardized quality products threatened to discontinue the Fordist virtuous circle. Since then, the debate on the so-called post-Fordist regimes of production suggested the emergence of various alternative modes of organization as appropriate for the 'post-industrial' era. Some of them, such as the craft production tradition based on skilled labour who produce a variety of customized goods for a market of varying product demand (Piore and Sabel 1984), are sharply contrasted to Fordism. Correspondingly, the social regulatory

---

[5] In his analysis of property, Roy draws from Zeitlin (1989).
[6] Roy's political sociology of the origin of the corporation develops against the prevailing functionalist account by Chandler (1962, 1969), according to which, corporations arose because they were the most efficient way to administer economic functions as technological change created economies of scale.

regime that supports them shifts away from the consumption stabilizing social welfare state. Most 'new' organizational paradigms, though, are not complete alternatives, but mutations of the Fordist basis of mass production and its state-based social supporting structure, and hybrids of Fordism with its alternatives. For example, in many countries the organization of mass production became leaner, and experimented with alternatives to the centralized hierarchical control, as, for example, the matrix organization. It allowed for more worker autonomy at the workplace, but withdrew the social welfare provisions.

MANAGEMENT AS INSTITUTION

One of the most prevalent features of organizations in the Western world at the beginning of the twenty-first century is that they are governed through a particular professional rationality oriented towards efficiency in a free market environment. Management is taken-for-granted as a rational way of steering action not only in business organizations, but increasingly also in any other social domain. Unlike other forms of governing, for example, through the command of the proprietors of organizations or through a system of political command, management is considered the most suitable way to promote the fundamental principles of economic growth in the capitalist system, mainly efficiency and innovation.

In organizational theory and management studies, it is widely accepted that management emerged as the dominant feature of modern organizations because of its fitness to the capitalist economic system, and gained its prevalence because of its proven superiority in relation to alternative forms of governing (Chandler 1962, 1969). Institutionalist analyses challenge this view, and show management as a system of meanings that has been created through the course of specific historical events. They point out that the pervasiveness of the managerial rationality as a generic professional specialism is significant not only as an effective means for running organizations—which is not always the case—but for the transition to a new system of socio-economic institutions. In the analysis of the contemporary capitalist socio-economic system by Lash and Urry (1987), the spreading of management is associated with the formation of a 'service class', which is a major force for breaking the capital–labour relationship of modern capitalism, thus responsible for what they call 'disorganized capitalism'.

Such an institutionalist view is substantiated best by Shenhav (1999), and his argument merits some attention here. Shenhav studied the American manufacturing industry in the period between 1880 and 1932, which he argues has been the most formative context and time of modern management. Indeed, 1932 is the year the 'managerial revolution' was crystallized in what became a classic book, *The Modern Corporation and Private Property* (Berle and Neans 1932).

In working out an interpretation of history which differs from the widespread literature on management and business studies, Shenhav points out the logical weaknesses of the view that the governance of organizations through professional managers is a natural consequence of the development of the capitalist economic system. Both the theoretical conception of the capitalist system by Adam Smith and the 'capitalists' of the late nineteenth century considered the delegation of control of business organizations to be detrimental to the creation of wealth. The owner of the means of production was considered best positioned to secure the interests of his business. Also, the principles of management, such as systematization of work practices and professional control of the production process were equally appealing to non-capitalist economic regimes, most notably in the Soviet Union.

Consequently, the question Shenhav investigates is: how did professional managerial rationality become the almost undisputed way of running business organizations and, more recently, an all-pervasive rationality for reforming non-business organizations, such as state administration or military services. The answer, he suggests, lies in the efforts of mechanical engineers to enhance and safeguard the interests of their professional position situated in the American political context at the turn of the nineteenth century.

In effect, in the United States mechanical engineers managed to secure their expertise on machines as an appropriate basis of organizing business organizations, in particular large corporations. The principles of systematization and standardization, first established against voices of opposition as the 'rational' way to produce mechanical parts, gradually won legitimacy as appropriate means for organizing work efficiently. Shenhav's research of the major engineering journals of that period provides evidence that establishing the engineering principles as the 'scientific' principles of organizing did not happen smoothly. It faced opposition within the circles of engineers, and, more importantly, by the business owners. It also took place against serious and long-lasting labour unrest.

Shenhav attributes a critical significance for the 'translation'[7] of engineering principles to the core logic of professional management to two political characteristics of the American social context: exceptionalism and progressivism. Exceptionalism refers to the American nationalist ideology of the nineteenth century, which entertained a belief in the uniqueness and superiority of the country stemming from the circumstances of its late creation on principles of 'rationality', liberalism, and democracy, and the values of affluence and broad opportunity. Shenhav argues that the engineering professionals both reinforced and capitalized on this ideology. They sustained the view that American manufacturing was superior to that of Europe in terms of worker productivity, machinery, and organization of business.

Progressivism was another aspect of a widespread ideology in the first seventeen years of the twentieth century, aspiring to revitalize the democratic values and restore equality through a pragmatic culture of pursuing efficiency, expertise, and systematic organization. It was believed that America could avoid political conflict and serve the needs of all. The progressivist ideology legitimized the roles of professionals, and engineers were well positioned to present their expertise on systematization and efficiency as tools capable of taking industry beyond chaos and creating prosperity for all. In short, progressivism allowed the engineering instrumental rationality to

---

[7] The technical meaning of 'translation' is explained in some detail in Chap. 2.

expand to human, social, political, and economic affairs. Management systems were seen as solutions to labour unrest and political instability. Organizations could be engineered and perfected as mechanical systems. And this is what F. W. Taylor did with 'scientific management'. As Shenhav puts it: 'During Exceptionalism, the class structure was depoliticized; during Progressivism, bureaucratization was depoliticized' (Shenhav 1999: 136).

Thus, what resulted from the social contest within a particular political culture was reified as a rational practice of universal validity. Concepts, such as efficiency, maximization, standardization, that were promoted by a social group trying to claim legitimacy for their expansion into taking charge of organizing activities acquired the status of objective, rational organizational norms. Since the 1980s there has been a strong tendency throughout the world to transfer managerial rationality into all kinds of organizations, including government administration, the military, and agencies such as universities which have had their own organizational logic. Public management became a platform for public sector reform in most countries (Heeks 1999; Lane 2000). Moreover, management is a thriving business, conducted by multinational corporations. In Europe and other advanced industrialized regions, this is a more or less self-chosen course of reform. In the developing countries, it is usually the result of influential international agencies such as the World Bank and bilateral aid agencies. The message Shenhav's institutionalist analysis puts forward is quite bold: governing organizations on the basis of modern management neither was technically/rationally developed nor does it necessarily lead to better outcomes over alternative ways of governing, such as politically determined formal rationality. Non-management governed organizations are not rationally inferior, but they are suffering a diminishing legitimacy within the context of an international economy under the hegemony of the United States.

ICT INNOVATION AS INSTITUTION

There are numerous 'rational' accounts for the significance of ICT in all fields of the social sciences. Influential publications have analysed its impacts on the performance of organizations and its potential to alter the socio-economic position of nations and regions (OECD 1988; Castells 1996; Mansell and Wehn 1998). Some studies portrayed a more sceptical attitude, showing factors which may inhibit the release of the potential of ICT, either at a national or an organizational level (see e.g. Landauer 1996). However, the momentum of ICT diffusion appears unbounded by critical analyses of its value.

From an institutional point of view, ICT is not seen as a set of material products functioning according to the technical rules embedded in their physical components, but as products of a social network embedded in social institutions. The current theoretical debate on the socio-technical networks constituting information systems is discussed in more detail in Chapter 3. Here, I point out the perspective that sees ICT as an institution in its own right, taking shape in relation to other institutions of modern society.

From an institutional perspective, it is significant that ICT has captured the hopes and fears of people in their professional roles as well as in their personal lives. ICT occupies a central position in the discourse of socio-economic change, such as on post-industrial society (Bell 1973), information society (Webster 1995), or globalization (Giddens 1990). Such discourse provides an underlying rationale about the value of ICT innovation, indeed so powerful that it creates a sense of inevitability regarding ICT innovation. Although the merits of particular information systems may be fiercely contested within organizations (see e.g. Silva and Backhouse 1997), the wisdom of expanding computer uses in ever more organizational activities is hardly challenged in any organization. ICT applications are taken-for-granted as fixtures of contemporary organizations. Their value has become a 'rational myth'.

A good indication of the extent to which ICT innovation is taken-for-granted as a necessity is found in the context of developing countries. There is little doubt regarding the developmental role of ICT, even in the poorest countries of the world. Earlier concerns relating to unemployment, opportunity costs, and dependency have disappeared from the discourse on socio-economic development and ICT. In contemporary development reports, the low diffusion of computers and telecommunications in desolate regions such as Sub-Saharan Africa is used as one of the main indications of their plight.[8] International aid institutions, through funding, educational and regulatory influence, take it as part of their mission to assist poor countries to decrease their ICT gap from the ever faster innovating industrialized countries. A few impressive examples, such as the modernization of the economy of Singapore and the innovation initiatives of Malaysia, became icons of success. A closer look to consider the way such technology diffusion impacts on the economic, social, and organizational context of specific developing countries tends to reveal rather bleak pictures of 'failed' projects, and unused technologies often demoralizing rather than 'enabling' development. Yet, such findings hardly curtail the belief in the value of ICT in order for developing countries to prosper in the global economy.

The institutional influences that have been shaping and spreading ICT have been studied in two rather distinct fields of literature, one that is concerned with innovation as a macro-level social phenomenon and another that is focused on innovation as a process situated in organizations. The former elaborates on the economists' process of invention, innovation, and diffusion and seeks to understand why certain societies have been successful in promoting ICT innovation as a basis for socio-economic development while others have failed to do so. It is primarily intended to inform policy and intervening action of national, regional, and international government entities. The latter is mainly part of the information systems literature, and reveals the significance of the non-technical/rational aspects of information systems development and use in organizations.

---

[8] This issue is discussed further in Chap. 3.

Macro-level Institutional Elements of ICT Innovation

King et al. (1994) list a number of sources of institutional forces at the macro-societal innovation level. They include government authorities; international agencies; professional, trade, and industry associations; research centres; trend-setting powerful domestic or multinational corporations; financial institutions; labour organizations; and religious institutions. Such entities—institutions in their own right—exert influence or enact regulation that affect market supply and demand.

Of these, particular attention has been given to national government policy. In most cases such policies have a double concern to assist the exploitation of the industrial potential in producing technologies and services, and to promote the use of the new technology in order to achieve beneficial economic and social effects. A mutual reinforcement of innovation in production and use is assumed: the development of a local ICT industry enables widespread and innovative usage of technologies, while the demand that is created from widespread use is also beneficial for the local industry.[9]

Addressing the action of particular types of organizations, such as government agencies, in the macro-dynamics of innovation does not necessarily imply a recognition of institutional forces. Most policy analyses guiding government action on technology innovation are exercises of technical economic theory (as for example many of the chapters in the volumes by Dosi et al. 1988; Foray and Freeman 1993). In contrast,[10] institutional analyses of macro-level innovation processes elaborate on the social, cultural, and political aspects of the entities involved. One such example is the literature that emphasizes the significance of cultural conditions, such as trust and socially acquired tacit knowledge, for the cumulative learning involved in successful 'national systems of innovation' (Lundvall 1988, 1992). Another example is the study of R&D

---

[9] Nevertheless, different governments and international institutions have addressed these areas in different ways, and with different degrees of commitment. Earlier policy interventions were concerned primarily with building national computer industries, taking a range of measures to that end, such as public funding of computer manufacturers, large-scale purchasing of computers for the public sector, and R&D programmes. In the 1980s, attention shifted towards facilitating technology diffusion, while attempts to interfere with the global oligopolistic forces of the computer industry were limited—although, as is discussed in Chap. 4, government involvement in the IT industry continued to be pursued rather successfully in South-East Asian countries. Industrial policy targeted the liberalization of national telecommunication companies. A variety of measures for technology diffusion have been taken, including direct promotion of specific technologies—such as the Minitel case in France (Cats-Baril and Jelassi 1994)—legislation to create a conducive environment for ICT use, such as data protection and intellectual property protection legislation, and dissemination of technical information to influence 'good practice', such as the publications of the OECD (1986, 1987, 1988). In the 1990s international and national efforts for the liberalization of telecommunications intensified as this industry formed links and started becoming enmeshed with another cluster of lucrative industries, generally identified as 'information', or 'content' industries. A series of initiatives—such as the much publicized initiatives of former Vice-President Al Gore on 'Information Superhighway' in the USA, the European Union on 'Information Society' <http://www.ispo.cec.be/infosoc/backg/bangeman.html>, and Malaysia's 'Superhighway'—have been launched with the common aim to spread ICT infrastructures and applications and the loud message that the spread of such technologies is a vital matter for 'progress' both in economic and social terms.

[10] Most often institutional aspects are highlighted not 'in contrast', but as complementing technical economic analyses.

initiatives launched by national and international government agencies as networks formed by the mobilization of powerful actors (Callon, Laredo, and Mustar 1997).

The political dimension of the macro-level institutions of ICT innovation has been prominent in the history of innovation of most countries and regions. A good example is the friction between the two government agencies that have orchestrated ICT innovation in Japan in the last three decades of the twentieth century (King et al. 1994). Another case with clear political dimensions is the launching of collaborative R&D programmes in Europe, analysed by Cram (1997). In the early 1980s, the European Commission launched ESPRIT, a collaborative R&D programme in ICT which involved research centres and major computer companies of the member states of the European Economic Community (EEC).[11] Since then the European Commission has sponsored a series of 'framework programmes' for R&D with main emphasis on ICT. It masterminded their technical and economic objectives, mobilized resources, convinced major companies of the European ICT industry to participate, and curbed the reluctance of national governments. The R&D programmes served political goals, as they provided a vehicle for the enhancement of cohesion within the Union through promoting partnerships among member states. Moreover, with these initiatives the European Commission legitimized its own existence in the European political arena.

Institutional Aspects of Information Systems

At an organizational level, ICT innovation is a combination of technical tasks and social negotiations. Some technical tasks, such as the use of methodologies in systems development practice and methodical evaluation have an institutional character (Avgerou 2000). There has been little research on the extent to which systems development methodologies contribute to building systems which serve better the needs of an organization. But it is clear that the effort to systematize technical practice serves other purposes in addition to the immediate task of building and implementing an information system to support an organizational set of activities. Methodologies made possible the professionalization of systems development by assigning technical roles such as the analyst, the designer, the project manager, or the programmer, with predefined skills (Avgerou and Cornford 1993). They are used for the training of large numbers of 'experts' required to sustain a booming industry. They established rules of 'good practice' to develop a system, without having to assess results. Indeed, it is well known that formal information systems evaluation is rarely practised, and when it is practised it may be only to legitimize decisions on systems development which have already been made on the basis of intuition and often

---

[11] European Economic Community (EEC) is the early name for the European Union. The name European Union was adopted in the 1990s to signify the increasingly significant political role undertaken by this regional institution. European Commission (EC) is a particular administrative body in the governance of the EU.

vested actor interests, rather than the technical merits of a particular IT innovation (Farbey, Land, and Targett 1993).

Furthermore, institutional forces are significant in shaping the perception of organizational opportunities for the exploitation of ICT, what Swanson and Ramiller call an 'organizing vision' (Swanson and Ramiller 1997). Information systems innovation is partly a matter of interpretation of the potential benefits and risks entailed by a technology for the organization concerned, and partly a matter of sharing a vision about such potential with a wider inter-organizational community. Various forces contribute to the formation of common visions about ICT uses and associated organizational changes. Among them Swanson and Ramiller include the rhetoric and interventions of macro-level institutions, the practices and language of information systems professionals, the practice of business and management.

It is important to highlight here the significance of management for the shaping of organizing visions for information systems innovation, an issue that I discuss in greater depth later in this chapter. The rationalization attempted by mainstream information systems research and practice by linking information systems to management practice, for example, by means such as aligning ICT innovation to business strategy, closely associates ICT innovation to the dominant institution of organizing.

THE NATURE OF ENDOGENOUS INSTITUTIONAL FORCES OF ORGANIZATIONS

Viewing organizations, management, and ICT as institutions does not deny that action and structure in organizations, their governing principles, and ICT innovation involve calculated choices driven by concern for efficiency and problem solving. But it questions the status of efficiency as a de facto driver for organizational action, and it juxtaposes efficiency-concerned accounts of organizations with the social constitution of the organizations themselves and their social environment (Berger and Luckmann 1967). The sketchy presentation of organizations, management, and ICT as institutions above demonstrates several social, political, and cultural forces involved in their formation and sustenance. For example, the institutionalist account of the rise of the formal bureaucratic organization refers to its function in relation to its broader social and economic system, and considers the way this was assisted by other social institutions, such as legislation. This, however, is only a partial explanation. The symbolic and cognitive aspects of social relations within the bureaucracy, as well as of the bureaucracy understood to be a 'rationally' organized entity within its social environment, have been crucial in maintaining its legitimacy even when its functional merits became questionable. Important in the sustenance of the hierarchical bureaucratic organizational form are also the power relations, both within the bureaucratic organization and among the institutional actors of the modern industrial economies at large, such as between management, labour, customers or politicians, corporate activity, and amorphous market. In presenting management as an institution, Shenhav emphasizes the political dynamics, whereby one social category shaped the legitimacy of a particular way of organizing that favoured their interests. The case of ICT shows that functional elements, such as the practices of professional experts, are reinforced by the symbolic, such as methodological jargon and rituals. It also shows the significance of cognitive processes, that is, of sense making as a collective process of forming a vision for ICT innovation.

But the distinction among social, political, and cultural elements is unclear in most institutional analyses, in which all three are seen as contributing to the formation, continuation, and transformation of institutions (Friedland and Alford 1991; Meyer and Rowan 1991; Scott 1991; Zucker 1991). Also it seems it is often assumed that, whatever these aspects are, they are in harmony in social institutions. To some extent this assumption is responsible for the perception of the institutionalist theory as a theory of stability and uniformity. But when these elements are not in harmony, they may create uneven and conflicting institutional forces and, consequently, institutional transformation trends. Therefore, disentangling the possible relationships of these forces is important in order to explore the roots of organizational diversity.

Culture is a vague concept in social theory, generally defined unhelpfully very broadly as the system of values and beliefs in a society.[12] Nevertheless, the debate on what culture is has addressed questions about how it is related to the functional and political aspects of a society, which are the significant issues here. One category of theories, the socio-cultural theories in cultural anthropology, considers culture as a component of the social system striving to improve its materialistic condition (Allaire and Firsirotu 1984). In such theories cultural elements, e.g. myths or rituals, are seen as serving functional necessities for the satisfaction of human needs or for maintaining structures of social order to that end. In contrast, the so-called 'ideational' theories in cultural anthropology consider culture as a system of ideas and symbols which cannot be explained in terms of serving a social function and maintaining the structure through which a social system is distinguished from and survives within its environment (see e.g. Geertz 1973). According to the ideational view, systems of symbols and ideas both reflect and contribute to the creation of social 'reality'. The symbolic and cognitive aspects that sustain an institution acquire significance and legitimacy in their own right, irrespective of whether they contribute to functions and social relations that serve the material interests of the members of the institution. Indeed, often the opposite can be observed: functions and structures in social institutions are maintained to fulfil their symbolic character. And when the symbolic and cognitive forces in an institution are not in harmony with the functional and structural forces of its social system, the stability of the taken-for-granted behaviour and role of institutions is challenged from within.

---

[12] In organizational studies and information systems, culture sometimes refers to deeply ingrained values and beliefs that govern actions in an organization, and sometimes to the behavioural manifestations of such ingrained values and beliefs (Fiol 1991). Prevalent in the information systems literature is Hofstede's definition of culture as a programming of mind. In itself this definition of culture through a metaphor of the computer is revealing for the cognitive ways this field deploys to make sense of social aspects of information systems. Such definitions though are not very helpful to understanding the relationship of cultural aspects, such as particular enactment of information-related jobs at the workplace, with social and structural characteristics, such as established structures of authority and forms of governance.

Similarly, the symbolic and cognitive aspects of an institution are neither void of politics nor the inevitable consequence of sedimented power relations. The view of culture as a system of shared understandings and values reached through social consensus is common in theories of cultural anthropology as well as in the literature on organizational studies. However, 'critical cultural' studies have pointed out the formation of systems of values and ideas through power relations and political processes that are not necessarily consensual (Deetz 1985; Knights and Willmott 1987). The meanings and significance of institutional symbols and ideas are manipulated, contested, and reinterpreted by individuals and other institutions. And the stability of an institution is challenged by the politics of 'truth', whereby the meaning and value of taken-for-granted behaviour are confronted by 'subjugated' meanings and values.[13]

Early institutionalist writers (DiMaggio and Powell 1991; Meyer and Rowan 1991) paid relatively little attention to incompatibilities between the cultural systems and functional aspects or the power relations in organizations. They suggested that organizations are historically produced social systems, whose formal structures and processes are sustained by systems of shared meanings. In other words, as a result of the circumstances of their genesis, organizations develop their own values, symbols, ideologies, rituals, and myths, which are widely shared by their members and sustain organizational life. But the relationships between the formal social structures and processes of organizations and the cultural systems they involve—as well as those in their environment—may well change over time, and founding shared meanings may subsequently be challenged. Power relations and dominant symbolic and cognitive systems may change by the reflexive behaviour of actors in the organization and its environment. Actors in the organization may develop and strive to impose new definitions of the organization's situation. Moreover, the organization's members, through their efforts of interpretation and sense making of emergent new conditions, continuously shape and reshape their meanings and value systems (Allaire and Firsirotu 1984; Zucker 1991).

The degree of institutionalization—in the sense of stability and taken-for-grantedness—of a social domain depends on the extent to which the individuals' actions in an organization have a shared meaning and value and accepted legitimacy. In highly institutionalized domains of action, we can expect to find cultural persistence,

---

[13] Influential social theories differ regarding the notion of power itself, the nature of social struggle, and the way certain systems of value become dominant or are challenged. Marxist-inspired theories see power relations and cultural distinctions along the lines of class structures. Foucault develops a very different notion of power relations, as being immanent in the symbolic and cognitive forces of social institutions. Such an all-pervasive notion of power exposes connections between power and discourse, which through history become relations of domination by 'subjugation of knowledge' (Foucault 1977). Foucault's notion of power recognizes that counter action and resistance are constituent forces in the formation of the cognitive and symbolic elements of institutions. However it leaves unclear where such resistances stem from, and his analyses of institutions, such as prisons and the psychiatric hospital, portray a pessimistic state of impotence of subjugated knowledge to effect change. Giddens's structuration theory too considers asymmetries of power as pervasive in social relations and as encompassing human agents' systems of meaning, but in comparison to Foucault, Giddens places more emphasis on the capacity of human agency to alter sedimented power relations (Giddens 1984).

which involves transmission and maintenance of ways of acting through chains of actors, and resistance to attempts to change them. De-institutionalization and institutional transformation can take place when established meanings and action in an organization are discredited, either as a result of competing meanings and actions or because they are seen as failing to contribute to the institutional *raison d'être*. However, recognition of the possibility of incongruities among the social, cultural, and political elements that constitute an institution suggests another institutional possibility. Castoriadis points out that institutionalized action may acquire 'its own inertia and its own logic, that, in its continuance and in its effects, it outstrips its function, its "ends", and its "reasons for existing". The apparent plain truths are turned upside-down: what could have been seen "at the start" as an ensemble of institutions in the service of society becomes a society in the service of institutions' (Castoriadis 1987: 110). The main example Castoriadis had in mind for such a state of 'alienation' of society from its institutions was the post-Second World War Soviet Union. But there are many other cases of dysfunctional institutional inertia, particularly in the micro-institutional world of the formal organization, as is shown in the case studies in Part II of this book. Methodical practices, formal authorization or supervision procedures, and codes of behaviour often come to define what the organization does, irrespective of whether all these fulfil its declared objectives. The problem pointed out here is that in certain social contexts formal organizational institutions, management, and technical innovation may exist almost entirely on the basis of their symbolism and their imaginary value.

INSTITUTIONAL INTERACTION

In addition to elaborating on the nature of the endogenous forces contributing to the continuity and transformation of institutions, institutionalist analysis highlights the significance of the interactions among institutions. Most institutionalist organizational literature has been concerned with the influences organizations receive from other organizations in their environment, stressing in particular the isomorphic effects in clusters of organizations. This is a limited view though[14] with misleading messages regarding ICT innovation and organizational change. Two limitations are identified and discussed here. First, tracing influences in clusters of organizations misses the complex dynamics of globalization as a multifaceted phenomenon. Second, the focus on the formal organization as the main social institution ignores the emergence of management and ICT as institutions in their own right and therefore cannot account adequately for the processes of transformation of organized activities in modern society.

---

[14] One explanation for the emphasis given to isomorphic effects in institutional theory is as a manifestation of the parochialism of the American organizational theory (Boyacigilier and Adler 1991). Ghoshal and Westney note: 'Modern organization theory (OT) has been dominated by Americans, and ethnocentrism has characterized the theory, as it has American business and society ... research on organizations in California or Ohio has led to propositions that have been implicitly stated and accepted as universal' (Ghoshal and Westney 1993: 6).

Isomorphism and Variation

One of the core theoretical propositions of institutional analysis is that organizations tend to be clustered in fields, and within each field they tend to develop similar structures and processes. The clusters are referred to by terms such as the 'organizational field' (DiMaggio and Powell 1991), 'functional organizational field' (Scott 1987), or 'societal sector' (Scott and Meyer 1991), although the term 'organizational field' seems to be more commonly used. An organizational field is understood to be constituted by organizational actors competing in the production of similar products or services, their suppliers, sources of funding, professional and trade associations, consumers, and regulatory agents. The participants in an organizational field may be located in the same geographical location or be dispersed. Apart from the technical exchanges among them, such as contract-based or financial transactions, they exert normative and cognitive influences upon each other, sharing similar sets of activities.

This argument of 'isomorphism' is not new in organizational theory or unique to institutional theory. Rational analysis of competitiveness under market conditions both assumes and suggests the existence of common optimal structures and behaviours of organizations. Without denying the merits of such analyses, institutionalist theorists look beyond classical economics and emphasize the social, cultural, and cognitive forces that shape common structures and processes within organizational fields.

DiMaggio and Powell (1991) identify three distinct mechanisms through which institutional isomorphic change occurs: coercion, imitation, and normative professional conduct. 'Coercive' pressures may be formal or informal, exerted through force or persuasion. They sanction the legitimacy of organizational structures, processes, and outputs. The clearest source of coercive pressures is government mandates and the legal framework of the regional, national, or international context of an organizational field. For example, organizations are obliged to adopt specific accounting practices, work safety procedures, data protection measures, and pollution avoidance mechanisms. Regulation has been the most prevalent mechanism determining the structure, processes, and mission of public sector organizational fields, such as schools, and until recently in most countries telecommunication services. But it is also highly significant in the functioning of market-controlled fields. Indeed, the liberalization of industries such as banking and telecommunications involves the substitution of strict monopolistic legislation with more complex regulatory regimes that determine what is considered a legitimate balance between 'fair competition' and customer (or citizen) access to services of fundamental importance in modern society.

'Mimetic' mechanisms refer to the voluntary acquisition of particular characteristics of structure and process by emulating other organizations seen as successful. It is seen as a way of coping with problems which do not have clear technical solutions, or addressing uncertainties and ambiguous threats or opportunities. More generally, organizations tend to model themselves after other organizations, rather than to design totally new structures and patterns of behaviour on the basis of efficiency plans.

'Normative' pressures refer primarily to the effects of professional practice. Professionals convey a combination of cognitive and regulatory norms that legitimize their occupational autonomy. Such norms are produced and maintained through formal education and training, as well as through professional associations. The isomorphic effects of professional standards are particularly important when particular activities with on-the-job socialization (that is learning and perpetuating 'the way we do things here') become autonomous professional occupations and a business in their own right. In such cases professional standards justify the existence of specialist organizations, and are maintained with continuous training, trade magazines, and affiliation to professional societies that expose employees to common pools of knowledge and standard skills.[15]

The argument that organizations become similar to each other as they respond to common regulatory and normative pressures, or as they copy the structures and imitate the processes of other organizations that are considered successful leaves many grey areas. Are isomorphic influences always converging? How far does institutional isomorphism spread? Do isomorphic forces transcend national borders and organizational fields?

To begin with, the 'organizational field' is an ambiguous and constraining unit of analysis. The boundaries of an organizational field can be defined relatively accurately only for an organization with a single output under the influence of one institutional system. But organizations and the influences they receive are more complex than that. They often produce many different outputs under different controls. This is what happens in large diversified corporations, e.g. a retail firm may also trade financial services, as well as in public service providers, e.g. most universities provide vocational training and research programmes.

The institutional forces of an organizational field may be contradictory rather than confluent. Different institutional agencies in the local environment of organizations may exert conflicting pressures; an organization may receive both local and international or 'foreign' institutional pressures or models for imitation; and particular aspects of the historically constructed taken-for-granted structures and processes may be in conflict with emerging new rationalized myths in its environment.

The limitations of the 'organizational field' as a unit of institutional studies are more obvious in the case of multinational corporations and the so-called 'global industries', as pointed out by Westney (1993). By straddling two or more countries' organizational fields, such organizations cope with different isomorphic pulls. By competing against and imitating other multinational companies, they contribute to

---

[15] Scott (1991), using different terminology, proposes a set of institutional mechanisms which partly overlap with, but also extend those proposed by DiMaggio and Powell. A variation of coercion is inducement, whereby an organization is given incentives to adopt particular structures or activities. Also, acquisition of common organizational characteristics may result through more subtle ways than coercion, imitation, or standardized professional intervention, through unplanned, historical processes of adaptation of organizations to the most salient features of their context. Moreover, Scott argues, organizations may act similarly because they share common beliefs, common cultures, even if they are structured differently. For example, his research indicated that the coherence of American schools was based more on an agreement about the nature the school system rather than common organizational structures, thus arguing that 'cultural controls can substitute for structural controls'.

the formation of global organization fields with unclear implications for the organizational fields of their 'local' competitors, suppliers, customers, and regulators.

In general, institutionalist literature is ambivalent regarding the significance of conflict between local and international institutional forces and shows limited awareness of the variation in formal organizations and their broader institutional fields in different national contexts. Studies addressing national institutional characteristics are often based on the assumption that the contemporary organization of the public domain of national societies, the 'modern polity', is a replica of the Western polity and the formal organizations sustained within contemporary nation societies are the same as Western formal organizations. As Jepperson and Meyer explicitly state, institutional studies of the interdependence—what they call 'interpenetration'—of the formal organization with the institutional mechanisms of the nation state and the wider world system, 'rely upon . . . [the assumption] that a distinctive polity form, a creation of the Europe-based world system, develops and expands worldwide' (Jepperson and Meyer 1991: 207).

Such an assumption of hegemony of Western political and economic norms reflects the geopolitical world situation at the beginning of the twenty-first century. Through long historical processes, the governance mechanisms of the West have acquired a global legitimacy. Moreover, a network of formal organizations, such as the various agencies of the United Nations, the World Bank, the IMF, exert coercive and normative pressures for the spread of the institutions that comprise modern Western society. Nevertheless, the spreading of nation state and economic institutions through isomorphic pulls is only part of the change processes occurring in countries with different socio-political histories. Copied social institutions—such as democracy, free market, formal organization, management—either on grounds of efficiency or through politico-economic hegemony, are subject to local social, cultural, and political processes. The combination often results in formal organizations incapable of either locally meaningful or globally effective action. The modern nation states of Africa provide dramatic examples of distorted rationalization and institutional alienation (Mutahaba 1989). The imposition of Western-type modern polity institutions led to highly inefficient organizations, an unreconcilable split between the rationalized form and the taken-for-granted collective values, and disastrous political and economic consequences.

On a more positive note, institutionalist studies show that inter-societal influences can result in locally meaningful and effective organizational development if the mimetic influences are accompanied by local adaptation. Westney's study of the emulation of Western organizations in the making of the modern nation of Japan in the late nineteenth century shows a complex process of selection of organizational forms and adaptation within the local social, cultural, and cognitive systems (Westney 1987). The result of this process was innovation and diversity, not isomorphism. Successful local institutionalization of features transferred from across organizational fields entailed adjustments and innovation rather than across-field isomorphism. The Japanese emulation and adaptation resulted in organizational forms that are now seen as sufficiently different from those of the West. In another empirical study, Orrù, Biggart, and Hamilton (1991) show that business groups in

South Korea, Taiwan, and Japan operating under different institutional contexts exhibit distinct organizational structures.

National variation in organizing business and government has been highlighted in many studies across economics and sociology (see e.g. Lash and Urry 1987; Guillén 1994; Whitley and Kristensen 1997). There are significant national variations in the industrial organization of mass production, which are most visible in comparisons between Western industrialized countries and developing economies. Many developing countries which adopted industrialization based on mass production have never developed an effective system of state support, such as welfare provisions.

Within industrialized countries, the formation of patterns of work organization is shaped and sustained by institutions such as trade unions, education and training systems, and state authority structures and policies (Whitley 1997). Local variations are also prevalent in management, despite the mimetic and normative pressures exerted by consultants, business schools, and the international business literature on globalization and competitiveness. While there is a risk of making too much of national stereotypes in identifying national patterns of management, nevertheless, the historical formation of particularities of management practices in some major industrialized countries, notably Germany, France, Britain, and Japan, have been adequately researched to support the argument of their relative distinctiveness.

For example Grint (1995) points out the short-termism of management in Britain and discusses the institutional forces that contributed to a professional tradition which is reluctant to pursue rational/instrumental planning, systematization and efficiency in the way other industrialized countries do, with the prime example being the United States, as discussed above. Grint traces the idiosyncratic characteristics of 'British management' to the historical circumstances of the shaping of the laissez-faire society with long rooted class structures. Unlike the American context, engineering—and consequently professional management—in Britain did not find fertile ground in an economy of rather small family businesses and a social system dominated by an aristocracy unenthusiastic about getting involved in organizing a manufacturing industry. In the ideological and political context of Britain in the early twentieth century, the techniques of scientific management were considered inhuman and rejected. More recently, with increasing concern about the country's decline in the international economy, British management has felt a more pressing need to follow more typical rational instrumental orientation. Indicatively, it was as late as in the 1990s that Cambridge, one of the two top universities of the country introduced a management programme.

In Germany, where the formal Tayloristic standardization of work fitted well with a pre-existing formalistic bureaucratic organizing tradition, professional management took hold easier. However, generic professional management was not allowed to supersede the legitimacy of the old professions in controlling their areas of expertise. Moreover, the state remained prevalent, enjoying high influence and esteem over organizational matters (Lash and Urry 1987).

Another much noticed example is Japanese management, which although influenced by American principles of efficiency and systematization has developed unique features that are considered responsible for the economic performance of the country—whether admired or criticized. In response to industrial conflicts in the inter-war period, Japanese corporations developed the notion of 'enterprise as community' to secure worker commitment. This involves a seniority system, life employment, and company unionism. Moreover, unlike the US business context, management is much less a matter of independent professional practice. A strong involvement of the state in the market and direct presence of capitalists in the organ-ization of production complicates the case of Japanese management.

Such examples suggest that institutional influences are unlikely to be isomorphic beyond well delineated fields, such as those formed by national economies. In effect, having exposed multiple and often conflicting pressures and aspirations that organ-izations derive from their interaction with their contexts, institutionalist theory inevitably confronts the generation of variation.

Institutional Alliances

The institutionalization of ICT needs to be understood in association with the quest for new principles and structures for the formal organization and the establishment of management as an institution in its own right. The point made in this section is that ICT finds its strongest support in management, and the alliance of these two institutions forms a formidable force in the context of globalization.

ICT and the Formal Organization
While the main impetus for the invention and building of the first computers was the working out of computations required in sciences and military programme logistics, their pervasive diffusion owes a great deal to their use as data processors in large hier-archical organizations. ICT acquired the legitimacy of an enabler for any organiza-tional rationalization, and became one of the most significant factors in justifying and enacting organizational change. In the last forty years of the twentieth century, ICT has been fostered largely within the formal organization, initially assisting the bureaucratic form to increase its efficiency and strengthen its coordination and control mechanisms.

However, the merits of the hierarchical bureaucratic structure have been questioned in the last few decades; even the dominance of the large corporation has been chal-lenged (Piore and Sabel 1984; Roy 1997). ICT has been associated with the emergence of new organizational forms (Drucker 1988; Powell 1990; Bjørn-Andersen and Turner 1994). Yet, seeking a universal pattern and isomorphic trends for a new organizational form fit for the contemporary economy has proved futile. Indicatively, reporting the findings of a large survey undertaken in the early 1990s, Applegate suggested that organizations are moving towards a 'hybrid' model that combines features from the hierarchical bureaucratic model with alternative more flexible organizational types that had been identified in the management literature. While the characteristics of the hybrid model remained vague, major significance in its performance was attached to its networked information infrastructure (Applegate 1994). Two years later, Applegate reported at the International Conference on Information Systems (ICIS) that her continuing research on IT and organizational forms suggested the persistence of the hierarchical structure, rather than its replacement.

The question of organizational reform in the late twentieth century became more complex than the transformation of the unitary hierarchical organization. While such organizations continue to dominate the organizational fields in many Western countries, they coexist with inter-organizational partnerships, such as the conglomerates between banks and producer companies in East Asian countries, with clusters of small independent firms, as well as with clusters of interdependent firms often supported by government agencies.

The inconclusiveness regarding a new dominant organizational pattern is significant in the institutionalist analysis of ICT and organizational change. While the institutionalization of ICT is well advanced, self-justified, and irreversible, organizational changes of structure and process lack a commonly accepted orientation, and are easily challenged by alternative organizing models (Avgerou 2000). With pervasive uncertainty regarding the principles of effective organizational structures, the fundamental dictum of information systems practice that technology should be designed to fulfil well-specified organizational requirements and to serve well-defined organizational needs is inapplicable. Organizations lack confidence regarding the direction of change to provide unambiguous requirements for information systems development.

ICT and Management

What continues to gain ground across the variety of organizational forms, however, is the managerial rationality. Even with significant variations from region to region and among organizational fields, and often mixed with other rationalities, such as legal norms, professional managerial governance is unquestionably regarded as the most appropriate way of running organizations in the contemporary context of globalization. Many of the ideas and practices of management are short lived, contributing transient changes, rather than creating incrementally new norms for organizing (Abrahamson 1991, 1996; Pettigrew 1998). Yet, the status enjoyed by management as a way of governing organizations efficiently is undiminished.

ICT as an institution is linked closely with management. In the United States, information systems training and research takes place predominantly in business schools, and in many countries information systems training emulates the American information systems curriculum. Information systems academics of all countries gain kudos from publishing in the 'international' American journals, which have a clear business studies orientation. Ever since the early 1980s, the information systems literature has adopted the discourse of management, shifting focus from engineering-oriented research agenda to addressing business-oriented concerns (Avgerou, Siemer, and Bjørn-Andersen 1999). Relatively little is written about information systems in organizations which are not governed by a managerial rationality.

At the same time, management became increasingly dependent on the rational myth of ICT. Widely influential new ideas in the literature of management, such as business process re-engineering and e-commerce are centred on ICT. The rationalization vision that underlies management has been strengthened by accommodating the efficiency potential of the computer and telecommunications and has been translated into a vision of perpetual innovation.

The mutually reinforced institutions of ICT and management are not damaged by the crisis of the formal organization, on the contrary, they contrive to its erosion. Management and ICT are no longer constituted only as functions of the formal organization. They have been externalized, developed a corporate status, and constitute a thriving consultancy services multinational industry. With continuous management innovation, linked with ICT best practice in software and implementation services, such as enterprise resource planning (ERP), organizations rely increasingly on outsourcing. Such externalization cripples the unitary formal organization. Inasmuch as the allied ICT and management institutions are in the business of creating and spreading visions for new organizational arrangements for production and trade that do away with the integrity of the unitary formal organization, they further de-institutionalize it.

The interaction between and co-development of these two institutions under the influences of business studies and computer science and the multinational services industry constitutes an institutional field in the same way that interaction among organizations constitutes organizational fields. Unlike the organizational fields that are geographically identifiable, ICT and management operate in a mode which is not determined by space-bound social institutions. Although the ICT and management practices enacted in specific organizations are shaped by the institutional features of the organization concerned, the ICT innovation and management knowledge is institutionalized through the multinational IT business, the international mobility of professionals, and international business school teaching. This disembedded institutional mode will be discussed in some more detail as an aspect of globalization in Chapter 4.

Thus, the interrelated processes of ICT innovation, management, and organizational restructuring are unequally sustained by their respective institutional elements. The taken-for-granted inevitability of technical progress of ICT, and increasing confidence in the soundness of technological expertise and managerial efficiency are unmatched by the ambivalent orientation of change in organizational structures and processes.

CONCLUDING REMARKS

The institutional perspective discussed in this chapter suggests that organizational diversity is the inevitable consequence of context-specific historical processes of the formation and transformation of social institutions. The way in which formal organizations are structured and function could have been otherwise. Indeed, it is different across the notional boundaries of organizational fields, and the geographic boundaries of countries and regions. By expanding the analysis of organizational formation and change beyond the technical/rational perspectives of organizational behaviour to address social, cultural, and cognitive influences, institutionalist theory exposes not only isomorphic forces, but also sources of conflict and variation. The neat argument on isomorphism stated in the institutionalist literature is confronted by complex accounts of conflicting interrelations of organizations and multiple organizational fields in studies of different organizational contexts.

Thus, organizational diversity is not a transient aspect and information systems innovation cannot be understood in terms of the capacity of ICT to contribute to an organization's efficiency and competitiveness. Recognition of the institutional nature of ICT and management implies that ICT innovation cannot be adequately accounted for by considering the technical potential of technologies, the methodical activities of the information systems professionals, and the declared strategies of management. The tasks performed by the actors involved in ICT innovation are institutionally shaped, for example, through training, professional standards, work experience, trade journals, the history of power relations in the organization concerned and in its organizational fields. In this sense, innovation involves *institutional actors*, not just individuals applying their particular skills and technologies, but networks of actors who are immersed in institutions.

My main argument in this chapter is that the institutional alliance of ICT and management—the historical product mainly of the specific organizational field of the United States—has created a very distinct knowledge and practice of information systems innovation. However, the aligned ICT/management knowledges, disembedded from their formative environment, have acquired universal validity through the dynamics of globalization and in particular the consultancy services industry, and are invariably transferred to other social contexts. Consequently, as the case studies in Part II show, information systems innovation often manifests the confrontation between the powerful ICT/management alliance with multiple other social institutions, some of a local, others of global extent, and others without specific geographic reference.

References

Abrahamson, E. (1991). 'Managerial Fads and Fashions: The Diffusion and Rejection of Innovations'. *Academy of Management Review*, 16: 586–612.

——— (1996). 'Management Fashion'. *Academy of Management Review*, 21: 254–85.

Allaire, Y., and Firsirotu, M. E. (1984). 'Theories of Organizational Culture'. *Organization Studies*, 5(3): 193–226.

Applegate, L. M. (1994). 'Managing in an Information Age: Transforming the Organization for the 1990s', in R. Baskerville, S. Smithson, O. Ngwenyama, and J. I. DeGross (eds.), *Transforming Organizations with Information Technology*. Amsterdam: North-Holland, 15–94.

Avgerou, C. (2000). 'IT and Organizational Change: An Institutionalist Perspective'. *Information Technology and People*, 13(4): 234–62.

——— and Cornford, T. (1993). 'A Review of the Methodologies Movement'. *Journal of Information Technology*, 5: 277–86.

——— Siemer, J., and Bjørn-Andersen, N. (1999). 'The Academic Field of Information Systems in Europe'. *European Journal of Information Systems*, 8: 136–53.

Bell, D. (1973). *The Coming of the Post-Industrial Society*. New York: Basic Books.

Berger, P. L., and Luckmann, T. (1967). *The Social Construction of Reality*. London: Penguin.

Berle, A. A., and Neans, G. C. (1932). *The Modern Corporation and Private Property*. New York: Macmillan.

Bjørn-Andersen, N., and Turner, J. A. (1994). 'Creating the Twenty-First Century Organization: The Metamorphosis of Oticon', in R. Baskerville, S. Smithson, O. Ngwenyama, and J. I. DeGross (eds.), *Transforming Organizations with Information Technology*. Amsterdam: North-Holland, 379–94.

Boyacigilier, N., and Adler, N. (1991). 'The Parochial Dinosaur: Organizational Science in a Global Context'. *Academy of Management Review*, 16(2): 262–90.

Bransson, N., and Olsen, J. (1998). 'Organizational Theory: Thirty Years of Dismantling, and Then. . . ?', in N. Bransson and J. Olsen, *Organizing Organizations*. Bergen-Sandviken: Fagbokforlaget, 13–43.

Callon, M., Laredo, P., and Mustar, Ph. (1997). 'Technico-economic Networks and the Analysis of Structural Effects', in M. Callon, P. Laredo, and P. Mustar, *The Strategic Management of Research and Technology: Evaluation of Programmes*. Paris: Economica International, 385–429.

Castells, M. (1996). *The Rise of the Network Society*. Oxford: Blackwell.

Castoriadis, C. (1987). *The Imaginary Institution of Society*. Cambridge: Polity Press.

Cats-Baril, W., and Jelassi, T. (1994). 'The French Videotex System Minitel: A Successful Implementation of a National Information Technology Infrastructure'. *MIS Quarterly*, 18(1): 1–19.

Chandler, A. D., Jr. (1962). *Strategy and Structure: Chapters in the History of the Industrial Enterprise*. Cambridge, Mass.: MIT Press.

——(1969). 'The Structure of American Industry in the Twentieth Century: A Historical Overview'. *Business History Review*, 43: 255–81.

Ciborra, C. U., and Andreu, R. (1998). 'Organizational Learning and Core Capabilities Development: The Role of IT', in R. D. Galliers and W. R. J. Baets (eds.), *Information Technology and Organizational Transformation*. Chichester: John Wiley, 87–106.

Cram, L. (1997). *Policy Making in the EU*. London: Routledge.

Deetz, S. (1985). 'Critical-Cultural Research: New Sensibilities and Old Realities'. *Journal of Management*, 11(2): 121–36.

DiMaggio, P. J., and Powell, W. W. (1991). 'The Iron Cage Revisited: Institutional Isomorphism and Collective Rationality in Organizational Fields', in W. W. Powell and P. J. DiMaggio (eds.), *The New Institutionalism in Organizational Analysis*. Chicago: University of Chicago Press, 63–82.

Dosi, G., Freeman, C., Nelson, R., Silverberg, G., and Soete, L. (eds.) (1988). *Technical Change and Economic Theory*. London: Pinter.

Drucker, P. (1988). 'The Coming of the New Organization'. *Harvard Business Review*, Jan–Feb., 45–53.

Farbey, B., Land, F. F., and Targett, D. (1993). *IT Investment: A Study of Methods and Practice*. Oxford: Butterworth-Heinemann.

Fiol, C. M. (1991). 'Managing Culture as a Competitive Resource: An Identity-Based View of Sustainable Competitive Advantage'. *Journal of Management*, 17(1): 191–211.

Foray, D., and Freeman, C. (eds.) (1993). *Technology and the Wealth of Nations: The Dynamics of Constructed Advantage*. London: Pinter.

Foucault, M. (1977). *Power/Knowledge*. New York: Pantheon.

Friedland, R., and Alford, R. R. (1991). 'Bringing Society Back: Symbols, Practices, and Institutional Contradictions', in W. W. Powell and P. J. DiMaggio (eds.), *The New Institutionalism in Organizational Analysis*. Chicago: University of Chicago Press, 232–63.

Geertz, C. (1973). *The Interpretation of Cultures*. New York: Basic Books.

Ghoshal, S., and Westney, D. E. (eds.) (1993). *Organization Theory and the Multinational Corporation*. Basingstoke: Macmillan.

Giddens, A. (1984). *The Constitution of Society: Outline of the Theory of Structuration*. Cambridge: Polity Press.

—— (1990). *The Consequences of Modernity*. Cambridge: Polity Press.

Granovetter, M., and McGuire, P. (1998). 'The Making of an Industry: Electricity in the United States', in M. Callon (ed.), *The Law of Markets*. Oxford: Blackwell, 147–73.

Grint, K. (1995). *Management: A Sociological Introduction*. Cambridge: Polity Press.

Guillén, M. F. (1994). *Models of Management: Work, Authority and Organization in a Comparative Perspective*. Chicago: University of Chicago Press.

Hammer, M., and Champy, J. (1993). *Reengineering the Corporation: A Manifesto for Business Revolution*. London: Nicholas Brealey.

Hannan, M. T., and Freeman, J. (1989). *Organizational Ecology*. Cambridge, Mass.: Harvard University Press.

Heeks, R. (ed.) (1999). *Reinventing Government in the Information Age: International Practice in IT-enabled Public Sector Reform*. London: Routledge.

Jepperson, R. L. (1991). 'Institutions, Institutional Effects, and Institutionalism', in W. W. Powell and P. J. DiMaggio (eds.), *The New Institutionalism in Organizational Analysis*. Chicago: University of Chicago Press, 143–63.

—— and Meyer, J. W. (1991). 'The Public Order and Construction of Formal Organizations', in W. W. Powell and P. J. DiMaggio (eds.), *The New Institutionalism in Organizational Analysis*. Chicago: University of Chicago Press, 204–31.

Jessop, B. (1991). 'Thatcherism and Flexibility: The White Heat of a Post-Fordist Revolution', in B. Jessop, H. Kastendiek, K. Nielsen, and O. Pedersen, *The Politics of Flexibility*. Aldershot: Edward Elgar, 135–61.

King, J. L., Gurbaxani, V., Kraemer, K. L., Mc Farlan, F. W., Raman, K. S., and Yap, C. S. (1994). 'Institutional Factors in Information Technology Innovation'. *Information Systems Research*, 5(2): 139–69.

Kling, R., and Iacono, S. (1989). 'The Institutional Character of Computerized Information Systems'. *Office, Technology and People*, 5: 7–28.

Knights, D., and Willmott, H. (1987). 'Organizational Culture as Management Strategy: A Critique and Illustration from the Financial Services Industry'. *International Studies of Management and Organization*, 17(3): 40–63.

Landauer, T. K. (1996). *The Trouble with Computers: Usefulness, Usability, and Productivity*. Cambridge, Mass.: MIT Press.

Lane, J. E. (2000). *The Public Sector: Concepts, Models and Approaches*. London: Sage.

Lash, S., and Urry, J. (1987). *The End of Organized Capitalism*. Cambridge: Polity Press.

Lawrence, P. R., and Lorsch, J. W. (1969). *Organization and Environment*. Homewood, Ill.: Richard D. Irwin.

Lundvall, B.-Å. (1988). 'Innovation as an Interactive Process: From User–Producer Interaction to the National System of Innovation', in G. Dosi, C. Freeman, R. Nelson, G. Silverberg, and L. Soete (eds.), *Technical Change and Economic Theory*. London: Pinter, 349–69.

—— (ed.) (1992). *National Systems of Innovation: Towards a Theory of Innovation and Interactive Learning*. London: Pinter.

Mansell, R., and Wehn, U. (eds.) (1998). *Knowledge Societies: Information Technology for Sustainable Development*. Oxford: Oxford University Press.

March, J. G., and Olsen, J. P. (1989). *Rediscovering Institutions: The Organizational Basis of Politics*. New York: Free Press.

Meyer, J. W., and Rowan, B. (1991). 'Institutionalized Organizations: Formal Structure as Myth and Ceremony', in W. W. Powell and P. J. DiMaggio (eds.), *The New Institutionalism in Organizational Analysis*. Chicago: Chicago University Press, 41–62.

Mutahaba, G. (1989). *Reforming Public Administration for Development: Experiences from Eastern Africa*. West Hartford, Conn.: Kumarian Press.

OECD (1986). 'Trends in the Information Economy'. Paris: OECD.

——— (1987). 'Science and Technology and Internationalisation: Opportunities and Constraints for Balanced Development and Implications for Government'. Paris: OECD.

——— (1988). 'New Technologies in the 1990's: A Socio-economic Strategy', I. Paris: OECD.

Orlikowski, W. J. (1992). 'The Duality of Technology: Rethinking the Concept of Technology in Organizations'. *Organization Science*, 3(3): 398–427.

Orrù, M., Biggart, N. W., and Hamilton, G. G. (1991). 'Organizational Isomorphism in East Asia', in W. W. Powell and P. J. DiMaggio (eds.), *The New Institutionalism in Organizational Analysis*. Chicago: Chicago University Press, 361–89.

Pettigrew, A. M. (1998). 'Success and Failure in Corporate Transformation Initiatives', in R. D. Galliers and W. R. J. Baets (eds.), *Information Technology and Organizational Transformation: Innovation for the 21st Century Organization*. Chichester: John Wiley, 271–90.

Pfeffer, J., and Salancik, G. R. (1978). *The External Control of Organizations: A Resource Dependence Perspective*. New York: Harper and Row.

Piore, M., and Sabel, C. (1984). *The Second Industrial Divide: Possibilities for Prosperity*. New York: Basic Books.

Porter, M., and Millar, V. (1984). 'How Information Gives You Competitive Advantage'. *Harvard Business Review*, 63(4): 149–60.

Powell, W. W. (1990). 'Neither Market nor Hierarchy: Network Forms of Organization'. *Research on Organizational Behavior*, 12: 295–336.

——— and DiMaggio, P. J. (eds.) (1991). *The New Institutionalism in Organizational Analysis*. Chicago: University of Chicago Press.

Roy, W. (1990). 'Functional and Historial Logics in Explaining the Rise of the American Industrial Corporation'. *Comparative Social Research*, 13: 19–44.

——— (1997). *Socializing Capital: The Rise of the Large Industrial Corporation in America*. Princeton: Princeton University Press.

Scott Morton, M. S. (1991). *The Corporation of the 1990's, Information Technology and Organizational Transformation*. New York: Oxford University Press.

Scott, W. R. (1987). *Organizations: Rational, Natural and Open Systems*. Englewood Cliffs, NJ: Prentice-Hall.

——— (1991). 'Unpacking Institutional Arguments', in W. W. Powell and P. J. DiMaggio (eds.), *The New Institutionalism in Organizational Analysis*. Chicago: University of Chicago Press, 164–82.

——— and Meyer, J. W. (1991). 'The Organization of Societal Sectors: Propositions and Early Evidence', in W. W. Powell and P. J. DiMaggio (eds.), *The New Institutionalism in Organizational Analysis*. Chicago: University of Chicago Press, 108–40.

——— ——— (eds.) (1994). *Institutional Environments and Organizations: Structural Complexity and Individualism*. Thousand Oaks, Calif.: Sage.

Shenhav, Y. (1999). *Manufacturing Rationality: The Engineering Foundations of the Managerial Revolution*. Oxford: Oxford University Press.

Silva, L., and Backhouse, J. (1997). 'Becoming Part of the Furniture', in A. S. Lee, J. Liebenau, and J. I. DeGross (eds.), *Information Systems and Qualitative Research*. London: Chapman & Hall, 389–414.

Swanson, E. B., and Ramiller, N. (1997). 'The Organizing Vision in Information Systems Innovation'. *Organizational Science*, Sept./Oct., 458–74.

Walsham, G. (1993). *Interpreting Information Systems in Organizations*. Chichester: John Wiley.

Webster, F. (1995). *Theories of the Information Society*. London: Routledge.

Westney, D. E. (1987). *Imitation and Innovation: The Transfer of Western Organizational Patterns to Meiji Japan*. Cambridge, Mass.: Harvard University Press.

—— (1993). 'Institutionalization Theory and the Multinational Corporation', in S. Ghoshal and D. E. Westney (eds.), *Organization Theory and the Multinational Corporation*. Basingstoke: Macmillan, 53–76.

Whitley, R. (1997). 'The Social Regulation of Work Systems: Institutions, Interest Groups, and Varieties of Work Organization in Capitalist Societies', in R. Whitley and P. H. Kristensen (eds.), *Governance at Work: The Social Regulation of Economic Relations*. Oxford: Oxford University Press, 228–60.

—— and Kristensen, P. H. (eds.) (1997). *Governance at Work: The Social Regulation of Economic Relations*. Oxford: Oxford University Press.

Zeitlin, M. (1989). *The Large Corporation and Contemporary Classes*. Cambridge: Polity Press.

Zucker, L. G. (1983). 'Organizations as Institutions', in S. B. Bacharach (ed.), *Research in the Sociology of Organizations*. Greenwich, Conn.: JAI Press, ii. 1–47.

—— (1991). 'The Role of Institutionalization in Cultural Persistence', in W. W. Powell and P. J. DiMaggio (eds.), *The New Institutionalism in Organizational Analysis*. Chicago: University of Chicago Press, 83–107.

2

The Socio-technical Nature of Information Systems Innovation

A long effort is discernible in the information systems literature to establish an understanding of 'information systems' as a notion that does not mean only technology. In the early 1980s several authors voiced concern that the bulk of information systems research and professional know-how were limited to setting principles of engineering for the cost-effective construction of reliable technical artefacts. Significant efforts were made to conceptualize and organize the practice of information systems development as an intervention in organizations that is concerned with work processes and the distribution of control over work (Mumford and Weir 1979; Kling and Scacchi 1980; Land et al. 1980; Mumford et al. 1985). To that end, it was suggested that information systems should be considered as social systems which rely on technology (Land and Hirschheim 1983).

Those early efforts to shift the emphasis of computer applications development in an organizational context from the technical to the social formed the intellectual and ethical underpinnings of the 'socio-technical approach' to the practice of systems development, which became more widespread within the Scandinavian countries' industrial politics.

The socio-technical approach rarely became a fully-fledged practice, an alternative to the primarily engineering perception and practice of systems development. Nevertheless it sensitized the then emerging academic field of information systems to the significance of the social aspects of organizations in which computer applications are embedded. Systems development methodologies that were instrumental in the articulation of the roles of professional information systems experts (Avison and Fitzgerald 1996) came to accommodate ideas suggested by proponents of the socio-technical approach such as user participation (Land et al. 1980), although not always wholeheartedly (Beath and Orlikowski 1994).

The prevalence of managerial influences in the research agenda of the information systems field in the late 1980s, discussed in Chapter 1, marginalized the socio-technical approach discourse on information systems. Emphasis was put overwhelmingly on 'business management under increasing competition' concerns, and the association of employee job satisfaction with business success made by the socio-technical approach in Europe lost credibility. The technical artefact came to be seen, above anything else, as an instrument in the hands of managers striving for success in the market; it became a 'competitive weapon'.

The social effects of technical innovation continued to be recognized, as for example in methods that attempted to measure the people-dependent aspects of the business value of information systems (Parker, Benson, and Trainor 1988). Moreover, as organizational change came into the centre stage of information systems research in the early 1990s, the social aspects of information systems acquired renewed attention. As was noted in the Introduction, the main thrust of such research too has been to guide management on how to harness the social context and ICT-led organizational reform to improve business performance in a free market context. Most business information systems literature in the 1990s paid attention to socio-technical issues only to the extent that they can be managed for business success. Indicatively, IT-associated employee 'empowerment' was accommodated in the managerial discourse instrumentally, as a good-for-all management strategy, stripped from its political connotations.[1]

Nevertheless, in the 1990s, new research interest in the social dimensions of ICT-based information systems emerged, this time aimed at building understanding of the interrelationship between the processes of information systems development and use and socio-organizational change. The new 'socio-technical theory' in information systems—feeding into, and informed by, pragmatic concerns about the way new technologies mediate almost all situations of modern life—has drawn from several theoretical and epistemological traditions (Walsham 1993; Hirschheim, Klein, and Lyytinen 1996; Bloomfield et al. 1997; Introna 1997).

The current efforts to build socio-technical theory abandon some of the most fundamental principles of the socio-technical approach as systems development practice. To begin with, socio-technical theory has pursued critical theoretical perspectives which are not intended to translate directly into systems development activities. Moreover, the new theoretical investigations have a social science orientation that favours interpretative analyses. This is very different from the way the ICT functionality and organizational change were analysed in systems theory terms that underpinned much of the socio-technical approach. Nevertheless, there is a continuity of concern regarding the relationship of the technical to the social in the spreading of ICT, and although the theoretical arguments and the analysis of the case studies in this book draw most explicitly from the concepts of the new socio-technical theory, they are also influenced by earlier literature of the socio-technical approach.

Thus, the remainder of this chapter first outlines and discusses the intellectual and political character of the socio-technical approach and then proceeds to present and discuss key ideas underpinning current perceptions of the relationship between ICT and society. The aim of the review of socio-technical concepts and theory is to derive a way of accounting for ICT innovation and organizational change which is capable of addressing diversity. The two final sections of this chapter elaborate on this question.

---

[1] Empowerment had a clear presence in the information systems literature of the 1990s (Hammer and Champy 1993; Hoffman 1994; Jenkins 1996; Psoinos, Kern, and Smithson 2000). Nevertheless the democratization intentions of the earlier socio-technical literature were usually absent. See e.g. Jones (1994) for a critique of the notion of 'empowerment' in Business Process Re-engineering.

THE SOCIO-TECHNICAL HERITAGE

There are several accounts of the socio-technical ideas and practices of the 1970s and early 1980s (Iivari and Lyytinen 1998; Mumford 1999; Kling 2000; Mumford 2000), and they reveal country differences of research focus and of the extent to which socio-technical ideas were put into practice. In the 1970s, in the United States some first efforts were made in the development of participative systems design practices (Greenbaum 1979) and early conceptions of what became later known as 'social shaping' of computer technology were put forward (Kling and Scacchi 1980). Such research took place against a background of some industrial interest in increasing organizational effectiveness and quality of working life (Davis and Cherns 1975) and considerable academic concern about the possible negative impact of computerization at the workplace (Mowshowitz 1980).

Nevertheless, the most visible socio-technical practice emerged in Europe and was concerned, mainly, with systems design in tandem with work processes redesign. The basic principle of socio-technical design was to cater for interesting, multi-skilled jobs as part of designing technical systems. To do that, the design task was understood to extend beyond machine architectures and software and to include the rearrangement of the work organization that was seen as surrounding the technology. The notions of quality working life and job satisfaction were crucial for this design effort.

The socio-technical notion of designing work organization in order to achieve a positive association between the technical and social systems of production originates in action research conducted by the Tavistock Institute of Human Relations in London after the Second World War.[2] The main innovative ideas of the Tavistock socio-technical research were the design of technology-supported work arrangements that allowed for multi-skilled jobs in working teams responsible for a range of activities. In this way, the socio-technical practice broke away from the Tayloristic tendencies of work organization that were prevalent at that time. In information systems, these ideas are best exemplified in the systems development methodology ETHICS proposed by Enid Mumford in the 1970s (Mumford and Weir 1979). ETHICS involves a double design effort: the design of a technical system—typically a system of software applications—and the design of work processes. The two design efforts unfold separately at the beginning. The design of software follows technical systems analysis methods, while the design of work processes involves an effort to determine the 'job satisfaction' requirements of the workers involved, and the application of work quality principles, such as multi-skilled jobs. The two streams of design are then matched to achieve a socio-technical optimization.

---

[2] Socio-technical ideas pre-date the Second World War. In the 1930s the founder of the Tavistock Institute of Human Relations, Eric Trist, associated technology 'rationalization' in the jute industry in Scotland with social problems, such as unemployment and alienation. After the war the socio-technical theory of the Tavistock researchers was developed with action research studies in coal mining (Mumford 1999).

A principle developed by socio-technical proponents in the field of information systems that was widely adopted in practice was user participation (Land et al. 1980; Land and Hirschheim 1983). In its strongest form, participative systems development requires intended users to take an active part in all systems development tasks, including technical design. But, participative practices became popular in a much weaker sense, often as user consultation in systems analysis aiming at eliciting information about the tasks a technical system is going to support (Land et al. 1980; Land and Hirschheim 1983).

The socio-technical ideas of the Tavistock Institute found particularly fertile ground in the socio-political conditions of the Scandinavian countries. In the 1960s the principle that technology innovation should improve work conditions as well as productivity was introduced in the 'Norwegian Industrial Democracy Project', which sought to give employees power and resources to organize their own jobs. Socio-technical approaches to information systems development similar to that suggested by Enid Mumford in the United Kingdom were tried in Denmark and Sweden (Bjørn-Andersen and Eason 1980; Hedberg 1980). Nevertheless, they were not as welcome in practice as their proponents expected, and a number of those committed to the democratic socio-technical ideals realized that

Socio technical designs are not enough. Lasting improvements must also involve changing values, rewards, and power structures. . . . As long as managerial perspective[s] dominate problem formulations, design tasks, and reward systems, resulting systems will at best improve organizations from a managerial point of view . . . Managerial perspectives, and systems must therefore be confronted with worker perspectives, and systems must be designed participatively. (Hedberg 1980: 32, quoted in Iivari and Lyytinen 1998: 145)

Consequently, several socio-technical researchers considered information systems development to be a potential area of conflict between management and labour, aligned themselves with the interests of labour, and initiated action research aiming to give workers a say in the systems design process.

In the social-democratic regimes of the Scandinavian region, aligning research and professional systems development to workers' interests was politically feasible. Powerful trade unions and 'co-determination' legislation ensuring employee rights to participate in decisions affecting their workplace provided conditions conducive to attempting the design of computer applications according to democratic ideals. Several well publicized projects—NJMF in Norway, DEMOS in Sweden, DUE in Denmark, UTOPIA in Denmark and Sweden—involved academics and 'users' in action research aimed at accommodating employees in design practice in order to promote industrial democracy and quality of work life (Kyng and Mathiassen 1982; Ehn and Sandberg 1983; Sandberg 1985; Bødker et al. 1987; Kyng 1998).

Such research produced systems development methods and design tools to facilitate active participation of non-technical experts in technical tasks. But the radical attitude diminished with time. The perception of conflict between industrial management and trade unions lost its prominence and the voices claiming work condition rights against managerial uses of new technology to increase productivity were softened.[3] Even though users' participation continues to be routinely practised in major information systems projects, this has been more of a method for the success of management-set innovation objectives, for example drawing from workers' tacit expertise or securing their gradual acceptance of the innovation. In the 1990s, systems development action for the democratization of the workplace, whereby workers are given resources to develop and juxtapose their preferred designs, 'almost totally disappeared' (Kyng 1998: 15).[4]

The decline of the socio-technical systems development approach, which sought to improve working conditions either in harmony or in confrontation with management-set objectives, was not confined to the Scandinavian countries. In the 'tough' business context of global capitalism of the 1990s, the socio-technical design efforts that emerged in the national social-democratic regimes of the 1970s began to be seen increasingly as utopian. Pursuing technology design and the rearrangement of work processes with the intention to improve work conditions, and through these to improve the performance of an organization as a whole, ceased to be a convincing course of action.

In retrospect it became clearer that the socio-technical approach has three basic weaknesses. First, it takes a narrow perception of the duration and scope of innovation; second, it takes a limited view of context; and third, its instrumental view of technology innovation and social change is sociologically naive.

As Suchman notes in her friendly critique of the Scandinavian socio-technical efforts, both technology and work practices often take shape after technology implementation, during use (Suchman 1998). And, as it became increasingly recognized in the 1990s, technology innovation and organizational change are often improvised and emergent rather than designed (Ciborra and Lanzara 1994; Orlikowski 1996).

Moreover, concentration on the 'micro' context of the immediate environment of work tasks that are directly affected by an artefact misses significant institutional forces of both the technology and an organization's field. This omission became more obvious as the assumed macro-context changed, that is as the social conditions of regulated national economies and unionized labour within which the socio-technical approach emerged became less prevalent. Mumford traces the roots of the retreat of such ideas and practice to the changing business 'climate' (Mumford 2000). She observes that in the 1970s business organizations in North American and North European countries were short of labour and made efforts to retain and

[3] Many consider the action research efforts that sought to serve the interests of the trade unions as distinct from the socio-technical approach of the Tavistock research that perceived technology as harmoniously achieving job satisfaction and productivity increases (Iivari and Lyytinen 1998). Nevertheless, such a distinction is debatable (Bjerknes and Bratteteig 1995). In the political context of Scandinavian countries providing technical resources to the trade unions and striving for improved quality of working life were not thought of as incompatible with industrial growth and did not constitute a particularly radical position.

[4] Some notable exceptions emerged in the 1990s, e.g. the Australian Union Research Centre on Organisation and Technology (URCOT) (Snelling and Jolly 1994, quoted in Kyng 1998), and the research on the implementation of Enterprise Resource Planning systems in the merger of the Canadian telecommunication organizations (Truex and Ngwenyama 2000).

empower their employees. In the 1980s and 1990s surplus labour and pressures for 'lean' production made democratization of the workplace irrelevant for profitability and management commitment to earlier democratic industrial relations principles weakened. The argument that satisfied workers increase productivity and improve quality of industrial output lost its appeal.[5] In short, the socio-technical approach was a product of a particular socio-political regime. It lost its strength, and even its relevance as that regime was de-institutionalized. Without a stable, taken-for-granted outer context, strategies for change in the workplace require effort to trace the changing broader socio-economic dynamics.

Finally, the underpinning theoretical fundamentals of the socio-technical approach proved unduly optimistic regarding human capacity to combine technology and social engineering and achieve social ideals. Even when the confrontational political nature of the innovation context is acknowledged, as in the case of the Scandinavian 'trade unionist' projects that sought to create 'contexts for design' conducive to social change (Kyng 1998), the socio-technical design approach had an instrumental character. It attempted to guide action towards particular 'desirable' work organization effects through ICT innovation.

The socio-technical approach relied mostly on systems theory, which for decades after the Second World War appeared to offer a very promising way to study, construct, and control complex entities—whether machines, societies, or their combination. It was used to engineer technologies, as well as to structure the organization of socio-technical entities. On the basis of systems thinking, for example, job enrichment could contribute positively to both employee satisfaction and organizational output. Autonomously managed groups could do even better, as sub-systems linked to optimize the behaviour of the larger system they were part of. The influential ideas from the Tavistock studies brought together a whole range of disciplines to tune sub-systems into the optimization of larger systems: psychoanalysis would enhance self-understanding, psychology would provide information about individuals' job satisfaction needs, and organization theory would accommodate such knowledge into the design of effective organizational structures.

The certainty of systems theoretical studies as to what constitutes a desirable work organization was challenged by interpretivist accounts of social systems. What changes are desirable for the workplace, what technology does, and whether it is a benefit or not could be seen as matters of interpretation. Peter Checkland's 'soft systems theory' is the best example of such a theoretical position. The researcher, as well as the practitioner, should allow multiple interpretations to be manifested. They should, nevertheless, be capable of facilitating consensus decisions by parties holding different 'world-views' (Checkland 1981).

---

[5] There are signs of revival, or at least perseverance, of the socio-technical systems development principles in the work of several groups of researchers and practitioners committed to assisting in fairer representation of interests in the workplace or social settings introducing ICT innovation. (See e.g. the special issue of *Human Relations* on socio-technical systems theory (1997), 50(2), and Clement 1994; Suchman 1994; Eijnatten and Zwaan 1998.) Participatory design ideas have been influential in Computer Supported Collaborative Work (CSCW) technology applications and Human Computer Interface (HCI) design.

This position too was challenged by more critical social theories, which emphasized power as a reality that distorts both the professionally designed systems relations and the professionally facilitated processes for reaching consensus among different stakeholders, each with their own interpretations (Bloomfield and Danieli 1995). According to current critical views, the mission undertaken by the socio-technical approach to design job arrangements in order to improve the position of a social group at the workplace is suspiciously instrumental. The belief that technology, if appropriately designed, is capable of altering social relations has an element of naive determinism. It is also prone to manipulation, as indeed happened with the trivialization of the core socio-technical ideas during the 1980s and 1990s (Beath and Orlikowski 1994; Jones 1994; Mumford 1999).

Thus, almost completely discarding the experience of the 'socio-technical approach', the association of ICT innovation and social change in organizations became prominent in information systems in the 1990s. Research efforts have been drawing from and joining in ongoing debates in contemporary social sciences.[6] This wave of socio-technical research has brought an unprecedented awareness of theory in the information systems field which, throughout its history either as engineering or as a branch of business studies, has been more keen to inform practice than to explain socio-technical processes.

THEORETICAL PERSPECTIVES OF THE TECHNOLOGY/SOCIETY RELATIONSHIP

The core theoretical position—whether explicit or implicit—in any study of ICT innovation and organizational change is the postulated relationship between technology and social institutions. A fundamental distinction can be made between deterministic theories assuming a relationship of causality between technology and societal structures, and 'structurational' theories assuming some sort of interplay between technology and human action in an institutional setting that defies cause and effect relationships between material properties and social processes or structures. The former can be either in the form of technology determinism, whereby particular states of social systems are thought to be 'effects' due to the properties of particular technologies, or social determinism, whereby specific technologies are the result of particular social structures.

Technology deterministic assumptions are widespread. They are manifested in professional discourse, e.g. promising organizational qualities such as 'accountability' as a result of the implementation of particular computer-based information systems, and populist political discourse, e.g. associating the democratization of China with

---

[6] There is of course a great deal of ongoing research on systems ideas. Two active strands of systems theory in organizational theory and information systems are on critical systems theory (Flood and Jackson 1991; Urlich 1995) and autopoiesis (Von Krogh and Roos 1995). See also the discussion on systems thinking in the 1990s by Galliers, Mingers, and Jackson (1997). However, the new socio-technical theories have been more interested in exploring non-wholistic concepts of social relations, and the concept of network is more prevalent than the concept of system in current socio-technical studies.

the spread of the Internet. Social determinism is discernible in the writings of authors who seek to explain or predict the course of technical innovation on the basis of existing social structures and deterministic views of the course of social history. Examples of this position are found in several Marxist analyses of the 1970s, which consider technology innovation as an instrument in the struggle of social classes within capitalism (such as Braverman 1974). They perceive computer technology as an oppressive instrument in the hands of the management of capitalist institutions.

On the whole, the information systems literature has avoided bold hypotheses of causality between ICT innovation and particular organizational or societal effects.[7] As early as the 1970s, theoretical investigations of the relationship between computer innovation and the social fabric of organizations suggested that social contexts have formative effects for technology, but at the same time technologies have constraining or enabling effects due to their material features. Influential have been Kling and Scacchi's research on 'web models' (Kling 1987) and Kling's subsequent analyses (Kling 1987, 1991), which elaborated on the connections between a technology and the social, historical, and political contexts in which this technology is developed and used. Nevertheless only as recently as the 1990s the theoretical question of the relationship between technology and society became more prominent in information systems research, and was linked with the broader stock of social science theory, first with Giddens's structuration theory (Giddens 1979, 1984) and more recently with theories from science and technology studies (see e.g. Law 1991; Bijker and Law 1992).

According to structuration theory people are skilled 'agents' who produce, sustain, and transform social life. Social structure—the organized sets of rules and resources of social systems—is produced by actors and at the same time provides the resources and restrains the outcome of their interaction. In this sense 'action' and 'structure' are in a recursive relationship, each iteratively shaping the other, and this is the meaning conveyed by the term 'structuration'.[8] These fundamental ideas on the relationship of social structure to action were introduced in information systems studies in order to break away from technology deterministic conceptions and form an explanatory theory of the interdependence of ICT and its social context. A pioneering

---

[7] I refer here to the theoretically aware literature. A great deal of literature in information systems has a prescriptive and predictive character, aiming to influence management and technology experts' behaviour, and has an implicit deterministic view of ICT. Nevertheless, in the established jargon of the general information systems literature, ICT is considered an 'enabler' of desirable organizational effects, meaning that such change depends on the organization's circumstances.

[8] It should be understood that Giddens's ideas on 'structuration' form a very general theory—seen by many as a meta-theory (Giddens 1979, 1984). They have been elaborated in an effort to reconcile a fundamental division between two traditions of thought in the social sciences: one which emphasizes the pre-eminence of the social whole over its constituent actors, the human subjects, and the other which makes the study of subjective experience the foundation of the social or human sciences. The most dominant schools of thought in sociology, functionalism and structuralism, despite their difference of approach, tend to study 'structures' of social phenomena, such as patterns of social relations, and they pursue a naturalistic, objectivist perspective. In contrast, the hermeneutic school of thought studies social phenomena by focusing on action and meaning in human conduct. Whereas functionalism and structuralism see human action constrained by the structures of societal totalities, hermeneutics do not pay much attention to constraint of human action.

comparative case study of the introduction of computer tomography in two hospitals by Barley, which demonstrated that people's actions in using the new technology are influenced by the institutionalized traditions and power relations within organizations, influenced several information systems researchers (Barley 1986). Barley's study suggested that in order to explain the interaction between technology and its organizational context, it is necessary to consider the history which formed the social context of the organization in the first place.

Subsequently, a series of studies adopted the basic ideas of structuration theory on the relationship of institutional structure to human action (see e.g. Orlikowski and Robey 1991; Orlikowski 1992; Yates and Orlikowski 1992; Walsham 1993). They put forward the concept of technology as constructed and enacted by human agents, and at the same time as having properties which both constrain or enable human action. Also, they provided empirical evidence to demonstrate the structurational concept in the case of ICT innovation. Nevertheless, it has been difficult to elaborate on such a fundamental conceptual position and to work out more focused theories on the way the interplay between ICT innovation and organizational change occurs and the problems encountered as such an interplay unfolds (Monteiro and Hanseth 1996; Jones 1999). Rather than opening new insights of the cases studied, often the cases studied were used to explicate the theory. The introduction of structuration theory in the information systems literature had an educational effect, as it exposed the rather a-theoretical field to one of the most influential contemporary social theories, but did not shed much light on issues of concern to information systems research and practice. Questions such as how ICT innovation is implicated in the changing of contemporary organizations found only vague answers in structurational analyses. For example, structurational studies maintain that the organizational impact of technology depends partly on the material properties of the technology and partly on the actions of people appropriating and changing it. Therefore the choice of technology for deployment is a crucial decision for an organization. But, can organizations implementing carefully chosen technologies for capturing 'best business practice' expect to gain the technology in-built benefits in their own circumstances? In what way may in-built patterns of organizational processes and social relations be changed during implementation or use?

Such questions are more effectively addressed by drawing from the field of science and technology studies, which—while generally consonant with the most basic premisses of structuration theory—have developed conceptual constructs to deal with the processes through which technologies are developed and influence societies. Science and technology studies form a multidisciplinary field with a relatively short history but, unlike the field of information systems, have devoted most of their endeavours to theoretical and explanatory studies, without assuming an intellectual responsibility for guiding professional practice.

Information systems studies have drawn mostly from one approach in the science and technology field, the 'actor-network theory' (ANT). Although many of the theoretical propositions of actor-network theory are debatable, a rather eclectic use of its conceptual vocabulary, and to a lesser extent its methodology, is thought to provide a promising theoretical vehicle for information systems research (Walsham 1997).

It is important to see actor-network theory not as complete in itself and well developed theory, but as a theoretical position within the broader debate of the studies of the sociology of technology. With this in mind, before presenting some key concepts of actor-network theory, the following section summarizes the basic ideas from another variant of science and technology studies, the 'social construction of technology' (SCOT). Although many accounts of actor-network theory and social construction of technology stress their differences, their similarities are perhaps more important for the formation of a theoretical background for ICT innovation and organizational change.

Social Construction of Technology

Social constructionists deny any self-evident explanation of the effects stemming from the functional attributes of technologies. Constraining or enabling effects are a matter of interpretative action from people in their social context.

Much of the literature on the social shaping or social construction of technology elaborates on the social interactions during the design of technology. In the design process possible features of technical artefacts are contested, and the final constructed object embodies the balance of interests of the social forces involved. This is a very familiar story for information systems scholars and practitioners. The anything but straightforward task of information requirements determination, the strategies and counter-strategies to cope with resistance to change, the difficulties of managing user participation are some of the manifestations of the struggle taking place during systems development. This is what the socio-technical approach proponents have stressed all along (Mumford and Weir 1979; Ehn and Sandberg 1983; Howard 1985; Ehn 1989), and this is what the work-oriented systems design proponents continued to argue about in the 1990s (Clement 1994; Suchman 1994).

The question that is more controversial for social constructionism and of greater interest currently in information systems research is whether, once designed, technical artefacts impose the social structures prefigured at the design process wherever they are subsequently implemented and used. To what extent are technologies, often with 'generic' features such as software packages, amenable to further shaping according to the circumstances of the context where they are implemented? Is the technology of information systems capable of empowering or trapping organizational actors, centralizing or decentralizing control in organizations, according to their designed properties? Or is the social shaping continuing at the implementation and use site, overriding at least some of the potential effects of the technologies' in-built properties? As the software market gets established and in-house systems development becomes the exception rather than the norm, do organizations have any chance to shape their information systems to match their circumstances, or are they forced to comply to the 'best business' work processes and social relationships built into the packaged technology? Furthermore, does technology transfer imply the unnegotiated transfer of organizational and social relationships as well? Is there a closure point, after which the transformative effects of a technology on a social system should be considered fixed, a predictable consequence of the use of the technology?

Social constructionists argue that technology continues to be shaped and reconfigured beyond its design. To begin with, Woolgar observes, designers do not have adequate knowledge of the 'user', and they leave loose ends at the boundary between the machine and its user that take shape during trials and implementations. This is certainly the case of many software mega-packages, such as the various 'Enterprise Resource Planning' software packages, which include redundant functionality, allowing for the contingencies of different usage requirements. Implementation, i.e. *in situ* configuration, becomes almost as critical a task for the shaping of such technologies as defining requirements for design, and involves both technical experts and users. But this can be dismissed by a sceptic as a technical stage, part of the technical fine-tuning of a computer application, and much more under the control of technical experts than the 'users'.

The social constructionist argument pushes the scope of users-shaping-technologies process further, arguing that the capacity and effects of technology introduced at the workplace are a matter of interpretation by human actors according to their social conditions. An analogy is suggested between the relationship of technology and its users to that of a text and its readers. Users continuously interpret the inherent capacity of a technology introduced in their context and negotiate their practices. The constraining or enabling character of the technical artefact in the workplace is not a matter of the material qualities, where their designed political nature is embedded, but a matter of interpretation of the actors that implement and use them.

Grint and Woolgar, pursuing the machine/text analogy, suggest a substantial hermeneutic freedom for the user. Not all interpretations are equally valid, of course. Appropriateness of interpretation is determined by the social context within which interpretation is exercised: 'Users are free to make what they will of the machine, but can only do so "appropriately" within an interpretative context. This "context" does not exist in isolation from the machine; it is instead defined by the social relations which make up the machine' (Grint and Woolgar 1997: 93). Emphasis here is shifted overwhelmingly to the 'making up' of the machine at the place of use. Interpretations are not judged as valid or invalid on the basis of the nature of the technical artefact, but on the basis of the meanings sustained by the social context of its use.

Also, the extent to which particular effects are attributable to technology is a matter of interpretation. On this question Grint and Woolgar are much more bold in their argument, trying to eliminate any trace of the conviction that technologies have, as part of their essence, the ability to 'cause' particular 'effects'. They argue that the causes and the nature of particular 'effects' are always subject to social interpretation. In an impressive thought exercise they expose layers of social factors intermingled with attributing death by being shot at a Russian roulette game (Grint and Woolgar 1997). The interpretivist social constructionist argument is here spelt out clearly: there cannot be any specific 'effects of technology' attributable to the material qualities of technologies. The 'effects' can always be interpreted otherwise.

Actor-Network Theory

While sharing the social constructionist view that structures and actions of a social setting cannot be deduced through an account of the material properties of its technology, actor-network theory forms a different conceptual perspective by making no analytical distinction between the social and the technical. By taking a position of 'symmetry' between humans and artefacts, it challenges the distinction between 'natural' and social entities, proposing a 'sociology' to accommodate both on the same terms. On the principle that the technical is inseparable from the social, actor-network theory developed an elaborate vocabulary of concepts to describe and explain socio-technical phenomena (Latour 1988; Callon and Law 1989; Callon 1991; Akrich 1992; Law and Callon 1992). It is mainly through this vocabulary that actor-network ideas come to influence socio-technical theory in information systems, and this section traces its key notions and their meaning.

The fundamental idea is that human and non-human actors[9] interact to form the networks of heterogeneous entities of the world we live in. Actors interrelate to each other and define each other by circulating intermediaries. Actors and intermediaries can be technical artefacts, texts, conventions such as money, people, or hybrids of these entities.

An example of such a hybrid actor network quoted in Callon (1991) is a nuclear power station, seen as a heterogeneous network constituted by associations among many different actors—atoms, machines, operators, engineers, managers. Not only is a nuclear power station a conglomerate of heterogeneous actors, but is also a collective actor itself, as when it is referred to as a threat, without referring to its constituent parts. Similarly, Callon explains, in the services sector a package holiday operator is a complex hybrid network of '(c)omputers, alloys, jet engines, research departments, market studies, advertisements, welcoming hostesses, natives who have suppressed their desire for independence and learned to smile as they carry luggage, bank loans and currency exchanges . . . and many more', playing the role of an intermediary between a person and a holiday break (Callon 1991: 139).

The process through which actors interact with each other to build networks or change them is called 'translation'. Translation refers to both the process of 'translating' an idea into reality and the result of such a process. Thus, the notion of translation extends the common understanding of 'action'. The results of action involved in a translation process are inscribed in intermediaries which, subsequently, 'black boxed' participate in further translations. Intermediaries embody 'scripts' or 'scenarios', conveying an intended change. For example, a machine introduced by management at the workplace carries inscribed new work operations that define new roles for workers. The machine is the intermediary through which a translation of work processes is enacted.

The process of translation that builds and changes networks is political in nature. It begins with a certain 'problematization', when an actor identifies and explores a 'problem' and attempts to persuade other actors in the network that the problem is significant enough to dedicate resources for its solution. This may involve negotiations about the nature and scope of the problem. Actors put forward their favoured

---

[9] More accurately called 'actants', to denote 'whatever acts or shifts actions', thus avoiding anthropomorphic connotations of the term 'actor'.

solutions, 'scenarios' for their favoured translation. In effect they develop and contest the scripts for another network, and try to enrol allies from within or outside the network for its realization. Finally, resources are mobilized to sustain commitment for the new network that results from the translation.

Networks are inherently unstable. Translations may not result in a stable new condition, and the network may reverse to being contested by alternative scripts. A translation that is successfully carried through leads to alignment of actors' interests, and as a result their network has a high measure of convergence. Otherwise, if translations are challenged and do not succeed, alignment among actors of a network is weakened, and coherence of the network is jeopardized. The validity of translations depends on institutions, such as conventions or regulations that have been produced in past interactions. Legislation, local informal norms, or technical norms determine legitimate actors and valid translations. The existence and significance of such conventions determines how strongly coordinated a network is, and consequently strong coordination contributes to a high degree of convergence.

With the notion of convergence actor-network analysis considers the ability of a network to perform tasks effectively through the aligned and coordinated actions of its heterogeneous actors. A convergent network is like an effective Tower of Babel, Callon remarks, where everyone 'would speak their own language, but everyone else would understand them' (Callon 1991: 148).

Successful translations lead to a network which not only is robust, but it has the potential to prolong its life and extend its scope. The durability and robustness of heterogeneous network entities depend on whether translations that brought the network to its current state can reverse back to a point where they were not highly aligned or coordinated, and whether the network can resist alternative translations. Durability is achieved by aligning as many of the inscriptions of the intermediaries that define the relationships of its entities as possible. A memorable example of such alignment of the inscriptions of multiple actors is Latour's observation of the way hotel managers achieve customers' compliance to their request to return the key of their room to the reception desk before they leave. Polite oral reminders, notices on the walls, and loading the key with a bulky weight that makes it uncomfortable to carry are all mobilized as intermediaries aligned towards making customers leave their keys on the desk, without offending them (Latour 1991).

High irreversibility implies standardized actor and intermediaries behaviour, constrained by general or local norms. Normalization further aligns actors and intermediaries making the future predictable, and when a network's dynamics are highly normalized it can be considered as a black box, an actor with predictable behaviour that can be punctualized in the contexts of other networks.

Where does this stream of concepts lead us as far as the relationship between technology and its social context is concerned? Technologies, Akrich (1992) explains, are intermediaries, embodying scripts of particular behaviours determined through the 'interessement' and enrolment processes of a particular network, that is under the socio-technical circumstances of the societies that created them. Latour sees technologies' scripts as significant allies for the stability and irreversibility of social relations, adding to the durability of social networks. Scripts successful to the completion of a translation can then be black-boxed, 'described', transferred to other networks. Their transfer into another context triggers a process of another translation, which has the potential to change social relations, to translate them into new socio-technical conglomerates. In technology transfer, Akrich argues, technical objects may be reinvented and reshaped in use, as 'technical objects and people are brought together into being in a process of reciprocal definition in which objects are defined by subjects and subjects by objects' (Akrich 1992: 222).

It should be noted that the actor-network theory takes an interpretative stance, as social constructionists do. However, unlike social constructionists, actor-network theory recognizes the material embodiment of 'scripts' in technology as significant. Of course inscriptions of technologies are contested, their meaning is negotiable at the enrolment process, and networks are inherently unstable, reversible. But properties of technical artefacts carry their own weight, and the mobilization of suitable technology actors can make the difference to socio-technical translations and their durability.

ICT INNOVATION AND ORGANIZATIONAL CHANGE IN CONCEPTS OF SOCIO-TECHNICAL THEORY

One could observe that the new socio-technical theories have not led to truly new perceptions of information systems. Often theoretical accounts of information systems have done little more than to express case studies in terms of an elaborate set of concepts, without adding new understanding over what is already known in the field about the socio-technical relations involved in information systems. Moreover, such theoretical studies of information systems have been criticized as not being entirely faithful to the original theoretical corpus they draw from (Walsham 1997). Indeed, often the theoretical interests of the information systems researchers appear to be, in some respects, at cross-purpose to the interests of their main proponents. For example, actor-network ideas were put forward with a background of social theory that had no adequate way to account for technology (Callon 1987; Law 1991) and their principle of symmetric treatment of nature and society sought to point out the significance of material entities in social systems. Information systems researchers use actor-network theory primarily because they wish to account for the social dynamics in technology innovation. Overall socio-technical theory marks a new theory-conscious orientation to IS research, tapping social sciences for making sense of information systems questions.

For the purposes of the investigation pursued in this book, the theoretical debate under way provides a set of useful concepts and theoretical insights. First, it is possible to clarify the meaning of the *and* in 'ICT innovation *and* organizational change'. Structuration, social construction, and actor-network theories, all suggest that ICT innovation should be considered *in interaction* with the changes undergone or pursued by other actors (people, institutions, other socio-technical hybrids) in an attempted organizational change. More specifically, in the vocabulary of actor-network concepts, the object of enquiry of this book is the formation of the heterogeneous networks of ICT-supported organizational processes.

The concept of 'heterogeneous network' conveys more accurately what the expression 'information systems as social systems' was meant to connote in the information systems literature of the 1980s. It suggests that what is generally called an 'information system' cannot meaningfully be restricted to computer or communications applications within an independently delineated social environment. Technical artefacts, such as hardware, software, data in paper or electronic form, carry with them engineers with the conventions of their trade; industries that sell, install, and support them; users who judge their significance and interpret the way they should be put to action according to their circumstances; consultants who claim that they can convert them from symbol manipulating machines to competitive advantage. In effect the concept of heterogeneous network is a way to refer to ICT in its institutionalized constitution, as discussed in Chapter 1, rather than in a laboratory abstraction. Thus, more appropriately, 'information systems innovation' should be understood to refer to ICT innovation and organizational change, whereby both the ICT items and the individual organizational actors involved are part of institutionalized entities, that are historically formed durable, but dynamic, heterogeneous networks.

This notion of information system entails the methodological position stated in the Introduction that does not distinguish the processes of technological development from the organization where they are enacted in terms of content and context. The study of information systems innovation needs to address the way technology actors make (or break) alliances with organizational actors in the course of translations set in motion for a range of reasons. Abandoning the separation of technology as content and society as context avoids oversimplified argumentation over whether technology affects society or vice versa. The concept of translation guides attention to the decisive process of the deployment and use of technologies where the material and symbolic capacity of technologies, interpreted, misinterpreted, or modified by other actors will become an ally or an enemy to other actors with particular organizational change strategies.

Potentially, the notion of an actor network provides the methodological mechanism to expand the study of a particular information systems innovation instance— a particular socio-technical translation—to trace the dynamics of its outer context, which is itself a larger socio-technical actor network. As Callon notes (1987), the notion of network does not delineate entities by boundaries, it is expandable to consider links with other entities, thus allowing the linking of the inside and the outside, the micro and the macro. Few actor-network studies demonstrated this potential in a convincing way, though; most concentrate on the details of micro-level translations. Indeed, concentration on the details of an actor network, with little attention to the broader social structures and processes within which a network translation unfolds is one of the major criticisms of actor-network theory more generally (Habers 1995; Walsham 1997).

On the whole, actor-network proponents and social constructionists are reluctant, and sometimes explicitly unwilling to trace explanations in large-scale socio-technical dynamics. They make no assumptions about and have no intention to find out why socio-technical actors interact in the way their studies show they do or what the consequences of such kinds of interactions are. Although recognizing the political nature of the socio-technical processes, power dynamics of an actor network do not account for the origins of the scripts of translation over which the battles are fought, the politics evolve, and the interpretations of the technology options are articulated.

Thus, actor-network and social constructionist analyses have a relativistic attitude regarding the causes and implications of socio-technical change that leave one disconcerted (Russell 1986; Fujimura 1991). While convincing that the formation or disturbance of socio-technical order are not following technological imperatives, that 'it might have been otherwise' (Star 1991), they do not offer particularly useful guidance to trace forces that result in the supremacy of one actor's translation script over another's.

This is an important point of criticism for the object of study of this book, which is concerned with the way diversity may be addressed. The assumption made in the Introduction that diversity as a social condition cannot be ironed away with universalistic theories and practices implies a relativist stance. But the question that needs to be addressed is how a relativist standpoint in research and practice can overcome the paralysing 'anything goes' attitude that is often manifested in front of the multiplicity of networked social settings that actor-network studies demonstrate so eloquently.[10]

Verran's search for a satisfactory way of explaining and coping with difference[11] offers useful insights (Verran 1999) for an approach to address this question. Influenced by ideas in feminist epistemology, she associates difference with the embodiment of social practices, that is, the simultaneously material and symbolic experiences of people in their life conditions. Her concept of the 'embodied' refers to 'routines of collective acting by multiple participants'.[12] Difference, therefore, is neither the manifestation of a defect in drawing rational interpretations from a physical reality and concrete social practices nor an arbitrarily reached cultural gesture. Material conditions shape, originally, the enacting of social routines, repetitions, and rituals. And '(t)he outcomes of these routines, repetitions, and rituals are more routines, repetitions, and rituals' (Verran 1999: 148). Therefore, to understand the logic of actions that appear different we have to trace back the shaped—or patterned in Verran's language—actions and recognize them as expressions of embodiment, that is symbolic manifestations of their lives' material conditions.

Although Verran presents her analysis as taking issue with both the universalist and relativist positions, to my understanding hers is a relativist thesis, and the importance of her analysis lies in providing a way of overcoming a 'neutral' recognition of difference. Recognition of the embodied nature of difference leads to addressing the historically developed ideological character of social practice.

---

[10] This question is discussed also in more general theoretical terms in Chap. 3.

[11] In her article (1999), Verran is concerned with the differences of understanding and learning basics, such as quantification, which she met as a teacher in Nigeria.

[12] Verran uses the term 'participant' as equivalent to the 'actor', or 'actant' in actor-network theory, whether human or non-human.

Following Verran's reasoning, the processes of translation undertaken in incidents of information systems change should be understood against their background of 'routines, repetitions, and rituals', which need to be traced back in order to understand their significance. In other words the institutional forces, the interrelation of which forms the locality of information systems projects, should not be accepted with indifference to the material and social conditions that gave rise and sustains them. The sociology of translation of information systems should not be limited to revealing the mechanisms of the interrelations of humans and technology under power relations which just happened to be so, that is, without considering the history of social conditions that have shaped them. The formation of the actor network, the translations that succeeded, and those that failed can be understood in relation to their historically shaped broader social context.

CONCLUDING REMARKS

It might be helpful at this point to summarize what lessons are retained from the above discussion of socio-technical theory. Furthermore, it is necessary to consider how these concepts and ideas can be of value in the analysis of ICT innovation and organizational change in conditions of diversity.

To begin with, socio-technical concepts—and in particular concepts from actor-network theory—provide theoretical fundamentals for non-deterministic analyses.[13] The definitions of 'information system' and 'information systems innovation' proposed in the previous section are a starting point to that end. Also, the argument that is invariably advanced by the contemporary theories of technology and society and outlined in this chapter, namely that technology does not determine social and organizational change, has clear implications on the issue of diversity. If, as such theories suggest, technology does not convey organizational imperatives by virtue of its material characteristics, the spread of ICT around the world does not result in universal patterns of organizational structure and activities by means of the technical inscriptions in ICT. No homogenization effects can be attributed to the essential nature of ICT. Heterogeneous engineering is inherently political and contingent.

Nevertheless, it is important not to jump from this to the conclusion that ICT does not convey any organizational isomorphic influences at all. While ICT does not constitute an imperative towards a standard socio-technical order by virtue of material properties and software inscriptions, isomorphic pressures may be exerted by other actors mobilized along with ICT in the socio-technical arena. It may be that market forces inexorably lead to techno-economic networks that are comprised of uniform organizational forms and made durable by the spread of ICT applications. The question

---

[13] This is disputed in debates of the sociology of technology. Social constructionists are suspicious that the symmetry principle of actor-network analysis has deterministic consequences, as it attributes socio-technical results to the 'essential' material properties of technology (Grint and Woolgar 1997). Nevertheless, the most widely accepted position in information systems is that recognizing that the properties of technologies matter does not necessarily imply a technology deterministic thesis. The importance of actor-network concepts is that it provides a vivid way to describe the interplay of the social and the technical.

of diversity in the study of information systems innovation is not fully answered by the contingent nature of heterogeneous engineering. It requires also consideration of the patterns of behaviour afforded to other actors involved in the information systems translation process.

In general, the new socio-technical theory and methodology does not offer a satisfactory way to study the other actors involved in information systems innovation, because it does not link theoretically the situated studies of incidents of translations in organizations with broader contextual forces. Actor-network theory does not attempt to explain the nature and significance of the diverse situations it reveals. Thus, the methodological ability to consider multiple contexts in order to account for the condition of diversity in information systems innovation needs to be combined with concepts and theories capable of accounting for the actors' behaviours and relations.

Such a study can be pursued by making use of the concepts of ICT and organizations as institutions. Considering ICT as an institutional actor, rather than as an object with material and symbolic inscriptions, adds different analytical possibilities. The translation process can be seen as a process of alliances and conflicts which are not incidental, but it is subject to institutional dynamics. From such a perspective, the argument made in Chapter 1 about the institutionalization of ICT in close linkage with management adds a significant dimension to actor-network analysis of information systems innovation. In actor-network terms, ICT tends to enter information systems translations bound with managerialism, bearing its script. The most significant inscription here is not the functionality embedded in the material technology, such as the software, but the taken-for-granted shared rationality of their institutional alliance.

And while actor-network analysis is contextually myopic, that is, it does not have a vision of the social concerns and dynamics within which networks emerge, grow and stabilize, or languish and perish, the institutional perspective offers a view of the missing contextual background. The link between an organizationally situated network and its broader context can be made with the concept of institutional field, which encompasses the institutions that coerce or influence the problematizations and the legitimacy of translations undertaken. Networks involving institutional actors do not grow at random, but result from alliances and tensions of forces at the junction of the institutional fields in which an information systems innovation takes place. I examine the extent of relevant organizational fields and their articulation in Chapter 4, and a more detailed account of a contextual analysis which associates socio-technical translations with multiple institutional contexts is presented in Chapter 9. At this point it suffices to note that the introduction of institutional actors in actor-network translations provides a methodological mechanism to trace the origins and meaning of the scripts circulated in a particular instance of information systems innovation.

References

Akrich, M. (1992). 'The De-scription of Technical Objects', in W. E. Bijker and J. Law (eds.), *Shaping Technology/Building Society*. Cambridge, Mass.: MIT Press, 205–24.

Avison, D. E., and Fitzgerald, G. (1996). *Information Systems Development: Methodologies, Techniques and Tools*. Oxford: Blackwell.

Barley, S. R. (1986). 'Technology as an Occasion for Structuring: Evidence from Observations of CT Scanners and the Social Order of Radiology Departments'. *Administrative Science Quarterly*, 31(1): 78–108.

Beath, C. M., and Orlikowski, W. J. (1994). 'The Contradictory Structure of Systems Development Methodologies: Deconstructing the IS-User Relationship'. *Information Systems Research*, 5(4): 350–77.

Bijker, W. E., and Law, J. (eds.) (1992). *Shaping Technology/Building Society*. Cambridge, Mass.: MIT Press.

Bjerknes, G., and Bratteteig, T. (1995). 'User Participation and Democracy: A Discussion of Scandinavian Research on System Development'. *Scandinavian Journal of Information Systems*, 7(1): 73–98.

Bjørn-Andersen, N., and Eason, K. D. (1980). 'Myths and Realities of Information Systems Contributions to Organizational Rationality', in A. Mowshowitz (ed.), *Human Choice and Computers*, 2. Amsterdam: North-Holland, 97–109.

Bloomfield, B. P., Coombs, R., Knights, D., and Littler, D. (eds.) (1997). *Information Technology and Organizations: Strategies, Networks, and Integration*. Oxford: Oxford University Press.

——and Danieli, A. (1995). 'The Role of Management Consultants in the Development of Information Technology: The Indissoluble Nature of Socio-political and Technical Skills'. *Journal of Management Studies*, 32(1): 23–46.

Bødker, S., Ehn, P., Kammersgaard, J., Kyng, M., and Sundblad, Y. (1987). 'A Utopian Experience: On Design of Powerful Computer-Based Tools for Skilled Graphic Workers', in G. Bjerknes, P. Ehn, and M. Kyng (eds.), *Computers and Democracy*. Aldershot: Avebury, 251–78.

Braverman, H. (1974). *Labor and Monopoly Capital*. New York: Monthly Review.

Callon, M. (1987). 'Society in the Making: The Study of Technology as a Tool for Sociological Analysis', in W. E. Bijker, T. P. Hughes, and T. Pinch (eds.), *The Social Construction of Technological Systems: New Directions in the Sociology and History of Technology*. Cambridge, Mass.: MIT Press, 83–103.

——(1991). 'Techno-economic Networks and Irreversibility', in J. Law (ed.), *A Sociology of Monsters: Essays on Power, Technology and Domination*. London: Routledge, 132–61.

——and Law, J. (1989). 'On The Construction of Sociotechnical Networks: Content and Context Revisited'. *Knowledge and Society*, 9: 57–83.

Checkland, P. (1981). *Systems Thinking Systems Practice*. Chichester: Wiley.

Ciborra, C. U., and Lanzara, G. F. (1994). 'Formative Contexts and Information Technology: Understanding the Dynamics of Innovation in Organizations'. *Accounting, Management and Information Technology*, 4(2): 61–86.

Clement, A. (1994). 'Computing at Work: Empowering Action by "Low-Level" Users'. *Communications of the ACM*, 37(1): 52–63.

Davis, L., and Cherns, A. (1975). *Quality of Working Life*. Glencoe, Ill.: Free Press.

Ehn, P. (1989). *Work-Oriented Design of Computer Artifacts*. Hillsdale, NJ: Lawrence Erlbaum Associates.

——and Sandberg, A. (1983). 'A Local Union Influence on Technology and Work Organization: Some Results from the DEMOS Project', in U. Briefs, C. U. Ciborra, and L. Schneider (eds.), *Systems Design For, With and By the Users*. Amsterdam: North-Holland, 427–37.

Eijnatten, F. v., and Zwaan, H. v. d. (1998). 'The Dutch IOR Approach to Organizational Design: An Alternative to Business Process Re-engineering'. *Human Relations*, 51(3): 289–318.

Flood, R. L., and Jackson, M. C. (1991). *Critical Systems Thinking: Directed Readings*. Chichester: Wiley.

Fujimura, J. (1991). 'On Methods, Ontologies and Representation in the Sociology of Science: Where Do We Stand?', in D. Maines (ed.), *Social Organization and Social Processes: Essays in Honor of Anselm L. Strauss*. New York: Aldine de Gruyter, 207–48.

Galliers, R., Mingers, J., and Jackson, M. (1997). 'Organization Theory and Systems Thinking: The Benefits of Partnership'. *Organization*, 4(2): 269–78.

Giddens, A. (1979). *Central Problems in Social Theory*. London: Macmillan.

——(1984). *The Constitution of Society: Outline of the Theory of Structuration*. Cambridge: Polity Press.

Greenbaum, J. (1979). *In the Name of Efficiency—Management Theory and Shop-floor Practice in Data Processing Work*. Philadelphia: Temple University Press.

Grint, K., and Woolgar, S. (1997). *The Machine at Work: Technology, Work and Organization*. Cambridge: Polity Press.

Habers, H. (1995). 'Book Review: *We Have Never Been Modern* by Bruno Latour'. *Science, Technology and Human Values*, 20(2): 270–5.

Hammer, M., and Champy, J. (1993). *Reengineering the Corporation: A Manifesto for Business Revolution*. London: Nicholas Brealey.

Hedberg, B. (1980). 'Using Computerized Information Systems to Design Better Organizations and Jobs', in N. Bjørn-Andersen (ed.), *The Human Side of Information Processing*. Amsterdam: North-Holland, 19–33.

Hirschheim, R., Klein, H. K., and Lyytinen, K. (1996). 'Exploring the Intellectual Structures of Information Systems Development: A Social Action Theoretical Analysis'. *Accounting, Management & Information Technology*, 6(1/2): 1–63.

Hoffman, G. M. (1994). *The Technology Payoff: How to Profit with Empowered Workers in the Information Age*. Burr Ridge, Ill.: Irwin.

Howard, R. (1985). 'Utopia: Where Workers Craft New Technology'. *Technology Review*, Apr.: 43–9.

Iivari, J., and Lyytinen, K. (1998). 'Research on Information Systems Development in Scandinavia: Unity in Plurality'. *Scandinavian Journal of Information Systems*, 10(1/2): 135–86.

Introna, L. D. (1997). *Management, Information and Power: A Narrative of the Involved Manager*. Basingstoke: Macmillan.

Jenkins, D. (1996). *Managing Empowerment: How to Make Business Re-engineering Work*. London: Century Limited.

Jones, M. (1994). 'Don't Emancipate, Exaggerate: Rhetoric, Reality and Reengineering', in R. Baskerville, S. Smithson, O. Ngwenyama, and J. I. DeGross (eds.), *Transforming Organizations with Information Technology*. Amsterdam: North-Holland, 357–78.

——(1999). 'Structuration Theory', in W. L. Currie and B. Galliers (eds.), *Rethinking Management Information Systems*. Oxford: Oxford University Press, 103–35.

Kling, R. (1987). *Defining the Boundaries of Computing Across Complex Organizations*. Chichester: John Wiley.

——(1991). 'Computerization and Social Transformation'. *Science, Technology and Human Values*, 16(3): 342–67.

——(2000). 'Learning about Information Technologies and Social Change: The Contribution of Social Informatics'. *The Information Society*, 16: 217–32.

——and Scacchi, W. (1980). 'Computing as Social Action: The Social Dynamics of Computing in Complex Organizations', *Advances in Computers*, issue 9.

Kyng, M. (1998). 'Users and Computers: a Contextual Approach to Design of Computer Artifacts'. *Scandinavian Journal of Information Systems*, 10(1–2): 7–44.

—— and Mathiassen, L. (1982). 'Systems Development and Trade Union Activities', in Bjørn-Andersen (ed.), *Information Society, for Richer, for Poorer*. Amsterdam: North-Holland, 247–60.

Land, F. F., and Hirschheim, R. A. (1983). 'Participative Systems Design: Rationale, Tools and Techniques'. *Journal of Applied Systems Analysis*, 10: 91–107.

—— Mumford, E., and Hawgood, J. (1980). 'Training the Systems Analysts of the 1980s: Four Analytical Procedures to Assist the Design Process', in H. Lucas, F. F. Land, T. Lincoln, and K. Supper (eds.), *The Information Systems Environment*. Amsterdam: North-Holland, 239–56.

Latour, B. (1988). 'Mixing Humans and Nonhumans Together: The Sociology of a Door-Closer'. *Social Problems*, 35(3): 298–310.

—— (1991). 'Technology is Society Made Durable', in J. Law (ed.), *A Sociology of Monsters: Essays on Power, Technology and Domination*. London: Routledge, 103–31.

Law, J. (ed.) (1991). *A Sociology of Monsters: Essays on Power, Technology and Domination*. London: Routledge.

—— and Callon, M. (1992). 'The Life and Death of an Aircraft: A Network Analysis of Technical Change', in W. E. Bijker and J. Law (eds.), *Shaping Technology/Building Society*. Cambridge, Mass.: MIT Press, 21–52.

Monteiro, E., and Hanseth, O. (1996). 'Social Shaping of Information Infrastructure: On Being Specific about the Technology', in W. Orlikowski, G. Walsham, M. R. Jones, and J. I. DeGross (eds.), *Information Technology and Changes in Organizational Work*. London: Chapman & Hall, 325–43.

Mowshowitz, A. (ed.) (1980). *Human Choice and Computers*, 2. Amsterdam: North-Holland.

Mumford, E. (1999). 'Routinisation, Re-engineering, and Socio-technical Design: Changing Ideas on the Organisation of Work', in W. L. Currie and B. Galliers (eds.), *Rethinking Management Information Systems*. Oxford: Oxford University Press, 28–44.

—— (2000). 'Socio-technical Design: An Unfulfilled Promise or a Future Opportunity', in R. Baskerville, J. Stage, and J. DeGross (eds.), *Organizational and Social Perspectives on Information Technology*. London: Kluwer, 33–46.

—— and Weir, M. (1979). *Computer Systems in Work Design: The ETHICS Method*. London: Associated Business Press.

—— Hirschheim, R., Fitzgerald, G., and Wood-Harper, A. T. (eds.) (1985). *Research Methods in Information Systems*. Amsterdam: North-Holland.

Orlikowski, W. J. (1992). 'The Duality of Technology: Rethinking the Concept of Technology in Organizations'. *Organization Science*, 3(3): 398–427.

—— (1996). 'Improvising Organizational Transformation over Time: A Situated Change Perspective'. *Information Systems Research*, 7(1): 63–92.

—— and Robey, D. (1991). 'Information Technology and the Structuring of Organizations'. *Information Systems Research*, 2(2): 143–69.

Parker, M. M., Benson, R. J., and Trainor, H. D. (1988). *Information Economics: Linking Business Performance to Information Technology*. Englewood Cliffs, NJ: Prentice-Hall.

Psoinos, A., Kern, T., and Smithson, S. (2000). 'An Exploratory Study of Information Systems in Support of Employee Empowerment'. *Journal of Information Technology*, 15: 211–30.

Russell, S. (1986). 'The Social Construction of Artefacts: A Response to Pinch and Bijker'. *Social Studies of Science*, 16: 331–46.

Sandberg, Å. (1985). 'Socio-technical Design, Trade-Union Strategies and Action Research', in E. Mumford, R. Hirschheim, G. Fitzgerald, and A. T. Wood-Harper (eds.), *Research Methods in Information Systems*. Amsterdam: North-Holland, 79–92.

Snelling, L., and Jolly, C. (1994). The work mapping technique. PDC' 94, Chapel Hill, NC, CPSR.

Star, S. L. (1991). 'Power, Technologies and the Phenomenology of Conventions: On Being Allergic to Onions', in J. Law (ed.), *A Sociology of Monsters*. London: Routledge, 26–56.

Suchman, L. (1994). 'Working Relations of Technology Production and Use'. *Computer Supported Cooperative Work*, 2: 21–39.

—— (1998). 'Strengthening our Collective Resources: A Comment on Morten Kyng's "A contextual approach to the design of computer artifacts"'. *Scandinavian Journal of Information Systems*, 10(1–2): 45–52.

Truex, D., and Ngwenyama, O. K. (2000). ERP Systems: Facilitating or Confounding Factors on Corporate Telecommunications Mergers?, in H. R. Hansen, M. Bichler, M., and H. Mahrer (eds.), the proceedings of the 8th ECIS conference A Cyberspace Odyssey, Vienna, 3 July, 645–51.

Urlich, H. (1995). 'Critical Systems Thinking for Citizens: A Research Proposal'. Hull, University of Hull Centre for Systems Studies.

Verran, H. (1999). 'Staying True to the Laughter in Nigerian Classrooms', in J. Law and J. Hassard (eds.), *Actor Network Theory and After*. Oxford: Blackwell, 136–55.

Von Krogh, G., and Roos, J. (1995). *Organizational Epistemology*. Basingstoke: Macmillan.

Walsham, G. (1993). *Interpreting Information Systems in Organizations*. Chichester: John Wiley.

—— (1997). 'Actor-Network Theory and IS Research: Current Status and Future Prospects', in A. S. Lee, J. Liebenau, and J. DeGross. *Information Systems and Qualitative Research*. London: Chapman & Hall, 466–80.

Yates, J., and Orlikowski, W. J. (1992). 'Genres of Organisational Communication: A Structurational Approach to Studying Communication and Media'. *Academy of Management Review*, 17(2): 299–326.

3

Multiple Situated Rationalities

In Chapter 1, I discussed organizational practice and ICT innovation as historically shaped within institutional contexts. In Chapter 2, drawing from socio-technical theory, I argued that information systems innovation is a contingent practice, depending on situated alliances of actors who are themselves embedded in institutions. One might think at this point that I put too much emphasis on circumstantial irrationalities and historical biases in people's actions and that I neglect the rational behaviour of individuals and organizations. In this chapter I address this fundamental concern and make the argument that rationality itself is a cognitive state derived from the history of social relations in the context of an organization.[1]

This is not a new thesis; it has been repeatedly made, particularly in connection with postmodern analysis of organizations and management (see e.g. Cooper and Burrell 1988; Clegg 1990; Hassard 1996). Nevertheless, it continues to be considered a radical and unsettling position, as it contradicts fundamental assumptions of much of the existing knowledge on organizations, management, and technology innovation. Conceding that rationality is embedded in the history of societies rather than being a universal capacity is confronted with a deep-rooted predisposition of the contemporary world. Therefore, a non-universalist view of rationality in information systems innovation needs to be drawn by understanding the broader debate on the meaning and significance of rationality.

Before I review the main perspectives of this theoretical debate, it may be helpful to clarify the general meaning of rational behaviour in organizational theory and social science. Studies of the rational behaviour of organizing have addressed two levels of rationality, the decision making of individual actors and the behaviour of organizations as collectivities of individuals. In a very general sense, at the individual level decisions and actions are rational if they are logically consistent within a system of beliefs or a system of desires. The best example of such a study is Simon's analysis (Simon 1955), which considers rational behaviour as a case of decision making. At the collective level organizations are understood to behave rationally if the actions of their individual members are coordinated effectively to achieve a predetermined goal that is good for the organization. Again, a good example is Herbert Simon's seminal analysis of administrative behaviour (Simon 1945).

---

[1] Following Granovetter's critique (1985), the view of context-dependent rationality is distinguished from both the under-socialized theories of organizations and innovation which assume that individuals and organizations act according to an economic logic, and the over-socialized theories which assume some overall social or cultural imperatives to explain organizational action. See also the relevant discussion in Clegg (1990: 6–7).

Such studies are concerned with what Elster (1983) calls the 'thin' meaning of rationality.[2] They do not account for the rationality of the beliefs, desires, and goals of individuals and organizations. These are value choices, whose rationality—what Elster calls the 'broad' meaning of rationality—is much more rarely addressed in studies of organizations. The technical/rational perspective postulates the self-interested individual and the efficiency-pursuing organization. In most theories of organization it tends to be assumed that rational individuals are interested above all in improving their material position within a social context,[3] and that organizational goals are ultimately determined by the operations of the market. Political action and organizing is often acknowledged, but it is assumed that they serve the same purpose, collective maximization of benefits that are consequently translated to individual benefits.

Information systems innovation brings along another aspect of rational behaviour in organizations, that of scientific reason. There is a powerful combination of common beliefs behind the continuous technical innovation efforts. Information and communication technology is considered to be the triumph of progress of scientific reason unbound from mystical traditions and untainted by subjective human condition. Furthermore, the wide diffusion of computers and telecommunications and the development of today's unprecedented infrastructure of data and communication channels within and among organizations across the globe have taken place within a socio-economic regime committed to creating wealth by increasing efficiency. These

[2] In the thin sense of logical consistency, an action is rational if the agent's beliefs or desires are reasons for the action; if the beliefs and the actions cause the action for which they are reasons (the action has not been accidental); and if they cause the action 'in the right way' (the action is the direct and intentional outcome of the beliefs and desires, rather than a side effect of the agent's beliefs and desires). But, this view implies that the rationality of an action depends on the rationality of the beliefs and desires from which they stem. Also, the criteria of the thin rationality of beliefs and action are limited to criteria of consistency: the set of beliefs and desires which are reasons for an action must not involve logical, conceptual, or pragmatic contradictions.

The thin notion of collective rationality is a matter of aggregating or coordinating individual rationalities, or eliminating their contradictions. Elster explains that two manifestations of this are the economic notion of collective rationality and the political notion of collective rationality. The former implies that people's individually rational actions bring about an economic outcome that is good for all, or at least not bad for all. The political notion of collective rationality complements the economic notion, concerned with the concerted action that people may follow to overcome these contradictions. The political rational action is a mechanism of avoiding the irrationalities stemming from what economists call 'externalities' of the inherently rational market system.

A lot of theoretical work in economics and political science has elaborated on the thin conception of rationality. Rational choice, utility theories, or game theory have developed formal-logical and probability criteria on the consistency of sets of beliefs and preferences of actors engaged in economic or political behaviour and the consistency of the plans of action stemming from such beliefs and preferences. Social choice theory is concerned with the problem of how a socially optimal outcome is achieved on the basis of given individual preferences. But such theories do not have a way of examining whether the beliefs of individuals are true or their desires are ethically good. As Elster notes, the consistency criteria of rational behaviour can apply equally well to actions such as suicide, homicide, genocide, or consulting the horoscope before investing in the stock market. They only need to be consistent with a consistent set of beliefs of desires, no matter how unfounded these beliefs and desires are (Elster 1983).

[3] The view of people as actors employing their capacity of reason to serve their interests leaves a great deal of human behaviour condemned as irrational and unexplained. Elster (1989) addressed this issue by

two courses of action—scientific advancement and the quest for economic efficiency and growth—are not only compatible, but reinforce each other in a virtuous relationship. Technology has been one of the most significant factors in economic growth, and the economically strong societies have been investing in continuing research and development. The view that the virtuous relationship between scientific advancement and the quest for economic efficiency and growth is a matter of universally rational action—that is, action seen as desirable and applicable in all societies and all domains of action—is the basis of the techno/economic rationality that has been driving much of the information systems innovation.

But the validity of this view has been subject to a very long debate, both in academia and among people with different cultural traditions and different social status. In the Western world the debate on what is rational and how people's ability to reason relates to other fundamental human abilities—mainly the emotional and the aesthetic—has a history of at least two and a half millennia. The juxtaposition of Aristotle's and Plato's views on rationality had already advanced the main contentious distinctions that underpin the debate on this issue ever since: 'pure reason' against the messy human experience; and formal, abstract, timeless and universal rationality against situated reasoning and action (Toulmin 1990). Non-Western cultures have sustained their own convictions about the essence of rationality and its relationship with other human capacities (see e.g. Feenberg 1995; Upadhyaya 1995).

The literature on rationality is bewildering, as questions of reason and reasoning underlie the development of ideas in philosophy, economics, political science, psychology, and sociology. The exploration of this long and rich history of ideas is outside the scope of this book, and this chapter is limited to discussing some of the most salient aspects of the debate on rationality in the twentieth century, and in particular in relation to modernity and its critique.[4] With the emergence of the discourse of late modernity or postmodernity in the last three decades of the twentieth century, a context-dependent view of rationality that supports the belief that different cultures and historical periods sustain different ideas of reason and rationality, became more prominent.[5] It is from these ideas that I draw to elaborate on a contextualist position regarding the rationality of organizing. But the contemporary critical debate on

discussing the relationship between rational behaviour and social norms. He proposed several examples of social norms which are apparently irrational, such as: consumption norms that regulate manners of dress, of table, etc; norms that determine acceptable or non-acceptable uses of money, e.g. the norm that dictates that buying votes is unacceptable; norms of reciprocity or retribution; norms about work and workplace behaviour; norms about fair distribution of income and goods. An assumption often put forward for social-norm-driven behaviour is that indirectly they too are instruments of individual, collective, or generic optimization, and therefore, in more careful analysis, they are a manifestation of economic rationality. While in many cases this may be true, Elster provides many examples in which social norms, although harmful for the interests of individuals and their communities, hold strongly and are perpetuated through generations.

[4] Modernity here refers to the dominant ideology in the Western world, which began with the Enlightenment movement in the mid-17th cent.

[5] Toulmin (1990) argues that, far from being a new phenomenon, a rationality appealing to reason in the sense of 'reasonable' under particular social, cultural, and intellectual conditions (contextually reasonable rather than universally rational) had started becoming prominent at the humanistic period of the Renaissance that was interrupted with dramatic events in the European political scene of the 17th cent.

rationality cannot be understood without the background of orthodox and critical theory of rationality of the twentieth century, mainly Weber's formal rationality and its distinction from substantive rationality and the Marxist critiques of the instrumental character of rationality in modernity. And this is where the following section focuses before examining the contemporary critiques.

FORMAL AND SUBSTANTIVE RATIONALITY

While the origins of today's emphasis on rationality in Western society are generally located in what is known as the Enlightenment age of the late seventeenth and the eighteenth centuries,[6] it is Max Weber's work of the early twentieth century that has had profound direct effects on contemporary social practice.

Weber's analysis did not address questions on the essence of rationality of individuals and collectivities in an abstract sense of thin reasoning, and did not elaborate on the fundamental value choices of individuals, although he shared the basic assumption of the existence of a 'rational self-interest' of individuals. He was interested in understanding the institutional organization of modern society, and was, therefore concerned with collectivities—either societies or organizations. There are three different notions of rationality intertwined in Weber's work: formal rationality, which is primarily a methodological device for purposes of typological analysis; substantive rationality, which acknowledges the ultimate ends towards which a particular course of action is oriented and which should be taken into account in order to make sense of it and judge its appropriateness; and institutionalized rationality, which refers to the institutional conditions that effectively sustain a particular course of action.

Weber's methodology in the course of his sociological analysis of economic life and structures of authority consisted of constructing ideal categories of social settings and determining courses of rational action for their particular ends. Such an abstract 'purely rational' course of action was intended to serve as a basis of comparison with actual, observed action to account for deviations from the line of conduct which would be expected on the hypothesis that the action were purely rational. Within this framework of analysis a particular behaviour or action is to be considered irrational if it deviates from the conceptually pure type of rational action. In other words, action not conforming to the rational means of serving the end assumed by the ideal model of action, is irrational.

As far as economic action is concerned, formal rationality determines what course human action should take to be in accordance to an ideal model if it were completely and unequivocally directed to the single end of the maximization of economic advantage. But such a 'rationalized' economy, where people orient their decisions towards maximizing efficiency and weighing costs and benefits is based on a particular

---

[6] The Enlightenment movement was founded on a cluster of underlying beliefs and expectations about the role of reason in the improvement of the human condition. In that context reason had the meaning of the opposite of custom and religion, which formed the core of the established order at that time in Europe.

Newton's and Galileo's science showed the way reason could produce liberating results. The displacement of theological thinking by scientific reason that combined Empiricism and Rationalism promoted the basic

Theory

mentality that involves the ethical sanction of acquisitive activity and a propensity to seek new solutions to problems rather than to adhere to traditions.

The limited nature of formal rationality becomes clear with the notion of the substantive rationality, which provides a wider perspective of rational action. The issue here is to understand how a particular rational course of action satisfies the value choices of a society. Thus, the outcome of economic action is judged differently in relation to different underlying ends, which may include ethical, political, or utilitarian considerations, such as social equity, social justice, and furtherance of power of a political unit. For example, a particular course of economic action may be successful in terms of social equity within a social group, but inadequate in terms of the overall power of the social group vis-à-vis its political rivals. In terms of substantive rationality, economic activity itself may be of secondary importance, or in conflict with the attainment of the social values of a society.

A fundamental premiss in Weber's work is that there is no single rationality that in a substantive sense captures the logic of human social behaviour. Consequently, his comparison of ideal types of rational systems of social action is an exploration of the institutional conditions that favour and maintain the prevalence of one particular set of values over others. It is along such lines that he undertook the analysis of economic activity and authority. The former articulated the formal rational institutional characteristics of the free market economic system, and the latter led to the definition of the characteristics of the legal rational bureaucratic administrative system.

Weber's analysis of the institutional structuring of economic interests and activity identifies and contrasts two economic systems: the modern market economy, based on the values of economic rationality, and the pattern of social structure and behaviour which is based on what he called communal rationality, referring mainly to the family-based economic structures of traditional societies. Rational economic activity under market conditions is based on the development of profit-making enterprises oriented to 'capital accounting', that is striving to increase the money resources at the command of the enterprise. In listing the institutional conditions for such 'capital accounting', Weber (1947) described the fundamental social conditions of the modern capitalist system, which differentiate economic activity from other kinds of action.[7] In contrast, in societies oriented to a communal rationality economic activity

tenets that natural science and theoretical abstract knowledge can serve practical needs. Science took the mission to search for facts that everybody can agree are true in order to produce objective and universal knowledge. Emulating the task of the natural sciences, the social sciences sought to study the regularities of facts observed in society and to formulate them as universal laws, untainted by the subjective human condition. Inductive and deductive reasoning methods, ideally expressed in mathematics, produced secularized theories of nature and society which at that time had a subversive character. The Enlightenment was a critical, reforming movement, spreading the belief that 'man' can govern himself and breeding revolutions to sweep away the social and political orders and the forms of organization of the Middle Ages. In that context, commitment to science and technology to discover the forces of nature as well as to understand the laws of society, empowered individuals to 'criticize princes and priests and to defend their own ideas and preferences' (Touraine 1995: 32).

[7] Weber identified the following social conditions of the modern capitalist system: (1) complete appropriation of all non-human means of production by owners and absence of formal appropriation of opportunities for profit in the market (i.e. market freedom); (2) autonomy in the selection of management by

is not clearly differentiated from other action, nor does it involve the formal calculated arrangements of 'capital accounting'. Mutual responsibility among members of the community—often the extended family—solidarity and common welfare of members prevail over the freedom of enterprise to accumulate capital. Moreover, affectual, emotional, and traditional ties are legitimate motives for action.

His analysis of authority structures was concerned with the way authority is legitimized within organizations. He identified three ideal types of authority: charismatic, which is based on the personal qualities of a leader; traditional, which relies on custom; and rational-legal, which follows a system of rules and procedures in order to achieve specific goals. The legal-rational bureaucracy, an 'ideal' institution of administration by appointed officials, was suggested as the modern organizational form that would apply in all types of organizations.[8]

Weber did not claim it is desirable that human life is driven in accordance with the formal rational types he identified. Indeed he considered it as a danger for social sciences to pursue rationalistic interpretations, that is, to assume the predominance or general desirability of the courses of action he determined in his abstract ideal rational categories. From his analytical perspective, modern Western economic order is not a 'natural order', but only one possible line of social development. In addition to the traditional communal rationality Weber identified, another now obvious example of an alternative economic type is the 'command economy' towards which socialist societies aspired for a good part of the twentieth century. In its ideal form, this is a non-market economy where a central authority owns all the means of production, rations consumption, and assigns labour at predetermined wages.

Further research on the lines of Weber's analysis of ideal types identified historical situations that demonstrate the dominance of alternative economic and non-economic rationalities and suggested various formal classifications and comparisons. An example of a classification of alternative types is Polanyi, Arensberg, and Pearson's suggestion drawn on research evidence on the economic activities of historical societies, including Mesopotamia, Greece, Mexico, and India. They identified

---

the owners; (3) absence of appropriation of jobs by workers and, conversely, absence of appropriation of workers by owners (i.e. free labour market); (4) absence of substantive regulation of consumption, production, and prices, or of other forms of regulation; (5) calculability of the technical conditions of the production process; (6) calculability of the functioning of public administration and the legal order and legal guarantee of all contracts; (7) complete separation of the enterprise from the household or private budgetary unit and its property interests; the capital at the disposal of the enterprise should be clearly distinguished from the private wealth of the owners, and should not be subject to division or dispersion through inheritance; (8) a formally rational monetary system.

[8] The ten characteristics Weber identified for the legal-rational bureaucracy were summarized by Albrow as follows: (1) the staff members are personally free, observing only the impersonal duties of their offices; (2) there is a clear hierarchy of offices; (3) the functions of the offices are clearly specified; (4) officials are appointed on the basis of a contract; (5) they are selected on the basis of a professional qualification, ideally substantiated by a diploma gained through examination; (6) they have a money salary, and usually pension rights, which are granted according to position in the hierarchy. The official can leave the post and under certain circumstances it may also be terminated; (7) the official's post is his sole or major occupation; (8) there is a career structure, and promotion is possible either by seniority or merit and according to the judgement of superiors; (9) the official may appropriate neither the post nor the resources which go with it; (10) he is subject to a unified control and disciplinary system (Albrow 1970).

two main patterns of economic action in addition to the exchange mechanisms in the market context familiar to Western societies (Polanyi, Arensberg, and Pearson 1957). The first is reciprocative, in which goods and services are exchanged without economic calculation, price payments and wages. Only a very loose principle of balancing the giving and receiving of goods and services is discernible in such reciprocal exchanges. The second is redistributive, in which goods and services are collected to a central source, such as government, and then redistributed throughout the members of the society. Rather than economic calculation, this pattern of activity is driven by principles of social justice and equity. It should be noted also that such ideal economic patterns, even when derived from empirical evidence, do not exist in actual terms. The pure 'command economy' model has never been implemented, and the exchange, reciprocative, and redistributive rationalities usually coexist, although one particular rationality may be more dominant than the others.

Yet, Weber saw the development of the formal rational institutions of free market capitalism as well as the rational bureaucracy as inevitable. And, despite his concerns for the features he considered undesirable, e.g. the inherent tendency in legal rational bureaucracies to accumulate power and curtail democracy, his analysis of these 'ideal' types has had a normative character.

Weber's analysis was far more preoccupied with the formal types of rationality than with substantive choices of societies. Subsequently, the ideal categories he identified in his analysis acquired normative status and the substantive notion of rationality has been greatly overlooked. Indicative is the narrow use of the notion of irrationality, which, by being determined only in relation to the formal rationality, suggests a misleading dichotomy between rational and irrational. Such a dichotomy ignores the possible validity of multiple rationalities stemming from different value choices.

In the substantive sense, the modern Western economic rationality that values productivity and efficiency in a free market setting of a global economy represents the dominance of one set of values over others. This thesis has been echoed in many other studies that look at the economic activity within a social system. For example, Parson and Smelser (1956) argued that societies differ with respect to the degree to which they temper economic productivity and efficiency in relation to other values. As a result, in different historical settings different mixes of economic and non-economic rationalities prevail and are perpetuated through institutional mechanisms.

Strange made the same point in the context of the study of the international political economy (Strange 1988). She identified four fundamental values coexisting as concerns in every society: wealth, security, freedom, and justice. While all societies provide for these values, societies in different times and places differ in terms of the degree of significance they attach to each of these values. One value often dominates and renders the others subordinate.

Consequently, Strange suggests, rather than assuming that economic action, and in particular the Western type of rationalized economic action, is of general value and of global legitimacy, there is a need for analytical methods raising such questions as what values are rated the highest in a society, and who benefits from the maintenance of particular biases to certain values over others or from the overthrowing of the status quo. Similarly Smelser (1978) suggests the need to understand the way different kinds of rationalities that may govern the production, distribution, and consumption of economic goods and services such as efficiency, social justice, social security, military defence, are incorporated in the complex economic and social processes of particular societies, either local or global.

CRITICS OF INSTRUMENTAL RATIONALITY

The formalization of reason, which constitutes the intellectual engine of modernity as exemplified in the theoretical work of Max Weber, was strongly criticized by Marxist theorists, mainly Horkheimer and Adorno (Horkheimer 1947; Horkheimer and Adorno 1972), at the aftermath of the devastation of Europe from the Second World War. In the context of modernity, Horkheimer argued, reason is 'an intellectual faculty of co-ordination, the efficiency of which can be increased by methodical use and by the removal of any non-intellectual factors, such as conscious and unconscious emotions' (Horkheimer 1947: 9). Such instrumental rationality that endeavours to optimize the means, but has nothing to say on the validity of ends, can serve any means, good or bad. This criticism is concerned with the relativization of substantive rationality, the lack of discourse on the values lying behind the particular rationalities pursued by the formally rationalized institutions of modernity, mainly science, technology, and the free market economy.

This point of view was voiced more clearly by Marcuse in his critique of the cognitive foundations of modernity. Marcuse associated the instrumental nature of the rationality of modernity with the prevailing political system of his milieu. He saw the rationality of science and technology as serving a particular structure of power and class interests, reinforcing the way the rationality of the free market maintains the unequal relations fostered by capital accumulation. Thus, he argued, far from being universal and independent of social and historical conditions, the scientific-technical rationality in the context of modernity is a political system of domination (Marcuse 1964).

Marcuse saw a sinister character in the 'technological' rationality: in particular instrumental rationality in a technocratic society ceases to be the means that serve the specific demands of capitalism, or any other chosen economic system. Instead it establishes and maintains a system of domination in its own right. The pursuit of efficiency through scientific-technical rationality dominates over choices of human value, transforms social action to action bound by the requirements of the technology itself, and ultimately imposes its own authoritarian system. In this process the methods of reasoning of science are the universal instruments of domination of a particular civilization. They lead to the domination of nature and, through technology, they perpetuate and extend their domination and absorb all spheres of culture. The 'objective order of things' created by technological rationality is so pervasive that it renders any alternative to the existing socio-economic conditions utopian, despite gross faults of inequality, waste of natural resources, and lack of individual freedom.

In short, Marcuse saw the advanced industrial society of the 1950s and 1960s as a 'rationally totalitarian society', whereby the existing system of domination is secured by technological imperatives.

In their analyses, Adorno, Horkheimer, and Marcuse saw the rationality of instrumental reasoning, and technology in particular, as an ideology—a view which is held by most critics of modernity since then, but not with the same negative connotations. The rationality of modern society, enshrined in its economic institutions and technology, is an ideology in the sense that extended reliance on them hides, distorts, and makes impossible the consideration of relevant options to the present social conditions, as well as the present relationship of society to nature. The essential problem with instrumental reasoning in the advanced industrialized society is not that it leads to false beliefs and non-prudent action, but that it hinders people's reflective ability to assess and challenge the validity of their beliefs and prudence of their actions (Pippin 1995).

Beyond the common view of these three critical theorists on instrumental reason and technology as ideology they differ on whether and how this condition could be overcome. Adorno and Horkheimer remained deeply pessimistic about the instrumental way through which reasoning limits human existence. Marcuse saw the possibility of reversing the inherent irrationality of the dominant 'technological rationality' through social action. For Adorno and Horkheimer the most glaring evidence that instrumental rationality was the Enlightenment's seed of self-destruction was the way technologically educated masses reversed enlightened civilization to such acts of barbarism as the Holocaust. Their critique suggested resistance, but did not find grounds to indicate how alternatives to the state they criticized might come about. Marcuse's attitude was much more optimistic, suggesting that a 'new science' and 'new technology' might be possible. To that end, to the instrumental reasoning he juxtaposed 'dialectical thought' which precludes abstraction and is preoccupied with the 'concrete content of its objects'. Dialectical reasoning could be the means for understanding the contradictions, the opposition forces and tendencies of a historical world 'in which the established facts are the work of the historical practice of man' (Marcuse 1964: 141), thus revealing the irrational character of the existing societal order.

Indeed Marcuse perceived automation as a potentially liberating mechanism, which under an appropriate social regime could allow people to regain their freedom from the system of production, and he considered the possibility of non-Western societies or social movements, such as feminism, to develop liberating rather than dominating technologies. In the Western world a 'revolution' could reinstate different social choices creating a 'new science' with liberating effects for both society and nature (Marcuse 1972). Nevertheless, as Vogel points out (Vogel 1995), Marcuse too linked his utopian view to an overall universal value, the perception of some inherent 'objective qualities of nature'.

Marcuse's ideas were radical for his time and fuelled the political struggles of the left in Europe and North America but, as Marxist thought and radical political action were increasingly discredited in the following decades, his critical views were subsequently marginalized. However, similar views are held by more recent streams of critical thought on rationality, more attuned with the contemporary political milieu.

A widely influential contribution to the debate on the nature of the rationality of modernity, its limitations, and the way to overcome them is found in the writings of Habermas. His basic position is that the rationality of science and technology that, in modernity, drives action in the domain of work reflects human interest in predicting and controlling nature, but has not brought up its promised emancipation. Following Weber's institutionalized rationality norms, Habermas accepts that work is rational if it is efficient and productive (Habermas 1972), and he considers the emergence of such a purposive rationality a positive development which lies at the core of modernity.

He finds problematic, though, that the logic for the rationalization of work has expanded to the domain of human interaction, and this, he suggests, is where changes are needed to overcome the distortions in human interaction caused by the interests of money and power. An important line of his critique, sharing Horkheimer's concerns, focuses on the self-sufficient subjectivity of reason in modernity. He proposes non-coercive intersubjectivity as a different basis of rationality. Reason can be reconstructed through mutual understanding and reciprocal recognition.

The new orientation that Habermas suggests for the critique of instrumental reason and the overcoming of its shortcomings is founded in the communicative use of language, the 'ideal speech situation'. Rationality in this case is in the pragmatic logic of argumentation. In this way communicative reason addresses one of the main questions of the 'subject-centred' reason that constituted the modernity of the Enlightenment, namely what criteria should be used to measure the truth for knowledge and the success of purposive action: 'Communicative reason finds its criteria in the argumentative procedures for directly or indirectly redeeming claims to propositional truth, normative rightness, subjective truthfulness, and aesthetic harmony' (Habermas 1987: 314). In this way, he believes, communicative reason can go beyond the formation of a formal reasoning process concerning the means and provide the substantive basis for consensus on social life-processes.

The way Habermas proposes to retain the positive elements of the instrumental reason while avoiding its negative consequences finds many critics. For example, Feenberg and Vogel (Feenberg 1995; Vogel 1995) question the validity of the distinction Habermas makes between two modes of human life, 'work' and 'interaction' (or in his more recent writings success-oriented action and communicative understanding) on the basis of which he separates a positive from a problematic domain of the subjective purposive rationality of modernity. Another line of criticism pursued by Elster (1983) concerns the extent to which the 'ideal speech situation' is realistic and effective as a transformation strategy to overcome the shortcomings of selfish subjective action for the achievement of common good: it is reasonable to believe that ideal speech can be the outcome of such a transformation which succeeds in abolishing political and economic domination, but it is questionable whether it can be the mechanism to enact the transformation.

CRITICS OF THE UNIVERSALIST RATIONALITY
OF MODERNITY

Rationality as Reflexivity in Late Modernity

Another stream of critical thought on the role of reasoning in contemporary society has been developed by Giddens, Beck, and Lash (Giddens 1990, 1991; Beck 1992; Lash 1993; Beck, Giddens, and Lash 1994). They observe that increasing production of knowledge about the natural and social world has not led to greater certainty in the conditions of contemporary life. The ambition for control of the natural world produced unintended side effects which amount to unprecedented risks, such as the risk of ecological catastrophe. The effort to liberate individuals from the bonds of tradition has brought us to a state of facing complex contingencies of potentially widely destructive futures. The growth of human knowledge created more uncertainty and unpredictability. Giddens, Beck, and Lash associate this 'diagnosis' of the contemporary situation with the concept of 'reflexivity', each with a different meaning though.

Central in Giddens's theory of late modernity is the process whereby human beings continuously monitor the circumstances of their activities. Monitoring is a constituent of both the institutions of modernity—such as organizations, the nation state—and individuals. Particularly important in this self-monitoring of institutions and individuals is the knowledge produced by systems of experts, which penetrate all aspects of social life, from technological expertise (scientists and engineers) to social relations and the intimacies of the self (social theorists, economists, doctors, counsellors, and therapists). Systems of expert knowledge underlie the condition of 'trust' that Giddens believes is fundamental for day-to-day actions, lifted out from their local context due to time/space separation.[9] In this sense reflexivity is a state of continuous revision of social activity and material relations with nature in the light of new information or knowledge (Giddens 1991). Thus, in late modernity expert knowledge does not accumulate to create certainty, but it feeds into two modes of reflexivity: the transformation of organized environments of action by the routine incorporation of knowledge or information (institutional reflexivity), and the constitution of self-identity by the reflexive interpretation of an agent's biography (reflexivity of the self).

Beck holds a more critical view of reflexivity, suggesting a 'reflex', in the sense of unintentional and unconscious self-confrontation of modernity with the undesired side effects of its instrumental knowledge creation, rather than a state of 'reflection' in the light of knowledge and information. Central in this thesis is his analysis of 'risk society' as the contemporary phase of modern society in which the social, political, economic, and individual risks escape the institutions for monitoring and protection of the industrial society (Beck 1994). In this conception reflexivity is not the result of expert knowledge, but almost the opposite: it results from the inadequacy of scientific knowledge to predict the consequences of the activities it supports. Beck does not preclude the development of self-awareness and the action through conscious cognitive

---

[9] Giddens's notions of the distance of time and space and disembeddedness are briefly explained in Chap. 4 as fundamental concepts for his view of globalization.

reflection—and in particular reflection on the self-dissolution and self-endangerment of the industrial society—but he does not consider it a necessary response to the experience of the manifestations of risk. This view suggests the 'ambivalence of modernity': reflexivity may lead to corrective reflection, but it may, as well, lead to further self-destructive response, such as violence, nationalism, and wars.

Lash takes yet a different view of reflexivity, linking it to cultural or hermeneutic processes. Reflexivity, he argues, is not only a cognitive process resulting from sciences and economic forces, but it is also a mimetic 'aesthetic' process, manifested in such aspects of contemporary everyday life as the behaviour that constitutes consumer capitalism. His notion of the aesthetic dimension of reflexive modernization emphasizes the cultural character of the institutions of modernity. His argument involves the following three points: cultural drivers, differentiated from political and economic rational ones, become increasingly more prevalent in contemporary social institutions; cultural institutions, such as education and the media, become increasingly influential; and as an increasing proportion of social interactions involve extra-institutional communicative exchanges—for example in between-firms production relations—the individuals' semantic backgrounds and personal lifestyles acquire increasingly greater significance.

These three notions of reflexivity share the view that the instrumental rationality of modernity has had damaging effects, creating to a large extent uncertainty and unpredictability regarding the future. But from this observation Giddens, Beck, and Lash derive different understandings regarding the capacity for rational action and its significance. Giddens, despite acknowledging the inherent risks of the global techno-economic system appears optimistic about the capacity of reason and science-informed action to address the risks and drive action with positive effects. His notion of reflexivity as self-monitoring reflection based on the appropriation of expert knowledge retains somewhat of the character of the instrumental rationality of early modernity. Faith is once again put in the rationality of science, technology, and the free market for overcoming their faults.

Beck's position is more critical of instrumental rationality, seeing it primarily as the cause of distraction, and not putting a great deal of faith in its capacity to generate self-control mechanisms. Beck does not suggest an alternative view of the 'rational' or a different relation between the rational, the emotional, and the aesthetic. His notion of individualization as a new process in the arena of political relations is a pessimistic view, suggesting lack of faith in the human capacity to gain control of the unpredictable forces of instrumental rationality.

Lash's notion of cultural reflexivity attempts to find a way out of the dead-end of instrumental rationality through culture, the mimetic aesthetic aspects of human action. However, this perspective seems to fall short of a cultural critique and is unclear about the relation of the aesthetic with cognitive reflexivity. His notion of information accumulation and his analysis of contemporary capitalist developments in terms of information and communication structures do not consider differentiating contextual qualities, such as human judgement and local knowledge. The extension of the cognitive to include the aesthetic seems to suffer from similar shortcomings.

Despite referring to hermeneutic capacities, the aesthetic is presented as a matter of informational signs, images, and narratives, without much effort to relate them to historical contexts.

The Social Messiness of Science

The core belief of modernity that science and technology are driven by objective reason for the discovery of the laws of nature and the development of technologies that bring socio-economic progress has also been a subject of considerable controversy. Science is in many ways affected by the social setting within which it is practised. Governments might starve science from the resources required for research, or neglect to train the youth adequately to carry the scientific baton. Religion may condition people to care more about afterlife and spiritual aspects, and therefore restrict the commitment required to discover the laws of nature and improve the material human condition. Many intellectuals disputed the belief that science is the realm of pure reason, finding misleading both the claim that science discovers the laws of nature 'out there', and the idea that technology brings progress. Also, many pointed out negative effects of technology, such as unemployment, damage to the environment, even dehumanization of people (Ellul 1964; Mumford 1966; Braverman 1974).

In the last three decades, the studies of science and technology shifted attention from the social structures that affect science and technology to the microcosm of science and technology practice as such, revealing a different kind of complication to the assumption of scientific reasoning (see e.g. Hughes 1983; Shapin 1992). In the late 1970s, Latour and his colleagues began scrutinizing how scientists work, 'invent', and publish (Latour and Woolgar 1986). He traced the details of what a practising science researcher goes through, showing the partiality of the actions and decisions of scientists and engineers (Latour 1987). Not only science is affected by its macro-social context, such as economic interests, but the practice of science at the micro-scale—in the laboratory or the field trip—is not as pure reason-based as it has been thought, it involves actions whose nature is social, political, and cultural.

Many of the scientists' choices are controversial, Latour showed, made with limited knowledge, without full consideration of alternatives. The establishment of the truthfulness of scientific findings does not depend only on achieving demonstrable results and internal rational consistency. Controversies crop up in scientific research, which are resolved by the formation of alliances of heterogeneous entities such as skilled technicians, and machine equipped laboratories, reviewers, financial sponsors, and institutional bodies. Once the controversies of the making of scientific results are settled and the processes that produce them are black boxed, their acceptance as undisputed facts is a matter of rhetoric and technicalities employed by the scientific community. Scientific texts are presented in a positive rhetoric, hiding the dubious choices involved in experimental conditions and field work. Technicalities of language, such as mathematical notation, restricts scientific discourse to formal correctness, discouraging broad debate on substantial choices. Furthermore, the 'universal laws' of science do not have a universal applicability on their own. They require a network of common technical practice and infrastructure to spread. Thus, Latour argues, scientific facts are 'constructed', they are not discovered (Latour 1993).

In short, Latour's and other studies of science have pointed out the inconsistency between the partiality and impurity of scientific practices and the 'matter of fact' quality attributed to published scientific findings. They challenged the established distinction between the social and the scientific arenas. The superiority of knowledge achieved by scientific practice is not a matter of pure, objective reason, but a matter of strength of alliances mobilized to support this knowledge. The results of scientific and technological work could be 'otherwise'.

The Postmodern Critique

In the last three decades of the twentieth century, the most radical views about the rationality that has sustained modernity have been put forward by authors associated with the ideas of postmodernism. This is a diverse spectrum of views concerning the status of art, literature, and social order, and this section is confined to some basic ideas of one of the key figures of postmodernism, Jean-François Lyotard, about the status of scientific knowledge (Lyotard 1984).

Lyotard argued that neither the faith of the Enlightenment that the search for knowledge liberated by tradition can lead to social order, nor the critical views that condemn the instrumental nature that reason acquired in pursuit of this faith are relevant any more. With the dominance of the market system of advanced liberal capitalism and the possibilities opened by computer technologies, knowledge itself has become a commodity and its practice is driven by the principle of 'performativity', that is by efficiency in converting input to output.[10] This, he argued, marks a significant change to the way scientific knowledge has derived legitimacy. In modernity the legitimacy of science was derived from a 'meta-discourse' of some idealist notions or humanistic values provided by philosophy; in the new state he called 'postmodern', there is a disbelief—incredulity—towards meta-narratives, and science is pursuing the pragmatic aspirations of a performance-oriented institutional system of power. But, without a justification provided by a 'grand narrative', science is as valid as any other discourse. Moreover, such a view challenges the alleged qualities of objectivity of the abstract reasoning of scientific method and Lyotard saw science as engaged in 'agonistics of language games'.

Lyotard identified two different meta-narratives for the legitimization of science in modernity. The first is what he called the 'speculative narrative', the idealistic philosophical belief that the commitment of scientific activity to the search for truth is driven by its own ideal ultimate goal, and that this search coincides with the pursuit

[10] It is interesting to note that many of the rather speculative claims Lyotard made when he wrote his book in the 1970s about the availability of knowledge resources in public data banks became more obviously relevant with the abundance of Internet-based information resources almost thirty years later. The significance of such wide access to vast information resources on the status of scientific knowledge remains to be seen. It may well erode the prominence of scientific discourse, which is esoteric and elitist, privileging alternative discourses with more popular appeal.

of just ends in moral and political life. The alternative meta-narrative sees scientific knowledge as providing the means for emancipation and self-governance of the human subject. Lyotard recognized the first, speculative-idealist meta-narrative as the one initially inscribed in the university systems in Europe and the United States, although later weakened with the political requirements for science to deliver practical ends. But, in contemporary society, Lyotard argued, both the speculative idealist and the emancipatory narratives have lost credibility.

For Lyotard the seeds for the delegitimation of these two grand narratives can be found inside them rather than in their socio-economic context. The speculative self-justifying knowledge 'harbors a certain skepticism towards positive learning'(Lyotard 1984: 38). More importantly, perhaps, the delegitimation of the emancipation narrative stems from the difficulty of translating the 'truths' derived from scientific endeavours into emancipatory prescriptions: 'There is nothing to prove that if a statement describing a real situation is true, it follows that a prescriptive statement based upon it (the effect of which will necessarily be a modification of that reality) will be just.' (Lyotard 1984: 40).

Technology, however, gained a different legitimacy in modernity, contributing more directly to wealth creation through efficiency. And so long as technology serves systems of power—whether nation states or corporations—as means for their efficient performance, science is expected to provide relevant knowledge to that end. The new legitimacies of scientific knowledge do not stem from discovering what is true, but from contributing utility, efficiency, and ultimately being 'saleable'. Moreover, in the postmodern era, technological innovation becomes self-justified, merely on the basis of its novelty. Advanced science confronted with its limitations such as undecidable situations, or the limits of precise control, is a generator of ideas by imagination, just as another 'storyteller', rather than the discoverer of truth by the superior capacity of reason.

Lyotard's arguments on the delegitimization of scientific discourse, along with similar ideas of other postmodernists, have been met with a great suspicion from across the social sciences and from philosophy. Most social scientists find the idea that science cannot be the basis for universally valid knowledge on the merits of its own embedded rationality as an offence against the very existence of social science. The implications of the postmodern claim that there is no grand narrative capable of securing the grounds of objective knowledge is that knowledge can claim only localized validity. Rather than universally rational knowledge, there is a plurality of rationalities, 'islands of order in a radically contingent world' (Feenberg 1995). And such relativism creates a great deal of uneasiness.

Rationality as Regime of Truth

Another influential position regarding rationality was developed in the work of Michel Foucault.[11] For him rationality is neither the human capacity for discovering

---

[11] The views of Foucault on rationality are best presented in Foucault (1980).

truth, as the Enlightenment proponents suggested, nor an instrument for determining the means that serve unquestioned ends, as the Marxist critical theorists argued. Rationality is a constituent part of the ubiquitous politics of determining what is true and what is false. Fundamental in Foucault's analysis is the conception that knowledge and power are constituted in interdependence to each other, and his studies trace the history of how particular types of discourse in particular domains such as sexuality, criminality, madness, came to be considered rational. He uses the term 'regime of truth' to capture the socially constructed, power constituted determination of what is rational—in other words, of what is a valid way to distinguish between true and false. Regimes of truth are the rules according to which truth is determined and specific effects of power are attached to the true.

Foucault does not examine the intrinsic rationality of scientific and economic practices, their overall capacity to determine what is true in nature and social affairs, and their general effects on the human condition. He does not try to understand whether certain general kinds of rationality are a fundamental mechanism for the organizational and institutional order, or represent repression, coercion, and violence, and therefore form a mechanism for social domination. Instead he considers particular discourses shaped under particular political, economic, institutional regimes of the production of truth. Fundamental in his approach is a conceptualization of power as something which cannot be a priori judged either as positive or negative.

Foucault's studies simply implicate power in the formation of regimes of truth, which he considers essential for the structure and functioning of societies. Power is present in all discourses, interwoven with all kinds of relations, such as kinship, sexuality, or production, and in multiple forms, either negative such as prohibition, or positive such as protection. General conditions of domination are created by such multiform localized power-laden relations integrated into overall strategies. But, relations of power are always accompanied by resistances, which are also multiple in form and can be integrated to form larger strategies. Indeed, Foucault's historical analyses of rationality attempt to uncover the 'knowledges' that, in the struggles and conflicts of the formation of particular social institutions, were disqualified as inadequate and naive, what he calls the 'subjugated knowledges'. Thus, he pays attention to forms of domination as well as to the resistances encountered.

And this is where the radical nature of Foucault's work lies. By uncovering the subjugated knowledges in the history of the formation of prevalent modern social institutions, by tracing the omnipresent effects of power that condition reason, he strips the most well-respected domains of knowledge and practice, such as those on which medical and penal systems are based, of their rationality privilege.

The Rationality of Modernization as 'Development'

The concepts of rationality and the critiques outlined above have been proposed to account for the social context of industrialized Western societies, but they have clear implications for the so-called developing countries. Modernity's instrumental way of reasoning on socio-economic development first determines the problems to be solved: the irrationalities of tradition, the injustice of authoritarian regimes, and the limitations of local inefficient production practices to feed the local population. Consequently, it defines the solution: courses of action to be taken in order to perform according to the formal ideals of progress, as they have been pursued in the advanced Western economies. But if the techno-economic rationality of modernity is not a neutral and objective way of reasoning and is, instead, an aspect of the culture of Western civilization, and thus inextricably bound to its history, the changes brought by modernization into the life conditions of the poorer and politically weaker require a closer examination. There have been many voices critical of the way the universalist rationality of Western modernity in its various forms—colonialism, economic modernization, socialist totalitarianism—affected the social fabric of communities around the world (see e.g. Freire 1970; Nandy 1987; Said 1994; Gandhi 1997). To the failure of the reason of efficiency, growth, and science to sustain a satisfactory state of human life such voices juxtaposed the local and traditional logics of the sacred, the symbiosis with nature, and self-sufficiency. Here I will only review briefly Escobar's critique of the development interventions, which draws directly from the Western critiques of the rationality of modernity reviewed above.

Escobar (1995), following the critical line of Foucault, analysed the notion and policies of socio-economic development pursued since the 1940s as a discourse, that is as a space of thought and action within which only certain things can be said, done, or imagined. Examining the political dynamics, theoretical ideas, and the practical interventions that have constituted development, he argued that the adoption of free market rationality and its institutions, and the cognitive instruments of science and technology in developing countries were socially constructed rather than naturally chosen.

The organizing premiss of the discourse of development has been the belief that modernization, based on the two pillars of science-technology and capital, is the only force capable of destroying archaic superstitions and relations, and that it should be applied at whatever social, cultural, and political cost. Within this discourse, institutions and professionals of development have determined and classified problems by applying the concepts and techniques of the sciences that sustain modernity—economics, public administration, management—and formed policies of change.

Presented as a detached rationality capable of improving the human condition, the modernization discourse has created a regime of truth, passing judgement on social groups, determining their needs, and prescribing how they should change. Social life has been conceived as a technical issue, and its improvement is entrusted to technical experts, thus becoming subject to rational decision making and management.

Escobar's analysis points out that, instead of delivering universal improvement of the human condition as was initially expected, indiscriminate application of instrumental rationality in the second half of the twentieth century eroded poor people's ability to define and take care of their own lives even further than the erosion of past colonial regimes. The transfer of the rationality of modernity carried with it the transfer of values and institutions. For example, the need for foreign exchange and investment influenced the promotion of cash crops to the detriment of food crops for domestic consumption; targeting efficiency and competitiveness in the global economy imposed industrialization—or post-industrialization—interventions over local production and trade patterns.

Moreover, Escobar noted, a discourse that privileges a modern culture of Western values and modes of knowledge and action is destructive in a deeper manner. It considers local cultures, predominant values, and politics responsible for backwardness. Most interventions of modernization have paid little attention to the historically derived system of values that sustain social systems—such as an economy, a business organization, a public service institution—which are irrational from the point of view of the rationality of modernity.

UNIVERSALISM AND RELATIVISM

At the beginning of the twenty-first century, social theory seems disillusioned with the science and technology that has triumphed in Western societies. In substantive terms, the institutionalized techno-economic rationality of the modern Western societies is highly controversial. There is a great deal of concern that it is destructive of the human habitat and creates a social order which leaves vast numbers of people in intolerable conditions.[12] Yet, despite the theoretical critiques and quite widespread awareness of its potentially catastrophic consequences, the techno-economic rationality of modernity continues to be dominant in all affairs of the Western societies, and tends to be transferred worldwide in the globalization phenomenon. In social sciences, as well as in the professions, there is a reluctance to adopt a pluralistic epistemology. The hesitance underlying the wider acceptance of the notion of socially shaped rationality is clearly manifested in the debate on ideology, which merits some further attention at this point.

All critiques of modernity allude to its ideological nature, but as was indicated in the discussion of the Marxist critics, there are differences about what is meant by ideology and whether ideology is an undesirable state to be overcome by reason, or as the nature of all beliefs and action. In general abstract terms, Elster (1983) explains that ideology is a bias, whereby a set of beliefs or values can be explained as perceptions of the interests of a social group. Ideological beliefs, often embodying 'an understanding of the whole according to the logic of the part' (p. 145) may be held by a social group although they do not serve their interests, or even the interests of other dominant social groups who manipulate them. For example, the belief of oppressed social groups that their oppressors are their protectors is clearly against the interests of the oppressed and it may not be in the best interest of the oppressors

---

[12] The most prevalent concern at the end of the 20th cent. has been the destruction of the earth's natural resources. Pippin (1995) lists five additional contemporary concerns: concentration of a new form of power—the power invested in scientific knowledge—in a few hands; deskilling of the labour force through automation; the narrowing of democratic debate as increasingly policy issues are considered complex technical matters; the extent of administrative power over aspects of private daily life; the use of science and technology for military purposes to create weapons of mass destruction of an unprecedented scale; and the dehumanization of life environments as technology invades all areas of culture.

either. This understanding of ideology as a case of limited capacity to develop beliefs through valid causality processes, that is, as a case of formal cognitive 'irrationality', is perhaps non-controversial.

But views are divided between those who attach negative connotations to the manifestation of this irrationality and discuss it as a state that should be overcome by rational thinking and action, and those who accept it as the pragmatics of social action. The former consider ideology as a disturbing 'false consciousness' that takes a social group astray from the correct route of action for its benefit. The latter consider ideology as historically developed systems of shared meaning and therefore pragmatically an unavoidable state of social knowledge. Consequently, the negative view requires efforts to rectify the faults of the collective cognitive processes. As corrective mechanisms Adorno and Horkheimer suggested resistance to the instrumental reason of modernity, Marcuse suggested the fostering of a different relation to nature, Habermas believes the solution lies in communicative processes. The alternative view neither believes in the possibility of rational corrective measures for the faulty rationality nor requires them. Very dissimilar analysts seem to share this attitude.[13] Weber, despite the normative character of his formal institutional types, was sceptical of the capacity of rationality as a cognitive process and the rationalistic structures that one might work out to lead to desirable social states. Foucault finds meaning only in the historically situated discourses that constitute the regimes of truth, the other postmodernists accept knowledge as a localized and transient form of rationality. Escobar highlights the chauvinistic character that general rationalities develop if they are ahistorical and a-contextual. From this perspective, the techno-economic rational order of modernity is an ideological state that emerged in the history of Europe and grew strong roots in North America.

These attitudes to the understanding of the rationality of modernity as ideology are associated with the fundamental division in social science and philosophy regarding universalism and relativism, objectivism and subjectivism. In its extreme form, the universalist, objectivist thesis bears the conviction that it is possible to determine what is true, real, and right in universal terms, unrelated to the specifics of history of social groups. Consequently, it implies the search for universal knowledge capable of improving the human condition irrespective of particular circumstances of the social actors, or—as is the case of critiques of modernity such as that by Habermas—by rationally reconciling the differences stemming from particular circumstances. The subjectivist, relativist thesis is based on the conviction that truth and perception of what is real or right can only be the result of specific forms of social life and culture which are a product of history. It accepts that there are many equally true conceptions of reality. From a critical point of view, the knowledge sought by the universalists is

---

[13] Many analysts of modernity and postmodernity do not use the concept of ideology, considering it inappropriate for the contemporary era. For many postmodernists, such as Lyotard, Baudrillard, and Foucault, this position is taken in order to break from the Marxist thought and its modernist concept of ideology as false consciousness. But I share Larrain's view that 'while they try very hard to get rid of the concept of ideology' they implicitly utilize it in their arguments against meta-narratives and universal theories (Larrain 1994).

utopian and often harbours totalitarian tendencies, imposing a uniform mode of thinking, believing, and acting which robs individuals and social groups of their ability to make their own choices. In contrast, subjectivism is feared to sanction arbitrary choices and chaotic behaviour of social actors.

The differences between these concepts and their implications are more complicated than the dichotomy between objectivism/subjectivism suggests. Universal knowledge does not reject the freedom of the 'subject', and relativist knowledge is not equivalent to individualistic, knowledge. The goal of universal knowledge in Western modernity involves 'subjectivization', that is, the assumption of free to decide, self-interested, and creative individuals. But it also assumes that it is possible to capture the behaviour of such free individuals in general laws and therefore in subject-independent theory, and consequently to work out action prescriptions that are good for all. The relativism of most post-Marxist and postmodern thinkers neither assumes an arbitrary individualism of 'free choice' nor is it based on the existence of independent 'self-interested' individuals. Rather, the multiple conceptions of reality manifest different regimes of truth, collective perspectives shaped by the historical power relations of social groups.

Relativism is an unsettling attitude, suspicious of anarchy There are pragmatic reasons why the challenge of the possibility of universal knowledge makes social theorists, political actors—such as politicians and policy makers—and practitioners alike uneasy. Social scientists take for granted a 'nomothetic' role legitimated by virtue of the universal and objective knowledge they are supposed to develop. The role of policy makers in contemporary national, and now international, decision-making centres incorporates the assumption that universally valid knowledge and principles of social intervention are possible. And most professional practice is formulated on standardized practices based on objective principles, derived from uni versal knowledge. A relativist epistemological orientation requires the redrawing of most of the learned, codified knowledges and practices. So far, Western societies have been extremely hesitant to do this. In their historically developed understanding of the world and their position in it, their well-being is thought to be served better by the rationalized myth of objective knowledge that holds universal validity.

Such a position is not universally valid, though. Even in the Western world the techno-economic rationality does not serve everybody well. The power relations maintained by the contemporary techno-economic regimes of truth leave a variety of social groups locked in frustrating life conditions with a very limited range of options. From a global perspective, as it is discussed in Chapter 4, relativism takes a different significance.

ORGANIZING REGIMES

Let us now turn to examine what rationality assumptions can be made in organizing and information systems innovation. The review of the debate on the rationality of modernity so far in this chapter makes it clear that the economically self-interested individual as a basic element for organizational behaviour in the free market context is a far-fetched abstraction. Similarly, the assumption that technological innovation is the consequence of scientific invention and an instrument for the attainment of the collective goals pursued by organizations is, at best, a convenient (for some) simplification of complex processes taking place in the context of modern societies.

Most studies of organizations and information systems moderate the assumption of universalist techno-economic rationality, and a stream of research has elaborated on the messiness of organizational behaviour. Herbert Simon's notion of bounded rationality (Simon 1945) set the tone for recognizing the limitations of organizational reasoning even in technical/rational studies. Others studied the way social, cultural, and political behaviours complicate the fundamental techno-scientific rationality, without, however, always challenging it as the underlying principle of organizing. This is the case with many institutionalist studies, which reveal such complications and moderate, but do not abandon, the technical/rational behaviour thesis. They still 'appear to regard the spread of "western" norms of rationality as almost inevitable given the development of world markets, . . . [and] do not discuss whether there may be alternative variants of such rationality' (Whitley 1997: 290).

Nevertheless, there have been studies that highlighted examples of organizations in which individual and collective action clearly does not comply with the assumption of such principles of rational behaviour and which exhibit what Clegg calls alternative 'modes of rationality' (Clegg 1990). The organizational behaviour patterns in East Asian countries—mainly Japan, South Korea, and Taiwan—have been repeatedly discussed as examples of alternative underlying substantive rationalities (see e.g. Hamilton and Biggart 1988; Clegg 1990; Orrù, Biggart, and Hamilton 1991; and Chapters 1 and 4 in this book). It has been pointed out that the organization of Japanese industry in groups of firms is based on a communitarian ideal, which involves consideration of what is good for the collectivity, not for individual firms. South Korean conglomerates are an expression of a patrimonial principle, whereby an authoritarian leader acts in the mode of a patriarch and his children. Taiwanese groups of firms are based on familial relations which, however, are not under the control of a single patriarch. Many other examples of alternative modes of rationality can be found in studies of organizations in Latin America (Caldas and Wood 1997; Pérez-Lizaur 1997), or South Europe (Clegg 1990; Kumar and van Dissel 1998).

Generally in such studies, alternative modes of rationality are seen as derived from long-term broader social experiences within which the organizations under study are embedded. For example, differences in the degree to which rational action is driven by trust and cooperation or competition and antagonism are traced in broader, historically formed, structures of social relations (Fox 1974; Dore 1983; Gambetta 1988).

The recognition of multiple, historically developed, substantive rationalities and congruent modes of organizing provides an orientation towards a non-universalist perspective in the study of information systems innovation. Rather than aiming to develop general knowledge and practice to conform to a-contextual rules of rational behaviour, the recognition of differences in substantive rationality directs attention to local meanings and legitimate action. But, with all the importance of an epistemology that overcomes the rigidity of universalist conception of rationality, this is a crude thesis for three reasons. First, associating modes of rationality with the historically developed social relations of a locality, whether a country or an otherwise defined region, entails the risk of stereotyping and oversimplifies the multiple institutional influences discussed in Chapter 1. Second, emphasizing the difference among underlying substantive rationalities creates the impression of homogeneous beliefs and behaviours, overlooking the coexistence of multiple beliefs, in particular ignoring the subjugated beliefs and knowledges. Third, a question still remains on how individual rational behaviour within an institutionalized organizational context should be understood, in other words, how the subjective is related with the institutional.

Starting from the latter, and drawing from contemporary critiques of modernity, individual rational behaviour can be understood as reflexive reasoning rather than a search for what is true or false. Rational situated acting can be best expressed in Weick's concept of enactment (Weick 1979). According to the notion of enactment, individuals and groups are not passive recipients of influences from their institutional context, they 'construct, rearrange, single out, and demolish many "objective" features of their surroundings' (ibid. 164). However, individuals' interaction with their organizational context by enactment is very different from the notion of action pre calculated to produce efficiency benefit. In enactment, members deal with the 'here and now', according to their desired outcomes which stem from their beliefs, according to their perceptions of entailed gains or risks. These perceptions and beliefs are neither arbitrary nor reducible to universal fundamentals of human nature or social history; they are derived from life conditions—the embodied life experiences, in Verran's vocabulary (Verran 1999). There is therefore a continuous interaction between the behaviour of subjective rational actors and social institutions. Individuals and groups' actions form, sustain, and change the institutions in which they are embedded and which subsequently feed into their perception of resources and constraints afforded to their action. This understanding of rationality in an organization's context is taken in a number of information systems studies, most prominently by Ciborra, Orlikowski, and Suchman (Suchman 1987; Ciborra 1991; Orlikowski 1996; Ciborra 1999).

Organizing entails the steering of individuals' enactments in collective action. The achievement of such a congruence of subjective situated behaviour is partly a matter of institutional influences of the environment—either by the shaping of substantive rationalities or by coercion—and partly internal institutionalization processes—again a matter of culture and/or coercion. A point that needs to be emphasized is that organizing is subject to multiple external influences and multiple internal enactments, therefore it cannot be seen as the result of common perceptions, common values and desired outcomes, and a single knowledge. Rather, organizing entails a regime of truth in Foucault's terms, with multiple knowledges streamlined in particular enactment coordinations under historically formed power relations. Paraphrasing this sentence, the rationality of an organization is a particular organizing regime.

I discuss the limitations of the association of an organization's mode of rationality with the social institutions of the locality within which an organization is situated in Chapter 4. At this point, it suffices to point out that the rationality of organizing behaviour is shaped by influences of institutional fields extended beyond the organization's locality—whether this is understood as the country or the region. More importantly, as I discussed in Chapter 1, social institutions are not culturally, socially, and politically harmonious and homogeneous. There too, manifested dominant rationalities hide subjugated knowledges. To wit, an organizing regime is woven from multiple enactments and institutional influences. And while particular rationalities are dominant in shaping the overall consistency of the collective organizational behaviour, other substantive rationalities, other perceptions of truth, are still present, even if not engaging in active resistance.[14]

CONCLUDING REMARKS

Bringing together the concepts drawn from the theoretical explorations so far, information systems innovation processes can be seen as translations that involve the enactments of multiple actors within organizing regimes shaped through power relation histories and under the influence of multiple social institutions. The problematizations that trigger an information systems translation can therefore be traced to the rationalities of the actors involved: their beliefs and desires, moulded through their membership in social institutions and challenged by their imaginary possibilities of change. The translation process may strengthen or challenge the institutionalized conditions of power/knowledge, that is, the existing organizing regime.

Even when it expresses the dominant rationality of an organization, the setting in motion of an information systems innovation network requires the mobilization of others—the users, the customers, the law, the various categories of professionals involved in the institutionalized organizing practices. Being shaped by different institutional histories, each of the network's actors may have different material concerns, different understandings of the consequences of innovation that matter, different symbolic expressions of what they know and what they want.

From such a perspective, the mainstream knowledge on ICT use of information systems professionals and the rationality of efficiency and competitiveness driving management can be seen as constituting a widespread institutionalized regime of truth. This organizing regime is constantly contested, and the results of the innovation scripts circulated by this alliance of ICT and management depend on the outcome of many situated confrontations with subjugated knowledges. To account for the diversity of outcomes of information systems innovation we need to be able to account for the alternative knowledges of the actors on whose enactment the information systems translation relies.

---

[14] Scott's study of power relations from the perspective of subordinate groups in society shows that resistance to domination can take many subtle forms (Scott 1990). In other words, subjugated rationalities are omnipresent and manifested in the multiple enactments of social institutions.

There can be no general a priori dichotomy between rational and irrational, rational and ideological, true and false, success and failure. Nevertheless, in the arena of the multiple contesting rationalities of the actors' institutionalized conditions, some rationalities have more legitimacy than others. Conversely, the techno-economic rationality of ICT and management is more compatible with certain organizations' organizing regimes and more alien in others. This is a general problem in the so-called technology transfer cases, in which technologies and organizational practices that are shaped and legitimized in one social setting are introduced in another. The literature of development studies is littered with accounts of the friction that takes place in the receiving organizations (Westney 1991). This problem is also demonstrated in the case studies in Part II and is further discussed in Chapter 9.

References

Albrow, M. (1970). *Bureaucracy*. London: Macmillan.

Beck, U. (1992). *Risk Society: Towards a New Modernity*. London: Sage.

——(1994). 'The Reinvention of Politics', in U. Beck, A. Giddens, and S. Lash, *Reflexive Modernization*. Cambridge: Polity Press, 1 55.

——Giddens, A. and Lash, S. (1994). *Reflexive Modernization*. Cambridge: Polity Press.

Braverman, H. (1974). *Labor and Monopoly Capital*. New York: Monthly Review.

Caldas, M. P., and Wood, T., Jr. (1997). '"For the English to see": The Importation of Managerial Technology in Late 20th-Century Brazil'. *Organization*, 4(4): 517–34.

Ciborra, C. U. (1991). 'From Thinking to Tinkering: The Grassroots of Strategic Information Systems'. *Proceedings of the 12th International Conference on Information Systems*, New York, 283–92.

——(1999). 'A Theory of Information Systems Based on Improvisation', in W. L. Currie and B. Galliers (eds.), *Rethinking Management Information Systems*. Oxford: Oxford University Press, 136–55.

Clegg, S. R. (1990). *Modern Organizations: Organization Studies in the Postmodern World*. London: Sage.

Cooper, R., and Burrell, G. (1988). 'Modernism, Postmodernism, and Organizational Analysis: An Introduction'. *Organizational Studies*, 9(1): 91–112.

Dore, R. (1983). 'Goodwill and the Spirit of Market Capitalism'. *British Journal of Sociology*, 34: 459–82.

Ellul, J. (1964). *The Technological Society*. New York: Vintage.

Elster, J. (1983). *Sour Grapes*. Cambridge: Cambridge University Press.

——(1989). 'Social Norms and Economic Theory'. *Journal of Economic Perspectives*, 3(4): 99–117.

Escobar, A. (1995). *Encountering Development*. Princeton: Princeton University Press.

Feenberg, A. (1995). *Alternative Modernity: The Technical Turn in Philosophy and Social Theory*. Berkeley: University of California Press.

Foucault, M. (ed.) (1980). *Power/Knowledge: Selected Interviews and Other Writings 1972–1977*, ed. C. Gordon, trans. C. Gordon, L. Marshall, J. Mepham, and K. Soper. New York, London: Prentice Hall.

Fox, A. (1974). *Beyond Contract: Work, Power and Trust Relations*. London: Faber and Faber.

Freire, P. (1970). *Pedagogy of the Oppressed*. New York: Seabury Press.

Gambetta, D. (ed.) (1988). *Trust: Making and Breaking Co-operative Relations*. Oxford: Blackwell.

Gandhi, M. (1997). 'The Quest for Simplicity: "my idea of swaraj"', in M. Rahnema and V. Bawtree (eds.), *The Post-Development Reader*. London: Zed Books, 306–7.

Giddens, A. (1990). *The Consequences of Modernity*. Cambridge: Polity Press.

——— (1991). *Modernity and Self-Identity*. Cambridge: Polity Press.

Granovetter, M. (1985). 'Economic Action and Social Structure: The Problem of Embeddedness'. *American Journal of Sociology*, 91(3): 481–510.

Habermas, J. (1972). *Knowledge and Human Interests*. London: Heinemann.

——— (1987). *The Philosophical Discourse of Modernity*. Cambridge: Polity Press.

Hamilton, G. G., and Biggart, N.W. (1988). 'Market, Culture, and Authority: A Comparative Analysis of Management and Organization in the Far East'. *American Journal of Sociology*, 94: S52–S94.

Hassard, J. (1996). 'Exploring the Terrain of Modernism and Postmodernism in Organization Theory', in D. M. Boje, R. P. Gephart, Jr., and T. J. Thatchenkery (eds.), *Postmodern Management and Organization Theory*. Thousand Oaks, Calif.: Sage, 45–59.

Horkheimer, M. (1947). *Eclipse of Reason*. New York: Continuum.

——— and Adorno, T. W. (1972). *Dialectic of Enlightenment*. New York: Herder and Herder.

Hughes, T. P. (1983). *Networks of Power: Electrification in Western Society, 1800–1930*. Baltimore: Johns Hopkins University Press.

Kumar, K., and van Dissel, H. G. (1998). 'The Merchant of Prato—Revisited: Toward a Third Rationality of Information Systems'. *MIS Quarterly*, June: 199–226.

Larrain, J. (1994). *Ideology and Cultural Identity: Modernity and the Third World Presence*. Cambridge: Polity Press.

Lash, S. (1993). 'Reflexive Modernization: The Aesthetic Dimension'. *Theory, Culture and Society*, 10(1): 1–24.

Latour, B. (1987). *Science in Action*. Cambridge, Mass.: Harvard University Press.

——— (1993). *We Have Never Been Modern*. New York: Harvester Wheatsheaf.

——— and Woolgar, S. (1986). *Laboratory Life: The Constitution of Scientific Facts*. Princeton: Princeton University Press.

Lyotard, J. F. (1984). *The Postmodern Condition: A Report on Knowledge*. Manchester: Manchester University Press.

Marcuse, H. (1964). *One-Dimensional Man*. Boston: Beacon Press.

——— (1972). *Counterrevolution and Revolt*. Boston: Beacon Press.

Mumford, L. (1966). *The Myth of the Machine: Techniques and Human Development*. New York: Harcourt Brace Jovanovich.

Nandy, A. (1987). *The Intimate Enemy*. Bombay: Oxford University Press.

Orlikowski, W. J. (1996). 'Improvising Organizational Transformation Over Time: A Situated Change Perspective'. *Information Systems Research*, 7(1): 63–92.

Orrù, M., Biggart, N. W., and Hamilton, G. G. (1991). 'Organizational Isomorphism in East Asia', in W. W. Powell and P. J. DiMaggio (eds.), *The New Institutionalism in Organizational Analysis*. Chicago: Chicago University Press, 361–89.

Parsons, T., and Smelser, N. J. (1956). *Economy and Society*. New York: Free Press.

Pérez-Lizaur, M. (1997). 'The Mexican Family Enterprise Faces the Open Market'. *Organization*, 4(4): 535–51.

Pippin, R. B. (1995). 'On the Notion of Technology as Ideology', in A. Feenberg and A. Hannah (eds.), *Technology and the Politics of Knowledge*. Bloomington: Indiana University Press, 43–61.

Polanyi, K., C. Arensberg, and Pearson, H. (eds.) (1957). *Trade and Market in the Early Empires.* New York: Free Press.

Said, E. (1994). *Culture and Imperialism.* New York: Vintage Books.

Scott, J. C. (1990). *Domination and the Roots of Resistance: Hidden Transcripts.* New Haven: Yale University Press.

Shapin, S. (1992). 'History of Science and its Sociological Reconstruction'. *History of Science*, 20: 157–211.

Simon, H. (1945). *Administrative Behaviour.* New York: Macmillan.

——(1955). 'A Behavioural Model of Rational Choice'. *Quarterly Journal of Economics* 69: 99–118.

Smelser, N. J. (1978). 'Reexamining the Parameters of Economic Activity', in E. M. Epstein and D. Votaw (eds.), *Rationality, Legitimacy, Responsibility: Search for New Directions in Business and Society.* Santa Monica, Calif.: Goodyear Publishing Company, 19–51.

Strange, S. (1988). *States and Markets.* London: Pinter Publishers.

Suchman, L. (1987). *Plans and Situated Action.* Cambridge: Cambridge University Press.

Toulmin, S. (1990). *Cosmopolis: The Hidden Agenda of Modernity.* Chicago: University of Chicago Press.

Touraine, A. (1995). *Critique of Modernity.* Oxford: Blackwell.

Upadhyaya, P. (1995). 'The Sacred, the Erotic and the Ecological: The Politics of Transformative Global Discourses', *Journal of Organisational Change Management*, 8(5): 33–60.

Verran, H. (1999). 'Staying True to the Laughter in Nigerian Classrooms', in J. Law and J. Hassard (eds.), *Actor Network Theory and After.* Oxford: Blackwell, 136–55.

Vogel, S. (1995). 'New Science, New Nature: The Habermas–Marcuse Debate Revisited', in A. Feenberg and A. Hannah (eds.), *Technology and the Politics of Knowledge.* Bloomington: Indiana University Press, 23–43.

Weber, M. (1947). 'Sociological Categories of Economic Action', in T. Parsons (ed.), *Max Weber: The Theory of Social and Economic Organization.* New York: Free Press, 158–323.

Weick, K. (1979). *The Social Psychology of Organizing.* New York: McGraw-Hill.

Westney, D. E. (1991). 'International Transfer of Organizational Technology', in R. Robinson (ed.), *The International Communication of Technology.* New York: Taylor and Francis, 167–82.

Whitley, R. (1997). 'The Institutionalist Approach, Review of the *Institutional Environments and Organizations: Structural Complexity and Individualism* by W. R. Scott and J. W. Meyer (eds)'. *Organization*, 4(2): 279–302.

4

The Global, the Local, and the Disembedded

My main objective in this chapter is to examine how the historically developed diversity of organizing regimes under which information systems innovations unfold is affected by the trends of institutional changes known as globalization, and therefore to identify the relevant contexts for the study of information systems. To that end, the perspective of globalization taken here is broader than that usually found in the information systems literature so far. Inasmuch as I take the view that information systems innovation involves the interplay of multiple substantive rationalities the contextual changes that matter cannot be confined to the economic processes of globalization.[1] In a more fundamental way, I need to begin by exploring what is meant by globalization, to trace its constituent dimensions, and to look at its emerging consequences.

Concern about social and economic processes across the globe and interest in matters international are not new, but in the last couple decades of the twentieth century the global has taken on a new theoretical significance across the social sciences. In a very general sense globalization is understood to refer to an increasing disassociation of social life from territoriality (Waters 1995). This contemporary conception of globalization is closely associated with the diffusion of ICT innovation. The expansion of communication systems is considered to be at the root of the socio-economic changes of globalization—changes that many analysts consider to be as revolutionary as the most visionary technology innovators have foreseen: no less than the 'overthrow of the old order', according to Giddens (1999), one of the most influential theorists of globalization.

Giddens (1990) associates globalization with the 'disembedding' of social relationships from their local context of interaction that started happening as early as the emergence of modernity. Time became a universal identifier, measured by the mechanical clock independently from the seasonal cycles of particular geographic locations and the rhythms of the daily lives of particular communities. Also space became universally defined along the dimensions of the globe. The disassociation of

[1] Globalization features prominently in the information systems literature of the 1990s. With few notable exceptions (e.g. Walsham 2000 *a*, *b*), the information systems studies are concerned with the ICT-mediated internationalization of economic activities (Currie 2000) and the information infrastructure of the multinational corporation (Ives and Jarvenpaa 1991; Bradley, Hausman, and Nolan 1993; Hanseth and Braa 2000).

time and space from specific social reference allowed the separation of the two concepts, so that people's activities could be organized across large temporary and spatial distances by business and state organizations. It is the 'disembedding' of human activity from locality that ICT innovation accentuated according to Giddens, thus becoming a powerful mechanism of globalization.

Harvey (1989) too finds that the changing relationship between time and space, that he calls the 'time-space compression', plays a fundamental role in globalization. The shortening of the time it takes for transport and communication makes distance in space insignificant. For example, the distance between London and Tokyo becomes unimportant when performing a business transaction through telecommunications or watching a media event instantaneously in the two places. In other words the space distance between the two places is annihilated by time compression.

The significance and consequences of the new possibilities for technology-mediated social interaction pointed out by Giddens and Harvey need to be understood in association with the socio-economic regime that accommodates them. And this is what most theories of globalization have been concerned with: the social processes through which ICT and other technologies—such as transport technologies—acquire significance and within which they are mobilized for economic or other social purposes.[2]

Most prominent among the theoretical perspectives of globalization are those which seek to explain it in terms of the logic and the logistics of the economic system in modern society. Globalization is seen as a fundamentally economic phenomenon and is analysed in economic concepts, such as the free market, the relations of production, or patterns of consumption. But socio-economic perspectives vary on two accounts: first the extent to which they subordinate the social to the economic postulating that everything is a consequence of economic imperatives, and second the social vision they aspire to. Liberal economic ideas fuel a widespread discourse on the imperatives of the new 'global economy' oriented towards the free market ideal— what Beck calls 'globalism' (2000). Marxist-inspired efforts to explain the globalization processes trace the changing structures of production and consumption inherent in the perpetuation of the capitalist system, and they too tend to assume that economic relations determine social structures and possibilities of action (see e.g. Lash and Urry 1987; Sklair 1991). Such a perspective is also discernible in Wallerstein's widely known theory of 'world system', which conceptualizes the world as a single capitalist economy governed by the principle of profit maximization (Wallerstein 1980).

Several recent analyses shifted emphasis and, while acknowledging the significance of the capitalist socio-economic context, they explored new elements, which are not reducible to the economic logic. Harvey, for example, attributes the compression of time and space to efforts made to overcome the crises of the capitalist socio-economic

---

[2] In contrast, there is a plethora of speculative technocratic writings on ICT and globalization, which predict social states on the basis of technological potential, a good example of which is Negroponte's futuristic scenario of technology mediated life conditions (Negroponte 1995).

system, and he moves on to analyse the contemporary industrial conditions. He observes that spatial barriers have collapsed through a combination of a flexible accumulation production organization, technology innovation, and the removal of regulatory obstacles so that capital flows follow the relative advantages of particular space locations, such as lower cost labour (Harvey 1989). A similar view is put forward by Castells who sees globalization occurring through the process of capitalist restructuring (Castells 1989, 1996, 1997, 1998). The technological potential for information processing and communication that emerged in this historical period becomes the fundamental source of productivity and power for the restructuring of a socio-economic system prone to crises. Social and cultural dynamics play an important role in this restructuring.

Other theories, though, begin from non-economic assumptions about the nature of the processes of change comprising globalization. Political scientists point out the significance of power institutions in the shaping of the liberal international economy and elaborate on the emergence of international political authorities which challenge the sovereignty of the fundamental political structure of modernity, the nation state (Rosenau 1990; Held 1996). In cultural theory, attention shifts to the way cultural 'signifiers', whether products or symbols loaded with life values, cross borders through mass media, international business, and increased travelling and erode national identities. Such studies show how cultural processes are implicated in the 'breakdowns and new departures'[3] of the contemporary world (King 1991; Hall 1992; Robertson 1992; Friedman 1994; Appadurai 1996).

Clearly it is not a matter of finding a single cause or dominant logic for the phenomena collectively perceived as globalization. Rather, globalization is better understood as comprising the interplay of multiple processes.[4] And contrary to the quite popular view that the world market overrides the historically created cultural and political processes,[5] a common conclusion in theoretical studies of globalization is that its constituent processes are multifaceted and contingent, and do not result in a homogeneous world. Socio-theoretical analyses such as by Harvey and Castells quoted above are not mono-causal accounts of economic rationality. A good example to clarify the way social theorists account for multiple dimensions of the globalization trends is Bauman's discussion of this complex phenomenon (1998). He begins with the observation of the contemporary relationship of capital and labour, pointing out the asymmetry between the mobile shareholder capital—free from community and social welfare obligations to move to locations where investment

---

[3] See Beck 2000: 48.

[4] Analyses that conceptualize and assess the significance of globalization tend to cluster specialized observations of causes and processes in a few dimensions of trends. For example, in his analysis Giddens (1990) identified four dimensions of the globalization process: the nation state system; the world capitalist economy; the international division of labour; and the world military system. More dimensions could be added, of course, and Beck (2000) highlights the cross-border consciousness of the ecological side effects of industrialization. Also, Giddens's list does not include changes of cultural identity, which have attracted a great deal of attention by other authors.

[5] See Fukuyama (1992) for the 'end of history' thesis.

yields higher dividends—and the vast numbers of locally bound people. He highlights the non-economic aspects of the global economy and points to its social consequences. He stresses that the creation of the global economy involves the disempowerment of the nation state, and the development of a 'new world order' with new cultural distinctions between those who live their lives in global mobility and those who are powerlessly tied to their locality.

With the understanding that globalization cannot be accounted for in simple cause and effect relationships, the disentangling of the main 'dimensions' of contemporary large-scale social change can, nevertheless, be helpful in tracing the contexts that matter in information systems innovation. Thus, the following section looks separately at the three trends widely perceived as comprising globalization, namely increasing international economic activity, pressures that diminish the power of the nation state, and increasing cultural flows.

ECONOMIC PROCESSES OF GLOBALIZATION

The basic observation regarding globalization in the economic arena is that national borders, which have traditionally determined a pattern of distinct economic territories on the globe, are gradually losing their significance and economic activities are conducted in a way that defies geographic distance. Globalization is manifested through increases in cross-border trade and capital flows, production chains, and transfer of labour and professional expertise.

The growth in cross-countries economic exchanges and collaboration has been documented with an abundance of statistics. Indicatively, the value of the exports of industrial countries grew at an average rate of 12 per cent a year between 1964 and 1992, while lending and borrowing across national borders through banks grew at 23 per cent per year (Haggard 1995). Import tariffs have been reduced in all countries. In the United States tariffs on industrial goods were reduced from an average of 60 per cent in 1934 to 4.3 per cent in 1987. At that time Japanese tariffs were at an average of 2.9 per cent and European Union tariffs were 4.7 per cent.

Manufacturing of goods often involves production chains through companies around the world. An indicative example may suffice here. Browne (1994) described the production of televisions by the Japanese company Hitachi for the US market in the early 1990s as follows. Hitachi estimated the numbers and models of television sets their distributors in the United States would need in six weeks, and according to this estimate issued an order to a Singaporean subcontractor who manufactured the specified transistors. The transistors were shipped to a subcontractor in Malaysia who assembled circuit boards. The circuit boards were then shipped to another subcontractor in Taiwan who, according to Hitachi's mix instructions, assembled controller chassis. The chassis from Taiwan, a number of components ordered from Hitachi affiliates in Japan, and other components made by a Dutch company in the United States were all shipped to Mexico to be assembled in television sets, tested, and packaged before they were finally shipped to the distributors in the United States.

Labour mobility and transfer of professional expertise are particularly noticeable in services, the most value adding economic activities in the current 'post-industrial' era. International consultants' services, university education, and specialized training are some of the activities that sustain a vibrant international services market.

Such observations of increased cross-border economic activity create powerful images of business conduct determined by global market competition, a global free market, and economic growth prospects across geographic regions with historically unequal patterns of industrialization. But international business is not unrestrained by social institutions. The economic flows are not the result of the invisible hand of free market alone. And economic disparities are not decreasing in the world economy; on the contrary, gaps between the 'rich' and the 'poor' are deepening both at the global scale and within nation states. The remainder of this section looks closer at each of these misconceptions about the organizational dynamics, political mechanisms, and the economic consequences of the global economic flows, in order to understand the social forces that enable and constrain the economic processes of globalization.

International Business and Social Institutions

Chapter 1 discussed the institutional aspects of organizations at some length, pointing out the national variations of organizational patterns and management. This section looks at the two types of organization of business activity which are often discussed as best fit for the global economy, the multinational (MNC) and the network organization.

The MNC is broadly defined as a dispersed firm with individual components located in a number of countries (Ghoshal and Nohria 1990). It is widely seen as the pillar of the contemporary global capitalist system, and often as a perpetrator of homogenization. But MNCs vary significantly in terms of the density of integration of their global units and several typologies have been suggested to capture their variations.[6] All MNCs, though, can be seen as integrated international organizational networks, parts of which are nested in national organizational fields (Ghoshal and Bartlett 1993). An important question, therefore, is how their subunits are held together while maintaining their degree of autonomy and their differences. According to institutionalist theory, the circumstances of their genesis in the country of ownership are significant in forming a long-lasting corporate culture. Moreover, the relative power of the country of ownership in the world economy is considered

---

[6] Best known in the 1990s was Bartlett and Ghoshal's identification of four different types of multinational corporations: the 'multinational' corporation that builds its presence in many countries through sensitivity and responsiveness to national differences; the 'global' corporation that builds cost advantages through centralized global-scale operations; the 'international' corporation that exploits parent company knowledge and capabilities through worldwide diffusion and adaptation; and the 'transnational' corporation that encourages shared decision making to manage global efficiency, responds to local differences, and promotes innovation (Ghoshal and Bartlett 1998).

significant in determining the extent to which the 'headquarters' impose homogeneity and exercise control over a uniform structure and culture. However, the local national environment is in many ways influential, creating differences among subunits. Possibilities for subcontracting, variations in traditions of trust and social networking, differences in state regulations and trade union activities, differences in authority and decision-making characteristics, different education environments and skills available, different tacit knowledge mechanisms are some of the conditions accounting for the heterogeneity of their subunits (Nelson 1993).

Inevitably, the study of the MNCs exposes the institutional conditions for the conduct of business in different countries. Not surprisingly, a study looking at the country imprinting found in the MNCs, observed that '[t]here is no optimal arrangement of human affairs or organized economic activity that can serve as a template because social knowledge is evolutionary and embedded in the social relationships that prevail' (Kogut 1993: 144). And while MNCs are often seen as conduits of best practice, this should not be understood as uniform practice. Diversified MNCs operating in heterogeneous environments are faced with conflicting organizing practices: whatever is considered international best practice and the local wisdom of doing business. For some of them, at least, 'best practice' is not a generalizable quality, but a geographically and socially specific condition.

Another configuration frequently associated with the emergence of the global economy is the organizational network. It is often argued that the network model is an effective structure for the corporation, and in particular for MNCs. It is open-ended, flexible, and possible to expand in any direction without the burden of hierarchical control and production processes. Castells, a main proponent of the 'network' structure, draws from the Japanese analyst Ken'ichi Imai to suggest the best way to organize MNCs is as cross-border networks, that is as sets of companies in different institutional environments without overall control from a national basis (Castells 1996).

The concept of network is also extended beyond the structure of a corporation to refer to inter-organizational relations. Such networks vary substantially in their synthesis and may involve small enterprises as well as MNCs. In some cases they are composed mainly from small enterprises that complement each other's production and share the services of common agencies. Examples of this type are found in the networks of Emilia Romagna which are studied in the 'flexible specialization' literature (Piore and Sabel 1984; Pyke, Becattini, and Sengenberger 1990) and are discussed in some detail in the case study described in Chapter 7. In other cases, a large corporation becomes the focal unit that sustains the business of hundreds of local subcontractors (Schienstock 1997).

In industrial economics and policy studies, particular interest has been shown in the networks of organizations that form the basis of the impressive economic growth of the South-East Asian countries in the last three decades. For example, two types of networks were identified as playing a significant role in the Japanese economy. The first is networks of large firms, such as Mitsubishi and Mitsui, each of them involving banks as their own sources of financing and competing in all main sectors of activity. The second type of networks, the *keiretsu*, is built around a large specialized corporation, e.g. Toyota or Hitachi, and comprises hundreds or thousands of suppliers and subcontractors. Thus, the Japanese economy is understood to be based on financial interdependency, market agreements, personnel transfer, and information sharing among the partners of a dense network of organizations (Castells 1996). In Korea, hierarchical networks (*chaebol*) of large companies coordinated in a centralized manner and controlled by family-owned central holding companies compete for the market of the country under considerable government patronage. Almost the opposite in terms of size of component organizations and role of government is the networks of the Taiwanese economy. There, small family-owned firms are linked with each other in highly personalized and informal exchanges and financial dependencies through alliances between families.

What lessons can be learnt from such examples? The network structure of economic activities is a generic, abstract concept. The main message the use of this concept conveys is that non-monolithic and non-centrally controlled organizations are very likely to excel in regional and global markets, particularly when supported effectively by ICT. But the actual form of the network enterprise or the industrial network is contingent upon social and political circumstances, thus giving rise to very diverse types of work organization and business partnerships. To wit, the literature on the network society demonstrates that economic activity remains polymorphic, very much depending on the institutions of the local society. MNCs may strategically redeploy their resources and actions across borders, and policy makers may design network-type industrial structures, but the success of such interventions—as will be seen in the case of the attempt to restructure manufacturing in Cyprus in Chapter 7—largely depend on the social institutions that are mobilized to realize them, or are expected to support them.

Market and Political Institutions

The increased flows of capital, goods, production components, and labour are generally attributed to two mutually reinforcing developments: technology innovation and the reduction of government barriers that segmented the world economy. Technology innovation, that changed the significance of time and space, would not be so effective without policy reform towards lowering the fences of the national economies and allowing free trade and capital investment. Since the end of the Second World War, the relaxation of border restrictions on trade and foreign investment has been relentlessly pursued by the multilateral economic institutions—the World Trade Organization and its predecessors, the World Bank and the International Monetary Fund (IMF). Indeed, in the 1990s most countries, notably in Latin America and South-East Asia, abandoned their decades-long policies of import substitutions and production protection and pursued trade liberalization processes. Moreover, the adoption of economic reform policies and adjustments by nation states, such as intellectual property rights legislation or environmental policies, have been reducing national differences in the rules of competition. Examples of successful economic growth, such as of Singapore or Chile, have strengthened the conviction of many academic and policy analysts that freer trade and commercial liberalization improves economic performance.

The question that arises here is to what extent such changes are the result of political forces serving particular economic interests rather than the free market ideal which is assumed to provide opportunities for all. Economic liberalization invariably involves pressures, which are not determined by the rules of macro-economic theory alone, but are part of a changing system of political power—as will be discussed in the following section. The effects of the pressures of international institutions on regional economies are not always clearly positive. The most noticeable case of concern is the so-called structural adjustment programmes by the World Bank and IMF that exert pressure on developing countries to adopt market policies and reform their economies according to the global economy requirements. The results of such efforts are highly controversial (Herbst 1998; Ravenhill 1998), raising questions of whether the economic integration of open market policies pursued by the international development agencies benefit developing and advanced economies alike.

Haggard, for example, highlights the external political pressures that contributed to the adoption of economic liberalization policies in the two developing regions, Latin America and South-East Asia (Haggard 1995) His analysis suggests that during the 1980s developing countries adopted economic integration policies under powerful external economic and political constraints, namely: their external debt, the constraining lending policies of the international financial institutions and bilateral donors, the commercial policies of advanced industrial states, and the conditions they used to enforce compliance to regulations of their interest.

Crises in repaying accumulated debts obliged many developing countries to adopt economic and political reforms in order to regain access to foreign investment. To the extent that commercial lending and foreign direct investment was in retreat, international financial lenders, such as the World Bank, and bilateral assistance from advanced industrial countries acquired great importance; but such lending and assistance was accompanied by conditions of domestic policy reforms. At the same time, there were pressures from advanced industrial economies, and in particular the United States, through sanctions and regional economic collaboration agreements to open the markets of developing countries for export and investment opportunities. The international regime of 'freer' world trade and investment was also enforced by the offering of reciprocal trade concessions by the advanced economies to countries willing to comply with policies favouring their commercial interests, such as intellectual property rights.

The identification of such pressures for the development of the current global economy not only exposes some darker moral aspects of coerced 'development', but also raises questions about the sustainability and social consequences of the new economic regime. As Haggard points out, to the extent that compliance with the global free market regime is a result of external pressures and privileges the more internationalist elite groups of a country, it is uncertain whether integration with the global economy results in broad social improvements.

Economic Inequalities

The most glaring aspect of diversity of the contemporary economic globalization is that of its resulting effects. In industrialized countries a few large cities have emerged as the new international economic centres, concentrating financial, legal, accounting, and management consultancy services—the specialized high value activities of the post-industrial economy. Mega-cities form a transnational network, oriented towards the world markets rather than their local economy, and they tend to be poorly integrated with their regional economy. Within mega-cities there is a trend of polarization with rich elites co-existing with acute poverty, and prosperous mega-cities may exist in the midst of not-very-prosperous countries. Poor 'inner cities' exist next to the richest commercial centres. At the urban perimeters there are often immigrant ghettos, as well as well-off suburbs (Sassen 1994).

In developing countries in-country inequalities are a striking feature, particularly in cases of cities with rapid economic development, such as Bangalore or Shanghai, through linking to the global economy. Such large cities continue to grow, mainly as a result of migration from rural areas, becoming global hubs of services in the middle of regions with much slower economic growth trends. They are also polarized themselves, with a globally oriented elite and a vast population of very cheap labour trying to survive by offering devalued services at the margins of the newly developed affluent society. With all the admiration India's hub of software industry and China's services industry have attracted recently, these are also exemplary cases of social inequality and human deprivation.

Sweeping changes in the world economy as a whole have accentuated the difference between 'developed' and 'underdeveloped' countries and regions. The collapse of the socialist economies of East Europe, the rapid economic growth of Japan to become the second most wealthy country of the world after the United States, the emergence of the small South-East Asian economies out of poverty as dynamic players of the global economy, and the further decline of poor economic regions, such as Africa, have changed the clustering of countries in first, second, and third world that was formed after the Second World War. In the post-colonial and post-cold-war era some regions have done well in finding a position in the global competitive economy, but others have become even more marginalized, unable to organize effective economic activity and sustain effective social institutions. The contrast between the economic development of Japan and the South-East Asian economies and the stagnation of Africa demonstrates the current state of disparity in the global economy.

The impressive economic growth of the South-East Asian countries in the last three decades of the twentieth century, which challenged the historical economic dominance of Western nations, has particular significance in the current perception of the globalization trends. It is widely mentioned as an exemplar of the opportunities of the global economy, and frequently considered in comparative policy studies in order to derive lessons for other regions and countries. Japan was gradually transformed from an economically backward esoteric society, devastated from the Second World War, to become the second largest economy of the world. A cluster of neighbouring small countries, the 'newly industrialized Asian economies' of Singapore, Taiwan, South Korea, and Hong Kong, emerged out of poverty to account for a disproportionately large for their size percentage of the world's industrial output and exports.[7]

In a nutshell, since the 1950s the Japanese government pursued a combination of effective policies to promote trade and technology innovation and to secure financial resources for the creation of powerful business networks that became mighty competitors in the world market. Legendary is the role of the Ministry of International Trade and Industry (MITI), and, more recently, the Ministry of Posts and Telecommunications (MPT) in coordinating the formation of giant corporation networks, securing credit, building technological infrastructures and competencies. A strong nationalist identity, cultural homogeneity, a competent state bureaucracy, management/labour cooperation, and industrial relations conducive to high productivity are some of the factors highlighted by analysts of the Japanese economic growth (Bradshaw and Wallace 1996; Castells 1998).

The Japanese economic success has been followed by the emergence of the four Asian 'tigers'—Singapore, Taiwan, South Korea, and Hong Kong. They were transformed from desolate economies with no domestic markets, energy resources, or industrial and technological capacity to the most competitive producers and exporters in the world market. For about three decades they sustained the highest rate of GNP in the world (Castells 1998). In 1997 Singapore had US$32,810 GNP per capita (lower only than Japan's), Hong Kong, China (SAR) US$25,200, South Korea US$10,550 (UNDP 1999). Other countries of the South-East Asian region—Thailand, Malaysia, Indonesia—have also been developing at an unprecedented pace.[8]

Analysts of the spectacular economic development of the four newly industrialized Asian countries point out a number of common characteristics (Hobday 1995; Castells 1998). Most noticeable is the influence of the state, with authoritarian but competent government regimes, orientation towards global exports, and emphasis given to science and technology innovation. Nevertheless, comparisons of the development trajectories of these four countries invariably stress also their significant differences in economic structures and development policies. Singapore, with a succession of consistent government strategies, pursued a sustained effort to attract foreign capital, becoming an export platform of multinational corporations, and shifting the basis of its economy from local trade towards advanced services. South Korea, with the active involvement of a nationalistic authoritarian government and with substantial American military support, attracted foreign loans and nurtured a number of highly successful large companies. Taiwan, under strong state guidance, formed effective networks of small

---

[7] In 1998 the newly industrialized Asian economies, with 1.3% of the world's population exported 9.3% the world's goods and services, achieving a share of 3.2% of the world's GDP. In comparison, 27 other Asia countries (excluding Japan and the Middle East), with 52.2% of the world's population had only 8.1% share of the world's exports of goods and services, and 22.8% of the world's GDP (IMF 1999).

[8] Despite the major setback of the 1997 financial crisis that hit the economies of most South-East Asian countries, most international economic analysts are optimistic that this region's economic performance is improving.

and medium family-owned producers, state agencies, and foreign trading companies and exports a range of efficiently manufactured products, including high technologies such as microelectronics. Hong Kong, with an economy composed of small firms and stressing flexibility in manufacturing and competitive prices, became an international business centre under a 'benevolent' colonial government that facilitated access to world markets and subsidized collective consumption.

From a Western point of view, the authoritarian nature of the governments that have fostered the economic growth in most of the countries in the South-East Asian region causes some concern, but overall these countries are considered to be successful examples of globalization. The states' heavy intervention in the market is watched with apprehension, but the way these countries overcame market entry barriers to compete internationally in the electronics industry and, furthermore, came to play a pioneering role in shaping the vision and realization of the 'information society' is greatly admired.

In stark contrast to the impressive economic growth of the South-East Asian economies, the economies of most African countries have been stagnant in the last few decades, with deteriorating trade indicators. Africa's percentage of world exports was reduced from 3 per cent in 1950 to 1.1 per cent in 1990. Foreign direct investment also fell in the 1980s, and in 1992 it amounted to only 6 per cent of the total foreign direct investment in developing countries (Castells 1998). The total external debt of sub-Saharan Africa increased from US\$9 bn. in 1971 (14 per cent of the area's GNP), to US\$107 bn. (56 per cent of GNP) in 1985, and to US\$220 bn. (68 per cent of GNP) in 1997 (IMF 1999). Their trade balance declined from US\$7.1 bn. in 1990 to US\$−11.4 bn. in 1998 (African Development Bank 1999). The income gained from rich mineral resources, such as gold and oil, and the substantial funds of international and bilateral aid tend to be mismanaged by inefficient governments and not to be invested in developmental infrastructures. The decade of the 1980s was called the 'lost decade' for the African continent. The 1990s have not been any better.

The reasons for this decline are complex and include inappropriate economic policies, government deficiencies, lack of human resources appropriately trained to support modern industries, and lack of ICT infrastructure (Callaghy 1998; Castells 1998; Ravenhill 1998). The latter is an issue discussed in a dispersed literature on technology transfer, implementation, and policy problems (Kluzer 1990; Moussa and Schware 1992; Odedra et al. 1993; Minges and Kelly 1994; Audenhove 2000). The diffusion of computers has been anything but a priority in the indebted, mainly agricultural economies of Africa, and until the 1990s they were imported with high tariffs.[9]

---

[9] For many African countries the main way of acquiring computers has been aid-funded projects. These, however, have been almost exclusively concerned with the government sector, and had a short-termist attitude related to the deadlines, immediate objectives, and resources of particular aid projects. They have often neglected such substantial issues as compatibility of new systems with the technical resources of the organizations that hosted them, training of local personnel to operate the systems after the project consultants left, and resources for maintenance. The result has been numerous non-operational systems that added to the frustration and apathy of demoralized administrators. University training in IT only started in the 1980s in many African countries and has been unable to follow the fast development of the field; with the exception of South Africa, studies of information systems that associate computer technology with their organizational context hardly exist in African universities.

State telecommunications organizations, starved of funding, technical expertise, and management capacity have been totally incapable of coping with the flood of communications innovation.[10]

The inequalities exemplified by these two regions manifest some of the dilemmas of contemporary globalization. The opening of opportunities for growth by some tolerates the decline and further impoverishment of vast numbers of poor and many weak population groups. The global economy has a tail of stagnant regions in cities, in countries, and in the world at large, for which globalization is a negative experience of sliding more into debt and desolation. A large percentage of the world's population has little participation in the world economy. The global economic forces do little to accommodate the rural poor, the mega-cities' poor, and regions such as Africa or central Asia in the world economy.

In short, the literature examined in this section suggests that the economic processes and consequences of globalization depend on local social institutions and the interplay between local and international political forces. At the beginning of the twenty-first century the result of these contingent politico-economic processes is a world of very unequal economic conditions, both at the local and global scale.

POLITICAL PROCESSES OF GLOBALIZATION

Since the late eighteenth century, the world has been perceived as composed of autonomous monolithic nation states, empowered with legal authority and institutional mechanisms to govern the people on their territory. Increasingly, though, the neat structure of the world as a set of interrelated state actors is complicated by developments both internationally and within states. These developments include the following:

1. Various international institutions have been formed to pursue particular universal goals, such as economic liberalization, environmental protection, or

---

[10] Some innovations, such as mobile telephony, offer quick solutions to overpass severe lack of conventional telephone wiring networks, but their diffusion has been relatively slow in African countries. Similarly, satellite technology overcomes the problem of missing wiring infrastructure, but Africa does not have its own satellite, it buys services from the European Intelsat and some from the Arab Arabsat. This makes satellite communication services in Africa more expensive than in industrialized regions. Inefficiencies in procurement of telecommunication equipment and management make the cost of installing new telephone lines in Africa higher than other parts of the world (Minges and Kelly 1994). Overall, there is a severe shortage of the required funds to develop the telecommunications infrastructure characteristic of today's global economy. African countries have been slow to follow the universal trend of liberalization of telecommunications, and voice telephony remains under state monopoly in most countries. The debate on privatization of telecommunications in Africa is faced with the dilemmas inherent to a service which is both a fundamental public utility—essential to overcome social exclusion—and a business tool. There are compelling arguments for liberalization of telecommunications to create services for the small, but crucial in its role, business sector. But regulation of a privatized telecommunications sector in order to provide even rudimentary connectivity to the vast rural areas is a far more difficult problem. Indeed, connectivity continues to be almost non-existent outside the big cities of the continent. Technologically, there is a variety of possibilities to provide communications to rural areas (Pauw 1994; Nicola and Jarke 2000). But local telecommunications administration seems unwilling and incapable of implementing effectively alternative technologies, and such possibilities remain, at best, pilot cases.

individual human rights. It is argued that global risks make action and legislation of individual states ineffective and require international regulatory institutions and agencies. Moreover, supranational regional governments, such as the European Union, NAFTA, and Mercosur, complicate the overall picture, exerting pressure to the local economies to reform, innovate, and compete in the global market, but also adding another intermediate level of decision-making bodies.

National autonomy is weakened as governments are obliged to comply with decisions and courses of action that often compromise their interests. Supra-national governance institutions supersede the policy making of the nation states and erode their systemic unity and autonomy. In the international policy-making institutions, states act in a fragmented manner through their bureaucratic agencies, each pursuing its own agenda with minimal government coordination or control (McGrew 1992). Decisions are made on individual issues without consideration of the overall national interests.

2. There has been a resurgence of ethnic and sub-national regional communities, often claiming rights for self-governance. In only a few cases has the political construct of the nation state followed ethnic allegiances, with the result that only about a dozen contemporary states coincide with an ethnic group (Hobsbawm 1992). The ethnic 'impurity' of nation states has been further complicated with the uprooting and transfer of large numbers of people as a result of war, slavery, and more recently immigration. Nationalistic friction and ethnic revolts against central governments have not been unknown in modern history, but there is a general feeling that they are now becoming a dominant feature of the world politics. The recent 'devolution' gained by Scotland and Wales in Britain is indicative of the reshaping of world governance under way, even in long established and politically powerful nations. But, in many cases, reshaping of political authority has direct destabilizing effects for the nation state and often involves violence. The problem is particularly acute in nations formed by the colonial powers of the twentieth century, such as most African nations, and nations formed haphazardly with the decline of imperialist regimes, such as the Balkan states, and the new Central Asian states formed in the aftermath of the Soviet Union.

Contemporary ethnic unrest is understood to be associated with the forces of economic and cultural globalization. Many ethnic minorities or sub-regions experience the unequal consequences of economic restructuring entailed by globalization, outlined in the previous section. The nation state is in many cases unwilling and perhaps incapable of intervening in the dynamics of the global free market economy and compensating specific minorities or sub-regions for the negative impact of globalization. In addition, cultural processes of globalization contribute to the development of an accentuated sense of identity. The flows of people and cultural symbols often trigger processes of recovery of 'hidden histories' (Hall 1991) of social groups who have been oppressed or marginalized within the political project of the nation state.

3. The role of the state in advanced capitalist societies has been changing from protector, service provider, and industrialist to regulator and agent. The 'liberal' Western nation state of the mid-twentieth century intervened in the capitalist economy through multiple activities. It fostered a mixed economy, providing central

planning and economic management, and acted as an intermediary between employers and employees. It was directly involved in certain areas of industrial pro-duction considered either natural monopolies, such as telecommunications, or of strategic importance, such as computer manufacturing. Also, it maintained redis-tributive policies through progressive taxation and set up an extensive range of social welfare services to provide for the needs of those who cannot care for themselves, or cannot influence the choices made for them—children, the sick, the aged, the under-privileged. Towards the end of the twentieth century most of these areas of state activities were reduced or were left to the control of the market. Many of the areas which were considered natural monopolies in the 1960s became arenas of MNC competition in the 1990s, and the state now addresses oligopolistic risks through its regulatory capacity rather than by setting up service producer organizations itself. Moreover, the social welfare ideology of the European states has been challenged, and social policies seek ways to provide social services through the market.

As a result of such changes, the horizontally structured world in autonomous units of sovereign nation states is becoming more complicated. Rosenau perceives these changes as a structural bifurcation of two interrelated systems: while the system of states related to each other through diplomacy and national power continues to exist, there is also a system of various types of entities—whether organizations, groups, or individuals—which lies outside the control of any national state and form a trans-national society (Rosenau 1990).

Nevertheless, the extent to which the pressures summarized above diminish the autonomy and sovereignty of nation states is debatable. In international relations theory the nation state continues to be considered the primary actor of the world, although more systemic world perspectives tend to be adopted to understand its role and scope of action (Keohane 1986). The international economic liberalization trends and the new supranational governance mechanisms allow scope for national states to act autonomously and effectively to promote the interests of their people. Cases supporting this point are not only the powerful nations states of Europe and North America but also the counties of South-East Asia briefly discussed above, whose economic success is largely the result of interventionist national policies.

However, it is important to recognize that within the contemporary system of world governance nation states are granted unequal degrees of autonomy. Advanced capitalist economies have greater autonomy than others, and military might contin-ues to be significant in the 'integrated' and economically liberal world system. At the two extremes of the spectrum of autonomy, the United States plays a hegemonic role in world governance, and a large number of poor nation states are governed under conditions of dependency both from more powerful nations and international institutions. Hamelink's research on the international politics of communications, intellectual property rights, and transborder data flows amply demonstrates this last point (Hamelink 1994). He shows that world communication policy is increasingly shaped by trade and market standards and less by political considerations, as the locus of decision making shifts from intergovernmental bodies where all countries had delegations to forums of corporate actors of advanced economies. An indicative example given by Hamelink is the World Administrative Radio Conference in 1992 on the future shape of telecommunication services, in which developing countries were just bystanders.

CULTURAL PROCESSES OF GLOBALIZATION

A key question in the literature of globalization is what happens to the cultural differences among social groups as a global economy emerges and as the power of the nation state to command and inspire its citizens and order their social affairs is under challenge. The interest here is in culture as a distinguishing feature that marks group identity, rather than as an aspect of the substance of a social group (Appadurai 1996). The issue is whether the cultural processes of globalization imply the preservation, lessening, or disappearance of differences among social groups, including organizations.

Three main views are discernible in the current debate on globalization regarding this question. The first associates cultural difference with national states, seeing the world as continuing to be multicultural along national border lines. The second perceives a process of homogenization through cultural imperialism—more specifically as Americanization or Westernization—spreading the cultural products and behaviours of hegemonic regions all over the world. The third challenges both these views and suggests a rather chaotic process of hyper-differentiation through cultural hybridization.

National Cultural Differences

The association of cultural difference with nation states has been widespread. This is not surprising as studies of culture developed in a historical period when the nation state was a dominant and universal system of world governance, and 'society' was almost synonymous with nation state. Besides, it is not surprising to see the nation as the basis of cultural difference, since the state has various mechanisms to create a shared sense of identity among its citizens, through education and institutionalized rituals and symbols (Wallerstein 1991).

National cultural stereotyping, which assumes that a nation state is a distinct and homogeneous social group, is a widespread attitude in business, international relations, as well as national development projects. Hofstede's study (1984) that classified forty countries on the basis of a number of cultural indicators is a good example of national cultural markers of difference. Hofstede derived measures on four dimensions of culture: power distance, which refers to people's relation to authority; uncertainty avoidance, which relates to tolerance of the unpredictable; individualism, which refers to the relationship between the individual and the group; and the concepts of masculinity and femininity. His main data set was drawn from the subsidiaries of a multinational corporation, in order to reduce organizational difference as a source of variation for the values studied.[11]

---

[11] Hofstede's study treats cultural difference mechanically, using the metaphor 'mental programme' or 'software' to define culture. The assumption that culture is 'programmable' is widely endorsed in the

The view that nation states have a uniform culture dismisses distinctions among different sub-national or cross-national social groups, or differences due to religion, class, or gender, which are powerful cultural differentiators, and which the nation state has at best moderated, but not instrumentally controlled.

Globalization of Culture

Several logical arguments and empirical observations have challenged the widely held belief in the cultural distinctiveness of the nation state. One of the most vocal arguments is made by those authors who see global capitalism as the main driving force of globalization, and who tend to emphasize the homogenization effects of modern global economy. Sklair (1991), for example, considers the spread of the 'cultural ideology' of consumerism as a fundamental feature of global capitalism.

Others see a more complex set of forces contributing to the development of a global culture. It seems plausible that the spread of consumerism is a force that erodes national cultural differences, as people in all countries become customers for the same goods and services and audiences of the same messages and images broadcast by worldwide media. International media, instant and institutionally unmediated communication through the Internet, employment postings in different geographic locations in transnational corporations or international institutions, are all contributing to a cosmopolitan attitude and a 'citizen of the world' feeling for a large number of people. Rather than adhering to traditions, individuals negotiate lifestyle choices among a diversity of options (Giddens 1991).

Also, regional and global institutions, such as the European Court of Justice, or international human rights legislation, spread a set of fundamental values as universal, in defiance of local traditions, such as the caste system of social differentiation in India. The transnational corporation and international trade challenge local institutionalized ways of conducting business and exert pressures for adopting common business practices.

To what extent, though, do such trends imply homogenization effects through the worldwide imposition of the Western culture? Tomlinson (1991), distinguishing globalization from imperialism, makes the point that today's international cultural influences are different from the cultural imperialism that spread the cultural features of hegemonic nations to their colonies. More accurately, he argues, today's international cultural influences should be seen as a process of cosmopolitanism, whereby a variety of common cultural manifestations become shared values and common

---

management literature, where managers are expected to consider culture as a manageable 'soft asset' of the organization (see, e.g. Fiol 1991). It appears possible to develop professional capacity to manage and exploit culture for purposes of competitive advantage, particularly by multinational corporations. If the nation state has succeeded in 'programming' common value and behavioural features into the usually diverse and often conflicting social groups it comprises, it is thought plausible that the powerful corporation can manage such features to its advantage. As I discussed in Chap. 1, such a view has been rightly criticized as ignoring the political and material conditions through which cultural features develop and to which they contribute (Knights and Willmott 1987).

features of everyday life of people all over the world. American McDonald coexists with Indian restaurants and Italian pizza at the centre of the big cities on all continents. The global economy does not circulate only Western cultural products; it is keen to exploit the 'otherness' of local differentiation, and market the 'exotic' across the world. In international management, the spread of American business management was—for a while at least in the 1980s—paralleled by the spread of Japanese norms of running a successful business. Thus, unlike the cultural homogenization exerted by the colonial regimes of modernity, contemporary globalization does not impose the cultural features of one nation over those of others.

Cultural Hybridization

The term 'glocalization' has been proposed to emphasize a different view on the way cultural identities change, namely, that the local cultures do not give way to a uniform global set of values, symbols, and behaviours, but interact with each other and create a multicultural world (Robertson 1992). The view that globalization implies neither cultural homogenization nor the preservation of national cultural differentiation became prominent in the 1990s, and it has been shared by many scholars on culture (see e.g. Friedman 1994; Nederveen Pieterse 1995). The global should not be understood in tension with the local, Robertson (1995) argues. Rather, globalization should be seen as complemented by localization, processes of situated reflexive action, and the result is plurality and hybridization.

The thesis of hybridization is eloquently presented by Appadurai (1996). Homogenizing processes, such as transnational business, worldwide spread of consumer products and clothing styles, advertising techniques, and language hegemonies, are entangled with two other processes: indigenization and export of particular local cultural features (often indigenized global cultural features) through immigration, travel, or neighbouring hegemonies. Appadurai brings several examples of indigenization, such as the way Western pop-style music is mixed with local 'colour' and acquires different meanings in different places of the world. A much more complex picture of cultural variation emerges from his discussion of the cultural reproduction occurring in small groups of diasporas, deterritorialized communities, and displaced populations. The reproduction of the cultural features of their original community context is mixed with the cultural influences of their new 'home' and international media. At the same time they also influence both, their original communities, fuelling their dreams and fears, and the new 'homes', exposing them to their cultural particularities.

Thus, the erosion of the significance of national culture through the processes of globalization is not a matter of domination of one nation over others. Locality for Appadurai is relational rather than spatial, and 'local context' is: 'a phenomenological property of social life, a structure of feeling that is produced by particular forms of intentional activity and that yield particular sorts of material effects' (Appadurai 1996: 182). In terms of social consciousness, the national identity competes with allegiances to profession, religion, or ethnic origin, all of which have proved capable of mobilizing the imagination, motivating, and providing legitimacy for continuity or change.

Nevertheless, hybridization is not a process independent from the power relationships of globalization, and is not occurring uniformly. Hybridization occurs at the tension between majorities and minorities, the centre and the margins, the internationals, the nationals, and the locals. This process is destabilizing and subversive for the relationships of established social spaces, such as nations, the ethnicities, and religions (Nederveen Pieterse 1995). The creation of new cultural projections through hybridization is interdependent with the structural changes in the political and economic world order. It is therefore important to consider hybridization in terms of social relationships. From such a perspective, Bauman's observation that the process of cultural hybridization is disproportional in globally mobile elites and the vast numbers of locally bound, is significant (Bauman 1998). Cultural hybridization is the continuing politics of culture, the contemporary form of the power relationships of knowledge.

ORGANIZATIONS AT THE JUNCTION OF THE LOCAL, THE GLOBAL, AND THE DISEMBEDDED

What are, then, the contexts that matter for organizations and information systems innovation? To begin with, it is too hasty—and perhaps more generally a mistake—to dismiss the national society and its institutions as no more relevant, as is so often assumed in the discourse of information systems and business in relation to globalization. It is also misleading to put all emphasis on the disembedded, as if space-specific institutions and locality-related history do not matter. Rather, the context of action, and more specifically organizing action, should be seen as an interplay of institutions in multiple social spaces: the sub-national local, the national, the regional, the global, and the disembedded.

The national context continues to be influential in many ways. National collective memory contributes to the shaping of cultural identities. With formal education the nation state creates a strong sense of history, identity, and social allegiances in national terms. National policy is an effective way of mobilizing economic activity, including technology innovation.[12] The setting of legal and regulatory constraints defines the scope of socially permissible individual and organizational action.

But the national context does not express all that is in the local. The immediacy of relations in local communities—in sub-national community spaces—often with ethnic identity, has the capacity to mobilize or restrain action. A flexible industrial network is one example where the local takes significance and structures its own economic activities in relation to the global economic space.

Through globalization, larger geographical regions and the world at large are increasingly becoming prevalent as spaces of socio-economic action. Territorially determined supra-national institutions and global institutions with regionwide and

---

[12] This message is loud and clear in economic studies of innovation. Concepts such as 'national systems of innovation' convey the significance attributed to national institutions for creating innovation capacity, fostering research and development, laying facilitating infrastructures, and cultivating tacit knowledge spaces conducive to entrepreneurial and technology innovation action (Freeman 1987; Lundvall 1992; Nelson 1993; Archibugi and Michie 1997; Archibugi, Howells, and Michie 1999).

universal reach respectively are becoming increasingly significant as arbiters of localized conflicts, sources of standards and regulations, and creators of cosmopolitan identities and social elites. Regional institutions, such as the European Union and NAFTA are geographically constituted and exclusive in their ideology and action. In contrast, many global institutions are universalist in their principles. They aim at creating uniform values and behaviours across the globe, albeit more often than not they are biased towards the interests and values of their more powerful member societies.

The disembedded should be distinguished from such geographically determined institutional contexts. Phenomena such as the flows of finance, the MNC networks, management consultancy action, and some media multinationals are disembedded, as they neither have a mission for universal action, nor are they geographically bound. Their presence in space is opportunistic and constantly negotiated with the embedded institutions of the local, the national, the regional, and the universalist global. They often create local and national strongholds, such as in particular megacities, or the hegemonic entities, such as the United States, or the EU, thus often promoting their interests in alliance to national institutions.[13] Nevertheless, they are neither subservient, nor commanding of national or local institutions. They form alliances with them, sometimes very close ones, with ideological and material bonding, such as by sharing technological infrastructures, but they are distinct. The disembedded are constantly in search of relocation—or virtualization, to the extent that suitable technology makes it feasible.

Therefore, the multiple institutional forces exerted on organizations stretch over variable geographical spaces. Some institutional forces can be seen as layered, in the sense that the influence of the outer context goes through inner layers of context. For example, European Union regulations and guidelines, such as on labour rights or environmental protection, affect an organization when they are endorsed by the member state where it is located. Others, including ICT and management, are subject to disembedded flows of ideas, standards of practice, and mobile professionals. It is in the interplay between space-bound, history-determined organizational fields and the disembedded institutions of capital, technology, ideas, and images that information systems innovation occurs.

CONCLUDING REMARKS

Drawing from the theoretical investigations in these four chapters, it is now possible to suggest principles for a contextual situated socio-technical analysis capable of accounting for the diverse circumstances of information systems innovation.

Each organization hosting a process of information system innovation has its own historically developed regime of truth, which is an arena of multiple rationalities,

---

[13] A good example of that is the way the USA represented the interests of multinational pharmaceutical corporations in their dispute with Brazil, and the developing countries more generally, which violate patent law and produce locally generic drugs for diseases such as Aids. In 2001 the USA brought this accusation to the World Trade Organization, where only state institutions participate, and therefore MNCs do not have a say in their own right.

both instrumental and substantive. Thus, to begin with, contextualist analysis needs to be able to understand the organizing regime within which an information systems innovation effort takes place. For this, it needs to trace the enduring translation, that is, the collective actions that constitute the organization, which—with more or less consistency and effectiveness—achieves particular results loaded with social significance. The notion of translation is significant here because it captures the difference of the collective organizing action from the stated mission or the strategy of an organization, which express the official justification of the organizing regime. The translation results from the actors' perceptions of mission, which are formed under institutional influences and filtered according to their interests. In other words, an organization's translation is enacted according to the rationalities that govern actors' perceptions and life stratagems. As a process, the enduring organizational translation may be well established and highly institutionalized, but is rarely a monolithic state of affairs. It usually involves conflicts, destabilizing pressures, and subjugated desires for alternative translations, and therefore accommodates adjustments and changes. Often conflicts and pressures for countervailing translations mount up to a significant de-institutionalization challenge, and the enduring translation is distorted and collapses. It may be substituted by an alternative translation, or the organization may be in a turmoil and contest for the legitimacy of a new durable translation.

Information systems innovation can be seen as an attempt to alter the enduring organizational translation by the mobilization of multiple actors who are participants of various institutions, such as ICT and management professions, financial systems, or workers nurtured in specific national work regulation and social welfare systems. Whether intentionally or unintentionally, information systems innovations confront the regime of truth that sustains the enduring translation of the host organization with those of the institutions involved in the information system innovation process. The discussion of the literature on globalization in this chapter points to the contextual origin and span of such institutional forces. Institutional fields may be geographically defined, such as the internal conditions and norms of the organization undertaking the innovation, geographically specific 'foreign' centres of influence, and geographically disembedded, that is constituted by virtually geographically unrestricted economic, political, and cultural flows.

There can be no a priori framework to determine the institutional fields that matter in a particular incident of information systems innovation. The way multiple fields associate to each other in the perpetual dynamics of globalization has to be studied as a situated emergent phenomenon. And this is where the actor-network concepts provide a valuable analytical approach. Tracing an information system's translation processes reveals networks of actors and their behaviours. They may, for example, involve remote computers and telecommunication centres, technical specialists from service provider companies, lawyers, or moneylenders.

But the socio-technical study cannot stop there, it needs to understand the actors' behaviour as part of the institutional context that gives rise to it and renders it rational. Therefore the translation process needs to be understood by analysis of the relevant institutional contexts and their interactions. In other words, analysis of the emergent socio-technical network needs to be complemented by the study of the institutional fields which give rise to and sustain the enactments that form or reverse the attempted information systems translation.

References

African Development Bank (1999). *African Development Report: Infrastructure Development in Africa*. New York: Oxford University Press.

Appadurai, A. (1996). *Modernity at Large: Cultural Dimensions of Globalization*. Minneapolis: University of Minnesota Press.

Archibugi, D., and Michie, J. (eds.) (1997). *Technology, Globalisation and Economic Performance*. Cambridge: Cambridge University Press.

——Howells, J., and Michie, J. (eds.) (1999). *Innovation Policy in a Global Economy*. Cambridge: Cambridge University Press.

Audenhove, v. L. (2000). 'Information and Communication Technology Policy in Africa: A Critical Analysis of Rhetoric and Practice', in C. Avgerou and G. Walsham (eds.), *Information Technology in Context: Studies from the Perspective of Developing Countries*. Aldershot: Ashgate, 277–90.

Bauman, Z. (1998). *Globalization: The Human Consequences*. Cambridge: Polity Press.

Beck, U. (2000). *What is Globalization?* Cambridge: Polity Press.

Bradley, S. P., Hausman, J. A., and Nolan, R. I. (eds.) (1993). *Globalization Technology and Competition: The Fusion of Computers and Telecommunications in the 1990s*. Boston: Harvard Business School Press.

Bradshaw, Y. W., and Wallace, M. (1996). *Global Inequalities*. Thousand Oaks, Calif.: Pine Forge Press.

Browne, H. (1994). *For Richer, For Poorer: Shaping US–Mexican Integration*. London: Latin American Bureau.

Callaghy, T. M. (1998). 'Between Scylla and Charybdis: The Foreign Economic Relations of Sub-Saharan African States', in P. Lewis (ed.), *Africa: Dilemmas of Development and Change*. Boulder, Colo.: Westview Press, 382–99.

Castells, M. (1989). *The Informational City: Information Technology, Economic Restructuring and the Urban-regional Process*.: Oxford Basil Blackwell.

——(1996). *The Rise of the Network Society*. Oxford: Blackwell.

——(1997). *The Power of Identity*. Oxford: Blackwell.

——(1998). *End of Millennium*. Oxford: Blackwell.

Currie, W. (2000). *Global Information Society*. Chichester: John Wiley.

Fiol, C. M. (1991). 'Managing Culture as a Competitive Resource: An Identity-Based View of Sustainable Competitive Advantage'. *Journal of Management*, 17(1): 191–211.

Freeman, C. (1987). 'Technology Policy and Economic Performance'. *Cambridge Journal of Economics*, 18: 463–514.

Friedman, J. (1994). *Cultural Identity and Global Process*. London: Sage.

Fukuyama, F. (1992). *The End of History and the Last Man*. London: Penguin.

Ghoshal, S., and Bartlett, C. A. (1993). 'The Multinational Corporation as an Interorganizational Network', in S. Ghoshal and D. E. Westney (eds.), *Organization Theory and the Multinational Corporation*. Basingstoke: Macmillan, 77–104.

—— ——(1998). *Managing Across Borders: The Transnational Solution*. London: Random House.

——and Nohria, N. (1990). 'Internal Differentiation within Multinational Corporations'. *Strategic Management Journal*, 10(4): 323–38.

Giddens, A. (1990). *The Consequences of Modernity*. Cambridge: Polity Press.

——(1991). *Modernity and Self-Identity*. Cambridge: Polity Press.

——(1999). *Runaway World: How Globalization is Reshaping our Lives*. London: Routledge.

Haggard, S. (1995). *Developing Nations and the Politics of Global Integration*. Washington: Brookings Institution.

Hall, S. (1991). 'The Local and the Global: Globalisation and Ethnicity', in A. D. King (ed.), *Culture, Globalisation and the World System*. London: Macmillan, 19–39.

——(1992). 'The Question of Cultural Identity', in S. Hall, D. Held, and T. McGrew, *Modernity and its Futures*. Cambridge: Polity Press, 273–325.

Hamelink, C. J. (1994). *The Politics of World Communication*. London: Sage.

Hanseth, O., and Braa, K. (2000). 'Globalization and "Risk Society" ', in C. u. Ciborra and associates (eds.), *From Control to Drift*. Oxford: Oxford University Press, 41–55.

Harvey, D. (1989). *The Condition of Postmodernity*. Oxford: Blackwell.

Held, D. (1996). *Democracy and the Global Order: From the Modern State to Cosmopolitan Governance*. Stanford, Calif.: Stanford University.

Herbst, J. (1998). 'The Structural Adjustment of Politics in Africa', in P. Lewis (ed.), *Africa: Dilemmas of Development and Change*. Boulder, Colo.: Westview Press, 431–49.

Hobday, M. (1995). *Innovation in East Asia: The Challenge to Japan*. Cheltenham: Edward Elgar.

Hobsbawm, E. (1992). *Nations and Nationalism since 1780*. Cambridge: Cambridge University Press.

Hofstede, G. (1984). *Culture's Consequences: International Differences in Work Related Values*. London: Sage.

IMF (1999). 'World Economic Outlook: A Survey by the Staff of the International Monetary Fund'. Washington, DC.

Ives, B., and Jarvenpaa, S. L. (1991). 'Applications of Global Information Technology: Key Issues for Management'. *MIS Quarterly*, Mar.: 33–49.

Keohane, R. O. (ed.) (1986). *Neorealism and Its Critics*. New York: Columbia University Press.

King, A. D. (ed.) (1991). *Culture, Globalization and the World-System*. Basingstoke: Macmillan.

Kluzer, S. (1990). 'Computer Diffusion in Black Africa: A Preliminary Assessment', in S. C. Bhatnagar and N. Bjørn-Andersen (eds.), *Information Technology in Developing Countries*. Amsterdam: North-Holland, 175–88.

Knights, D., and Willmott, H. (1987). 'Organizational Culture as Management Strategy: A Critique and Illustration from the Financial Services Industry'. *International Studies of Management and Organization*, 17(3): 40–63.

Kogut, B. (1993). 'Learning, or the Importance of Being Inert: Country Imprinting and International Competition', in S. Ghoshal and D. E. Westney (eds.), *Organization Theory and the Multinational Corporation*. Basingstoke: Macmillan, 136–54.

Lash, S., and Urry, J. (1987). *The End of Organized Capitalism*. Cambridge: Polity Press.

Lundvall, B.-Å. (ed.) (1992). *National Systems of Innovation: Towards a Theory of Innovation and Interactive Learning*. London: Pinter.

McGrew, A. (1992). 'A Global Society?', in S. Hall, D. Held, and T. McGrew, *Modernity and its Futures*. Cambridge: Polity Press, 61–116.

Minges, M., and Kelly, T. (1994). 'The Paradoxes of African Telecommunications', in B. A. Kiplagat and M. C. M. Werner (eds.), *Telecommunications and Development in Africa*. Amsterdam: IOS Press, 11–30.

Moussa, A., and Schware, R. (1992). 'Informatics in Africa: Lessons from the World Bank Experience'. *World Development*, 20(12): 1737–52.

Nederveen Pieterse, J. P. (1995). 'Globalization as Hybridization', in M. Featherstone, S. Lash, and R. Robertson (eds.), *Global Modernities*. London: Sage, 45–68.

Negroponte, N. (1995). *Being Digital*. London: Coronet Books.

Nelson, R. (ed.) (1993). *National Innovation Sytems*. New York: Oxford University Press.

Nicola, M., and Jarke, M. (2000). 'Analysis of Wireless Health Care Information Systems in Developing Countries', in C. Avgerou and G. Walsham (eds.), *Information Systems in Context: A Developing Countries Perspective*. Aldershot: Ashgate, 153–67.

Odedra, M., Lawrie, M., Bennett, M., and Goodman, S. (1993). 'Sub-Saharan Africa: A Technological Desert'. *Communications of the ACM* 35(2): 25–9.

Pauw, C. (1994). 'Trends in Rural Telecommunications Technologies', in B. A. Kiplagat and M. C. M. Werner (eds.), *Telecommunications and Development in Africa*. Amsterdam: IOS Press, 187–97.

Piore, M., and Sabel, C. (1984). *The Second Industrial Divide: Possibilities for Prosperity*. New York: Basic Books.

Pyke, F., Becattini, G. and Sengenberger, W. (eds.) (1990). *Industrial Districts and Inter-firm Cooperation in Italy*. Geneva: International Institute for Labour Studies.

Ravenhill, J. (1998). 'Adjustment with Growth: A Fragile Consensus', in P. Lewis (ed.), *Africa: Dilemmas of Development and Change*. Boulder, Colo.: Westview Press, 400–30.

Robertson, R. (1992). *Globalization: Social Theory and Global Culture*. London: Sage.

—— (1995). 'Glocalization: Time-Space and Homogeneity-Heterogeneity', in M. Featherstone, S. Lash, and R. Robertson, *Global Modernities*. London: Sage, 25–44.

Rosenau, J. (1990). *Turbulence in World Politics*. Brighton: Harvester.

Sassen, S. (1994). *Cities in a World Economy*. Thousand Oaks, Calif.: Pine Forge Press.

Schienstock, G. (1997). 'The Transformation of Regional Governance: Institutional Lock-ins and the Development of Lean Production in Baden-Württemberg', in R. Whitley and P. H. Kristemsen (eds.), *Governance at Work: The Social Regulation of Economic Relations*. Oxford: Oxford University Press, 190–208.

Sklair, L. (1991). *Sociology of the Global System*. Brighton: Harvester Wheatsheaf.

Tomlinson, J. (1991). *Cultural Imperialism: A Critical Introduction*. London: Pinter.

UNDP (1999). 'Human Development Report 1999'. New York, United Nations Development Programme.

Wallerstein, I. (1980). *The Modern World System II*. New York: Academic.

—— (1991). 'The National and the Universal: Can There Be Such a Thing as World Culture?', in A. D. King (ed.), *Culture, Globalization and the World System*. Basingstoke: Macmillan, 91–105.

Walsham, G. (2000*a*). 'Globalization and IT: Agenda for Research', in R. Baskerville, J. Stage, and J. DeGross (eds.), *Organizational and Social Perspectives on Information Technology*. London: Kluwer, 195–210.

—— (2000*b*). 'IT, Globalization and Cultural Diversity', in C. Avgerou and G. Walsham (eds.), *Information Technology in Context: Studies from the Perspective of Developing Countries*. Aldershot: Ashgate, 291–303.

Waters, M. (1995). *Globalization*. London: Routledge.

PART II

INSIGHTS FROM CASE STUDIES

5

Pemex—Transforming a National Company

This chapter sketches the changing organization of Pemex, the Mexican oil corporation, and follows its computerization efforts since the 1960s, when the company introduced its first substantial computer applications and until the end of the 1990s. It is impossible to understand the case of Pemex without some knowledge of Mexico's recent politico-economic history. The history of this company has been closely linked with the economic conditions of Mexico and the struggle of its governments with two political orientations: continuing its traditional populist nationalism or opening the economy to the global market forces. Thus, my story in this chapter begins with a brief outline of Mexico's national context and then it traces the changes Pemex underwent in this period and the major information systems innovation efforts it pursued.

BRIEF INTRODUCTION TO THE NATIONAL CONTEXT

Throughout the history of Mexico a strong national identity has been important to keep the country distinguished from its powerful northern neighbour, the United States. For the last seventy years the country has had its own version of political stability, governed by one party, the Partito Revolucionario Institucional (PRI).[1] Traditionally run by an indigenously educated elite, the PRI's political machine managed to win elections, mainly through an elaborate system of clientelistic links with local political leaders and civil institutions such as the trade unions. Castells gives a vivid picture of PRI's mechanism of staying in power:

Each president would designate his successor, and step out of the open political arena for ever. And each president would betray his predecessor, but never criticize him, and never investigate his actions. Systemic, widespread corruption was orderly, played by the rules, and, in fact, was a major stabilizing factor in Mexican politics: each president renewed the distribution of political appointments in the entire structure of the state, leading to tens of thousands of new appointments every six years. (Castells 1997: 286)

Nevertheless, the PRI governments made genuine efforts to deliver their promises for jobs, welfare, and infrastructure services, creating a nationalistic populist ideology,

---

[1] The PRI was defeated at the elections of 3 July 2000, after 71 years of ruling the country. The presidency was won by the candidate of the conservative National Action Party (PAN).

and avoiding violence and repression. The struggle of politics had for decades been contained among the factions inside the PRI, and only in the 1990s opposition parties developed increasingly more realistic possibilities to break PRI's monopoly of power.

In the 1960s and 1970s the Mexican governments pursued import substitution policies to foster indigenous industrialization. Those policies were brought to an end in the late1970s, when the government borrowed heavily to expand oil production and exports. Pemex failed to take advantage of a period of high export prices, making insufficient profits to service its debts, and in 1982 Mexico renounced responsibility for the payment of its debt.

The 1982 crisis broke Mexico's nationalistic entrenchment, and triggered political changes within the PRI government. The international and US institutions started intervening in the economic affairs of the country, as it was thought it endangered the international banking system. A new cadre of technical economic experts, most of whom were educated in the United States, became indispensable in the offices of government and gained power in the country's political system. In the 1980s and early 1990s the country opened the economy, foreign investment increased and the Mexican economy grew substantially. With production costs lower than those in the United States, Mexican exports of manufacturing goods rocketed in the early 1990s. In 1993 Mexico entered in the North American Free Trade Agreement (NAFTA), thus becoming integrated into the North American economy. Nevertheless, still with a big trade deficit, the Mexican economy remained vulnerable to the international financial flows, and faced another crisis in 1994 when its currency was dramatically devalued. It recovered with a great deal of support from the United States and the IMF, becoming even more dependent on its powerful northern neighbour and the international economic institutions.

By 1997 Mexico was the sixteenth largest economy in the world and well linked with the global economy. However, at the end of the twentieth century, a large proportion of its population still lived in absolute poverty: 15 per cent of Mexicans survived on less than $1 a day (UNDP 1999). During the 1980s and 1990s the standards of living of a big part of the middle classes deteriorated. Politically, discontentment erupted with sporadic populist upheavals, such as the 'Zapatistas' movement in the south, and the university students' revolt in 1999. In the political debate, both within PRI and among the other parties which started gathering strength in the 1990s, the economic 'modernization' has not been strongly opposed. However, the extent to which the country should pursue the route designed by the new technocratic elite and the international centres of power has been constantly questioned. Administration has often taken a pragmatic position, responding to the international economic pressures with local adaptations, eventually maintaining a mix of traditional nationalistic ways of governing the economy and technical-rational reforms.

More details on Mexico's economic development efforts and its politics, the dilemmas that have faced the country in its recent history, the contradictions of its policies, and the challenges confronting the country at the end of the twentieth century are interwoven in the story of Pemex below. Whether one starts to unravel the history of the country or the story of the company, one almost immediately comes across the other.

ORGANIZATIONAL CHANGE AND INFORMATION SYSTEMS INNOVATION IN PEMEX

As in all organizations, change in Pemex has been a continuous process and information systems innovation unfolded with multiple projects in all its activities. Nevertheless, this section presents these continuous, multifaceted, and turbulent processes in a simplified form of four periods, in order to highlight the shaping of major trends of organizational change and the way they have been paralleled by information systems development efforts. The four periods are as follows: First, the period until the early 1970s, when the first major computer-based information systems were built within the traditional bureaucratic Pemex administration. Second, the period from the early 1970s until 1980, during which the company—under bureaucratic government-led management—expanded, without building an adequate information systems infrastructure. Third, the period from 1980 until 1992 during which Pemex began efforts to change its structure, processes, and mission and to integrate its information systems. And finally, the period after 1992 when the company was redesigned and adopted a market-driven status, with continuing efforts to develop information systems for its new structure.

The Early History of a Giant Company

Pemex was created in the late 1930s following the expropriation of American and British oil companies that operated in Mexico at the beginning of the twentieth century. Since then Pemex has been the country's largest state corporation and a symbol of national pride and strength. The events of the expropriation of the foreign oil companies and the taking over of management and operations by the company's employees under adverse conditions of international boycott set an organizational culture which saw oil production as a service to the country. Pemex was established as a non-profit oriented company, with a mission to provide for the economic development and the social welfare of Mexico. Moreover, during the first months that the company struggled to satisfy the oil demand of the country and to prevent the collapse of its economy, the oilmen's trades union was established as a significant power in the running of the company and a political force in the country's politics more generally.

By the end of the 1950s Pemex was a huge hierarchical state-owned bureaucracy. Its operations covered all activities related to oil exploration, refinement, and distribution of oil and primary petrochemical products. With increasing oil demand in Mexico and low international prices, exports were considered of secondary importance. Moreover, the government taxed heavily the revenue of Pemex to fund the industrialization of the country, leaving the company unable to invest in the technological innovations that the international oil industry was pursuing at that period.

Three centres of power were involved in the affairs of the company: the government, the company's management, and the oilmen's trade unions. These were interconnected, creating a complex mix of political and technical-rational decision making. Top management positions were government appointments, and the men who headed the production plants enjoyed a great deal of autonomy and had a high degree of local political influence. The 'oilmen'—workers and engineers in oil fields and plants—had a reputation of 'doing the job at all costs', but they also had a significant say in the running of Pemex through their trade unions. Thus, the company was governed by two coexistent sets of values and imperatives: engineering, to organize complex technical activities; and political, to serve the nation's development and the welfare of the oilmen and their families.[2] This combination of values, power, and competencies kept the company going under difficult circumstances and contributed to the country's industrialization, but it created tolerance to gross dysfunctionalities. In Mexico, as well as internationally, Pemex was notorious for its bureaucratic inefficiency and corruption.

Consecutive administrations until the 1970s were acutely aware of the company's increasing inefficiencies, but were unable to remedy the problem. Productivity deteriorated, operational oil reserves were overexploited and a number of wells were depleted. There were bottlenecks and problems of coordination between the various parts of the process of production, refinery, storage, and distribution. As an indication, gas was often burnt because the technical infrastructure for processing and distributing it was inadequate. From 1966 till 1973 Pemex stopped all exports, and at times the country needed to import crude oil, as well as refined products. Moreover, Pemex was heavily in debt and, without investment, its productivity continued deteriorating.

The First Uses of Computers
Computers were first introduced in the early 1960s, with the expectation that they would improve efficiency. The first computer applications were payroll and accounting, typical of the business use of computers at that time. Several such applications were developed in a number of different locations of the company around the country. Very soon computer units, staffed with programmers, analysts, and operators, made their presence felt in all sites of the company, and each of them developed its own applications. To coordinate the anarchic proliferation of computer applications, in 1965 Pemex created the Office of Computing, with a central unit at the headquarters of the company and seven regional offices in major locations of operations. The first major projects undertaken by the Office of Computing were a new payroll system and an inventory control system for the major warehouses of the company.

The central computerization of the payroll system aimed at overcoming chronic delays in processing fortnightly salaries. The technical project was completed

---

[2] Pemex created and maintained a whole infrastructure of social services, such as schools and hospitals for its labour force and the communities where their operations were located. Many of these communities were remote and isolated. Pemex was not only their only industrial employer, but also the only provider of modern social services.

successfully, making on time payment of wages possible. But implementation stumbled on established practices for calculating employee overtime, which allowed for (what was seen as) arbitrary estimates of overtime by supervising members of staff and covered up widespread fraud. The system was not welcome by the oilmen and on several sites there was violent reaction to its implementation by destroying printouts, breaking equipment, and threatening the computer staff. Indicative of the severity of the situation is that in one of the computer centres the system began operations with the protection of the army.

Similar conflicts were triggered by the system intended to rationalize the management of the warehouses and to overcome bottlenecks in production caused by poor inventory control. The 95 major warehouses of the company were often unable to respond to requests for items required for production, while they kept huge stocks of items with low demand. In addition there were coordination problems among warehouses, exacerbated by the use of different names for the same items. The warehouse managers were suspicious of the computer systems, afraid that they would lose control. However, systems developers discarded what they saw as concerns of biased interest interfering within the solution of clear mismanagement and inefficiency, and the project was implemented against opposition.

Those early 'successes' of computerization were achieved with indigenous technical skills and under protectionist government policies restricting the import of computers. At that time computer technology expertise was very limited in the country and the Pemex projects had a pioneering role, consistent with the general perception of the company as a leader in the country's industrial development effort. Indicatively, the development of the payroll system was led by a chemical engineer who held also a lecturing position at the national university.

The government, with aspirations to foster an indigenous computer industry, maintained an active role in the shaping of the use of the technology. Mainframe technology was procured by public bidding, subject to state regulations and authorization. Nevertheless, without much previous experience of computer projects in Mexico, and with the close links between Pemex and the government, the early computerization efforts of this company had a more general impact on the development of expertise in the country. Because of its size and the pioneering role in computer use, Pemex was in a position to negotiate its terms of services with computer vendors. One of the executives interviewed boasted 'they didn't sell to us, we bought from them'.

By the early 1970s the Office of Computing had launched a portfolio of projects for the development of administrative applications, mathematical programming techniques, and engineering systems for various areas of oil production and distribution. Systems development was considered an engineering activity, and the main concern of the project teams was to construct technically reliable systems. Resistance to the new systems was usually interpreted by the project management as cover up of fraudulent activities and suspect management practices and was addressed by exercising bold power, rather than by responding to user concerns.

The results of that first period of computer applications were mixed. Some projects did not deliver operational systems. For example a project for a data communication infrastructure linking five sites through a central node in Mexico City was abandoned, unable to meet its specifications. The efficiency effects of implemented systems were difficult to assess in a general condition of increasing inefficiency. But this was not particularly detrimental to continuing computerization. Computer projects were gaining momentum, in harmony with the engineering culture of Pemex. The development and operation of computer-based information systems became a visible new function within the company.

The Expansion of the 1970s

In the 1970s Pemex, following government policy, changed dramatically its market orientation towards exports, and its significance in the national economy took a new meaning. The flurry for export-oriented growth was triggered by the international oil crisis in 1973. As oil prices increased and the United States was looking for sources to substitute its lost oil supplies, the Mexican government recognized an unprecedented opportunity for oil export to finance the country's development. Pemex, being at that time a domestic company subsidized by the government, was not ready to satisfy such increased demand. Its financial recovery, productivity growth, and investment for exploration became a matter of top priority in the country's economic policy. During 1976–82 the management of Pemex pursued an ambitious plan to triple oil and petrochemical production, to double refining capacity, to expand distribution infrastructure, and to accelerate exploration for new reserves. All this growth required investment, which was secured through borrowing from the international financial markets. Initial goals were achieved, with the most dramatic results in exploration. Huge new reserves were located, and by the early 1980s Mexico became the fourth largest oil producer in the world.

Exposure to the opportunities and risks of the international market challenged the status quo of the 'company that served the nation'. Although still obliged to follow government policy, the management of the company acquired more autonomy, and the engineering imperatives became more prevalent than its political mission. The structure and management of the organization remained unchanged, though, and the expansion was achieved by a centralized hierarchical administration with severe problems of coordination among the various parts of the vast organization. Management was well aware of the company's increasing inefficiencies, but in the hectic period of expansion, no efforts were made to change established bureaucratic practices. In that oil boom period, while export oil prices were high, mismanagement did not seem to have dire consequences. The ratio of operational costs to revenue looked healthy in comparison to earlier periods, despite efficiencies and expensive imported oil production technology. The consequences of poor management and continued tax burdens were felt only when oil prices fell in the international market. Pemex, facing now competition, could not sell in the international market and was forced to reduce production and cut down prices. The days of export growth and high prices were over and Mexico, having borrowed heavily for the expansion of Pemex, was more dependent on foreign lenders than ever before.

Consolidation of the Information Systems Function and
Integrated Financial Information Systems

By the time the company was pursuing its ambitious expansion efforts in the second half of the 1970s, computer-based information systems were undisputedly considered to be necessary means for productivity and 'optimization of the decision processes' (Volkow, forthcoming). The Office of Computing was restructured and its status was upgraded, becoming Gerencia de Informatica (Department of Informatics). At first located in the Sub-direction of Technical Administration, and later in the Direction of Finance, this new central department made further computerization plans in a top-down fashion. However, such a tight centralized control of the information systems function could not cope with the demand for new computer applications in all areas of the company, and soon the Gerencia de Informatica was overtaken by 'unofficial' local computer centres developing their own information systems. Local managers were keen to develop their own systems, and computer installations with applications for a variety of tasks spread in all sites of operations and proliferated without coordination.

Despite widespread recognition that the expansion of the company's operations required effective information systems, computerization at the period of the oil boom did not keep up with the increasing information processing requirements of Pemex. Not because there was reluctance to deploy it this time, but because too many people in various parts of Pemex were keen to do so. The various fragmented computer-based information systems could not provide reliable information on the company's operations—a problem that has caused concern to Pemex headquarters ever since.

The root of the problem of poor management information at that period of expansion was that different areas of operation—such as oil production, distillation, distribution—reported incompatible information to the top management. For example, data on volumes of oil produced and channelled to other parts of the company or sold did not match with data reported by those other parts of the company on the volumes of oil they handled. Also, the structure of accounting data produced by the various operations of the company was not compatible with budget data, while yet different data was required in reporting the company's financial situation for the purposes of the government's National Accounts.

To a large extent such information deficiencies were a result of computerization. Proliferation of incompatible systems in the 1970s in large organizations which began using computers in the 1960s is well documented in the information systems literature (Nolan 1979). An anarchic spread of computers was observed as technology became available in smaller, affordable, and technically accessible units. Organizations developed an appetite for applications, which were within their technical reach, and which overloaded centralized information systems departments could not satisfy. But on closer examination, information incompatibilities in Pemex were symptoms of a more serious and less transient problem. The computer-based systems captured only the official administrative aspects of the company's operations, leaving their substantial informal dimensions unaccounted. The technically oriented systems analysts did not grasp the complexity of the work processes in Pemex, missing out the significance and resilience of the localized informal practices that complemented the bureaucratic norms. Everybody was aware of the existence of idiosyncratic informal practices, yet the computer systems were expected to maintain reliable accurate information by bypassing them.

The informal aspects of a large bureaucratic company with highly political administration could not co-exist with well-designed technical interventions. The information-based decision making that IT was officially expected to support was clashing with the covertly political way of managing the company. Accurate reporting and flows of reliable information among the various parts of operations were not compatible with the established practices of running Pemex. Control over information was a base of power that the local managers of the company were not keen to relinquish. Most oilmen considered the detailed data input required by the computer systems as an aspect of red tape rather than an intrinsic element of accountability in their work.

Thus, while the political basis of the management of the company had not been challenged, computers were assimilated by the formalistic blend of hierarchical deployment of engineering expertise and its employees' commitment to achieve set missions at all costs. The computer-based information systems of that period probably created localized efficiencies, but overall they generated additional unexpected inefficiencies, and did little to improve central management capacity.

The Making of a 'Modern' Corporation

In 1982 the Mexican economy collapsed due to its huge debt for the expansion of oil production in the previous decade and the deteriorating international oil market prices. The 1980s was a period of macroeconomic adjustments, renegotiations of the foreign debt with the international banks, fighting hyperinflation trends and the fleeing of private capital from the country. Facing the crisis and under pressure from the IMF, the government of that period, led by President Migel de la Madrid, took the first steps towards neo-liberal economic policies, abandoning earlier welfare development policies. The following President, Salinas de Gortari, who took office in 1988 was more bold in promoting economic liberalization with policies such as trade liberalization, reduction of the government in the economy, privatization of banks and telecommunications.[3]

With the crisis of 1982, the priorities of management in Pemex changed to regaining control over anarchic expansion, making the sites of operations accountable, readjusting the company from growth-at-any-cost to increasing productivity, and ultimately increasing profits to repay the foreign debt. In 1983 Pemex began sustained

---

[3] The economic modernization programme of President Salinas's administration comprised four basic goals. First, to control hyperinflationary tendencies through fiscal measures and retrenchment in public sector borrowing requirements. Second, to reduce government participation in the economy through continuing privatization. Third, to facilitate private business operations through deregulation in a wide range of economic activities. Fourth, to stimulate the economy's efficiency and generate foreign exchange through trade liberalization (Heath 1998).

efforts for reorganization which involved the redesign of its structure and work processes, downsizing, and development of company-wide computer-based information systems. A new business-oriented mentality challenged the adequacy of good engineering and 'service to the nation' values. New management appointments of graduates from American business schools started introducing business administration expertise that challenged the tacit ways of running the company. The new powerful slogan of 'modernization' projected the vision of a company responsive to the market rather than the nation. The power of the trade unions ought to be curtailed, life-long employment could no longer be guaranteed, and social welfare services were not legitimate business activities.

However, in the context of Mexico, the new orientation of the company was unclear, lacking coherent strategic objectives. It was a period of unsettling the old and developing a new vision, but there was no concrete goal for the process of change. What new structure would substitute for the bureaucratic hierarchy, what management style would be appropriate for a highly technical oil company, what kind of business administration would be possible within an industry still considered constitutionally as the responsibility of the state, were still unresolved questions.

Management in Pemex entered a new state, as the appointment of a cadre of business administration graduates led also to the extensive use of services by multinational consultancy firms. There was friction between the odernizers—consultants and new professional management, the oilmen whose trade unions were still powerful, the engineers, and the managers from the old administration. It was generally accepted that the company was inefficient and changes were needed, but the oilmen and the old administration were sceptical about the kind of changes the company was pursuing. They felt that the new managers and consultants disregarded valuable experience and mistrusted their methods. They also believed that the 'real' power structures had remained intact, and therefore the newcomer interventions would be ineffective.

The conflict between the trade unions and new management reached its highest point in the mid-1980s. Once again, this was a matter of national politics rather than organizational power relations. It was resolved by the Salinas government, which, reaffirming its commitment to economic modernization, launched an attack on the trade unions. The government jailed the leader of the strongest union, announced a target of nearly 40 per cent staff cuts, and made sure that the management of Pemex saw the decision through.[4]

Efforts for an Integrated Information Systems Infrastructure
The changes in the management of Pemex in that period were accompanied with renewed efforts for information systems innovation. Consultants started playing a prominent role in both the management of the information systems function and the development of new systems. A succession of international and local consultancy

---

[4] Most of the staff cuts concerned construction activities, which started being subcontracted, and the social welfare infrastructure.

firms were engaged in various projects simultaneously, introducing technical skills for the planning, management, and development of new generations of information systems. On occasions they acted as carriers of truly new ways of addressing the information systems needs of an organization that tried to get rid of dysfunctional management practices and put in place effective informed decision-making processes. More often than not, their analysis and suggestions only legitimated ideas which were already conceived by the executives of Pemex, but their acceptance was questionable within the company's structure of power.

In 1982 the consultants recommended that the company should recognize the services that the computer centres were unofficially operating in the various parts of the company. As a result, the Gerencia de Informatica which was striving for total control of information systems in all Pemex was abolished. A new unit was created, the Gerencia Institutional de Informatica, which, according to the then emerging views about information systems management, was to be responsible for the overall planning and regulation of the development of new information systems. The idea was that with an overall information systems plan and standards for systems development and performance, the various parts of the organization could develop their own applications while avoiding introducing further incompatibility problems.

Regarding its regulatory role, the new Gerencia addressed itself to two areas of standardization: the technology environment and systems development methods. After monitoring closely technical developments and market trends the IT managers of Pemex were convinced of the merits of Unix. Despite consultants' advice to adopt IBM standards, the new management decided to adopt open systems based on Unix and DOS. Indeed, Pemex pursued an open systems strategy relatively early in comparison to other organizations. The Gerencia was less decisive regarding systems development standards and, as a result, the consultants employed for particular development projects tended to follow their own methods.

In terms of systems development projects, the first effort of the new information systems management was to resolve the incompatibilities of data produced its various areas of operations and administration. A project was launched in 1982 to create linkages between operational and financial data. It involved the design of new company-wide standards for work practices and reporting responsibilities. But the managers in many areas of operations were reluctant to adopt the new work practices entailed by the new information system, and the project did not go very far. However, it prepared the ground for subsequent projects with similar objectives.

Soon, the Gerencia Institutional de Informatica stepped up its central information systems function and started initiatives for the development of corporate-wide systems. It created the concept of 'institutional systems' intended to cover all the financial functions of the company. The new systems strategy comprised a portfolio of eight company-wide systems, namely the management of contracts, the budget, human resources, treasury, costs, auditing, procurements, and warehouses. These systems development projects involved a great deal of trial and error in terms of both technical learning and relations with users and had varying degrees of success. They resulted in the implementation of a set of applications throughout the organization, although not in an integrated information system form as was rather ambitiously envisaged initially.

The size and complexity of developing those 'institutional' systems had been underestimated, and projects proceeded in an ad hoc and piecemeal rather than systematic manner. Without determining a common systems architecture for all projects, the company's 'open systems' strategy led to incompatible hardware installations. Nevertheless, data communication among the different systems was possible by a layer of interfaces. Thus, with the necessary tinkering, Pemex developed for the first time the technology to support its financial data flows.

It proved more difficult to sustain effective use of such a company-wide information infrastructure. There were technical inadequacies in maintenance practices and the quality of operational systems deteriorated. The expertise the Gerentia Institucional de Informatica had assembled for the development projects was lost at the completion of the projects when staff returned to their local information systems centres. The most important problems though stemmed from the limited acceptance of the new systems. The new systems were considered inflexible, unduly complicated, and many parts of the company were not able to use them as intended. Errors in data input affected both the efficiency of the systems—as efforts were made to correct detected errors—and the reliability of the systems—as many errors remained undetected and were manifested in incompatibilities of information from different areas of operation. Moreover, the information systems centres of certain powerful areas of the company, such as exploration and primary production, challenged the implementation of the company-wide systems and sought to demonstrate that their own financial administration systems were superior to the 'institutional' systems. In effect they accused the Gerencia Institucional's practice of defining standards centrally and developing company-wide applications information practices as ineffective and argued that information systems should emerge from evolving practices and in accordance to market opportunities.

The reaction to the Gerencia Institucional's efforts to rationalize the flows of company-wide financial information was symptomatic of the underlying conflict between the old and the new regimes of governance in Pemex. The 'institutional systems' represented the emerging new mentality, which encouraged the development of integrated management information systems and provided professional resources for technical developments. Indeed, the appointment of consultants and initiatives such as assigning a strategic and regulatory role to the central information systems management unit, the planning for integrated systems, and the adoption of open systems standards indicate that Pemex was at the frontiers of international 'best practice' of that time. Nevertheless, the open systems policy and the integrated systems plans did not deliver expected benefits in a company fragmented in terms of management loyalty. Retrospectively, the problems faced by the integrated financial systems seem hardly surprising. One can see that the development of company-wide systems was a futile effort to provide an integrated infrastructure for technical rational management in a company whose traditional administration regime, with powerful local managers acting in their best capacity, but idiosyncratically, was still holding strong.

Pemex continued to rely more on the old regime and practices rather than the new, and rationalization proclamations were paralleled by muddling through actions to carry out work that was seen as tasks that had to be done. At the background of policies, initiatives, and interventions to instil modern management practices and information systems, Pemex continued to perform its activities in the idiosyncratic way it had been used to. Shadow information systems development action continued too, and in many cases was effective in providing support for various tasks in the organization.

Thus, while the controversy on the development of the 'institutional systems' that would give Pemex the possibility to manage its finances as a modern business company was noisy, engaging general directors, technologists, and consultants, the company continued to build and rely on computer-based information systems in an ad hoc way. Some of these systems came to play a key role in the management of the company, in effect compensating for the rigidities of large-scale efforts to develop a functioning integrated information systems infrastructure. The following example of a system developed to support the reporting on the company's operations demonstrates the more pragmatic activities on which Pemex tended to rely (Volkow 1996).

As the inability of the company to report consistently on its operations and financial conditions became a source of embarrassment, damaging its public image, a specialist unit, the 'Unit of Basic Information', was set up in the Director General's office to maintain data and publish monthly reports on the production activities of the company. Initially this unit collected data on production only by phoning daily all the operations centres in the country. The officer in charge of this unit checked for inconsistencies, asked questions to verify the validity of the information received if it looked unconvincing or contradictory, and resolved problems in communication with the reporting operations centres.

This process proved effective, and the significance of the data collected by the Unit of Basic Information increased with time. Its database became the only reliable repository of information on the operations of the company and the main source for planning purposes, particularly for the transformation of Pemex in 1992 that is described in the next section. It continued to be used throughout the 1990s. Over time the categories of data stored increased, including indicators on levels of production and distribution, costs, revenues, human resources. However, the process of collecting and validating the data remained fundamentally the same, involving the intermediation of personnel in the office to secure the consistency and reliability of reported information. In the 1990s, data were collected monthly either on computer printouts or electronically, but such data were not entered into the database unchecked. They were inspected by what they called 'intelligence interface', a team of employees with wide experience in the company and with a network of connections in all its operations sites, able to raise queries with those reporting the data when they suspected inaccuracies. In other words, reliable data were created by negotiating the validity and meaning of the indicators on the computer-generated reports.

Pemex in the 1990s

With the Salinas government pressing ahead its economic modernization pro-gramme, in the early 1990s Pemex entered a period of major restructuring. First, the company's established structure in functional departments was redesigned on the basis of 'business lines', each business line comprising activities related to particular products. A much more radical transformation followed in 1992. The monolithic organization of Pemex was split into a corporation of four subsidiary companies— Exploration and Production, Refinery, Gas and Basic Petrochemicals, and Secondary Petrochemical Products—headed by a Corporate Office.

The division of Pemex was part of the government's broader policy of economic modernization, which at that time aimed at the privatization of state-owned enter-prises. There were legal obstacles in privatizing Pemex, though. According to the country's constitution, activities related to oil production and distribution were the responsibility of the state. The government redrafted the relevant article of the constitution and redefined the oil industry to restrict state responsibility to basic oil production activities only. The splitting of Pemex created possibilities for privatiza-tion of parts of the company, the first candidate being the secondary petrochemical plants.

The transformation process was planned and implemented by a transition committee, which involved executives and technical experts of the company in nine 'technical' subcommittees, responsible for nine broad functional areas. The technical committees decided on the allocation of assets, human resources, IT equipment and organizational data, financial commitment with contractors, running projects, accounts, invoices, debts, fiscal duties, plants, and pipeline infrastructures.

In addition, the planning of the structures and processes of the new corporation relied heavily on international consultants, thus reaffirming the shift from political decision making to technical management that the modernizing circles of the gov-ernment wished to achieve. The transformation plan provided a general organiza-tional model for the design of all subsidiary companies, which set targets in terms of structures, processes, and mission. Nevertheless, the transformation process was largely politically driven. It was carried out within the then hierarchical culture in the traditional spirit of Pemex that an order had to be implemented at all costs, and despite any difficulties. Each subcommittee contested—rather than technically calculated—as many resources as possible for the area of their responsibility. Continuing the old tradition, the directors of the four new companies were appointed by the President of the country and all but one were professional polit-icians. There was a widespread cynical view in the newly formed companies that their structures were designed to secure the allocation of all the people in the administration of the old Pemex into high ranking managerial posts in the new subsidiaries.

Throughout the 1990s the organizational context of Pemex remained ambiguous. Until the time of the writing of this case, in 2000, not one of the subsidiaries was privatized.[5] Plans to privatize the secondary petrochemicals company provoked political opposition and were abandoned. The Pemex companies are managed professionally as competitive concerns, but they are still under the financial and political control of the government. Export of oil continues to be the country's major revenue generator, and therefore the budget of Pemex is determined by the overall government economic policy. Thus, the companies' revenues are directly deposited to the Treasury, and their resources are allocated through the Federal Budget, after approval from the National Congress. The Corporate Office forms a link between government policy and the business strategy of the four subsidiary companies by exercising central financial control, setting organizational standards and regulations, and working out corporation-wide human resources and information systems strategies.

Undoubtedly the transformation of Pemex in 1992 was the beginning of a new era, as each subsidiary began its own efforts to overcome the inefficiencies inherited from the old company, and to implement a market-oriented mission.[6] The initial transformation was followed by a stream of managerial innovation. All companies continued to employ international management consultants and experimented with a range of management techniques, such as TQM and BPR, with mixed results.

The apparently vibrant environment of change hid a great deal of scepticism about the meaning and goal of the modernization effort. Many saw the innovation initiatives as transient, and informal ways of conducting work were a significant aspect of maintaining continuity and organizational memory. One year after the transformation I found three different attitudes among the directors that I interviewed. Some were convinced that their company was on route to become a world-class business corporation, although disappointed with delays and obstacles they thought unnecessary. Others, in a more reserved manner, were optimistic about the prospects to become a professionally driven business corporation, but expected that the effects of the transformation would take time, as the company would gradually develop new

---

[5] It is interesting to note that in the NAFTA negotiations the Mexican government defended its protectionist policy for the oil and petrochemicals industry and won agreement to reserve the right to control all activities and investment in the exploration, exploitation, refining, transportation, storage, and distribution of crude oil and natural gas, as well as primary petrochemicals. Despite some redefinition of 'primary' and 'secondary' petrochemicals, Mexico basically kept foreign investors away from Pemex, with the exception of its secondary petrochemical plants. The main area of compromise with the USA was that Pemex could not sell its products to domestic customer companies at lower prices than to foreign-owned companies operating in Mexico (Maxfield and Shapiro 1998).

The newly elected President in July 2000, Vicente Fox, announced that he does not intend to privatize Pemex. His government may sell the petrochemical plants, and may create competition by privatizing the electricity system, but at this stage it seems that the double-sided role of Pemex as a state-controlled and market-oriented company is going to continue (Economist 2000).

[6] The degree of market orientation of each company varies. Pemex Exploration and Production, and to a lesser extent Pemex Refining have increasing, although still limited market choice in the purchase of their capital goods, but not much in terms of level of production and sales, which are determined by national policy and international treaties. Pemex Gas and Basic Petrochemicals and Pemex Petrochemicals—which comprises seven subsidiaries that handle secondary petrochemical products—are less sensitive to national government control and face competition, either from abroad, or from alternative energy producers in the country.

market-driven strategies and work practices. Several directors, though, were more cautious about the essence of the transformation. For example the director of gas production had doubts about the significance of thinking in terms of market competition in his business area. He continued to think 'nationally' about the value of the business of Pemex, saw little opportunity for export, and was uncertain whether the new regime was ultimately offering benefits to the consumers in the domestic market.[7]

At the time of my next study in Pemex, four years after the transformation, it had become clear that 'modernization' in Pemex did not mean the de-linking of the corporation from the state. Nevertheless, the managers I interviewed at the headquarters believed that the market-oriented regime had created a strong concern for efficiency and had changed the way Pemex was governed. Technical business management approaches were employed routinely in all companies, albeit moderated by the managers' sense of the particularities of its status in the national context.

Such a pragmatic approach to business management was reconfirmed at my last visit to Pemex in November 1999. Characteristically, the planning director of Pemex Exploration and Production, the subsidiary which has the least prospect to face foreign privatization, saw the need for his company to match the performance of 'other companies of the world'. He indicated several 'drivers of change', including the need to secure investment, either from the international financial market or, potentially, by private ownership. Also, he emphasized the pressure of public opinion, which through media exposure was becoming sensitized to issues of pollution and safety, developing higher expectations of service quality, and demanding accountability of investment of public funds to overcome political corruption. He was keen for the use of benchmarking to compare Pemex's performance with others. But he was also clear about the particular conditions that make Pemex different from 'the others', therefore requiring a different type of management. The mission of his company, he explained, is to contribute revenue to the government. Operations of the exploration and production are dispersed in remote areas and rely on the traditional culture of the oilmen—good engineering principles with a sense of a service to the state. Moreover the trade unions and the government continued to exercise power when faced with management initiatives for organizational change.

Information Systems Innovation after the Structural Transformation
When Pemex was split in 1992, hardware and personnel resources were rather haphazardly distributed to the subsidiaries and the Corporate Office. Six of the modules of the 'institutional financial system' of the old Pemex were packaged and copied to each subsidiary. Nevertheless, as subsidiaries became self-managed organizational

---

[7] However, Pemex Gas has faced the threat of losing its domestic market in the north-western states. This was partly because it made economic sense to buy gas from nearby Texas and avoid the huge costs of transporting it from the other end of Mexico, and partly because Mexico had a shortage of refining capacity (Quintanilla and Bauer 1996).

entities, their use of the systems they inherited from the old Pemex varied. Some put them in operation as before, while others launched the development of new applications.

Most computers and technical staff of the Gerencia Institutional de Informatica, were relocated at the Corporate Unit of Financial Systems in the Corporate Office. As its name suggests, this unit focused on financial systems and its terms of reference were to 'consolidate' financial information produced by the subsidiaries and report to central government. From this key position, the Corporate Unit of Financial Systems tried to create for itself a strategic and regulatory function. The scope and legitimacy of such a centralized role were contested and the Unit had no formal power to control the information systems functions of the subsidiaries. Nevertheless, in the first few years after the division of Pemex, this Unit was the main visible location of expertise remaining from the old Pemex. The staff of the information systems centres of the subsidiaries, struggling to establish their services with limited resources, turned to them for assistance. Also, the Corporate Unit of Financial Systems maintained the role of defining standards for the whole corporation, mainly for hardware acquisition and information flows.

Subsidiary companies set out to develop their own information systems competencies and strategies, relying heavily on outsourcing. Their perceived priorities varied. In some, modernization of antiquated production and distribution support systems became a pressing task and absorbed significant investment. For example in 1999 Pemex Exploration and Production had a portfolio of information systems projects under way for production support applications, such as simulation and monitoring of oil deposits, measurement of oil flows in pipelines, logistics of production, investment appraisal, knowledge management, monitoring and protection of environmental pollution. In other subsidiaries, such as in Pemex Gas, the most pressing information systems requirements were in the functions that took priority in their new market-oriented mission, sales and marketing.

Despite such differences, there is one area of systems development activities which has been common in all Pemex companies in the last period of this study. All subsidiary companies maintained the old Pemex aspiration to develop integrated management information systems in order to derive reliable data for management and planning. In the first few years after the transformation such an objective proved as hard to realize in the new companies as it was for the old Pemex.

A good example of the problems faced is the efforts made in Pemex Gas to structure its information systems function and to address its information systems requirements 'strategically'. The information systems manager organized the information systems function in a decentralized way, devolving systems development and management duties to user departments, and retaining a strategic and facilitatory role for the central information systems unit. Following the latest 'best practice' on information systems planning, recommended in textbooks and practitioner guidebooks, he sought the involvement of the managers of the five divisions of the company to define their critical success objectives, and drafted a strategy for integrated information systems for the new company accordingly. Initially there appeared to be consensus both for the information systems management structure and the information systems development strategy. Yet, a year later no progress had been made with systems development, and the directors were loudly complaining that the information systems strategy would not deliver the systems they needed. Most of them already had alternative projects under way to develop applications for their business areas, relying on their own technical skills for information systems and substantial subcontracting.[8]

In the last five years of the 1990s the realization of this long-standing aspiration was pursued through the implementation of Enterprise Resource Planning (ERP) systems. The corporate-wide implementation of ERP was first suggested by the Corporate Unit of Financial Systems in 1994. The Director-General of Pemex, who had a positive experience with the building of information infrastructure while he was director in another state institution before coming to Pemex, promoted the idea enthusiastically. Pemex Secondary Petrochemicals was already implementing an ERP system using ORACLE software. All the other Pemex companies embarked on the implementation of SAP software and by 1999 they had in place an ERP infrastructure of a set of core SAP modules. The Corporate Unit of Financial Systems championed the SAP implementation projects and negotiated a general contract with the SAP vendors for all subsidiaries.

With the SAP implementation projects, Pemex started relying more heavily than ever before on consultants. Invariably, the implementation of the new systems involved two streams of projects, subcontracted to different consultants: the technical implementation of the SAP software, and the management of change towards new organizational processes required to make use of the new systems effectively. Moreover, these projects were loosely related with ongoing efforts of consultant-led organizational change that each company had continued to pursue since its formation in 1992.

The implementation projects were completed, but the extent to which the new infrastructure has affected the way the Pemex corporation conducts business is more difficult to judge. The first view from the personnel in the Corporate Office, where the SAP applications became operational in 1997, was that the new systems are not substantially different from the financial information systems they replaced. Two years later the management at the headquarters of Pemex Exploration and Production saw the systems as useful for 'record keeping', but without a significant impact for the management of the company.[9] Top management continued to apply

---

[8] The information systems manager was perplexed, since he was convinced that he had done what was professionally correct in order to set the course for effective systems development, and he believed he had achieved a consensus on his plans. A more careful examination of the situation, though, indicated that the lack of opposition to his proposed plan did not imply endorsement and commitment to implementation. The whole process of deriving an information systems strategy from business objectives was a professional ritual without substance, as none of the directors at that time had clear objectives to commit themselves to.

[9] The implementation of SAP in Pemex did not result in downsizing savings, as in other cases reported in the literature. The main benefit expected from implementing an ERP infrastructure in Pemex was to create a common IT platform for the recording and communication of data 'from the field'.

a pragmatic combination of formal information channels and informal negotiation with local production managers to assess the production process and align it to business plans.

THE EMBEDDEDNESS OF PEMEX AND IT IN MEXICO'S DEVELOPMENT CONTEXT

Pemex's continuous information systems innovation has not resulted in strategic gains of the kind IT is associated with in the business information systems literature. This company has developed generations of information systems applications, it has closely followed IT trends,[10] and it has applied 'best practice' of information systems management. Nevertheless, the impact of all such innovation efforts on efficiency and management information, the two major long-standing concerns of the company, is questionable. In the remainder of this chapter I argue that the mediocre exploitation of ICT in Pemex has been due to three interrelated aspects: the complex role of the company in Mexico's national development context; its organizing capabilities; and the institutional forces of ICT.

Linking the limited results of information systems innovation with the status of Pemex as a national oil company may seem a blatant statement, reminiscent of the technocratic criticisms often made against Pemex. Indeed, the basic argument of the international agencies that exercise pressure for the privatization of Pemex is that, in order to become a healthy world competitor in the oil industry, the company must disentangle itself from the Mexican state, both in terms of strategic mission and administration. This is probably a valid view, but an assessment of Pemex's information systems innovation on the basis of disembedded international market criteria of performance misses the legitimacy of the company's mission and organizational practice in the socio-economic context of Mexico. In contrast, my interest is in understanding information systems innovation in relation to the organization's own mission and practice.

There is a great deal of evidence that the developmental mission of Pemex continues to be highly legitimate. Randall (1989), who researched extensively the oil sector in Latin American countries, identified four ways through which Pemex has been contributing to national development: First, through buying domestically produced capital goods, which, until trade liberalization in the 1990s, were acquired at above world market prices. Second, through taxes; for example, in 1987 Pemex's taxes were estimated to be 49.4 per cent of its income. Third, through the sale of its products in the domestic market at below world market prices. Fourth, by the construction of

---

[10] Pursuance of 'best practice' is a prominent feature in the parlance of management of Pemex and bench-marking techniques are of great interest to its managers. Indicatively, in a list of completed information systems efforts, the implementation of an additional module for human resources to the Integrated Financial Information System in 1999 is highlighted in the company's 1999 annual report as the introduction of 'best practice' in this area of management.

roads, schools, and hospitals for the oil labour force, and indirectly for the country at large. Pemex has been the main source of income for the federal government: the oil sector's share of tax revenue was 27 per cent before the outbreak of the 1982 crisis, rose to 45 per cent in 1985, and was reduced again to 27 per cent after the liberalization measures of the 1990s (Quintanilla and Bauer 1996).

The most salient aspect of the partnership between Pemex's performance and the Mexican government's struggle for development in the last twenty years of the twentieth century has been the issue of the foreign debt. Pemex's debt increased from $439 million in 1970 to over $20 billion in 1981, and fell to $16 billion in 1985. Pemex's debt amounted to 13.3 per cent of the federal government's debt in the 1970s, 38.1 per cent in 1981, and 23.6 per cent in 1985. Randall estimates that Pemex could pay for its own investment in the 1970s. Its heavy borrowing from abroad was the government's indirect way of borrowing through Pemex rather than directly from foreign development banks. Moreover, foreign banks preferred to lend to Pemex than to the Mexican government. Although oil did not prove to be the short cut to economic growth it was thought it could be in the 1970s, Randall notes 'if Mexican oil had been privately owned, Mexico would not have been able to borrow as much, or as cheaply . . . [G]rowing firms and developing nations rely on borrowing to finance investment and economic growth'(Randall 1989: 164). Indeed, Randall suggests that, taking into account Pemex's contribution to the country's development, its notorious inefficiency and ineffectiveness of management are not as bad as they have been generally perceived.

Even after the open market economic orientation of the 1990s, and the abandonment of protectionist policies, the reluctance of all political parties to privatize Pemex indicates how important it is still considered in the concern for national development. Also, such reluctance indicates that the Mexicans are still keen to protect Pemex—which is weak in comparison to foreign oil companies—from international competition.[11] Paradoxically, Pemex has to create the conditions of its 'freedom' from the government partnership by first securing the development of the rest of the economy. In Randall's words '[o]nly by helping to develop the rest of the nation can Pemex gain increased autonomy as a firm' (Randall 1989: 194).

Thus, considering the continuing legitimacy of the role of Pemex as a company closely related with national development, the tortuous process of information systems innovation should be traced in the interaction between the organizational practice of enacting this always-under-challenge role and the institutional forces of ICT. As far as organizational practice is concerned, the mix of tradition, orders emanating from political authorities, engineering principles, and business management that 'governed' the company in the largest part of the last forty years has been

---

[11] A good example of the attitude to the privatization of Pemex is Quintanilla and Bauer's article (1996), which, although favourable to liberalization, assesses the productivity weaknesses of Pemex and concludes that '[e]xposing the Mexican oil sector immediately to a completely open market could be disastrous. It needs to be strengthened first.'

inadequate and, indeed, often dysfunctional for its perceived purposes.[12] Unlike the continuing legitimacy of the developmental role of Pemex, its traditional organizational practice has long been discredited and the company has been slowly developing organizational competencies matching the complexity of its role.

Such organizational limitations may, to some extent, explain why information systems innovation has not produced significant results. It is well understood that information systems innovation requires considerable organizational strengths (Strassmann 1985). However, Pemex's organizing capability is only one side of its story of information system innovation. Another side is the extent to which ICT as an institutional actor has been capable of addressing the particular circumstances of Pemex. ICT did not come into Pemex as bare hardware, software, and wires. It came loaded with notions of good business management, and an army of systems analysts and information systems consultants keen to apply them. The partiality of ICT as an institution oriented to serving the dominant ideology of business management in a free global market context limited its responsiveness to the requirements of the organizational context of Pemex. The explicit logic that has been accompanying information systems innovation, expressed in terms such as profitability, efficiency, and competitiveness, captured one side only of the concerns driving the operations and the management of the company. In other words, the bias of ICT towards a particular organizing regime limited the possibilities of its use to serve Pemex's complex role.

SOCIO-TECHNICAL INSIGHTS OF INFORMATION SYSTEMS INNOVATION IN PEMEX

The incongruity of organizing practice and ICT to the role Pemex has been entrusted within the Mexican context can be shown by tracing the way information systems translations in Pemex were shaped amidst the confrontation of alternative rationalities that emerged in the company's organizational fields. This section follows the chronological break of the long and continuous motion of change in Pemex in the four periods suggested in the above narrative, and draws four broad-brush pictures of the company's changing enactment and information systems translations. The aim here is to demonstrate the interplay of local and international forces that affected the legitimacy of the developmental mission of the company, its

---

[12] Pemex is not unique in its inability to develop appropriate organizational methods for its developmental role. There is a widespread crisis in development administration in general. For various historical reasons, the inefficiency of public bureaucracies in most developing countries is notorious. Structural adjustment interventions that attempted to minimize the activities of public organizations, privatizing as many tasks as possible and entrusting the market forces rather than hierarchical command and political reason left little room for experimentation with alternative, locally relevant modes of organizing. The significance of public organizations for development was reinstated in the 1980s, yet their effective management continues to be a problem (Uphoff 1994). The advent of non-governmental organizations (NGOs), although delivering valuable services in many areas, does not alleviate the pressing problems of public administration. There is hardly a cumulative knowledge tradition and mimetic practice in this area.

organizing practice, and the involvement of ICT as an institutional actor aligned with business management.

The Irreversible Presence of Computers

In the 1960s, the role of Pemex in the transformation of oil into fuel and revenue for the industrialization of Mexico was closely linked with the country's institutions, and weakly linked with international or global institutions. The internal bureaucratic organizing regime was sustained by powerful rational myths, stemming from the history of the company's formation as a national company that was striving for the country's independence from foreign exploitation and autonomous development. Oil was God's gift to the nation; the oilmen were heroes capable of fulfilling their duty to the country against any odds, and their trade unions safeguarded their well deserved 'rights'; the director and the managers of operations of Pemex were the link between the nation's government and the company; the engineers, close allies of both, the government-appointed management and the oilmen, brought into the company vital intermediaries for its enactment: technology and the skills to structure a technical task.

The influence of the national institutions on Pemex was both material and symbolic. The government received Pemex's revenue, set the market price of its product, decided its budget, legislated its operations, chose its managers, approved or disapproved the import of its technology. In addition, national politics and public opinion sanctioned the power of the oilmen's trade unions, maintained the nationalistic rhetoric that determined Pemex's mission as the people's company that served the development of the nation, praised the company's social welfare programmes, and designated multinational oil companies as 'foreigners'. Moreover, the oil demand, purchasing power, and expectations of the domestic oil consumers on matters such as service quality and pollution determined the scope, ambitions, and constraints of the company's activities.

But even at that period, despite the protective shield of national institutions that virtually separated Pemex from the international oil market, Pemex was not influenced by one single organizational field confined within the borders of the country. The international oil industry, although not an arena of competition for Pemex, was a source of mimetic influences, developing know-how and technologies relevant for the production and distribution of oil and its by-products. Moreover, the bodies of professional engineering expertise, with international spread and with powerful local institutional sources at the national universities, were major determinants of the organizational practices of Pemex.

Against such an institutional background, the first mobilization of computers in the 1960s was the result of a combination of local and international forces. Inside Pemex the problematization that introduced the first computers stemmed from a growing disconcertion about the company's methods, the waste of resources, the accusations of corruption, the growing inability to cope with local demand. The lurking disconcertion about the company's messy performance found a legitimate expression and solution in the emerging computer technology. It secured the *interessement* of engineers who could 'naturally' extend their expertise with machines and accept computers as tools for the solution to the company's problem of organizational order.

It is important to recognize that this particular problematization—the problem was inefficiency and it could be overcome with computers—was not the only logical way to perceive and address the company's messy performance. For example, the problem of the payroll system, which was one of the first to be subjected to the computerization solution, could be seen as corruption and be dealt with by law, or as overcomplicated salary regulations that needed simplification, or as understaffing and low staff productivity that could be dealt with by work reorganization interventions. That the problem was defined as inefficiency, treatable by computers, was to a large extent a mimetic act of the international trend to use computers in public bureaucracies.

Indeed, the particular form of problematization that expressed the object of disconcertion as inefficiency and saw computers as a solution was not an original local conception. In the 1960s computers, still valued mainly for their number crunching and bulk data processing abilities, were widely seen as appropriate tools for enhancing the performance of hierarchical bureaucracies.[13] At that period most countries, including most developing countries, introduced computers in their biggest government departments and state utility companies.

Among the crucial battles in the process of translation of the first computerization projects were getting permission to buy the computers and getting the programming right. To a large extent, winning those battles relied on Pemex's characteristics of the national company that was pioneering the country's development efforts. Pemex was an organization that had the muscle—engineering confidence, money, size, significance of mission, and political manoeuvring skills—to wrestle with both the government's protectionist bureaucratic machine, and the newcomer computer vendors to acquire the necessary machines, and could mobilize the skills to program them. Computers, as machines, were within the cognitive grasp of the oilmen and fitted well into the professional ethos of Pemex's engineers. Thus, the first computers in Pemex were not intended to challenge the dominant organizing regime that sustained the organization, but to strengthen it. Moreover, the actions required for the entrance of the first computers into the company did not introduce a new modus operandi. Overall, the first computer applications brought some efficiency benefits, but did not remedy the bureaucratic dysfunctions.

Nevertheless, in Pemex as everywhere else, computers were not neutral instruments of efficiency, and their institutional carrier, the Office of Computing, could not stay out of the stratagems of bureaucratic power. Why should the oilmen be told by computers how much they should be paid? How did systems analysts know how the warehouses should be stocked to keep Pemex running?

Two forces secured the irreversible presence of the newcomer in the network of power of Pemex. First, internally, central management saw it as an ally in putting

---

[13] See e.g. the views expressed in the papers collected in Kraus (1983).

order in the unruly actions of the dispersed organization and used its coercive mechanisms to impose the new systems against user dissatisfaction. Second, computers were accompanied by the latest international discourse on organizational performance. With computers, efficiency, coordination, optimization, and scientific management had a clear voice, distinct from the established order of loyalty, service to the nation at all costs. Analysts and computer experts, who 'knew' what computers could do to improve a large company took a place next to the men who 'knew' how to serve the country's needs for oil and revenue. By the 1970s, computers and computer professionals were unquestionable participants in Pemex, despite several setbacks of projects that did not deliver, or were abandoned.

Information Systems Innovation in an Anarchic Organizational Context

The unprecedented problematization that the international crisis of the oil industry triggered in Pemex in the 1970s led the company to make itself an actor in the international oil market, in effect engaging in an enactment very different from that of producing for the needs of the national industry. The organizational fields of Pemex changed. The government continued to be the most important source of sanction and coercion, a master which the company should obey. But the relative significance of the other institutions of the organizational field of the 1960s changed, and powerful new ones appeared on the scene. To begin with, the 'foreign' influences became much more important; they were not seen any more in purely negative terms. Foreign markets acquired significance, and, for the first time, Pemex was oriented towards selling to international customers rather than producing for the national industry. Foreign oil companies became competitors, and Pemex's strategy considered questions such as how much oil was sold, to whom, and at what price. The foreign governments were not so much national enemies or friends any more, but customers, competitors, and regulators of the oil business. Most importantly, at that period the international banks acquired an enormous significance for what Pemex could do and how.

Money became a crucial intermediary. Either as investment or as foreign debt, it began a perpetual wrestling with oil, the major actor at the core of Pemex's enactment. Each of them had its own institutional network. The former included international banks, foreign governments' economic policies, the Mexican government's economic policy and budget, Pemex's own finance departments. The latter included the oil-producing countries' cartel, Pemex's oilmen and engineers, the imported technologies for exploration, production, refining, and distribution. It proved easy to mobilize the international banks, but the company had to learn to manage a long-term relationship with a powerful international institution, a relationship that was particularly tricky with the mediation of that giant master and protector, the Mexican government.

Pumping more money from the international banks could produce more oil, but this was oil that had to obey the logic of money all the way through: it was valuable and could produce wealth when there was scarcity in the international market, it was the cheap product of hard labour when the international market was flooded by the oil of the 'competitors'.

Still, at that stage, the legitimacy of the mission of Pemex was not questioned. But the organizing regime in Pemex started being eroded as the company came under the influence of the organizational field of the international financial system, sustained by a radically different substantive rationality than that of serving the development needs of a poor country. In effect, the role of Pemex became more complex: serving the developmental needs of Mexico and acting in the international trade and finance scene. The mix of engineering and political decision making and practice intensified, exposing more glaringly its inadequacies and unable to generate an effective enactment of the new complex role of the company.

ICT had an obvious position in the new enactment, and the innovation processes that began in the previous decade were set to continue. Increase of production and expansion of markets reinforced the legitimacy of the discourse for optimization and coordination, and in the haste of expansion managers mobilized computers in all kinds of efforts. Computers were everywhere, but ironically, they added to the confusion of organizing practice rather than optimizing and coordinating it. A proliferation of computers created incompatible information systems of as many different knowledges as localized networks of enactment of engineers, managers, oilmen, computer analysts, oil production machines, and money. Analysts did their best to design systems that would bring efficiency, accountability, and control, breaking user resistances and, in most cases, seeing projects through according to the specified requirements. But, computers at that time proved to be opportunistic allies, which could be adapted in use to match idiosyncratic masters, caricaturing in practice their in-built specifications and 'rational' performance. They could be enrolled in any local project, rewarding them with local efficiency and control. And while through their proliferation the irreversibility of computers was completely secured, they did not assist the ailing mix of political bureaucracy and engineering to overcome its growing troubles.

ICT Aligned with the Newcomer Business Management Rationality

It was in the 1980s, while the balance of institutional forces that became influential for Pemex in the previous decade was consolidated, that the mix of traditional bureaucratic loyalty and engineering started being confronted by the rationality of modernization. As in earlier periods, the changes of strategy within Pemex were directly influenced by the decisions and actions of the government. The gradual change from a protective nationalistic economic policy and political discourse towards a market-driven economic modernization ideology had immediate effects on Pemex. The 'modernizers' appointed by the government as leaders of the company introduced, more substantially than ever before, the discourse of business. The blow to the trade unions changed the relative power between the traditionalist and modernizing actors and challenged dramatically the rational myth of the heroic oilmen. As the rhetoric and the enactment of the national political ideology shifted towards liberalization, expectations of the company's customers, employees, and financiers began to change. The role of Pemex as a competitive business firm in the global market became more prevalent.

The political opening of the economy brought more international institutions in the organizational fields of Pemex. In addition to the banks, the customers, and the competitors—each of them with foreign national allegiances—the disembedded flows of technical expertise and international business consultancy started playing a significant role in the shaping of the liberal economy, and of Pemex as a business corporation, in particular. Internally, changes in the balance of power among existing and new actors shifted the company's enactment process towards a business aspiring to competitiveness in the global market and driven by modern management. The power, 'rights', and pride of the oilmen were assaulted. A new generation of managers and technical advisers trained as professional business administrators, as well as management consultants became the visible carriers of the new rationality.

Despite the modernization initiatives and the entry of new institutional actors, the old regime of truth was still holding strong in Pemex. Efforts to make the company a global competitor had neither de-institutionalized its mission in the development of the nation, nor could they convincingly be seen as serving it. Pemex was obeying two masters, politicians and professional managers, and was speaking two languages, the political/bureaucratic—notably when reporting to the ministry—and the technical/managerial to run it as a business corporation. Organizational practice was now clearly torn by conflict. Obeying orders and shouldering individual responsibilities based on the political and engineering traditions clashed with interventions to reorganize operations and decision-making processes according to technical principles of business management. The old practice was guilty of such sins as waste, inefficiency, and 'corruption', but bore the vested interests of powerful actors, and could be trusted to 'deliver at all costs'. The new practice enjoyed the kudos of its international affiliations, but had not developed adequate allegiances in the organization and was still untested for producing results.

The official institutional actor for IT, the Gerentia Institutional de Informatica, followed the changing organizational enactment with new plans for corporate-wide information systems. It had to admit the existence and the strengths of its contenders, the many different systems and technology expertise centres that had cropped up in every functional division, serving the local information processes of various office holders. More significantly, the official institutional actor for IT in Pemex had to share the job of the technical expert in information systems translations with external consultants. However, the loss of exclusivity of technical authority to consultants was compensated by the overall power gained from the internationalization of their professional expertise as represented by the consultants. IT experts, frequently moving between Pemex and consultancy firms,[14] increasingly drew the legitimacy of their role from disembedded knowledge on IT and business, rather than technical knowledge of computing and the localized understanding of Pemex's enactment. The technical computer knowledge became inseparable from the technical business knowledge. IT experts did not only do analysis to understand information requirements of specific tasks and develop systems accordingly. They

---

[14] Not least because they were sacked by Pemex at times of 'rationalization' and then reappointed in different posts as the company or its subsidiaries launched a new generation of computerization projects.

drew IT plans, 'aligning' them with 'business strategy'—even though the latter was unclear or confused—and they 'knew' the latest fads of computers in international business, such as managing through 'business lines'.

Yet, ICT, with all its institutional forces—professional knowledge, books and packages of information-processing applications, the selling influences of vendors—could not compensate for the contradictory forces underneath the surface of information systems translations and the conflicts of organizing practice in Pemex. With the combination of the might of ICT actors and modernizing managers, the development of the integrated information systems to rationalize information flows for financial accountability and to set the infrastructure for business management was completed. But the results of this big effort were contested, the resulting systems were resisted, and the information order they sought to impose was not realized. The details of local business remained local knowledge, never translated into corporate data. They could be negotiated with central management, as for example with the Unit of Basic Information, but they could not be surrendered to a formal 'Management Information System'. Fragmentation of information and local order persisted; business management continued to be deprived of integrated data. Political steering continued to require negotiated information, in order to overcome the inadequacies of formal data input procedures and to 'correct' the errors in formally captured data.

Emulation and Pragmatic Adaptation in the Post-Transformation Era

Almost ten years after Pemex launched its organizational transformation, its multifaceted strategy juggled the traditional with the modern, national development with business, and political authority with managerial order. The Mexican government continued to be one of the most—if not the most—significant actors in the company's organizational fields, allocating its budget and appointing its executives. The 'globally oriented' business corporation had more reasons to feel national rather than global. Its operations continued to be located in the country and efforts to release the forces of global business through privatization were met with wide political resistance. Competition for most subsidiaries was limited to the domestic market and a major concern continued to be how to avoid being swallowed by the cash-rich competitors of the powerful national neighbour or a captive supplier to the industry of the United States.

But Pemex was not the national hero it used to be, and the nationalistic rhetoric on Pemex subsided. The oilmen learnt to work under business management, to participate in business reorganizations, and to negotiate their productivity with financial and marketing executives. They almost accepted the 'need' to be accountable for their efficiency, but they had their own view of what to account for and how, and how to be efficient. The new translation of natural resources to revenue—still channelled to the government before it was reallocated to Pemex—was driven by a combination of national political aims and market strategies.

Organizing practice was perpetually engaged in combinations of managerial technicalities with political manoeuvring, bureaucratic order, and engineering imperatives. Pemex was no longer resisting business management. It appointed large numbers of business school graduates, it used continuously international management consultants and applied various emerging management ideas and techniques. But it also learnt to temper all these actors and assimilate them in its own organizing regime. From their genesis the four subsidiary companies of Pemex have been governed by technical/rational business planning and decision making, moderated by the traditional ways of seeing demanding tasks through. The business discourse of efficiency, productivity, customers, strategy, investment accommodated also policy, public opinion, and loyalty.

Information systems translations followed the same tendency for adaptation. The information systems professionals—either Pemex employees or consultants—were enthusiastic participants in the discourse of business management. They could argue about efficiency, promise better data resources for decision making, make information strategies aligned with business strategies, install systems for speedier communication, design integrated management information systems. The new SAP infrastructure installed in three of the subsidiary companies and the corporate office was not an exercise of aligning ICT to business strategy, but the result of a process of internal negotiations, power fights, and patronage as well as external mimetic and normative influences. The 'strategic need' for an integrated infrastructure of financial information, championed by the Corporate Unit of Financial Systems, was resisted or ignored by the subsidiaries. In turn, the strategic plans of the subsidiaries were invariably resisted, or adapted by improvisation in their own divisions and remote operations. But a number of forces coalesced to make the implementation of an integrated information systems infrastructure seen as a necessity, and SAP the 'preferred choice' for Pemex. 1994 saw not only the enrolment of the new Director-General, but also the growing reputation of the packaged ERP software internationally, and more specifically the reputation of SAP as a tool of rationalization of large corporations. Resistances were bent and ERP modules formed a new infrastructure for the redesigned processes of all subsidiary companies.

Yet, in their use, the implemented systems did not have much of a strategic character and came to be seen as 'useful for record keeping'. Within Pemex's organizing practice, the integrated managerial information infrastructure became part of the fabric of the operations of the company, and nothing more. As an indication of this adjustment of the role of ICT, unlike the widespread association of ERP implementation with downsizing during the 1990s, Pemex did not see the new systems as a way to achieve savings by reducing its labour force (Truex and Ngwenyama 2000). In the post-transformation era of Pemex, ICT, aligned with the institutional forces of business management learned to adapt to political and bureaucratic pressures, in the pragmatic attitude so characteristic of the modern Pemex.[15]

---

[15] Pemex's moderation of business rationality and adaptation of business information systems is different from the emulation and innovation process described by Westney in her study of the development of the modern nation of Japan (Westney 1987). Pemex is neither particularly selective in its innovation nor deliberately creative to match its own circumstances. Rather, the adaptation of the emulated innovation of information systems in Pemex is the tacit confrontation of the rationality of the intended innovation with the regime of truth of the organization.

CONCLUDING REMARKS

What if ICT had not come into Pemex as an ally of business management, packaged with inscriptions of what an organization should aim for, how to organize work, what decisions should be made, and how to be a competitive business company? What if analysts unaffected by business rationality attempted to develop systems to meet the requirements of Pemex's strategy? There would still have been resistances, negotiations, accommodations, rejections, and improvisations. Moreover, in the context of Pemex, information systems developers would be naive to seek to support a particular category of actors in the name of ethics and with confidence that their intervention would contribute to the company's improved economic performance. In the absence of the industrial democratic context that provided the sociotechnical approach proponents in Europe with a political framework for a model of a desirable and effective working place, systems developers in Pemex would have a more difficult task at hand.

It is plausible that without imitating—or transferring, in the case of SAP—the systems of best business practice, ICT would mediate in a different way between the various actors in Pemex and its context, such as management and the oilmen or the government and the management. Systems might have different functionality. They might have included modules supporting employees' service to the community, managers' engagement in political activities, account categories for the hospitals of Pemex, they might have incorporated data to monitor against corruption, they might have built databases to tune the strategy of Pemex with the development indicators of Mexico. Or they might have included surveillance mechanisms, monitoring employees' work, trade union activities, or social conduct.

Whatever one might think about such ideas, the point is that they hardly make sense at the turn of the twenty-first century for a corporation. Such is the power of the dominant economic activity and its social significance that alternatives are unthinkable. This is why Pemex accommodates ICT with all its inscriptions of business management and twists them in its enactment.

References

Castells, M. (1997). *The Power of Identity*. Oxford: Blackwell.
Economist, The (2000). 'Happy Birthday, Senor Fox'. *The Economist* (London), 8 July: 71–2.
Heath, J. (1998). 'Original Goals and Current Outcomes of Economic Reform in Mexico', in R. Roett (ed.), *Mexico's Private Sector: Recent History, Future Challenges*. Boulder, Colo.: Lynne Rienner, 37–62.
Kraus, H. (ed.) (1983). *The Impact of New Technology on Information Systems in Public Administration in the '80s*. Amsterdam: North-Holland.
Maxfield, S., and Shapiro, A. (1998). 'Assessing the NAFTA Negotiations', in C. Wise (ed.), *The Post-NAFTA Political Economy: Mexico and the Western Hemisphere*. University Park, Penn.: Pennsylvania State University Press, 82–118.
Nolan, R. L. (1979). 'Managing the Crises in Data Processing'. *Harvard Business Review*, Mar.–Apr.: 115–26.

Quintanilla, J. M., and Bauer, M. E. (1996). 'Mexican Oil and Energy', in L. Randall (ed.), *Changing Structure of Mexico: Political, Social, and Economic Prospects*. Armonk, NY: M. E. Sharpe, 111–25.

Randall, L. (1989). *The Political Economy of Mexican Oil*. New York: Praeger.

Strassmann, P. (1985). *Information Payoff: The Transformation of Work in the Electronic Age*. New York: Free Press.

Truex, D., and Ngwenyama, O. K. (2000). ERP Systems: Facilitating or Confounding Factors in Corporate Telecommunications Mergers?, in H. R. Hansen, M. Bichler, M., and H. Mahrer (eds.), the proceedings of the 8th ECIS conference A Cyberspace Odyssey, Vienna, 3 July, 645–51.

UNDP (1999). 'Human Development Report 1999'. New York, United Nations Development Programme.

Uphoff, N. (ed.) (1994). *Puzzles of Productivity in Public Organizations*. San Francisco: Institute for Contemporary Studies.

Volkow, N. (1996). 'Building a System Within its Context: A Case Study of Petroleos Mexicanos', in M. Odedra-Straub (ed.), *Global Information Technology and Socio-economic Development*. Nashua, NH: Ivy League, 143–52.

——(forthcoming). 'Interaction between Organizational Change and IT Innovation: The Case Study of Petroleos Mexicanos'. Ph.D. thesis, Information Systems Department, London School of Economics.

Westney, D. E. (1987). *Imitation and Innovation: The Transfer of Western Organizational Patterns to Meiji Japan*, Cambridge, Mass.: Harvard University Press.

6

IKA—Striving to Modernize a State Bureaucracy

IKA is the largest social security organization in Greece, providing insurance benefits and health care to over 5 million people, almost half the population of the country. It is directly controlled by the government ministry responsible for its domain of services, the Ministry of Health and Social Security. It is also accountable to the Ministry of Presidency, which regulates public administration and to the Treasury. The social security part of the organization, which is the subject of this case study, employs about 4,000 staff, who are located in its central administration offices in Athens and nearly 300 regional and local offices. The social security services of IKA include old age and disability pensions for private sector employees and their families, as well as a number of non-means-tested benefits, such as for sickness, maternity, and rehabilitation. IKA is financed by employee and employer contributions, and is heavily subsidized by the state. Insurance contributions have been traditionally collected by issuing insurance stamps to employers, which is a very inefficient and fraud-prone method. About 20 per cent of its staff are 'controllers', visiting employer sites and checking compliance with social security regulations. The organization operates in a legalistic, highly bureaucratic manner that is typical of the public sector in Greece and needs to be understood in relation to the socio-political and administrative context of the country's government. Nevertheless, its operations are decentralized; regional and local offices have always had responsibility for the collection of insurance contributions and insurance benefits decisions.

It is deceptively easy to identify gross dysfunctionalities in IKA and get unequivocal common agreement about the need for fundamental changes of structure, operations, and service quality. Successive reform programmes have left the structure, services, and work processes of IKA intact. Computer technology has also been marshalled to the pursuit of reform, but information systems innovation projects have been assimilated by its bureaucracy rather than contributing to any of the improvements generally seen as required in the organization.

In this chapter the presentation of IKA's case proceeds as follows. First, I outline the organizational setting of IKA's information systems function, and present the story of major information systems projects until the end of the 1990s, as I traced it with research at four points in time over two decades (see Appendix for methodological details). The following socio-technical analysis discusses the attempts for information systems innovation in association with the conditions of state administration in Greece, the dominant views on required reform, and the reform efforts until the end of the 1990s.

THE ORGANIZATIONAL SETTING OF IKA'S INFORMATION SYSTEMS

IKA introduced computers in the 1950s and established a computer centre within its central administration function. In a period of two decades it created several computer-based data files to store information on members, employers, and contributions. It developed a payroll system and an application to record insurance contributions for the employees of the biggest port of the country, Piraeus, as the first effort to substitute insurance stamps with a computer-based method for collection of contributions.

In 1969 the Greek government created a computer centre, KHYKY, to serve all the social security organizations of the country and IKA lost its in-house computer resources. Social security organizations were no longer allowed to maintain their own computer facilities and develop their own applications. Most of their computer systems and technical staff were transferred to KHYKY. The creation of KHYKY was justified partly on the basis that the computer technology of that time supported economies of scale, and partly as a step towards the amalgamation of the various social security funds of the country, which was a major political issue at that time.[1] KHYKY was established as a quasi-governmental organization, not as tightly restricted by civil service regulations as IKA is. It enjoyed, therefore, more flexibility to recruit computer specialists and could pay higher salaries.

In 1980 the legal restrictions binding social security organizations to the services of KHYKY were lifted. However without in-house technical expertise and under civil service salary regulations that were hindering recruitment of specialist skills, neither IKA nor any other large social security organization was able at that time to take advantage of this legal change. IKA could not pay adequate salaries for the then emerging professional jobs of project managers, analysts, and programmers. Moreover, there were political and bureaucratic imperatives that obliged IKA to continue to rely on KHYKY for the operations of its computer applications, as well as for the development of new applications. Withdrawal of IKA's services from KHYKY would bring the demise of the latter, and the socialist government elected in 1981 was not prepared to face the political cost of redundancies associated with public sector employment.

Thus, administratively, responsibility for the information systems of IKA was shared by KHYKY and two divisions in IKA. The Computer Services division was acting as an operational link between the two organizations: collecting data forms

[1] In addition to IKA, which provides social security services for private sector employees, there are many other social security organizations in Greece: OGA, for the agricultural population; TEVE, for self-employed professionals and craftsmen; the civil servants insurance fund, for public sector employees; and approximately 100 other funds, covering small occupational groups, such as telecommunication workers, lawyers, engineers. The amalgamation of social security funds met with strong opposition of some of the richer (although small in terms of number of beneficiaries) funds, and was not realized.

from all social security local offices, checking for obvious errors and correcting them before typing them onto tapes, subsequently sent to KHYKY, and dispatching computer output from KHYKY to local offices. This involved hundreds of employees in tedious jobs, such as sight-checking for errors and data entry. The Computer Applications division had a more managerial role, striving to oversee the KHYKY services, to negotiate enhancements of existing systems and the development of new computer applications, and to participate in the analysis of new systems. It was poorly equipped for such tasks though, lacking both the technical and management skills required for the critical intermediary role between the two institutions.

The development of computer systems for IKA was further complicated by the bureaucratic procedures of the supervising ministries, which controlled computer procurement in the public sector. Purchasing hardware required approval from a technical committee at the Ministry of Presidency. Requests even for small systems had first to be approved by the Ministry of Social Security, then proceeded to the long queue of cases waiting for approval from the technical committee at the Ministry of Presidency. This procedure took, usually, over a year.

THE STORY OF IKA'S INFORMATION SYSTEMS PROJECTS

By the early 1980s KHYKY ran several batch mode applications for IKA, all of them with serious deficiencies and limitations. The core problem was the unreliability of IKA's data, kept in three poorly maintained and corrupted files: the employers register, the insured members register, and the insurance contributions file. Of these, particularly problematic, and a source of embarrassment for IKA, was the poor state of the insurance contributions file, which was crucial for the calculations of all social security benefits. During the 1950s and 1960s, records on the employment history of insured members were stored centrally on punched cards, while local offices' maintained records for their own population of insured members on paper cards. In the early 1970s the central file was redesigned to store more information, it was upgraded from a number of different data sources, and transferred onto magnetic tapes. The upgrade process destroyed the integrity of insurance data, messing up irrevocably the most fundamental resources of IKA's operations. A number of efforts to remedy the situation produced additional files containing corrections but, rather than solving the problem, they resulted in a complicated and still unreliable set of data resources. The problem was compounded by the decision in the late 1970s that local offices could discontinue their manual insurance contributions records.

The main computer applications in operation in the early 1980s were a payroll system, a pensions payment system, an accounting system, and an application for monitoring the issuing of insurance stamps to employers. Their centralized mode of operation had worsened rather than alleviating the inefficiencies of IKA's bureaucratic operations. For example, the centralized computer-based payroll system had slowed down the payment of salaries, a task that was previously contained in the local offices. The output of the accounting system—general ledgers, balance sheets, and income statements on the financial transactions of the regional units—was produced with such long delays that it was hardly of any use. The regional units of IKA have traditionally had a great degree of autonomy in their accounting tasks and kept analytical manual ledgers. With inefficient data collection procedures and centralized computer operations, in 1983 the accounting system was two months behind for monthly updates and six months behind for the completion of the annual balance sheet and income statement. The regional units continued to keep their own analytical manual ledgers. But the inefficiencies of the computer-based accounting system had serious implications for the central administration, which did not receive timely information on the financial situation of the organization.

The most important developments in the history of computerization of IKA have been concerned with the development of computer-based methods for the collection of contributions aiming to phase out the outdated method of insurance stamps. In the 1970s, a sustained effort started to collect employment data from employers' computerized payroll systems on computer tapes or floppy disks. Employers could supply employee insurance data on computer tapes or disks, on the basis of which IKA subsequently issued invoices for the payment of contributions. Although a welcome alternative to insurance stamps, in the early 1980s the efficiency of this method was low, mainly because of the incompatibilities between the employers' computer systems and those of KHYKY, as well as because data were often wrongly formatted. Such problems were gradually overcome by providing detailed guidelines for the type and format of data required, and by collaboration with employers' computer services to clear initial confusion.

A number of specialized systems were developed in the 1970s and 1980s for small groups of insured members in occupations with particular insurance conditions, such as open market sellers and stevedores. Although each of those small systems provided an efficient alternative to the insurance stamps for the population they served, they remained isolated applications. They were specialized in terms of employee data and benefit regulations and could not be generalized to the bulk of IKA's insurance operations. Moreover, the successful development, reliable data, and smooth operations of those systems were achieved with the active interest and continuing collaboration of the trade unions of the occupations they served, conditions that were unlikely to be found in the general population of IKA's insured members.

The first contributions application covering a population of a significant size was developed in the late 1970s to support the calculation of the annual benefits of construction workers. The construction industry is characterized by volatility of employment, frequent changes of employer, mobility across regions, and complexity of legislation governing its insurance contributions and insurance benefits. In 1983 the 'construction workers' application was presented to me as the most successful attempt IKA had made to develop computer-based information systems. Nevertheless, the implementation of the system compromised its initial specifications drastically: instead of its intended decentralized operations the system was run in centralized batch mode. Moreover, the system was restricted to the processing of data from a few regional offices only. Expansion of implementation to the rest of the country was at that time discontinued, because of limited funds and the launching of new plans for a general computer-based contributions collection method.

Overall, by the time of my first study in 1983, IKA had a bleak experience with IT. Through KHYKY they maintained a dysfunctional service of miscellaneous applications, which had not had any positive efficiency impact. On the contrary, computerization had introduced additional inefficiencies in the most fundamental tasks of the organization, most importantly accounting and the calculations of insurance benefits. The ad hoc computer applications consolidated the fragmentation of its complex legalistic operations. Also computers had worsened work conditions. The centralized computer services had created additional paperwork for employees in both central and local offices. Filling in paper forms with computer data was the only contact IKA employees had with computer technology. Most of the new jobs that the computer services had created were unskilled laborious data entry and data sight-checking for errors.

The mediation of KHYKY added to the alienation of IKA's staff from computer technology. With the cumbersome procedures of transferring data from local offices through the central IKA division of Computer Services to KHYKY, and the subsequent long line of backward and forward communication to rectify data errors, the 'electronic brain'[2] was a very remote and inflexible mechanism, alien to the daily operations performed in IKA. Relations between the computer specialists of KHYKY and the employees of the division of Computer Applications in IKA were frequently strained. IKA's computer 'experts' resented being paid lower salaries than their 'colleagues' in KHYKY. Moreover, without adequate technical knowledge they were in a position of inferiority when they negotiated new projects as well as when they participated in systems development tasks. Some of them had recently acquired additional technical training and were keen to be more substantially involved in systems development projects, but still the project managers of KHYKY did not involve them in technical tasks.

Employee morale was not high in KHYKY either. Salaries of the technical staff there were better in relation to those of the civil servants, but still well below those earned by computer specialists in the private sector. KHYKY's staff did not enjoy the benefits of civil service, such as a job guaranteed for life, with 'natural' career progression and relatively generous pension and health insurance provisions. They felt insecure, threatened by IKA's wish to develop in-house computer skills. More importantly, they felt that the bureaucratic environment of their clients, the social security organizations, did not provide them with opportunities to develop their technical expertise. While technology was developing fast with the advent of microcomputers, networks, and distributed computing, they were still working on batch mode technology.

1983: An Attempt at Information Systems Innovation and Radical Reform

At the time of my first study of IKA in 1983, the development of new information systems was associated with initiatives for organizational reform inspired by the

---

[2] 'Electronic brain' was the most common name IKA's employees used for the computer at that time.

political change that swept the country when its first ever socialist government took office in 1981. There were still strong echoes of the calls for radical 'change' of the society, the state, and the economy.[3] Greece had not developed a 'modern'— European type—social welfare state, and the socialist government declared the improvement of welfare services a priority within its overall reform strategy. The senior administration of IKA, appointed by the government, was keen to pursue a 'modernization' policy, and worked out plans to restructure the organization and improve the performance of its operations. A cadre of 'advisers' was employed to overcome the organization's lack of the expertise required to design performance-oriented work structures and practices. Decentralization and employee 'empowerment' were key aspects of the discourse of that modernization reform.

Computer applications were considered important means for the modernization objective. The policy documents of IKA associated the development of computer-based information systems with the following expectations:

- To provide better services to employers and insured members;
- To secure the financial resources of the organization;
- To improve the work conditions of the personnel of the organization;
- To provide information for decision making and planning.

With such ambitious rhetoric, in 1982 IKA launched a major effort for the development of a computer-supported system for the collection and recording of insurance contributions. A task force comprising the most competent of IKA's recently computer-trained employees, in collaboration with systems analysts from KHYKY, set out to design the so-called 'Revenue system'. The main objective of the Revenue system project was the improvement of IKA's accountability over its financial resources. It was also expected that decentralization of data processing would strengthen administrative decentralization more generally. In essence, it was an attempt to design new processes of interaction between IKA, employers, and insured members. After studying the methods employed for the collection of contributions by social security organizations in Germany, France, and the UK, the team designed the processes they thought best-suited for IKA, and drew specifications for an information system accordingly. KHYKY saw an opportunity to engage in a significant latest-technology project, and gave full support for the development of the Revenue system.

Within one year part of the system was implemented in two pilot offices, with very positive results. The regional offices of the two pilot sites accepted the new system without reservations, and central administration was very satisfied with the information produced. Yet implementation in the rest of the country was discontinued when the supervising Ministry did not approve procurement of the required hardware. The software was readjusted to run in batch mode on KHYKY's existing computers, and the system was never implemented for other offices beyond the two pilot sites. In fact, the whole programme of modernization in IKA was suspended later in

---

[3] The slogan of the socialist government at that time was 'alaghi', meaning change. Areas of promised change ranged from restoring political justice by overcoming the institutionalized outcasting of citizens with left-wing orientation, to radical public sector reform.

that same year, when the Director-General was displaced and an anti-modernizer was appointed at the top position of the organization. In IKA, at least, it was clear that no radical reform was foreseeable in the following few years.

1986: Planning Anew a Decentralized Information System

At my second research visit in 1986 there was not much talk about reform in IKA, or for that matter, in any other domain of public life in Greece. Various changes were happening at a rather slow pace, but they were not conceived or planned for radical results. They were adjustments of established structures and practices. The only area where profound change was contemplated was in the planning of new information systems. That time the lead was taken by KHYKY by developing a 'strategy' to re-organize the core operations of IKA through distributed information systems. The strategy echoed the ideas of local accountability and decentralization that were prevalent in the 'modernization' plans of the early 1980s. But the stated objective emphasized more narrowly the combating of fraud in the payments of contributions by employers' Improvement of services to the public became a secondary and vaguely expressed desirable side effect.

A new 'strategic' information systems plan had been worked out, called this time 'Revenue and Insurance system', thus making an attempt to decentralize the processing of employers' contributions and insurance benefits onto a network of regional computers. Each regional computer centre would serve a number of local offices, while at central level the system would store an index of all insured members with indicators to the regional centres of latest employment. The plan envisaged mini-computers installed in regional and large local offices, computer terminals for on-line transaction processing in smaller local offices and stand-alone microcomputers in very small offices; KHYKY would provide support for mini- and mainframe computers.

The prospective implementation of that strategic plan involved great uncertainties. KHYKY's technical experts were concerned that IKA might find it difficult to develop or recruit the skills required to support local installations; they were also worried about data security. It was not clear that the telecommunications infrastructure of Greece at that time would be able to sustain the data transfers involved in such a decentralized system, but the project leaders were confident that the Greek telecommunications operator would provide for such services in the near future. More significantly, there was still a great deal of uncertainty regarding the funding for the purchase of the required equipment.

Indicative of the attitude that governed the development of the Revenue and Insurance system as a technology innovation project, and the computerization efforts in IKA at that time more generally, is the lack of efficiency benefit targets. The resulting computer service was predicted to be more expensive than the current manual procedures, although the new decentralized information system promised overall effectiveness by introducing new administrative procedures and financial benefits by curbing fraud. Moreover, not much thought was given to the way IKA would adjust work processes to accommodate the new methods. The whole effort concentrated on the technical tasks to set up the software and hardware technologies, disjoint from any organizational reform endeavours. The ICT project was almost entirely a matter of KHYKY's initiative. IKA, unwilling to get actively engaged in any radical innovation to improve its much criticized poor services and financial state, went along with the view that ICT is a force capable of achieving the improvements which previous reforms had failed to realize.

1993: Starting Again

In following up the story of IKA's information systems in 1993, my first impression was that time had stood still for a decade. The organization continued to rely on the same systems that were operational ten years ago, and the great bulk of payments of insurance contributions were still done by the use of stamps, in cash. Most applications continued to run inefficiently, the worst being the accounting system, which by that time was producing totally useless output. The latest annual balance had been produced in 1988, four years earlier. The Revenue system of 1983 continued to run on a 'pilot' status in the same two regional offices.

On closer study, the performance of some of those old systems had improved. The collection of electronic insurance data from employers' payroll systems was now running quite efficiently, maintaining reliable data on employee career histories. Similarly, the system that supported the collection of contributions and the calculation of insurance benefits for construction workers was considered adequately efficient, and had been expanded to cover the whole country.

IKA had now merged the operational and managerial computer service divisions into one division of Information Technology. The new division was still severely short of technical skills, but had the capacity to build small-scale applications. Overall IKA continued to rely almost completely on KHYKY, which was carrying on with the development of the Revenue and Insurance system that was planned in the previous decade, and had reached the stage of pilot implementation in yet another two regional offices. It had also initiated a portfolio of other applications to support the operations of local offices in handling insurance benefit services. In short, the IKA–KHYKY alliance had assimilated all past efforts of innovation into the dysfunctional bureaucratic network of activities, carrying along a service that everybody saw as inadequate and anachronistic.

At the headquarters of IKA, though, the story was taking a different turn. The Director-General had decided to make a new beginning in developing information systems by outsourcing. He had already contracted out the development of a new information systems strategy, the 'information systems master plan'. Funding for this latest effort was provided by the European Union, through a programme aimed at improving public sector efficiency. The contract for the information systems master plan was won by a consortium of local and multinational information systems consultants, who delivered a plan for an integrated system comprising all the functional areas of IKA. That master plan superseded the areas of the Revenue and Insurance system that KHYKY had been busy developing for the past seven years.

The information systems plan in 1993 was developed in a political milieu dominated by a discourse on 'modernization' that had lost the connotations of social reform of the early 1980s. Reform of public administration—a crucial aspect of modernization—was inspired by a widely perceived necessity for efficiency and effectiveness. The aims stated in the call for tender were: to improve the services provided by IKA, to secure the collection of the organization's revenue, and to improve the work quality of its personnel. The three aims were very similar to those stated ten years before and, as in earlier computerization exercises, emphasis was clearly put on the second of the declared objectives. This was interpreted by the subcontractors as aiming to provide the information means for central administration to gain overall control of the regional offices.

The call for tender stressed the transfer of technical skills from the private sector, but consultants were not encouraged to redesign IKA's processes by transferring private sector organizational models and expertise. One of the main criteria of eligibility at the bidding for IKA's project was that the subcontractors should have experience from developing information systems in other public sector organizations, either in Greece or abroad.

Without any specific direction of desirable organizational targets, the subcontractors designed a system architecture that took the Director-General and his technical advisers by surprise. It was suggested that IKA needed a centralized information system, judging that a distributed system would be 'quite an immature recommendation', because the regional and local offices did not have adequate management and technical expertise to undertake responsibility for technically sophisticated data management, and a design was proposed that required little information management capability at the local level.

IKA's management was dismayed with the suggestion. A centralized structure was considered politically inappropriate in an organization which has always believed in the merits of the autonomy of its branches, and for almost fifteen years had wished to build decentralized computer services. A solution to the accountability problem at the loss of local discretion in decision making was not acceptable in a context sensitive to the centralization/decentralization debate. IKA's administration was also concerned that the proposed configuration was technically less advanced than the strategy conceived by KHYKY in the 1980s. In essence, a centralized information system, even if promising to bring more overall efficiency, did not seem to break from the past centralized data processing operations that IKA was so keen to get rid of. After negotiations a compromise was agreed, with a configuration that would allow local offices ownership of data, but with a substantial amount of information processing done centrally, in order to give the headquarters overall control of the organization's core functions.

After the temporary clash between the Director-General and the subcontractors regarding the latter's interpretation of the strategic priorities and the decentralization values of the organization, the information systems master plan was accepted by the management of IKA with optimism that it would form the basis for eliminating chronic inefficiencies. It was a remarkable blueprint for technology-driven organizational reform. In order to work out proposals for the technical information system architecture, the consultants devised sequences of operations for four task domains: contributions, benefits, health, and financial management.[4] In essence they worked out scenarios of processes involving employers, insured members, local office staff, and central administration in order to determine how data would be collected, where it would be stored, where it would be processed, and what tasks would be automated. They specified database, hardware, and communications configurations and estimated costs and implementation implications. They acknowledged that the implementation of the information system plan implied organizational changes, and the master plan included a section which briefly estimated how radical a change each of the suggested models implied. Structure and work processes would be further elaborated as part of the implementation of the technical system.

IKA's staff had minimal involvement in the formulation of the new information systems plans, apparently leaving it up to the consultants to introduce new ideas and expertise that the organization was lacking. Specifically, IKA's technical staff did not ask to take part in the planning process. The manager of the IT department told me he believed that IKA's staff should not bias the consultants with their views about the organizations' requirements, allowing them to design work processes according to their knowledge of best management practice. Some of the staff I interviewed, though, were sceptical of the potential of the consultants' proposals to be materialized or make any impact, and their distance from the new initiative was more an act of non-cooperation rather than trust. The staff of KHYKY, who had been ignored by this initiative, were cynical about the chances of the master plan being implemented, and not particularly alarmed that they had been bypassed. Continuing with the implementation of the Revenue and Insurance system, most of KHYKY's staff, including its director, believed that their long experience in serving IKA made them indispensable, while the consultants, who were unfamiliar with the bureaucratic conditions of the organization, would sooner or later prove unable to deliver the promised technology-based changes.

1998: Implementing the Information Systems Master Plan

Five years later IKA was starting to press ahead with the implementation of the 1993 information systems master plan. With funding from the European Union, they were continuing the outsourcing policy to build the technical infrastructure as means for effective operations in all the domains of the organization's activities. Lacking the necessary capacity to manage the demanding systems development and implementation projects, they subcontracted the management of the development projects to another consortium of management consultants. This involved two areas of responsibility: project management, i.e. the supervision of the systems development and implementation tasks, and human resources management, i.e. the preparation of

---

[4] The financial management and budgeting were considered a matter of urgency and their development was given priority over the implementation of the other modules of the master plan. It was subsequently decided to purchase and customize a software package for financial management.

IKA's staff for the operation of the new system and the new work methods it would involve, as well as the restructuring of the division of information technology.

Consequently, IKA invited anew contractors to bid for the development of the information systems of its master plan. Also, they invited organizational consultants to design additional organizational changes, complementary to those planned to be carried out by the implementation of the integrated information systems of the master plan. This time, the call for tender explicitly sought consultants to emulate practices from the private sector and to use benchmarking techniques. The supervising management consultants set the new scene of modernization to be pursued by the organizational changes in a new language:

• Upgrade IKA's operations, by reconsidering and redesigning its processes, functions, and structures;

• Efficiency optimization through systems of measurement aimed at securing the achievement of set targets;

• Maximum utilization of IT aimed at reducing the time taken in the delivery of services, and the optimization of quality and productivity;

• Effective management of change, with emphasis on the development of human resources, suitably trained for the implementation of the new organization and for pursuing continuous improvement.

Overall, the redesign effort was intended to proceed with the identification of administrative and regulatory factors inhibiting efficient operations, and the design of relevant structural and legal interventions to overcome them.

Thus, more than five years after the creation of the 1993 information systems master plan for an effective information infrastructure, the modernization forces seemed to gain momentum. There was a new optimism in IKA's headquarters that the implementation projects would at last deliver new computer-based operations.

CLASHES OF RATIONALITY IN IKA'S HISTORY OF COMPUTERIZATION

From the story of IKA's attempts to develop computer-based information systems, one might get the impression that until recently information systems innovation suffered from technical incompetence and lack of financial resources. Specifically, until the start of the implementation of the information systems master plan, major information systems projects progressed very slowly to deliver grossly distorted versions of their initial specifications. Successive projects since the 1970s began with high expectations but, starved of funding and technical expertise, failed to develop a reliable new technology infrastructure in this information-intensive organization. Overall the computer-based systems often worsened the organization's dysfunctional bureaucratic operations, as in the case of substituting the manual employee contribution records with computerized insurance data files.

The latest efforts to develop efficiently functioning systems appeared promising. With professional expertise from the consultancy services market, and having secured financial resources from the EU, the conditions for the development of new technology systems were better than ever before. Moreover, information systems development incorporated efforts to introduce management practices and to redesign the organizational processes and was, therefore, more likely to make an organizational impact.

On closer consideration, though, IKA's chronic difficulties in making efficient use of IT have not been due to lack of technical capabilities and financial resources only. The ineffectiveness of computerization in IKA is symptomatic of an institutional setting that has been fundamentally at odds to the organizational objectives that information systems development projects were expected to support. The conditions that marginalized and distorted information systems in the past may still be present. Thus, without taking into account the institutional characteristics of the context of IKA, predictions on whether the projects under way at the time of the writing of this book are going to make an impact in the organization are precarious.

IKA is an institution of the Greek government sector. It enacts public administration regulations and is financed by the state budget, but, more importantly, its dysfunctionalities, its resistance to reform, and its chances of overcoming them are inexorably linked with the Greek political and economic affairs. Thus, central to a socio-technical analysis of the predicament of IKA's information systems innovation initiatives must be an understanding of the Greek public administration context.

Greece emulated the state institutions of the advanced industrialized nations of Western Europe. But in comparison to Western European countries the Greek administration became too large, with inflated high echelons, and delivers fewer and poorer quality services. As in many countries in Southern European and most developing regions[5] public administration in Greece is a 'mock bureaucracy' (Gouldner 1955), a caricature of the emulated Weberian formal ideal organizational model of the state. Attempts for public sector reform have been made throughout the history of modern Greece but dysfunctionalities have persisted, and indeed at times worsened.

There is remarkable consensus across the party political spectrum in Greece on the impediments hindering the effectiveness of the public sector. They include the following (Makrydimitris 1996):

• Direct political control of public administration, with the top positions of public organizations filled by government appointees. This practice has two problematic consequences. First, the people leading public services are often unsuitable for such a role, lacking both appropriate qualifications and experience. Second, short-termism and frequent discontinuity of policy implementation as government reshuffling leads to replacements of the heads of public organizations.

• Ad hoc recruitment procedures that allow the government of the day to use public sector employment as a mechanism of social policy and to favour their supporters. Civil service recruitment has at times served purposes of social

---

[5] Sotiropoulos (1996) presents a brief comparative discussion of politics and state bureaucracy in Southern European countries—which he calls 'semiperiphery' because of their economic and geopolitical link to the core capitalist countries of North Europe—and Latin American countries.

policy, taking, into account for example such criteria as the family situation, or the region of origin of candidates. Most frequently though it is a blatant abuse of power of the political party in office to perpetuate its dominance. Civil servants have traditionally been the main arm of political clienteles, and public administration became a massive employer of semi-educated people, reproducing a coherent and stable patronage network. Lack of technical criteria in recruitment leads to high numbers of poorly qualified employees.

• Inadequate civil service training. Preparatory education for civil servants is generally considered inadequate and the School for Public Administration, which was established in the 1980s to provide for in-service training, has not been able to fulfil its demanding role.

• Politically influenced promotions and in-service transfers. Career progression according to seniority, subject to political influence, and without performance criteria, creates disincentives for employees. Civil servants enjoy a number of privileges, such as a job for life, relatively generous pensions, and other social security benefits. However, being poorly paid, they are unmotivated in their bureaucratic jobs, and they tend to supplement their meagre salaries with multiple employment in the flourishing informal economy of the country. Lack of any technical description of the tasks involved in the service and required skills leads to two further problems: work positions occupied by unsuitable employees, and uneven employee distribution over the country, with inflated central administration in the capital and severely understaffed offices in some districts.

• Formalistic functioning according to the letter of regulation. The code of practice in the Greek civil service gives major emphasis to obedience to the orders of superiors, discourages initiative, and results in avoidance of responsibility.

These features reinforce each other, creating a stable condition that poses enormous inertia against efforts to remedy particular dysfunctionalities. For example, the recruitment, promotions, and transfers of civil servants create disincentives for training on technical skills, which are of dubious value in the customary ways of climbing up the hierarchy ladder through seniority and political patronage. On the other hand, lack of technical competencies perpetuates the formalistic regime that is inimical to reform interventions.

The dysfunctionalities highlighted by contemporary scholars are a persistent situation in Greek public life, despite the fact that what is known in Greece as the 'crisis of administration' has for long been considered a major factor retarding the socio-economic development of the country[6] and almost all governments of the post-dictatorship era[7] have been keen to see the situation improve. A stream of

[6] Makridimitris and Michalopoulos's collection of the most important parts of the reports sponsored by the OECD and the Greek government in the post-Second World War period shows how persistent the negative features of the public sector have been and how similar the diagnoses of all 'experts' of the problems plaguing the Greek public administration have remained for almost fifty years (Makrydimitris and Michalopoulos 2000).

[7] The Greek Post-second World War history has been marked by a seven-year military dictatorship, 1967–74.

research studies regarding the root of the problem of public administration in Greece point to the contradiction between its explicit mission for the delivery of modern state services and its latent role as an employer of political patronage (Mouzelis 1978, 1995; Tsoukalas 1986, 1987, 1989). Throughout the history of the modern Greek nation[8], the state has been the most important white-collar employer. Moreover, at crucial historical periods, such as the early years of the formation of the new nation in the nineteenth century and the restoration of civil order after the civil war of 1945–1949, employment in public administration was used as a reward to those who were considered to have contributed to the national struggle. It is estimated that in the late 1940s and the 1950s more than 20 per cent of the non-agricultural economically active population was dependent on employment in the state (Tsoukalas 1989).[9]

State organizations have always been used as a mechanism for the consolidation of the political power of governing parties.[10] In recent history, after the civil war, the state bureaucracy was first used by the right-wing party governments to keep the centre and left parties out of power. Then, during the colonels' dictatorship, 1967–1974, the public sector became an instrument of an oppressive state, grossly discriminating against and prosecuting its employees on the basis of their political beliefs and behaviour. Employment conditions, such as recruitment, promotion, and transfers, were offending fundamental democratic principles. But even after the democratization reforms of the 'socialist' governments of the 1980s, the public sector continued to be used clientelistically[11] and hardly improved in terms of fulfilling its declared mission.

Work conditions have always been harsh for civil servants. Until 1910 they did not have tenure, thus depending completely on the alternating governing parties. They were frequently subject to arbitrary firing, disciplinary charges, and confiscation of wages. Since 1910 tenure was withheld at a number of critical periods, such as during the civil war (12% of the civil servants were dismissed) and during the dictatorship of 1967 (Sotiropoulos 1996). In Greece, the three principles common to the civil service of most countries—loyalty to the constitution, obedience to the ministerial hierarchy, and neutrality regarding party politics—constituted the means by which civil service became subservient to political authority.

Under such conditions, the attitude of employees in the public sector is defensive, hiding an anarchic behaviour behind a façade of complex regulations (Mouzelis 1978). Service to the public is regulated by rules which civil servants are supposed to follow strictly, yet the rules are bent daily to offer preferential service to people civil servants would like to favour—or just to simplify unnecessarily awkward tasks. Indeed, most Greek citizens try, if possible, to approach public services through

---

[8] The modern Greek nation was established in 1927, after liberation from the Ottoman empire.

[9] The share of public sector employment in the overall active labour force has gradually, although not steadily, increased since the 1950s: in 1958 it was 7.2%, in 1962 it fell to approximately 5.7, in 1976 it rose to 8.5, and in 1988 it reached 10.1% (Sotiropoulos 1996).

[10] See, e.g. Sotiropoulos's analysis of the relation of politics and bureaucracy in Greece (Sotiropoulos 1996).

[11] Clientelism, in this context, is the exchange of voters' political support with job-related favours from a politician.

social networks rather than as anonymous citizens; they seek contacts with individual civil servants, who will deal with their case personally.

It is important to note that the features outlined above are dysfunctionalities only in relation to the declared mission of the public sector. In relation to its covert, tacit mission the whole system functions remarkably effectively. From this latter perspective it is not irrational that politicians, civil servants, and even the wider population of Greek citizens have been both unwilling to and incapable of sustaining modernizing reform interventions (Mouzelis 1978; Tsoukalas 1986).

INFORMATION SYSTEMS DEVELOPMENT AND THE IDEOLOGY OF MODERNIZATION

Although quintessentially 'national', IKA has always emulated international, and in particular European, institutions. The first computer applications in the 1950s were developed following the international trend of using the then new mainframe technology for processing large data sets according to bureaucratic regulations. Without challenging the bureaucratic status quo, the newcomer fitted quite easily into IKA. Moreover, the older people I interviewed in 1983 believed that the early applications had assisted IKA to cope with an increasing population of insured members. Nevertheless, with time the new actor adapted to the institutional setting of IKA, losing its most salient capabilities of accuracy, speed, and even reliable memory. The presence of IT in IKA became irreversible, but this was IT institutionalized in the Greek public administration, with little resemblance to the IT that was becoming widespread internationally in the 1970s. KHYKY proved a powerless link between the growing and ever-changing IT institution of the international arena and the computer services in IKA. Concerned more with sustaining its position as an obligatory point of passage for IT in IKA, it was itself adapted to the norms of public bureaucracy and became gradually cut off from the fast-changing professional IT expertise.

The assimilation of IT by IKA's bureaucracy was challenged in the late 1970s. Again this was a result of mimetic influences from social security institutions abroad, where the new generation of mini-computers started being used in a decentralized mode, introducing new operational possibilities. Computers could be used to substitute for insurance stamps—a technology that had been long abandoned in other European social security organizations. But that innovation has been an enormously complex process in IKA, closely associated with the political discourse on 'modernization'.[12] Generally speaking, in public administration modernization is understood to comprise legal and organizational change with the objective of getting rid of bureaucratic dysfunctionalities and achieving an effective delivery of services. However, there has been a significant change during the 1980s and the 1990s in the

---

[12] Modernization is not a new idea in Greek politics. Tensions between modernizing and a traditionalist culture are as old as the double role of state administration, dating back to the first political formations of the modern Greek state. The modernizing culture has always aspired to Western institutions and values, while the traditionalist culture has been introvert, emphasizing the distinctive features of local history and culture, and always suspicious of the West (Mouzelis 1995).

political meaning of 'modernization' in Greece, and in the views about modernization of the public sector in particular.

IT and Modernization in the 1980s

With the coming to power of the socialist party, PASOK, in the early 1980s, modernization of state administration was seen as an effort with two goals: to stop political control by the right-wing conservative party, and to transform it to an effective mechanism for social change and economic development.[13] As efforts and passion were placed in the former—in the context of democratization and the taming of the politically abusive state—improvement of organizational effectiveness not only was not seriously pursued, but it was further frustrated. Roughly speaking, these two goals concerned the two roles of the public bureaucracy: its hidden role as an agency of political patronage, and its explicit role as service provider to a modern society.

There seemed to be a consensus among politicians, intelligentsia, and the large majority of the public that supported the socialist government that pervasive and radical reform of all aspects of social life was needed (Tzannatos 1986). The dominant political rhetoric argued that incremental improvements would not be sufficient to address the economic crisis the country was facing, and at the same time shake the status quo in society. Reform should be implemented throughout the political, economic, and social institutions of the country, and it should be implemented fast.

In the summer of 1983, the civil servants I interviewed were watching the implications of the reformist plans announced by the still new socialist government with apprehension. But it was already clear that this was not the challenge that would rid the public sector of political manipulation. Fearing that a state administration staffed with conservative party supporters would sabotage its socialist reform agenda and erode its power, the first PASOK government infiltrated the state bureaucracy with masses of its own supporters at both the top and the lower grades of the hierarchy.[14] Rather than achieving democratization of the state, the PASOK government adopted the same clientelistic practices it had criticized.[15]

Under the first PASOK government public sector reform began with legislation that deflated the top of the administrative ladder, eliminating two of the highest

---

[13] In Sotiropoulos's words PASOK's goals were 'to take control of the state bureaucracy and to professionalize it'. He adds as a third goal the 'transformation of the state bureaucracy into a prosocialist organization with the use of the state as an employment agency' (Sotiropoulos 1996: 79–80), but this seems to me a consequence of the goal of taking control from the patronage of the conservatives, rather than a separate goal.

[14] Most political analysts of Greece tend to agree that the use of the state as an employment agency for the supporters of the ruling party in the 1980s was not an accident in the democratization battle, but a consequence of the populist nature of PASOK. Various authors have discussed the nature of populism in Greece, and more specifically of PASOK, the party that has been in government for most of the period since 1981, which maintained clientelistic relations with its supporters and used state administration as its predecessor governments did (see e.g. Lyrintzis 1987; Mouzelis 1995; Sotiropoulos 1996).

[15] Tsoukalas estimates that the total number of civil servants increased by 21% between 1981 and 1989, thus accounting at the latter date for over 36% of the total number of wage earners (Tsoukalas 1995).

echelons, which exerted mainly political influence with little functional content. Later, new legislation on recruitment introduced a social welfare character to social administration employment, privileging candidates of particular social characteristics, such as family situation, rather than professional qualifications. Further legislative measures throughout the two terms of office of the socialist government in the 1980s sought to develop a new career structure and salary scale, reducing the distance between junior and top civil servants (Makrydimitris 1996).

The reforms juggled two ideologies that were historically subjugated in public administration: democracy and 'rational' administration. But the *interessement* of the political authorities and citizens alike was directed to the former at that period, while the latter, marginalized, became irrelevant and meaningless. The battle for the reversal of the old regime of political domination took a form that further frustrated administrative rationalization: the new government restored the subjugated political voices by giving their supporters too—and the 'left' more generally—the 'privilege' of public employment.

Thus, in 1983, efforts to develop distributed information systems were taking place in a context where 'reform' was fought as an issue of democratic recruitment, promotions, transfers, and service. Although the modernization discourse referred also to the introduction of management-oriented decision making and operations, modern management was alien to IKA's traditional bureaucracy. 'Radical reform' hardly changed the organizing regime. Indicative of the incompatibility of the organizational environment within which the Revenue system was developed is that systems analysts had to consult the organization's legal experts for even the most minor operational changes their specifications would imply. With the formal administrative logic rigid and distorted and the managerial rationality at an embryonic stage, IT had no credible organizational role to play.

As the democratization process retained and enhanced the clientelistic tradition of the organization, the managerial reform was already in reverse in 1983. The reorganization project was terminated after the removal of its sponsor, the Director-General, whose initiatives were seen by both the Secretary of the State and the civil servants in IKA as 'going too far'. By 1984, the Revenue project reversed too, becoming an unrecognizable distortion of its specifications. The staff that championed it were removed to jobs of lesser importance and status.

The contested issue was not the introduction of computers. At no point at that time was there resistance to computerization as such. In fact, it was widely believed that computers could facilitate routine tasks, assist the organization to offer better services, and improve its reputation, and even lessen their routine bureaucratic burden. This is surprising given that by that time the overall experience of computerization in IKA was so poor, it had messed up basic functions of the organization, and had added the most tedious kind of work for the civil servants. Yet, everybody I interviewed at that time in IKA believed that it was not the computers to blame for the poor results, but the lack of capability in their organization and in KHYKY to make them work effectively. Many people were pessimistic about the future of the new project too, and their instinct was correct.

What was resisted increasingly loudly was the organizational rationalization that was at odds with the battle the most significant participants of IKA's network were engaged in. To the civil servants and that part of the Greek society that demanded a fair share of the public sector employment, a secure job in the politically patronized and hierarchically formalized administration sector was the basis of a whole lifestyle. It made much more sense than a work context that calculated the needs of 'the service'. The Greek economy offered few promising alternative white-collar jobs, and even those, as for example in the banking sector, had no tradition of management. Indeed, there were no strong isomorphic institutional influences for managerial innovation in the country. There were too few professionally qualified managers and even the private sector of the economy was run either bureaucratically or entrepreneurially.

In short, the development of computer-based information systems, vaguely associated with 'progress', were hardly resisted. Instead, resistance was oriented to the reforms that attempted to shake the established organizational structures and processes, and within which the technical innovation was to be deployed. The holding on to posts attained through investment in a regime of political favouritism made the efforts to instil the logic of management meaningless and ultimately dangerous. Information systems projects that were intended to convey this logic were, by the same token, irrelevant. For ministers, their secretaries, and trusted officials alike, computers were, at best, a luxury and investments in computer projects were among the first to be restrained in the public budget. With the fading of commitment to the reorganizational efforts that made efficient information systems meaningful, information systems development was starved of resources leaving only relics in its two 'pilot' sites.

Information Systems and Modernization in the 1990s

In the 1990s 'modernization' lost the socio-political meaning it had in the first years of the previous decade and conveyed a narrower economic view of required reform: the main concern now was that public bureaucracy was an obstacle for an economically liberal society. There were several changes in the broader socio-political context of the country that fuelled the perception of urgency regarding such a modernization of public administration organizations. Mouzelis (1995), for example, notes that changes of the established political culture were discernible at three levels: above, below, and within the national political arena.

Above refers to supra-national influences and interventions, such as those of the European Union. The ineffective public sector that cost too much and delivered little became particularly unacceptable in terms of the neo-liberal policies of the European Union that Greece is part of.

Below refers to behavioural attitudes and preferences of citizens. An increasing number of Greeks came to see a large public sector as parasitic and hindering the economy. Moreover, the significance of public sector employment lessened as, with the gradual development of the information sector of the economy, state administration ceased to be the main source of white-collar employment.

Within refers to changes in the politics of the country, where ideological divisions among parties on the basis of class representation and distinctions of socialist and capitalist orientation were weakening. Since the early 1990s the country's arena has been split between 'modernists' and 'populists' across political parties. Overall, the populist arguments have tended to perpetuate the legitimacy of the role of administration as a massive employer and social welfare service provider. The modernists have argued for the necessity to follow the dominant international socio-economic trend of a lean state operating under norms of efficiency similar to those of the market-driven sector.

Throughout the 1990s, the discourse on modernization was concerned with the elimination of the inefficiencies and 'irrationalities' of the economy and public administration and was much less, if at all, related with social change. It aimed to synchronize Greece with the Western partners of the European Union, and the neo-liberal global economy. Influenced by the international tendency to introduce management as a more effective mode of governance, the discourse of modernization in Greece promoted the view that a management-driven public sector was an imperative of modern life. Since the late 1980s a constant recommendation in all studies regarding the improvement of the public sector has been the need to employ the methods and techniques of 'public management' (Makrydimitris and Michalopoulos 2000).[16]

Thus, in the 1990s, information systems innovation in IKA was accompanied by favourable institutional changes. The driving problematization was not very different

---

[16] Public management refers to a form of public sector governance that uses principles and practices of the private sector. Since the early 1980s many industrialized countries—mainly Europe, New Zealand, and Australia—implemented extensive public sector reform programmes by adapting theoretical principles from economics, such as the separation of the institutions of demand from those of supply and the introduction of competition in supply, to restructure public enterprises as well as key functions of the state. A similar trend took place in the USA with the slogan 'reinventing government'. Many countries embarked on wide-ranging programmes of privatization of utilities, such as telecommunications, electricity, garbage collection, etc., which in the past were part of public sector on the belief that they were 'natural monopolies'. In addition, the body of administration for the delivery of many government services shrank through contracting out many 'peripheral' tasks. Most importantly, leadership by an elite body of civil servants in life-long roles providing for the continuity of administration of public sector organizations despite changes of government was challenged by the appointment of professional chief executive officers (CEOs) hired on a short-term basis with the expectation of producing specific results. For example, in the UK the running of hospitals and educational institutions are contracted to professional managers.

In general, public management is oriented towards the efficient achievement of specific objectives and adopts management techniques from the private sector, which is preoccupied, at least in principle, with the maximization of efficiency. There has been a great deal of debate about the variations of public management, and the extent to which the public sector can benefit from adopting the principles of governance and practices from the private sector, and what kind of variations. From an economic point of view, institutionalist economists argued that many of the tasks of this sector are more efficiently delivered through hierarchies rather than markets. From a socio-political point of view analyses of the role of the public sector emphasized the significance of roles of state organizations which are not in accordance with the market logic, such as maintaining law and order, and redistributing wealth for the relief of poverty. Thus, it has been argued, even if market-oriented governance serves well the objective of efficiency, it does not necessarily satisfy the objectives of these two major roles, legality and equity (Eliassen and Kooiman 1993; Lane 2000).

from earlier projects: ICT was considered to provide the means for improving IKA's efficiency and effectiveness as a service provider. But this time efficiency and effectiveness were prominent ideas in the country's political modernization discourse. And the translation of IKA's operations to improve efficiency and effectiveness started being reinforced by initiatives towards adopting the principles of public management. IKA's adoption of ICT was increasingly aligned with the management innovation forces.

Moreover, the institutional character of ICT was strengthened in Greece. Although slow in earlier decades, throughout the 1980s and 1990s the diffusion of computers continued at a fast pace and telecommunication infrastructure expanded and changed image from a social service to an instrument for economic growth. The Greek media threw its spotlight on the European 'information society', creating a feeling of urgency to adopt new technology in order not to miss the benefits of the always imminent information revolution. Also, an ICT services sector was developed by the transfer of international professional practice, closely linked with management consultancy services. Consequently, IKA in this period managed to secure the resources required for large-scale computerization and found ample technical expertise in the consultancy market.

Overall, several powerful new actors in IKA's network were enrolled in its modernization, most notably private management and IT consultants, EU money, and EU directives. The old actors—civil servants, politicians, politically appointed directors, old cumbersome computer technologies, KHYKY, employers, and citizens as insured members—continued to be there, many of them with undiminished power, but the preferences and expectations of many of them were to some extent changing. For example, employers and insured members became more impatient with the inefficiencies of IKA's services, as they compared them with organizations whose services were gradually improving through public management interventions, such as banks and telecommunications.

Therefore, while the information systems innovation that started in the 1990s was still under design at the beginning of the new century, a crucial question is whether the forces that promoted the objectives and practices of managerial reform were effective in de-institutionalizing the regime of truth that had blocked and nullified the effects of earlier information systems innovations.

There were many signs that the changes taking place may not have built up adequate momentum to overthrow the traditional regime of truth. The length of time it took to proceed from the conception of the information systems master plan in 1993 to the mobilization of the implementation project in 1998 is not encouraging. Public sector reforms were sporadic and ineffective throughout the 1990s (Makrydimitris 1999). Few public sector organizations had adopted performance-oriented management methods, had hired professional CEOs, had practised extensive subcontracting, or had been faced with competition. Privatization was limited in comparison to other European countries that have adopted public management. The size of public bureaucracies continued to be huge. Socio-economic change in the broader Greek context may have been too slow to provide desirable alternative lifestyles to those of civil service employment.[17]

In the political arena, the victory of the 'modernists' over the 'populists' was a narrow one, as the national elections of 2000 showed. The vision of a liberal economy and society in tune with the perception of pressing globalization has not displaced the deeply rooted local rationality that still sustains the public sector as an instrument of party-political power and a particular style of life that values secure life-long employment in the state.

Thus, while it seemed a reasonable prediction that at the turn of the century IKA, with the mobilization of expertise from the private sector, would complete the implementation of new technology-based information systems, it remained uncertain whether such an innovation would make a difference to the efficiency and effectiveness of IKA's services. The possibility for a technically successful system with no significant organizational impact was still present.

CONCLUDING REMARKS

Over a history of thirty years, the development and use of computer applications in IKA did not contribute to the efficiency, productivity, effectiveness, and innovation of its services; computer-based information systems adapted to existing dysfunctional bureaucratic functioning, adding more dysfunctionalities.

Identification of obstacles such as lack of resources, weak leadership, and inadequate management of change refers only to factors on the thin surface of the processes that prevented the expected benefits of ICT innovation. Action with respect to these factors, for example recruiting technical skills, appointing competent project leaders, and allocating adequate funds were indeed impossible and meaningless in IKA until the 1990s. The discussion of the social aspects of the Greek state administration in this chapter traced the socio-political processes that gave rise to these factors.

Information systems innovation was always thought to be an issue of administrative functionality, that is, an issue of speeding up operations, or reforming operations to make them more efficient and more reliable. It was understood that this required more than a technology construction and implementation project effort, and information systems projects have been coupled with the design of operations and change management.

---

[17] Tsoukalas (1995) offers an interesting analysis of the reluctance of Greeks to embrace and support the modernization goal as an incongruence between the instrumental rationality in individual economic behaviour and the collective instrumental rationality of the modern state. He identifies the historical reasons for the 'prevailing behavioural patterns of the majority of Greek *homines economici*, who have never functioned as *homines civili*', in other words of Greeks doing well for themselves but badly for Greece. He is less convincing in his attempt to identify the pressures that may lead Greeks to adopt behaviour more conducive to the collective instrumental rationality of economic modernization.

But, information systems innovation in IKA proved to be much more than a change of administrative functions or processes. It was implicated in the struggle for the change of IKA's organizing regime, which is inseparable from the change of the social regime of the whole country. The official reliance on the alliance of ICT and management as the institutions of desirable change foundered upon subjugated knowledges of civil servants and the Greek citizens more widely.

In the 1980s, the reluctant organizational modernization attempts did not form a durable translation of IKA's organizing rationality towards which ICT could contribute. The innovation efforts of the 1990s, despite a clearer managerial orientation, were still of uncertain credibility and the traditional organizing regime persisted.

Overall, there has been a negative interdependence between information systems innovation and the wider socio-political reform processes. The anti-modernization forces created obstacles for the technical information systems intervention, distorted their outcome, and assimilated the technology-based information processing tools in the bureaucratic labyrinth. Inability to develop a functioning information systems infrastructure to support the declared mission of the organization as a social service provider let the traditional bureaucratic regime and its covert mission perpetuate.

References

Eliassen, K., and Kooiman, J. (eds.) (1993). *Managing Public Organizations: Lessons from Contemporary European Experience*. London: Sage.

Gouldner, A. W. (1955). *Patterns of Industrial Bureaucracy*. London: Routledge & Kegan Paul.

Lane, J. E. (2000). *The Public Sector: Concepts, Models and Approaches*. London: Sage.

Lyrintzis, C. (1987). 'The Power of Populism: The Greek Case'. *European Journal of Political Research*, 15(6): 667–86.

Makrydimitris, A. (1996). *Administration in Crisis: Texts on Administration and Society*. Athens: Nea Synora (in Greek).

——(1999). *The "Great Patient": The Reform and the Modernization of Public Administration*. Athens: Papazese Publications (in Greek).

——and Michalopoulos, N. (eds.) (2000). *Reports of Experts on Public Administration 1950–1998*. Athens: Papazese Publications (in Greek).

Mouzelis, N. (1978). *Modern Greece: Facets of Underdevelopment*. Chichester: MacMillan.

——(1995). 'Greece in the Twenty-First Century: Institutions and Political Culture', in D. Constas and G. Stavrou (eds.), *Greece Prepares for the Twenty First Century*. Washington, DC: Johns Hopkins University Press and Woodrow Wilson Center Press.

Sotiropoulos, D. A. (1996). *Populism and Bureaucracy: The Case of Greece under PASOK, 1981–1989*. Notre Dame, Ind.: University of Notre Dame Press.

Tsoukalas, C. (1986). 'Radical Reformism in a 'Pre-welfare' Society: The Antinomies of Democratic Socialism in Greece', in Z. Tzannatos (ed.), *Socialism in Greece*. Aldershot: Gower, 24–34.

——(1987). *State, Society, Employment in Post-War Greece*. Athens: Themelio.

Tsoukalas, C. (1989). *Social Development and State: The Composition of Public Space in Greece*. Athens: Themelio.

——(1995). 'Free Riders in Wonderland: Or of Greeks in Greece', in D. Constas and T. G. Stavrou (ed.), *Greece Prepares for the Twenty-First Century*. Baltimore: John Hopkins University Press, 191–219.

Tzannatos, Z. (ed.) (1986). *Socialism in Greece*. Aldershot: Gower.

7

An Experiment of Flexible Specialization in Cyprus

This chapter traces the story of an effort of industrial restructuring in the economy of the island of Cyprus, and examines the limited role attributed to ICT in that reorganizational process. The 'Cyprus Industrial Strategy'(Murray et al. 1987; Murray 1992) is a case of emulation of the industrial model of flexible specialization. Flexible specialization attracted a great deal of attention since the early 1980s as a way of organizing production suitable for the changing market context of advanced industrial societies and promising for the developing economies.

When I started studying this case in the early 1990s, I expected it to demonstrate the interaction between organizational development and information systems innovation. The flexible specialization model contains many of the organizational characteristics which in the information systems literature are associated with the kind of context where ICT acquires a strategic role. It involves extensive and complex inter-organizational relations, it acknowledges technology as a major factor for the sustenance of a competitive regional socio-economic network, it encourages the creation of rich data resources while it recognizes the significance of informal information communication based on a culture of trust. The initial aim in following the implementation of the flexible specialization model in Cyprus was to study the ramifications of ICT innovation in its enabling role in a case of extensive reorganization.

However with the first collected data in 1993 it was apparent that, in this case, there were no significant new information systems either under development or being planned. There were of course computers and computer-controlled machines in operation in most of the enterprises involved in the industrial restructuring initiative. But few of the people interviewed expressed appreciation of the strategic potential of ICT. They were rather surprised at our interest in their use of computers.

That ICT was used modestly in the organizations taking part in the industrial restructuring of the island and was not perceived as important by the owners/managers of the manufacturing firms was at odds with the influential dictum of information systems research and practice in the early 1990s that the enabling role of IT becomes most prevalent and significant in cases of extensive organizational change.[1] It was

---

[1] See e.g. Earl 1987. In the early 1990s seminal publications, such as Hammer (1990) and Scott Morton (1991), associated IT innovation with organizational change and had an immediate impact on business and information systems management alike. They reinforced the message that IT enables the achievement of 'strategic' gains that was spread during the 1980s and gave it a new twist: the potential benefits of IT are released by reorganizing business organizations.

particularly paradoxical that the implementation of one of the most promising socio-economic theories of industrial organization of the 1980s, which 'focused on the way in which the pursuit of economic growth through technological change affected economic organizations generally and the organization of work in particular'(Piore 1993: 323) involved such limited efforts for information systems innovation. Thus, our research began with the study of flexible specialization as a theoretical model and as a realized practice in the region of Emilia Romagna in Italy. In Cyprus we traced the history of the adoption of the flexible specialization strategy, and started monitoring the government initiatives to develop suitable conditions for its implementation, and the organizational changes taking place in furniture manufacturing, one of the sectors that adopted the restructuring recommendations.

In the second half of the 1990s it was clear that the initiatives taken under the banner of flexible specialization had lost momentum without leading to the intended boosting of the productivity and competitiveness of manufacturing in the island. Few of the reorganization changes were long-lasting and made an impact. Therefore, the lack of information systems innovation had to be examined in relation to the failed reform. The question I examine in this chapter is why throughout the 1990s the majority of manufacturing enterprises of the island resisted and distorted a major industrial rationalization intervention and remained indifferent to information systems innovation.

In the following sections I present the economic background of the island, the initial launching of the flexible specialization emulation initiative, the subsequent faltering organizational development, and the eventual decline of the new structures of the furniture manufacturing sector. Without major ICT innovation in this case the descriptions of information systems are thin. The main focus is on the socio-organizational milieu of the industrial restructuring attempt—or experiment—that was unconducive to ICT innovation, first looking through the lenses of the economic theory that inspired and guided it, and then through the analytical approach pursued in this book.

ECONOMIC BACKGROUND

The economy of the Greek Cypriot state had an impressive growth in the first twelve years after the Turkish invasion and the split of the island in 1974. Between 1975 and 1985 the country's real GDP grew by 121 per cent, with manufacturing contributing 18 per cent of the overall growth (Murray et al. 1987). Through highly protective policies, including import quotas and high tariffs, as well as a series of publicly funded reconstruction programmes—such as emergency housing for refugees, basic infrastructure, and subsidies for the development of tourism—the government was instrumental in developing a labour-intensive manufacturing sector. As a result, the consumer boom of the country's economic reconstruction was met largely by domestic production. In addition, a number of manufacturing industries, e.g. for clothing and shoes, expanded through exports, mainly to countries of the Middle East.

In the early 1980s the reconstruction boom subsided and the Cypriot exporters to the Arab countries faced growing competition from South-East Asia. Nevertheless, the development of tourism and the still emerging and growing demand in the Middle East markets continued to sustain the key manufacturing industries that flourished in the 1970s. Government protection continued, but plans to form a customs union with the European Community posed the first substantial pressure for opening the economy. By 1986 it was clear that the growth in manufacturing was falling. With fierce local competition, individual manufacturing firms were under-cutting each other's export opportunities. As internal demand was saturated, the government was held by the industrialists responsible for failing to reorient the economy towards export markets and facilitate the promotion of Cypriot products and services abroad.

In 1987 Cyprus joined the European Community customs union. With the prospect of dismantling its protective economic regime, the government sought the services of UNIDO and UNDP to develop an effective industrial strategy. A team of economists and sector specialists centred at the Institute of Development studies at the University of Sussex in the United Kingdom conducted a study and found that the country's labour-intensive industry was geared towards mass production, a strat-egy, they judged, that would not be competitive in international markets The secluded economy of the island was small and characterized by a large number of small firms. Of the 6,616 manufacturing firms in the country in 1985, 6,184 had less than 20 employees, and only 56 companies employed more than 100 people (Murray et al. 1987). The majority of business firms were family-owned and built on a craft tradition. It was estimated that about 13 per cent of total wages and salaries were paid to working proprietors, their partners, and family members.

Furniture Manufacturing

The manufacturing of wooden furniture was highlighted in the UNDP/UNIDO study as one of the five sectors that was under pressure and in need of reform. In the mid-1980s furniture manufacturing firms imported 61 per cent of their raw materials and exported just 2 per cent of their production. Despite high tariffs (70%–80%) on imported furniture, the import of furniture increased throughout the 1980s and a third of furniture consumption was imported in the mid-1980s. There was low production efficiency, lack of product specialization, and lack of management. At the root of the problem was the small size of the production firms. Of the 774 furniture-making firms, 10 had 50–99 employees, 47 had 10–49 employees, and 717 less than 10 employees, which gives an average of 3.9 employees per firm (Murray et al. 1987). In other words most firms were artisan 'workshops', each of which produced a large range of products to satisfy a varied customer demand.

The small size of firms has several direct consequences on their operations. First and foremost there was lack of professional management. The consultants noted: 'There is lack of managerial specialisation, with the manager (usually the proprietor and family) simultaneously trying to cover marketing, production control, accounting, design, labour relations, product development and materials purchasing' (ibid. 123). Second, there was poor utilization of production technology. Many firms had invested in electro-mechanical equipment capable of large batch production which were used at a fraction of their capacity, staying idle much of the time, while no firm could afford to buy electronically controlled machines. Third, there was little investment in design and development of new products; most firms imitated foreign designs. Moreover, the imitation involved only the drawings without much attention to materials used, method of production, or proportion in sizes, with the result of costly, poor quality products that could not stand international competition.

FLEXIBLE SPECIALIZATION

Flexible specialization is one of the best known models for the organization of production proposed in the 1980s as an alternative to the Fordist method of mass production, and considered suitable to provide for the changing pattern of consumer demand observed at that time. Thus, flexible specialization is usually described in juxtaposition to Fordism.

Fordism is characterized by hierarchically managed organizations, using specialized technologies to produce efficiently for mass markets. It assumes a virtuous circle of production and consumption: productivity increases based on economies of scale lead to rising wages which fuel rising mass demand, then increased profits due to increased demand for consumer goods, and consequently increased investment in capital goods increasing further productivity growth. In terms of organization, Fordism makes use of scientific management, which implies functional specialization, work specification, and centralized decision making separated from the performance of the work tasks.

As mentioned in Chapter 3, Fordism has been the dominant model for the organization of production in all advanced Western economies since the turn of the twentieth century. It has been reinforced with government economic policies that aimed to sustain and stabilize mass demand, and institutionalized with such taken-for-granted ideals as life employment. Craft production, using skilled workers to produce a variety of customized products had not disappeared, but was marginalized as an inefficient and risky way of organizing production.

However, fears for the stagnation of the world economy in the 1970s triggered growing uncertainty of mass demand and raised questions about the merits of Fordism. It was in this context that flexible specialization, which reinstates craft production to supply for diverse consumer tastes, was suggested as a viable industrial strategy (Piore and Sabel 1984; Piore 1993).

But the craft-based business units suitable for the contemporary volatile markets are not just independent small producers. Flexible specialization consists of networks of task-specialist organizations, or organization units, equipped with skilled labour and flexible technologies. It is suggested that such a network is capable of producing changing volumes of quality goods for volatile markets without loss of productivity resulting from unutilized workforce or machinery. Thus, in general, flexible specialization is associated with the following features: production driven by economies of scope rather than economies of scale; flexible machinery; niche markets; information-intensive production inputs; task integration and flexibility; network and informal, rather than hierarchical, management structures; close customer and supplier linkage; competition by innovation, rather than by capacity.[2]

The principles of flexible specialization have been demonstrated with several examples in various countries. Invariably such cases exhibit close cooperation among geographically concentrated firms, involving usually small or medium-size enterprises. Significant factors for the success of flexible specialization are considered to be a high degree of trust between employees and skilled workers, the provision of collective services through self-help, and often government-mediated organizations (Piore and Sabel 1984; Pyke, Becattini, and Sengenberger. 1990; Cooke and Morgan 1994).[3]

Flexible specialization has influenced policy-making initiatives throughout the 1980s. Emphasis on the clustering of organizations and inter-firm relations provided a new perspective for industries dominated by large numbers of small producer firms, which have been generally considered problematic in the context of global competition.[4]

Flexible Specialization in Emilia Romagna

In the literature, and for most of the policy interventions that follow the flexible specialization ideas, the industrial district of Emilia Romagna in Italy acquired an 'ideal model' status.[5] The area of Emilia Romagna, extending from the Apennines to the Adriatic has fifty industrial districts, each with a population of less than 100,000, and

---

[2] It is interesting to note that flexible specialization is not an economistic perception of industrial activity. By considering contextual features such as the cultural aspects in the behaviour of the economic actors and the role of government institutions, it recognizes the social embeddedness of economic activities.

[3] It is debatable to what extent the mode of production of flexible specialization presents a serious challenge to the dominance of the Fordist system. A brief review of the debate regarding network organizational structures and multinational corporation within the current trends of economic globalization is included in Chap. 4. More specifically, critics of flexible specialization have pointed out that it is unlikely that the craft-based industrial paradigm will acquire substantial significance within the world economy, and that powerful economic actors, such as multinationals, will continue to dominate markets through their grip over finance, market outlets, advertising, and so on (Amin 1994; Cooke and Morgan 1994).

[4] Although the model of industrial clustering of flexible specialization was developed on the basis of the study of European industrial districts, it has been particularly relevant for developing countries, which tend to have large numbers of small firms. Small firm industries are often seen as comprising an 'informal economy', unsuitable to serve developmental goals through formal economic policy. Nadvi and Schmitz (1994) reviewed several cases of industrial districts in developing countries in terms of their organizational form, the social context, links with the state, and their developmental effects. Although optimistic that the principles of organizational clustering of flexible specialization as identified through the European experience provide a promising model for developing countries, they avoided drawing conclusions about its developmental potential. Instead they argued for the need for further research to understand the validity of the model in different contexts and its possible variations.

[5] Numerous descriptions and discussions of this case have been published. From those in English, see, e.g. Brusco 1982, 1990; Pyke, Becattini, and Sengenberger 1990; Becattini 1991; Cooke and Morgan 1994. This section is based partly on published descriptions and partly on research reported in Chrysohos (1999).

with a predominance of small firms specializing in a particular sector. For example, in the late 1980s in Montegranaro there was a concentration of footwear-producing firms of an average size of 17 employees, and in Poggibonsi there was a concentration of small furniture producers with an average of 5.8 employees.

The firms in each district had formed networks of industry associations, cooperative consortia, and joint facilities. The consortia played a significant management role for their constituent firms, coordinating their production and serving them with access to external information sources, export promotion programmes, market research, and staff training. This allowed the small firms to further specialize, some producing particular parts, others assembling, while they were able to share out production to others if demand exceeded capacity. Moreover, through the consortia the artisans of the small firms had access to complex and expensive technologies such as art design machinery, and CAD.

The small firms participating in the consortia continued to be managed internally in a rather informal manner, but they had to move towards formalization of particular functions, such as sales and marketing, which were mediated by the services of the consortia.

Thus, three different types of organization were involved in the Italian model of flexible specialization:

1. Small producer firms, typically family-owned and largely informally managed.

2. Consortia, organized as federations of geographically concentrated producer firms, often belonging in the same industry. Consortia may provide a variety of services to their members, such as promotion of exports, collective acquisition of materials, financial support. They tended to have a simple organizational structure, managed by an executive committee of their shareholder members, and employing a small team of clerical staff. Their activities were often carried out through subcontracting. For example, the consortium Centro Unitario Forme comprised eighty producers of textiles and clothing, tiles and ceramics, and agricultural machinery based in the district of Modena. It employed specialized companies on a contract basis to provide marketing and export, purchase of materials, and finance and investment services.

3. Support agencies, involving government authorities, entrepreneurial associations, financial organizations, as well as the small businesses themselves. Central role was played by the regional development agency ERVET (Ente Regionale per la Valorizzazione Economica del Territorio), which involved as shareholders a wide spectrum of public and private organizations. It provided its services either directly through its network of support centres, or through independent regional organizations, such as university research centres. Some of these agencies focused on the needs of specific sectors—such as CITER, the information centre for the textile producers of the district of Carpi—others provided cross-sectoral functional services—such as ASTER, the centre for technological development of Emilia Romagna.

Analysts of the development of flexible specialization in Third Italy tend to emphasize the significance of the socio-cultural environment that fostered such collaborative industrial relationships that amount to collective entrepreneurship. A Catholic tradition combined with the prevalence of collectivist socialist ideology formed a socio-economic fabric that mixes traditional values and modern materialist aspirations. Such a culture facilitated the development of collaboration without the need of direct government intervention.

The organizational complexity of the industrial network of flexible specialization in Emilia Romagna required rich information flows, both formal and informal. While management information requirements of the specialized small and medium enterprise (SME) producer firms were modest, the consortia and the network of support organizations have had more complex information needs as they deliver multiple services to their diverse customers. Moreover, a data infrastructure was developed. The centre of technological development ASTER provided on-line search facilities to about 4,000 firms and consortia through connections with over 1,000 international information services. It disseminated data related to location, financial performance, products and activities of 55,000 manufacturing firms of the region. Another system maintained information on research and technology transfer facilities in the region, and allowed interested firms to identify partners for collaborative projects.

Moreover ASTER developed and conducted test studies for new technologies, such as the development of intranet for exchange of information among SMEs, and the socio-economic issues of EDI use by the networks of the region. It played a facilitator's role as an information systems centre, providing services of requirements analysis for innovative IT uses, such as teleworking, and technical assistance for industrial automation, and new process technologies. In short, ASTER acted as an information broker both to the industrial actors of the region, and to their potential customers.

EMULATION OF FLEXIBLE SPECIALIZATION IN CYPRUS

It is not difficult to see why the UNDP/UNIDO sponsored study that considered the Cypriot manufacturing sector in 1987 concluded that flexible specialization was a suitable model for its survival in the prospect of increasing competition. The small size of the population of the island, the structure of the manufacturing industry, and the social conditions they observed made it a promising case for the principles of flexible specialization. In particular, the consultants emphasized the family culture, the strong tradition of education, the national cohesion in response to the Turkish threat, the collectivist tendencies manifested in the popular support enjoyed by the communist and socialist parties, and the social pact between labour and employers. Also, they highlighted the entrepreneurial attitude of the industrialists, their interest in quality, design-led production, and their resistance to takeover offers by foreign companies (Murray 1992).

The consultants drew up the 'Cyprus Industrial Strategy' (Murray et al. 1987), a document containing the rationale for pursuing reforms according to the flexible specialization principles, and recommendations to that effect.[6] Taking the industrial development experience of the region of Emilia Romagna as a model, they recommended a set of activities at three levels: the small producer firms, industrial sectors, and the national economy as a whole (Murray et al. 1987).

Reforms in the individual manufacturing firms involved the following: multi-skilling of employees to create a flexible workforce, capable of working with a range of machines; small production batches, reducing buffer stocks in the production process; closer integration of design, production, and marketing; strategic planning; development of information systems to support production and management. The most substantial structural recommendation concerned the formation of cooperative entities of small firms in a number of industrial sectors. It was suggested that cooperative networking is a suitable organizational form for functions such as finance, production, marketing, research, and training that individual firms were too small to carry out effectively. Specifically, the UNDP/UNIDO team suggested that the small manufacturing companies would benefit from the formation of associations to carry out collective services for themselves, the development of funds for long-term strategic investment; a centre for the development of industrial design, and the creation of technology support centres.

Further developments regarding finance, design, training, and human resources were suggested at the national level. The strategy required an industrial banking system capable of taking a long-term development view. The Cypriot Development Bank was advised to play a central role in promoting industrial restructuring by acting as a front-line consultancy agency and providing firms with support to reorient their activities along the flexible specialization lines. In order to foster an innovative attitude for the design of new products and develop indigenous creativity for competing in fashion-sensitive sectors, such as clothing, footwear, and furniture, it was recommended that the Ministry of Education should mediate to strengthen education in design in secondary schools, offer scholarships for studying design abroad, and establish a link between a college of art and design and a museum of contemporary art. It was also recommended that the country's existing industrial training authority—sponsored by employers and supported by trade unions—should reorient its training programmes from promoting a division of labour and responsibilities characteristic of mass production to the development of the sophisticated multiple skills required by flexible specialization. Moreover, it was stressed that new labour policies were needed to transform the regime governing conditions of employment. Also, the UNDP/UNIDO study, reflecting the significance attributed to geographic concentration in flexible specialization, advised local and government authorities to plan for district industrial estates, which would provide common facilities and services to specific industries.

The social and cultural characteristics in Cyprus were expected to play a significant role in the success of these structural reforms. The island's craft tradition, high

---

[6] The government endorsed the report and the manufacturing industrialists accepted it as a promising new strategy.

percentage of educated population, strong presence of trade unions which had historically trusted the government and supported its policies, and strong family and local ties were considered promising factors for the success of a flexible specialization strategy. However, such a strategy required a substantial change in the relationship between industrialists and government. In the proposed model, the government had a significant facilitating role, particularly for setting up the national level institutions outlined above, but it had to abolish its protectionist policies. Reciprocally, business owners and their workforce were required to take initiatives in following the recommendations. In essence, the strategy sought to reorient the existing partnership between government and industry towards the abolition of protectionist practices, and a new facilitatory role for the government, attuned to a free market economic environment. The regime that nurtured the island's manufacturing with creation of demand in the domestic market, subsidies, and protection from imports was to be discontinued. The government was asked to let companies compete on their own strength. Its 'care' should be to assist them to build competitive strength: in the words of a government official, 'to help them to learn how to swim, rather than to supply them with life jackets'.

THE IMPLEMENTATION OF REFORMS IN THE FURNITURE SECTOR

The Cyprus Industrial Strategy required action for the development of the three types of organization identified in the Italian case of flexible specialization. Individual firms ought to reconsider their competitive position in the local and international market, and adjust their production and business operations to become part of local industrial networks. New cooperative organizational entities, consortia, had to be created for the first time, complementing the functions and rationalizing the performance of their individual firm members. Specialized service providers facilitating and promoting the tasks of both the producer firms and their consortia had to be established from scratch. A number of such initiatives were taken with varying degrees of success.[7]

In the furniture sector, the most visible area of activity was the formation of consortia. Much less was done for the development of service providers, while rather minor changes took place within the small firms as a result of the strategy. Many firms grew in size since the industrial restructuring experiment began in the early 1990s, but they continued to face increasingly more serious competitiveness problems in the local market. More significantly, they did not reorient their business towards export markets.

[7] The UNDP/UNIDO report triggered sporadic action in various sectors, but the government delayed the implementation of its recommendations for many years. A study conducted by the Department of Commerce and Industry on the problems of the manufacturing sector in 1993 showed that little had been done and the problems in the five key industries had worsened. The study echoed the same concerns identified six years ago and suggested the same approach to reform the industries and make them viable. Several of the initially recommended measures were subsequently taken, but some people I interviewed in the industry as well as in government believed that the slow government response was one of the factors that contributed to the poor results of the attempted reform.

Acquisition of new technology was a significant factor of motivation for the development of the new organizational scheme. In the sector of furniture, as well as in clothing and aluminium products, there were clear benefits to be gained through common investment in the latest production technologies, such as wood cutting and shaping, fashion design and tailoring, aluminium colouring. Less interest was shown in utilizing IT for management purposes. The following section traces the organizational changes and information systems development efforts that accompanied the formation of industrial networks in furniture manufacturing.

The Formation of SME Consortia

AtoZ

The first consortium created in the furniture manufacturing sector with the support of the Cyprus Development Bank was 'AtoZ'. It was founded as early as 1987 by twelve furniture-making firms based in Limassol. These firms varied in size from fifteen to forty employees. The purpose of the consortium was to promote common marketing for the twelve shareholder manufacturers. It built its management office in the industrial district of its SME members, and began operations by creating showrooms in all major cities in the island. The AtoZ consortium had an executive committee of five shareholders elected by the twelve shareholder members and an appointed executive director. It employed also a design manager, a marketing and sales manager, and a small number of clerical and support staff.

Murray (1992), one of the consultants involved in drafting the 'Cyprus Industrial Strategy' reported enthusiastically on activities of AtoZ in the early 1990s and the benefits it brought to its members. The firms that formed the consortium agreed to specialize their products—e.g. in kitchen furniture or children's furniture—thus having efficiency of production benefits. Murray reports that the unit costs in the specialized furniture production fell by 20–25 per cent. As joint retailing required careful costing, the consortium formed a costing subcommittee to check costing, materials, and production methods of member companies and advise on ways for cost cutting. Moreover, Murray presented indicative evidence of successful sales promotion and successful exporting in 1989 to the Soviet Union and Saudi Arabia.

At the beginning of its operations AtoZ had no formal information system for communication with its member firms. When an order was placed by a customer, a standard form was filled in and the details were communicated to the specialized producer, mainly by telephone. A number of problems were experienced, such as incomplete information and misunderstandings in communicating order details, which in turn caused delays in meeting delivery dates.

To overcome such problems the executive committee of the consortium decided to use computers for the processing of orders. Technically and operationally the computer-based information system developed for this task was relatively simple. A database was installed at the main office of the consortium, order details were transferred from the showrooms to the main office, entered in the database and consequently distributed to the producers. The system produced information lists on orders, delivery dates, customers, and selling prices; later it started to be used to implement a penalty system for late deliveries. It was generally thought that this system improved efficiency and reduced the number of errors.

Encouraged by this positive experience, the executive director of the consortium developed plans for two further technology projects: a network to connect the showrooms with the consortium headquarters, and a design system through which the furniture producers would be able to propose models and then display them at the showrooms of the consortium to solicit customer responses. But the shareholder manufacturing firms were not keen to support these ideas and they were not implemented.

Line-11

Another consortium, Line-11, comprising eleven small furniture manufacturers in the industrial district of Larnaca was established in 1991. It had the same purpose as AtoZ, to market the products of its shareholder members under a common trademark, and its operations and management were very similar to those of AtoZ. Indeed its first executive director was a former director of AtoZ. Line-11 did not develop any computer-based information systems, and relied largely on informal communications for the dispatching of customer order details. Telephone and fax were seen as perfectly adequate by its shareholders.

MFC

Substantially different from AtoZ and Line-11, MFC was established in 1994 with the aim of efficiently pursuing one particular specialized process of furniture making, panelling cutting, through utilization of computer-controlled production machinery. MFC involved four furniture manufacturers of approximately the same size, forty to fifty employees. The initial idea was to equip the consortium by pooling together existing machines and technical staff of its members. However, a number of problems emerged when the implementation of such a strategy was thought out. Existing machines were found to be obsolete, with limited capacity and capability, and incompatible with each other. Moreover, it was not easy to release employees from other duties in their firms and transfer them to the new organization. It was decided to set up MFC by purchasing new computer-controlled production machines, and by transferring only a few employees from the shareholder firms.

By 1996, the work of panelling cutting at MFC was carried out by nine workers trained to operate the computer-controlled machines, and supervised by a manager with the support of a secretary. Strategic management was the responsibility of a board committee comprising the owners/managers of the member firms and the MFC manager. Initially, the goal set was to achieve 60 per cent utilization of the capacity of the computer-controlled machines' optimal capacity within three years of operation. That target was met within the first six months, covering all the production needs of the four members of the consortium and allowing surplus capacity that could be used by taking orders from non-member firms.

Despite the success in achieving the initial goal of the consortium, there were significant inefficiencies in the use of the computer-controlled production technology.

Details on panelling cutting were received on manual forms, which included designs of the ordered products. Such order details were first entered into a system that ran an optimization algorithm and calculated the size of the panels to be used, thus minimizing waste of raw materials. Subsequently, and according to the production schedule, the output of the optimization application was retyped as entry into the production machines. As the production process involved several steps and different machines, data and software commands were reloaded at each step. Overall, the repetition of the same data entry was prone to errors, caused frequent delays, and reduced the 'optimization' benefits.

Yet, the managers of the SME members of this consortium interviewed in 1996 were not keen to upgrade its technology and integrate the operations of the computer running the optimization algorithm and the production machines. They were pleased with the savings they achieved through MFC, and were not interested in increasing its efficiency. They recognized the potential of MFC to become a profitable specialized company for panelling cutting, but this was seen as too marginal for their business interests to contribute funds for the required investment.

Support Service Providers

Several sector-wide and national service organizations were gradually developed in the 1990s, such as a design centre for the clothing industry, and training organizations for the dissemination of appropriate skills and finance opportunities for all industrial sectors. One such intermediary service provider of particular relevance to this case study is the Institute of Technology (IOT). It was established in 1992 as an agency of the Department of Commerce and Industry with the mandate to support the technological upgrading of the manufacturing industry, and to create new technology industrial units. Among the aims of the IOT was the creation of an information technology centre, and the provision of consultancy services on technology and organizational development. In 1996 IOT assumed responsibility for a government plan of subsidizing consultancy services on IT that was partly funded by the World Bank. There was limited demand for such services, though, and a large proportion of the funds remained unused and returned to the Bank.

The information centre of the IOT was intended to provide information on a wide range of areas, such as market research, trading, abstracts of research relevant to various industries, industrial policy and regulations of the European Union, trade statistics, academic and professional journals, programmes on human resources development. The producer firms and their consortia in the furniture industry did not make any substantial use of these resources. Demand was poor in the other industries too and the role of IOT as an information centre diminished.

By the end of the 1990s, IOT was concerned almost exclusively with assisting the organizational development of the local business firms. This involved both subsidies to business firms to use consultancy services and efforts to develop the professional standards of the market of such services. For example the Institute offered subsidies to business firms in all industries to appoint management consultants and had a system of evaluation and professional certification for organization consultants.

The Producer Firms

Initially the producer firms appeared to respond to the recommendations for change and take advantage of the new opportunities offered by the intermediary organizations set up by the government. For example several firms made use of the new financial schemes of the Development Bank to expand their business, and sought to upgrade the skills of their workforce through government sponsored training programs. They were particularly appreciative of the opportunities to enhance their production technology. Thus, the MFC consortium was created by the initiative of the owner of one firm and enjoyed a great deal of commitment from its member firms. Also, they showed interest in collaboration for schemes for marketing and sales, thus setting up AtoZ and Line 11.

But, the restructuring strategy required also the manufacturing firms to adjust their operations and develop their organizational capacity taking part in the wider network of agencies that would complement or support their business. The small producer firms of the furniture sector were reluctant to change their traditional ways of doing business, they did not trust the consortia or the service agencies.

The behaviour of the firms involved in the three consortia outlined above demonstrates the prevailing attitude. The firms taking part in the AtoZ and Line-11 consortia were intended to remain independent organizations, but to adapt their production and specialize by product. Some producers started doing so, but in just two years after the creation of the AtoZ and Line-11 consortia their members started acting antagonistically both to each other and to the consortia that were supposed to be their marketing and sales agencies. Although initially these consortia boosted sales of the products of their members, they could not absorb all their production capacity. The owners/managers of the small firms reverted to their pre-consortium state, each producing and selling on their own a broad range of products, rather than specializing by product. They became competitors as well as suppliers of their consortium. On many occasions they supplied their products to the consortia at selling prices higher than those they offered directly to their customers. By the mid-1990s AtoZ and Line-11 did not have a privileged status as selling outlets of the producer firms that formed them; these producer firms kept only an agreement to supply them with a particular line of products with a pre-specified price and delivery timing.

The attempted restructuring had negligible effect on the management of the small firms. The most significant changes concerned the rationalization of production that resulted from the use of computer-controlled machines. Producer firms had to standardize their product parts in order to be able to use the new machines. In turn, such standardization benefited the MFC consortium as an independent business organization, increasing the efficiency of its operations, reducing errors in orders, and releasing spare machine capacity for further business.

Overall, the producer firms did not develop an export orientation. The structure, management, and business culture in furniture manufacturing remained unchanged, mitigating rather than contributing to the industrial change initiative. The owners/managers of the firms retained total control of the business through direct communication with their staff and day-to-day decisions on task allocation. Unlike the trend exhibited in the case of Emilia Romagna, the small firm owners in the Cypriot furniture sector did not form partnership networks and did not develop significant demand for the services of support agencies. They were reluctant to trust professional management and third parties—such as the managers of their consortia—for the survival of their business. All the owners/managers we interviewed saw their firms as a family business. The founder of the business either had already passed control to a son or daughter, or was hoping to do so. They saw the changing government regime from providing protection and subsidies to offering facilitatory services pessimistically, as the end of the era they built their business. They were concerned that unaided, under market conditions, they could fail to survive. They had little appreciation for the supporting services and were not keen to use them.[8] Most firms' owners continued to run their business in the way they had established them: by direct involvement in all matters of the firm and by trying to undercut their competitors in the shrinking local market.

The information systems requirements of the producer firms remained very limited. Computers were used for internal administrative tasks, but there was no interest to exploit the potential of IT to support management decisions, formal communication, and information sharing with partners. As the inter-organizational links that the flexible specialization experiment initiated waned, there was no need for inter-organizational network communications. Moreover, without an export orientation international data communications remained largely irrelevant to the concerns of the local firm owners/managers.[9]

THE ECONOMICS OF INNOVATION OF THE CYPRIOT INDUSTRIAL EXPERIMENT

In 1996 government officials told us that the experiment of flexible specialization had failed, and government economic policy was shifting attention from manufacturing to services. By the time of my latest round of interviews with managers and government officials, in 2000, most of the restructuring initiatives of the early 1990s had long been abandoned.[10] Questions about the reasons the restructuring experiment failed and the wisdom of changing government policy are beyond the scope of this case study. Rather, of interest here is more specifically the relationship of the failed restructuring intervention to the poor utilization of ICT.

---

[8] An example of the lack of appreciation of the value of the supporting services is the poor attendance at the training seminars for new skills organized and funded by the industrial training agency. Many firm owners were unwilling to allow their staff to leave earlier and attend the seminars.

[9] However, towards the end of the 1990s the use of communication technology took a new impetus with the spread of the Internet. The new industrial policy of the Department of Commerce, Industry, and Tourism in 1999 included subsidies for Internet connections and development of webpages.

[10] Still, the prevailing view in June 2000 was that the principal diagnosis of the structural problems of the Cypriot manufacturing by UNDP/UNIDO in 1987 was correct. Too small producers without management skills would not be able to face international competition. However the remedies considered were different this time. A 'New Industrial Policy' announced by the Department of Commerce, Industry, and Tourism in 1999 provided incentives for the merger of small manufacturing firms and the development of professional management services.

This is not a simple causal relationship, of the form 'ICT was not used because the restructuring intervention did not get off the ground'. It can be assumed that, had the organizational restructuring been successful in creating industrial networks of closely collaborating producers and service agencies, there would have been pressing requirements for rich information flows and formal information communication channels. In other words, it could be argued that the need for information systems innovation did not arise because the institutional change was not successful. However, it may also be assumed that, had the enterprises involved been self-motivated and proactive in utilizing IT strategically to improve their competitiveness in a free domestic market and expand their exports, the industrial organization initiative would have been able to build the necessary links for the intended industrial network structure. In other words, it could be argued that the industrial restructuring was not successful because the participating firms made inadequate efforts to innovate products and processes, including their information systems.

Before I examine the socio-technical relationship between the organizational restructuring effort and the lack of information systems innovation, the following two questions lead to the literature on innovation in economics. What did the theory that guided the restructuring intervention say about information systems innovation and how may it help us to explain information systems development inaction in this case? And, how realistic was it to expect the small producer firms to pursue the required innovation of organizational processes or technology?

From its inception, the restructuring intervention was vague on information systems innovation. The analysis of the UNDP/UNIDO team drew attention to the significance of investing in technology and the owners in the furniture sector had no difficulty in appreciating the significance of investment in advanced production technology. Indeed, they grasped the opportunities for securing funds to invest in new machines, and were willing to collaborate with competitors to that end. They had clear efficiency expectations from these machines—faster production, savings in raw materials, less labour—and they could see them realized.[11]

Information systems innovation was another matter. In the UNDP/UNIDO report information systems innovation was specifically related to the need to improve management. But what would an 'improved management' be like, and how could it be achieved? It seems that the team of industrial development specialists has been at a loss on these questions. They wrote:

If for the moment we leave aside the general orientation of the firms, and concentrate on two of the traditional centrepieces of management, accounting and finance, and production, there

---

[11] Nevertheless, technology innovation in production was not a long-lasting attitude. According to the flexible specialization model, the regional network should have spurred processes of localized learning and tacit knowledge sharing that would have promoted technology innovation. Economic theory is less clear on how that would happen, and does not offer convincing explanations of why it fails to do so when it does (Nadvi and Schmitz 1994; Howells 1999). Indeed, the idea that flexible specialization is conducive to technology innovation, and in particular ICT innovation has been disputed, and empirical studies suggest that even successful districts of flexible specialization make limited application of advanced technology (Lazerson 1990).

is something of a policy enigma . . . The Government has pursued remedial policies . . . [has] run management courses, which have been well attended, and provided consultancy services which have been well used. . . . Yet on the basis of our visits, and the reports of other surveys, this approach has not been sufficient. (Murray et al. 1987: 247)

The action they recommended as one of the 'immediate priorities' of the government, reinforces the impression that they had low confidence in their understanding of how management in the small producer firms could be improved. They proposed the appointment of a senior consultant to draw up the details of an emergency programme for management; the establishment of an 'Emergency Management Unit', staffed by consultants and civil servants to supervise the emergency programme; a 'Management Consultuncy Fund' to provide 'the requisite consultancy services to firms'; and a Management Equipment Fund to subsidize the 'purchase of equipment necessary to improve management information systems and stock control'.

The same report highlighted also the importance of access to information resources on market and suppliers. But the underlying logic that linked investment in data resources and ICT with business success was to be found in management. Without a successful reorientation in the management of the firms, the introduction of new elements such as a database service, or the rationalization of order taking using computers, remained isolated incidents, which did not add up to contribute to an information systems infrastructure.

These shortcomings were not mistakes in the particular diagnostic exercise, but, on closer examination, they reflect gaps in the underpinning theory. The obvious difficulty the economic development experts faced in their attempt to prescribe how a management tradition could be developed, and to provide a convincing rationale for the significance of information systems to that end[12] is indicative of a more general vagueness in economic studies of innovation regarding organizational change. The flexible specialization theory offers a target organizational structure—district conglomerations of semi-autonomous producers, service providing producer partnerships, and government agencies—but it is unclear about the way such structure can be managed effectively. The main characteristics of successful industrial districts include the maintenance of a craft tradition, their institutional capacity for informal communication and sharing of tacit knowledge, and reliance on trust rather than formal contracts or hierarchical control mechanisms. The right mix of formal and informal information flows, explicit and tacit knowledge in running a business, reliance on trust or regulation is recognized as one of the most crucial factors in fostering technical innovation and economic growth, but is unspecifiable in general

---

[12] The lack of vision for information systems development in the report of the development experts is in stark contrast to the business and management literature of that period, which offered long lists of arguments about the strategic potential of technology innovation in information systems and prescribed methods on how such potential could be diagnosed and achieved (see e.g. Porter and Millar 1984; Earl 1987; Earl 1989). One could think that if the study of the boosting of competitiveness of the manufacturing firms in the island had been done by business consultants instead the recommendations might have put more emphasis and guidance on 'strategic' information systems. Whether such recommendations would have had better chances of being successfully implemented is another question, though.

terms.[13] This is recognized as a particularly acute problem in cases which emulate organizational arrangements and supporting institutional elements, what Dalum et al. call 'institutional borrowing'(Dalum, Johnson, and Lundvall 1992). In short, the guiding theory did not have the capacity to make effective recommendations on initiatives for information systems innovation. Linking information systems with management, a problematic aspect in the context of the manufacturing firms in Cyprus, could not provide an inspiring vision for ICT innovation.

Furthermore, the limited guidance on information systems and management interventions that the experiment of industrial change began with was compounded by the limited extent to which the owners of the firms of this case were willing to innovate. Throughout the period of this study, the striving-for-survival small firms did not take an interest in investing in technology-based information systems. Could it be otherwise?

In economics, we find contradictory views about small firms as innovators and economic players. On one hand, small firms are highlighted as the creation of 'Schumpeterian entrepreneurs', who are ready to take risks and exploit opportunities that more established firms with rigid management procedures would not venture to pursue.[14] On the other hand, most small firms do not survive very long, and part of the problem is understood to be their inadequate innovation capacity (Audretsch 1999). But If propensity for innovation is not a general intrinsic characteristic of small firms, what are its determining conditions?

Most economic accounts of innovation in small enterprises consider innovation as the result of adjusting business performance under conditions of competition. Technology, with its impact on efficiency, is seen as a factor that changes a firm's competitive position. Economic research, therefore, has tried to determine what factors spur innovative behaviour, considering, among others, availability of funding, size, intensity of competition (Cosh, Hughes, and Wood 1999). In an effort to broaden the perspective and take into account the behaviour of the entrepreneur, Casson, still looking at the success of a firm as a matter of rational choice, argues that the significant factor is the cognitive ability of the entrepreneur: his ability to synthesize information on markets, technology, and people.

---

[13] On the same grounds it is difficult to predict which industrial districts can develop successful organizational processes to sustain networks of flexible production. This point is reinforced by Sabel who observes that on the basis of empirical evidence 'there is no plausible list of the necessary and sufficient conditions—rare or otherwise—for the emergence of flexible economies' (Sabel 1989: 133). It is interesting to note that in the Cyprus case the problem diagnosed was lack of formal and accountable decision-making processes, and eventually it was conflict rather than trust that prevailed.

[14] Joseph Schumpeter's work on technical innovation and the dynamics of economic growth (Schumpeter 1939) has been one of the most influential theories that paid attention to organizational, institutional, and social psychology issues of economic activity. In his early work Schumpeter emphasized the role of the entrepreneurs and the small innovative enterprise (Schumpeter 1934). In the 1980s Schumpeter's ideas became the core of the 'Neo-Schumpeterian' school of thought, pioneered by Christopher Freeman and Carlota Perez at the Science Policy Research Unit, Sussex, which has been one of the main contributors to contemporary theory and policy on technology innovation (see e.g. Freeman and Perez 1988).

Such analyses exemplify what Granovetter (1985) calls the under-socialized theoretical perspectives of economics. The decision maker is considered to be preoccupied with an atomistic rational behaviour, unaffected by social influences of the context within which he is embedded. To have a better understanding of economic action, Granovetter suggests, one should try to trace its broader underlying rationality, and explain it as embedded in a social context. Studies of innovation economics which have taken a broader perspective and considered the institutional context within which small firms are embedded—mainly the economic policies and industrial structures of the national context—added important new dimensions to the competition-by-efficiency perspective, such as the interaction between producers and their customers, and government incentives or disincentives (see e.g. Unger 1988; Lundvall 1992; Hobday 1995). Still, such analyses of the institutional and structural social features of the national context of small firms tend to ignore what Granovetter (1985: 507) calls the 'proximate causes' of their action, meaning the network of social relations overlaid on their business relations. They also tend to miss what could be called the 'distant causes', that is, the beyond-the-national-borders social and institutional influences that theories of globalization brought to our attention.

SOCIO-TECHNICAL VIEW OF THE CYPRIOT INDUSTRIAL EXPERIMENT

The restructuring experiment sought to reorganize a set of organizations as a cluster, an 'industrial network' whereby the enactments of its participants ought to be closely interrelated in order to achieve internationally competitive manufacturing of furniture. The small producer firms responded with remarkable similarity of behaviour to the restructuring experiment, although not to realize the intended clustering and exports, but to preserve their autonomy and to maintain their salient institutional features, such as total control by the owner, direct contact of the producer with the customer, the intermingling of business and family affairs. It is therefore valid to look at these small firms as a category of organizational actors sharing common institutional characteristics and engaged in common enactments.[15]

In the late 1980s, most small furniture manufacturing firms were the life work of artisans, people who knew, primarily, how to make furniture. Their firms had been formed in the previous decade under the favourable circumstances of plentiful demand in the domestic market and government protection from foreign competitors. The making and selling of furniture created wealth for the owner, provided work to a number of other people, and served the needs of the reconstruction of the country's economy. The protagonist in this enactment, artisan/manager, negotiated his actions with a variety of other actors and intermediaries: wood and other raw materials, machines, designs, money, workers and administrators, customers, competitors, laws.

---

[15] A shortcoming of this abstraction is that Granovetter's 'proximate' social relations of individual firm owners, managers, and workers, cannot be accounted for in detail, but only as generally observed patterns exemplified by indicative evidence from individual organizations.

There were a set of interconnected organizational fields that sheltered the small firms, and set the norms and conditions of their business. The most important organizational fields were local: the island's furniture industry with its 'standards' such as wages, range and quality of products, fashion, selling prices; the local supplier industries for raw materials and machines, with their norms for quality, speed, and prices; the local customers—families and businesses—with their taste and buying habits; the island's family culture and solidarity for the reconstruction of the nation after the invasion, setting, for example, values for saving, investing, and achieving; the government striving to rebuild the nation's economy, maintaining the vision of the nation developing against the odds, setting rules, protecting, subsidizing, and sanctioning.

Much weaker and more nebulous were the international institutional influences. These included: the international furniture industry circulating its own quality standards, designs and prices; the customers in the Middle East with their own tastes, spending capacity, and alternative sources of buying from South-East Asia; foreign suppliers of wood and machines; international agencies exerting pressure on the government to lift its protective regime, and creating uncertainty about the future of local firms.

In the mid-1980s, uneasiness about the small furniture firms' strategy grew out of various changes taking place in several of the local and the international organizational fields. To begin with, with the boom of the post-invasion reconstruction subsiding, the Cypriot furniture industry was getting too congested. Moreover, local customers, having overcome the difficult economic times that followed the war and the split of the nation, had reached a certain degree of prosperity and were prepared to pay more for imported furniture. The government was readjusting its policy from rehabilitation after the wounds of the war towards economic growth earned in the international arena of trade, and towards a political identity of a nation that is part of Europe. In the world beyond the island the discourse of economic globalization was shaping visions and consolidated in rules. Academia and economic institutions were circulating new ideas about how economies develop, and international centres of power worked out and exercised rules and conditions for participating in the global economy.

It was in this situation that the UNDP/UNIDO team of experts was called in to contribute. They brought along the flexible specialization model as a powerful intermediary, which could illuminate the problem and lead to its solution. Indeed, it produced a translation blueprint for this: a set of recommendations for the mobilization of diverse actors—government agencies, banks, training institutions, entrepreneurs—and the circulation of a whole set of intermediaries—design, technologies, management techniques, databases, information systems.

There were good signs that the translation of the model of flexible specialization in the Cypriot manufacturing industry—and furniture manufacturing in particular—could produce results. There was no explicit resistance and the main actors appeared accommodating. The government was interested in the new role it was given to play for the development of the country's manufacturing. It was 'politically correct' because it abandoned protectionism, and it enjoyed intellectual kudos in the international economic institutions. The government ought, however, to do a lot for such a change. It should not come to the rescue of stressed industrialists, even if it risked losing their votes, it should allow the private sector to do jobs they were doing. But many of the private actors of the flexible specialization blueprint—the specialized service providers, the venture capitalists—were not there yet, and the government had to be instrumental for their creation.

The small producer firms found the diagnosis convincing and the solutions promising, though perplexing. The flexible specialization translation gave them an obligatory point of passage position, therefore seemed to guarantee their survival. But it required them to change in order to gain such a privileged position. They ought, for example, to install new technology, to introduce new activities—such as design, marketing, and management—to collaborate with their competitors, not to hassle the government for subsidies and protection, to find new customers from abroad. For such changes they were promised assistance: the government would create special agencies for the required retraining, and create new funding institutions. But it was a matter of serious concern for them that the government would not secure the territory of their market any more, and would not provide them with subsidies when faced with hardship.

The furniture manufacturing business firms in Emilia Romagna offered credibility to the new organizing vision. Italy—a European country that maintained its family-centred culture, as Cypriots would like to do—demonstrated that small business firms could prosper by following the proposed model. Cypriot industrialists travelled to Italy to see the prosperity of flexible specialization live: the thriving businesses, their consortia, and the agencies that assisted them in producing for export.

But the translation process never built an adequate momentum. Although ICT was prescribed as an intermediary in the reorganization blueprint, it was not brought into action by any of the interested actors. This inaction can be explained as follows. ICT was a stranger in the organizational field of the attempted translation, an actor that the participants in the Cypriot furniture manufacturing sector would not 'naturally' turn to for support. That this stranger was connected with the managerial rationality which was alien to the traditional way of running the small manufacturing firms did not help either. So long as the enactment of the small producers did not change to export-oriented business, the global institutional fields of management and information systems exerted weak influences on the actors of the attempted translation, and could be ignored. The remainder of this section elaborates on each of these observations.

ICT was an insignificant institutional force in the Cypriot organizational fields that influenced furniture manufacturing in the 1980s and early 1990s. The producer firms had remained largely unaffected by the rational myth that ICT innovation is a strategic weapon for doing business. There was no taken-for-granted necessity for a race of information systems innovations as in the advanced economies. There was no substantial IT industry championing it, no strong government and media propaganda for an imminent information society, and no government experience as an ICT innovator. This does not mean that computers were not ubiquitous. But their perceived value was limited to providing support tools for formal administration, and, therefore, the significance attributed to computer-based information systems in the flexible specialization translation was not obvious or unquestionably accepted.

The argument for the need of information systems that associated them with management added reluctance rather than convincing the small firms' entrepreneurs of the necessity of ICT innovation. The small firm owners and their trusted staff were not competent in computers or in the management inscriptions they were valued for and expected to transfer. They had to surrender control to professional managers, competitors/partners, and service-providing intermediaries. If computer information systems were added in such networks, the owners of the small firms would lose some of their ability to exercise control and make decisions crucial for their business. For example, if the small firm owners allowed the computer-based system in the hands of the AtoZ manager to determine what they could produce best for a customer, at what price, and by when, they would lose their direct bargaining power with customers, which they trusted as the most reliable way to sell profitably.

Even if the alliance of professional managers and information systems was promising to save the producer firms from bankruptcy, their owners saw the risk of their family business being diminished, and their duty and joy to secure the well-being of the inheritors, sons or daughters, in jeopardy. Thus, their inaction was not a matter of the extent to which they were 'rationally' convinced about the economic merits of management and information systems. It was a result of battling with the question 'How should we live?',[16] as they confronted an unfamiliar regime of truth. The answer to this question was restricted by the embodied enactment of their business: their vision of the future, their confidence in negotiating with their customers—including language—their ability to use the tools of their trade, their imagination of what new to produce and how, their sense of the value of their business in their life. Management, exports, and the information systems they required were outside their embodied experience.

There were resistances to the flexible specialization translation and inactions by various other actors. Most importantly, perhaps, the government delayed for years the creation of the agencies that were so important for the flexible specialization translation, and they were reluctant to abandon those enterprises which, at the mercy of market forces, were begging for subsidies. Moreover, the government officials did not feel comfortable themselves in enacting their new roles as mediators for the cooperation of entrepreneurs and management professionals. The few and isolated actions that took place under the banner of the intended translation started reversing after a few years.

The reversal of the flexible specialization translation left the 'traditional' enactment of the small manufacturing firms virtually intact, without visions for information systems innovation. As exports continued to remain a remote possibility there was neither a felt need nor additional institutional pressure from international organizational fields for management practice and information systems innovation.

---

[16] Quoted by Helen Verran (1999), who referred to Pyne Addelson's work (Pyne-Addelson 1994: 154), showing how collective action addresses the question 'How should we live?'

As far as information systems innovation is concerned, the failed flexible specialization translation completed a vicious circle.

CONCLUDING REMARKS

A question that emerges from this analysis is whether and how this vicious circle—irrespective of a value judgement of its consequences—may be broken. A look at the unfolding interaction of local, international, and global institutional fields provides some indications for what may happen in the future.

During the 1990s the forces of globalization became more prevalent in Cyprus, as the government protective measures were gradually being lifted, and the post-invasion generation—much more at ease to use computers, to speak the language of modern business, and visualize the world beyond the island's shores as their market—started assuming power. The infiltration of norms from international organizational fields into the local ones was too slow to make a difference for the translation of flexible specialization undertaken in the late 1980s, but any translation that may be attempted more than ten years later will be situated in a very different institutional context.

Several changes are taking place that may make a difference to any new attempt for organizational change and information systems innovation. There is a cadre of professional managers and an emerging services industry, including ICT consultancy. ICT itself has changed and, in its latest and more flexible form, the Internet, it is less closely linked with formal information processing practices and data infrastructures. The spreading information society discourse cultivates widely the image of ICT as the *sine qua non* for modern life. The growth of the Cypriot stock exchange affects the perception of success in business, encouraging entrepreneurs to surrender their absolute control and autonomy of their enterprises, to venture in mergers with competitors, and to employ formal management techniques.

It is a safe bet to predict that such changing institutional conditions will open the way to many new experiments of ICT translations in all the economic sectors of the island. But, as the other cases demonstrate, the effects of such translations can hardly be predicted by general trends. Rather, they will continue to be decided by actors struggling with the question 'How should we live?'.

References

Amin, A. (1994). 'Post-Fordism: Models, Fantasies and Phantoms of Transition', in A. Amin (ed.), *Post-Fordism: A Reader*. Oxford: Blackwell, 1–40.

Audretsch, D. B. (1999). 'Entrepreneurship and Economic Restructuring: An Evolutionary View', in Z. J. Acs, B. Carlsson, and C. Karlsson (eds.), *Entrepreneurship, Small & Medium-Sized Enterprises and the Macroeconomy*. Cambridge: Cambridge University Press, 79–96.

Becattini, G. (1991). 'The Industrial District as Creative Milieu', in G. Benko and M. Dunford (eds.), *Industrial Change and Regional Development: The Transformation of New Industrial Spaces*. London: Belhaven, 102–14.

Brusco, S. (1982). 'The Emilian Model: Productive Decentralization and Social Integration'. *Cambridge Journal of Economics*, 6: 167–84.

—— (1990). 'The Idea of the Industrial District: Its Genesis', in F. Pyke, G. Becattini, and W. Sengenberger (eds.), *Industrial Districts and Inter-form Cooperation in Italy*. Geneva: International Institute for Labour Studies.

Casson, M. (1999). 'Entrepreneurship and Economic Restructuring: An Evolutionary View', in Z. J. Acs, B. Carlsson, and C. Karlsson (eds.), *Entrepreneurship, Small and Medium-Sized Enterprises and the Macroeconomy*. Cambridge: Cambridge University Press, 45–78.

Chrysohos, N. (1999). 'Information Systems and Organisational Change: The Case of Flexible Specialisation in Cyprus', Ph.D. thesis (Dept. of Information Systems, London School of Economics).

Cooke, P., and Morgan, K. (1994). 'Growth Regions under Duress: Renewal Strategies in Baden Wurttemberg and Emilia-Romagna', in A. Amin and N. Thrift (eds.), *Globalization, Institutions, and Regional Development in Europe*. Oxford: Oxford University Press, 91–117.

Cosh, A., Hughes, A., and Wood, E. (1999). 'Innovation in UK SMEs: Causes and Consequences for Firm Failure and Acquisition', in Z. J. Acs, B. Carlsson, and C. Karlsson (eds.), *Entrepreneurship, Small & Medium-Sized Enterprises and the Macroeconomy*. Cambridge: Cambridge University Press, 329–66.

Dalum, B., Johnson, B., and Lundvall, B.-Å. (1992). 'Public Policy in the Learning Society', in B.-Å. Lundvall (ed.), *National Systems of Innovation: Towards a Theory of Innovation and Interactive Learning*. London: Pinter, 296–317.

Earl, M. (1987). 'Information Systems Strategy Formulation', in R. J. Boland and R. A. Hirschheim (eds.), *Critical Issues in Information Systems Research*. Chichester: John Wiley, 157–78.

—— (1989). *Management Strategies for Information Technology*. Hemel Hempstead: Prentice Hall.

Freeman, C., and Perez, C. (1988). 'Structural Crises of Adjustment, Business Cycles and Investment Behaviour', in G. Dosi, C. Freeman, R. Nelson, G. Silverberg, and L. Soete (eds.), *Technical Change and Economic Theory*. London: Pinter, 38–66.

Granovetter, M. (1985). 'Economic Action and Social Structure: The Problem of Embeddedness'. *American Journal of Sociology*, 91(3): 481–510.

Hammer, M. (1990). 'Reengineering Work: Don't Automate, Obliterate'. *Harvard Business Review*, July–Aug.: 104–12.

Hobday, M. (1995). *Innovation in East Asia: The Challenge to Japan*. Cheltenham: Edward Elgar.

Howells, J. (1999). 'Regional Systems of Innovation?', in D. Archibugi, J. Howells, and J. Michie, *Innovation Policy in a Global Economy*. Cambridge: Cambridge University Press, 67–93.

Lazerson, M. (1990). 'Subcontracting in the Modena Knitwear Industry', in F. Pyke, G. Becattini, and W. Sengenberger (eds.), *Industrial Districts and Interfirm Cooperation in Italy*. Geneva: ILO.

Lundvall, B.-Å. (ed.) (1992). *National Systems of Innovation: Towards a Theory of Innovation and Interactive Learning*. London: Pinter.

Murray, R. (1992). 'Flexible Specialisation in Small Island Economies: The Case of Cyprus', in F. Pyke and W. Sengenberger (eds.), *Industrial Districts and Local Economic Regeneration*. Geneva: ILO, 256–76.

—— Best, M., Evans, D., Humphries, J., Kaplinsky, R., Rafferty, J., Snell, P., and Zeitlin, J. (1987). 'Cyprus Industrial Strategy: Report of the UNDP/UNIDO Mission'. Brighton, Institute of Development Studies, University of Sussex.

Nadvi, K., and Schmitz, H. (1994). 'Industrial Clusters in Less Developed Countries: Review of Experiences and Research Agenda'. Brighton, Institute of Development Studies.

Piore, M. (1993). 'The Revival of Prosperity in Industrial Economies: Technological Trajectories, Organizational Structure, Competivity', in D. Foray and C. Freeman (eds.), *Technology and the Wealth of Nations: The Dynamics of Constructed Advantage*. London: Pinter, 322–31.

—— and Sabel, C. (1984). *The Second Industrial Divide: Possibilities for Prosperity*. New York: Basic Books.

Porter, M., and Millar, V. (1984). 'How Information Gives You Competitive Advantage'. *Harvard Business Review*, 63(4): 149–60.

Pyke, F., Becattini, G., and Sengenberger, W. (eds.) (1990). *Industrial Districts and Inter-firm Cooperation in Italy*. Geneva: International Institute for Labour Studies.

Pyne-Addelson, K. (1994). *Moral Passages*. New York: Routledge.

Sabel, C. F. (1989). 'Flexible Specialisation and the Re-emergence of Regional Economics', in A. Amin (ed.), *Post-Fordism: A Reader*. Oxford: Blackwell.

Schumpeter, J. A. (1934). *The Theory of Economic Development*. Cambridge, Mass.: Harvard University Press.

—— (1939). *Business Cycles: A Theoretical, Historical and Statistical Analysis of the Capitalist Process*. New York: McGraw-Hill.

Scott Morton, M. S. (1991). *The Corporation of the 1990's, Information Technology and Organizational Transformation*. New York: Oxford University Press.

Unger, K. (1988). 'Industrial Structure, Technical Change and Microeconomic Behaviour in LDCs', in G. Dosi, C. Freeman, R. Nelson, G. Silverberg, and L. Soete (eds.), *Technical Change and Economic Theory*. London: Pitman, 480–95.

Verran, H. (1999). 'Staying True to the Laughter in Nigerian Classrooms', in J. Law and J. Hassard (eds.), *Actor Network Theory and After*. Oxford: Blackwell, 136–55.

8

Medical Drug Utilization Information Systems in the United States and Europe

This chapter turns attention to the information systems of an area known as 'drug utilization', that is the activities involved in the use of medical drugs. The World Health Organization (WHO) defined drug utilization as the marketing, distribution, prescription, and use of drugs in a society, with special emphasis on the resulting medical, social, and economic consequences (WHO 1977). The three aspects of 'emphasis' suggested in this definition give an indication of the overlapping and not necessarily harmonious interests served by drug utilization activities. Consequently, the underlying general principle of drug utilization information systems to 'identify opportunities to improve care in populations of patients' (Armstrong et al. 2000. 511) is fraught with ambiguities and conflicts. Some drug utilization information systems serve a clear pharmacovigilance purpose, assisting pharmacologists in health and medical institutions to evaluate the efficacy and risks of medical drug interventions. Others have primarily an economic focus, monitoring the drug costs of prescribing doctors, or producing cost data for budgeting and planning purposes. But in many cases drug utilization systems are expected to play more complex and multifaceted roles, for example systems used for cost containment purposes may be used to spot mistakes in the medication of individual patients, such as conflicting drugs or overdosage.

As a *genre*, therefore, drug utilization systems are ill-defined, with varying functionality, technological features, organizational locality, and associated purpose. Also, their categorization is complicated with confusing terminology, as similar systems are known with different names in different countries (e.g. drug utilization in the United States, prescription systems in the United Kingdom) and similar terms refer to systems with significantly different functionality and intended uses (e.g. 'DUR' and 'DURG', as will be explained in the following section). What justifies their study as a category in this chapter is that collectively they form the information infrastructure that supports the use of medical drugs in a modern health care setting. Indeed, it is argued in this chapter, that the difficulty of defining the systems comprising this infrastructure is indicative of the multiple intertwined facets of modern health care. In the context of reforming health care systems in most industrialized countries during the past two decades, drug utilization systems acquired a range of 'built in' functionalities and have undertaken multiple and contradictory roles. Of interest here is to examine how particular drug utilization systems reflect the prevalent concerns of the institutional health care settings that sustain them.

The organizational context of this study is different from the other three case studies in this book. Most information systems concerning drug utilization are not confined in one organization, although they are hosted, or sponsored by specific organizations. They are inter-organizational systems that draw data—increasingly through computer network connection—from organizations prescribing or dispensing medical drugs, such as general practitioners' surgeries, community dispensing chemists, or hospital pharmacies. They may provide some utility to the organizations they draw data from, but their main value is through and for others, such as national and international health institutions, and health insurance companies. In addition, drug utilization information systems are of great interest to—and indeed some are 'owned' by—organizations involved in the production and distribution of drugs, notably pharmaceutical corporations and medical research centres.

Thus, the study of drug utilization systems takes us beyond the microcosm of particular organizations with their partly technically/rationally and partly institutionally shaped missions, processes, and structures, as those of the cases of Pemex and IKA. It even takes us beyond the set of organizational transformation concerns that globalization exerts on confined organizational fields, such as those of the small manufacturers in Cyprus. We do not have here the familiar setting of information systems being constituent components of one organization or a few partnering organizations, and we cannot make satisfactory sense of their existence, purposes, and performance in the customary way of analysing the information needs of certain business or work processes. Many drug utilization systems are self-identifiable entities, a service, or even a commodity, that constitutes the main line of business— the *raison d'être*—of the organizations that host them. Such examples that will be outlined in this chapters are the PACT system in the Prescription Pricing Authority in the United Kingdom, and the drug utilization information of Medco that was bought by the pharmaceutical company Merck in the United States.

Thus, drug utilization systems are a good example of the role ICT assumes in contemporary societies. They are part of the fabric of a modern society's information infrastructure, serving multiple and often contradictory purposes: a mechanism of scientific research to create new knowledge, sometimes a mechanism of control of professional practice, a mechanism of economic rationalization, or a mechanism for creating new business.[1] They are also a good example of studying the dialectics of the local and the global, as the global pharmaceutical industry and apparently global scientific knowledge are confronted with the variety of national health care settings and localized drug use practice.

---

[1] Inter-organizational information systems have been a major research topic in information systems since late 1980s, initially under the term Electronic Data Interchange (EDI), and later, propelled by the spread of the Internet, as electronic commerce, or electronic business. Drug utilization systems fall outside the area of current focus of inter-organizational information systems in two main respects: they do not necessarily rely on electronic communications, and although they often serve business purposes and result from economic concerns, they are also instruments of medical research and practice. Also, they cannot be subsumed in the emergent study of electronic government, both because they pre-date e-government, and because various drug utilization systems have been developed in non-government controlled health service contexts.

MULTIPLE TERMINOLOGY, VARIETY OF SYSTEMS, AND OVERLAPPING PURPOSES

Two similar sounding buzzwords are often heard in connection with information systems on the use of medical drugs: DUR and DURG. The former stands for Drug Utilization Review—or Drug Use Review—and refers to medication surveillance programmes concerned primarily with the monitoring and guiding of drug use through state or private insurance organizations, usually in the context of the United States. The latter stands for Drug Utilization Research Group, which was initiated by the World Health Organization (WHO) in the 1960s and triggered the development of systems on drug utilization in most European countries. It refers to groups of investigators and institutions engaged in studies regarding the safety, efficacy, costs, and appropriateness of drug consumption.

The American DUR systems are classified according to the point in the drug use process at which a review occurs. *Retrospective* DUR occurs after a therapy is completed; *concurrent* DUR occurs during a patient's course of therapy but after a prescription is filled; *prospective* DUR occurs before the drugs are dispensed, but after the prescription is written. Another term confusingly related to that of DUR in the US context is Drug Use Evaluation (DUE), which is understood as a process that monitors and analyses drug use patterns of a specific drug or class of products in a patient population. Data of DUE systems are used to monitor the validity and effectiveness of drug therapy of individual patients and is intended to guide interventions to change patients' therapy when necessary and possible. As there is no clear difference between DUE and prospective or concurrent DUR—despite various efforts to devise precise definitions that distinguish among the three—practitioners and authors often describe DUR as only retrospective, and use the term DUE for concurrent and prospective activities. Also, the term DUE is sometimes used to make the distinction between systems set up to contribute to medical studies of drug outcomes and those which are part of health insurance administration, processing prescription reimbursement claims (Armstrong and Terry 1992; Fish, Kirking, and Martin 1992).

In Europe many different terms are used to refer to information systems and techniques in the management of drug use. In the United Kingdom, systems supporting or monitoring doctors' prescribing are known as 'prescription systems'. The term 'Patient Medication Records' (PMR) refers to systems registering patient and prescription information during the dispensing process. Such systems contain information about drugs sold by pharmacies to individual patients. They can be used for medication surveillance, as DUR programmes do, e.g. to screen for adverse effects of particular drugs and drug to drug interaction (Nørgaard 1996). Prescription Event Monitoring (PEM) refers to studies which focus on specific drugs and, using data from prescription databases and resulting outcomes from general practitioners, check the occurrence of possible undesirable effects.

There is also a wide range of systems handling various aspects of the prescribing and dispensing process in more confined, but diverse locations, such as hospitals, doctor surgeries, or pharmacies (Glinn, Hubbard, and Pickup 1993; Lee and Morgan

1993; Linnarson 1993; Stork and Greene 1993; Thompson and Chantry-Price 1993). Information systems supporting drug use related activities are often part of more general information systems of organizations, such as hospital pharmacy systems and community pharmacy systems to control dispensing and stock control, or general practice systems keeping patients' records and assisting in patient consultation.[2]

The first initiative in collecting data on drug prescribing and sales was undertaken in the United States in the 1930s[3] as market research for pharmaceutical companies, aiming to identify fields of opportunity for research and development and to monitor their competitive position in the drugs market (Dukes 1993). Intercontinental Marketing Statistics created a flourishing business of documenting prescribing and sales of drugs in many countries and making data available to pharmaceutical companies for a substantial fee.

National health authorities also became concerned about the use of drugs at a relatively early stage of the rapid introduction of drug treatments, mainly because of the increasing level of expenditure they implied. They started collecting their own statistics on prescription costs and prices, both because they met obstacles in getting access to the data collected by or for the pharmaceutical industry, and because they mistrusted them.

In the 1960s drugs surveillance systems received a major boost as a result of epidemiological and health risk concerns. The thalidomide case[4] drew attention to the prescribing habits of doctors and drug-induced health risks. Moreover, research in the 1950s and 1960s indicated enormous international and regional differences in drug prescribing. Existing drug consumption data, which were oriented towards costs and prices, were not suitable for research in health and epidemiology. In 1969 WHO in Europe created the Drug Utilization Research Group (DURG), which has been influential in raising awareness on the need to monitor the use of drugs and in developing common methodological standards for drug classification and measurement in order to make international comparisons possible.

In the broad scope of the WHO concept of DURG, drug utilization 'studies' are confronted by complex issues of medical, social, and economic nature, bearing the potential to contribute to each of them. From a medical perspective drug use studies may address questions about medical benefits and risks of specific medication, such as their efficacy in preventing and curing diseases, their short-term and long-term adverse effects, and the extent to which inappropriate prescribing or use may reduce benefits and increase risks, as in the case of antibiotics. They may explore social

---

[2] The plethora of terms provides a first indication of the multiple institutional actors involved and their interests. They include the WHO, national health policy makers and administrators, private health insurance providers, pharmaceutical companies, chemists in community or hospital pharmacies, practising medical doctors in community surgeries or in hospitals, medical or pharmacology researchers.

[3] That period was the start of very rapid development of pharmaceutical drugs due to a combination of forces: the development of social security systems, national health services and schemes for reimbursement of the costs of drugs, and the aggressive innovation and promotion strategies of drug manufacturers.

[4] Thalidomide, a drug used for the relief of various problems at the early stages of pregnancy, had deforming effects on embryos.

patterns of health care, such as the causes and trends of drug abuse, improper use (such as non-compliance to dosage and length directions of use, or use for purposes for which they were not prescribed), or unequal availability of important drugs to different categories of population. From a health economics perspective they may monitor the cost-effectiveness of alternative drugs and of drug treatment in comparison to alternative medical interventions. From a management perspective they may assist in planning for the allocation of resources, they can monitor doctors' prescription habits against norms of cost and predetermined 'best practice'.

It is well understood among medical and health policy making professionals that the use of drugs is not driven by straightforward medical necessity. Drug consumption—as indeed the very fundamental perceptions and responses associated with health and illness—is subject to variation of cultural, scientific, and technological traditions, the structure of health services, the pricing and reimbursement policies, the existence of local pharmaceutical production industry, and the degree of regulation of pharmaceutical products more generally. In addition, drug consumption is affected by the promotional activities of the drug industry, through training of prescribers and dispensers, as well as by shaping public attitudes. Drug utilization studies, Laporte et al. suggest (Laporte, Baksaas, and Lunde 1993), are confronted by the 'community pharmacodynamics of drug use', which are delineated by national borders and are subject to the governance of national health care systems. Whatever the potential for drug use information systems may be, the actual systems found in operation, their uses and purposes are determined in the arena of health care systems. Thus, in the socio-technical fashion, the following examples of the drug utilization systems in the United States and European countries need to be understood in relation to these countries' health care institutions.

DUR DEVELOPMENT IN THE HEALTH CARE CONTEXT OF THE UNITED STATES

The United States has a market-driven health care system. Unlike most other industrialized countries the United States never 'designed' a comprehensive national health care system. The institutional structure and financing arrangements that comprise its current health care regime resulted inadvertently by a series of initiatives under the pressure of powerful actors—such as doctors, employers, and the insurance industry—and influential leaders, and legitimated by government legislative responses (Miller 1996; Reagan 1999).

In comparison to most European countries, the United States started to introduce health insurance relatively late. Government efforts to introduce compulsory health insurance in the first three decades of the twentieth century met with opposition from physicians, who were concerned that insurance would decrease their incomes. A market of health care boomed in the 1920s, offering services to the large middle classes on a pay-as-you-use basis. But the Great Depression that began in 1929 signalled the uncertainty of such growth and put an end to the first era of affluence in health services. Hospitals hit by financial insecurity started private insurance plans for hospitalization. From those plans, the American Hospital Association (AHA) created the Blue Cross, a private, but non-profit, hospital insurance system. The system grew quite rapidly, covering over 4 million people by 1940, and a similar system, the Blue Shield, was soon introduced to cover physician payments.

Blue Cross and Blue Shield health insurance coverage grew substantially during the Second World War. They were seen as local corporations providing an alternative to both government and commercial health insurance. However, for-profit insurers emerged and grew after the war and health insurance changed and expanded to become a huge industry in a highly competitive market. The Blue Cross and Blue Shield became almost indistinguishable from commercial insurance plans, and indeed their non-profit status was dropped in 1994.

Government-sponsored insurance was introduced in 1965 with two schemes: Medicare, providing services to the elderly, and Medicaid covering the very poor. These schemes expanded accessibility to the most needy parts of the population, but increased costs substantially. The expansion of high technology in hospitals and speciality care by physicians added to rapidly increased costs of health care.[5] At the same time the efficacy and quality of many treatments and tests in the expensive health care were questionable (Flood 2000). Cost containment became a major concern, and almost all government legislation on health care since then has aimed at controlling cost rather than expanding coverage.

Under such pressures a significant development in the American health care system has been the emergence of the various 'managed care' entities, such as health maintenance organizations (HMOs). In general, managed care refers to arrangements used by an insurer or purchaser of health services from various providers, such as family doctors (physicians) or hospitals, to influence the cost, volume, and quality of the supplied services. In the United States, managed care sought to establish a direct relationship and interdependence between the provision of health care services and their payment. While originally plans such as the Blue Cross and the Blue Shield were 'third party' organizations, paying for the services of independent providers, in managed care organizations care providing networks took responsibility and shared financial risk with the insurer for a population's medical services. For example, in the case of HMOs, health care service providers are paid in advance a preset amount for the services an insured population is estimated to need in a given period. Therefore, they have an incentive to minimize use of their services.

In 1973 the US government passed legislation that mandated the range of basic services included in HMO organizations that combined providers and insurers. Many other types of managed care organizations were developed, such as associations of practitioners which do not operate facilities but purchase hospital or speciality care services for their insured members from other organizations, often HMOs, and various ways of linking service provision with financial responsibility have been devised.

---

[5] As an indication of the high health care costs, despite low accessibility, in 1992 the US spending on health care services as a percentage of GDR was 66% more than the average OECD spending, while 16% of its population without insurance lacked adequate health care (Flood 2000).

All, however, apply one of the basic principles of managed care, the monitoring of the insured population's use of medical resources. 'Utilization review' is a general term referring to the application of diverse techniques to control resource use and monitor quality. Among the major concerns have been coordination of care to decrease variations and to standardize treatment, and the avoidance of misuse or duplication of services.

In the 1990s the Clinton administration proposed a set of radical reforms aiming to provide all Americans with access to health services, and curb the high costs of the existing system. Such objectives were to be pursued by the existing health care system of private insurance and private service delivery. For various political and tactical reasons the proposed reforms proved unsuccessful. Partly as a response to this challenge, the private managed care approach intensified and the rate of increase in health care costs was reduced. Accessibility, although a general concern of Americans,[6] remained a problem. Those insured were unwilling to risk the quality of health care services they received, and trusted the market more than the government to reduce costs.

Thus, the US health care system continued to be capable of developing and delivering the most advanced medical services of the world, but leaving a large part of the population (estimated to be 40 million in 1996 (Sultz and Young 1997)) without any or adequate health insurance. In 2000, a WHO study which examined and ranked countries' health care performance and expenditure (WHO 2000) found that the US health care system has a large gap between those insured and those without health care coverage: the top 10 per cent of its people are the healthiest in the world; the middle 80 per cent gets a 'mediocre' deal while the bottom 5 to 10 per cent 'have health conditions as bad as in sub-Saharan Africa' (quoted in *The Economist* (2000: 62)). The same article in *The Economist* observes, the WHO report confirms that '[m]ore than any other country, America has turned health care into a business. It boasts myriad sorts of health-care companies and patients who, at least some of the time, think of themselves as consumers. This heady mix often spurs innovation in health care. But the conflicting interests of all the different parties—and their deep political pockets—also make wholesale reform extremely difficult' (ibid. 67).

The Emergence of DUR Systems in the United States

In the United States, drug utilization review (DUR) is understood as a management programme aiming at drug use 'optimization' (J. Jones 1991). Retrospective DUR programmes collect data on drug use patterns and apply predetermined criteria and standards to analyse the use and cost of particular drugs in a specific health care setting, such as a pharmacy, a hospital, or an insurance company. Prospective on-line DUR systems at point of sale alert pharmacists to inappropriate prescriptions, such as dose, or duration.

---

[6] Flood (2000), drawing from Marmor (1994), notes that the majority of Americans were concerned over the unfairness of their health care system.

The first DUR systems appeared in the mid-1960s. They consisted mainly of surveillance activities, and were intended to control fraud and abuse in outpatient drug prescriptions. Initially they were implemented in—and for a long time restricted to—large-scale organizational settings, such as hospitals, large employers, and Medicaid. Early DUR systems examined also drug-to-drug interactions to check for prescribing errors. By the late 1960s they started addressing various other problems, such as inappropriate drug choice and mistakes in drug dose (Lipton and Bird 1993).

In 1969 the Joint Commission on the Accreditation of Healthcare Organizations (JCAHO) began requiring hospitals to develop DUR in order to receive accreditation. During the 1970s and the 1980s, the growth of health maintenance organizations which included drug benefits led to substantial increase of DUR. A number of regulatory actions from state and federal government agencies—e.g. by the 'Medicare and Medicaid Health Care Financing Administration' in 1974 and the 'Medicare Catastrophic Coverage Act' in 1988—as well as recommendations of professional medical and pharmaceutical associations, gave DUR a more prominent position in the American health care system.

Significant further growth of DUR programmes resulted from a federal government law which mandated the implementation of DUR activities by state Medicaid programmes. The Omnibus Budget Reconciliation Act of 1990 (OBRA '90) required that by 1 January 1993 states should provide for a DUR programme to ensure that prescriptions were appropriate, medically necessary, and unlikely to produce adverse effects (Zawistiwich 1991). In each state a DUR board comprising doctors and pharmacists was responsible for running a programme with three components: (a) prospective DUR, monitoring drug regimens by pharmacists before dispensing, and intended to be followed up by consultation with prescribers and patients when a problem is detected; (b) retrospective DUR, evaluating claims submitted by pharmacists to identify anomalous patterns of patient behaviour, pharmacist dispensing, or physician prescribing, and intended to be followed up by appropriate interventions; and (c) educational interventions according to the results of the retrospective reviews, mainly in the form of academic detailing, or as one-to-one discussions between a drug expert and the prescriber (Schulke 1991). Although federal government policy was criticized for not keeping up the requirements for DUR (Flanagan 1994), most states developed DUR programmes on their own initiatives.

In the meantime, increases in prescription drug coverage and drug costs led private health insurance plans too to make efforts to rationalize the use of drugs. It was estimated that by 1993 nearly 20 Medicaid DUR programmes were implemented and nearly 75 per cent of health maintenance organizations ran formal DUR. While 58 per cent of them had the capacity to detect inappropriate use of the drugs monitored, and drug-to-drug interactions, the main focus of these systems was on drug costs (Lipton and Bird 1993; Moore, Gutermuth, and Pracht 2000).

Also, a variety of DUE type systems were introduced, serving purposes of drug use quality control in a variety of medical settings and for particular drug categories (Dasta, Greer, and Speedies 1992; Grasela et al. 1993; O'Connell, Chance, and Bowman 1994). Such systems varied in effectiveness, as they were loosely linked with information systems of a broader scope in their medical setting—such as patient record systems and hospital administration systems.

In comparison to the retrospective DUR databases and DUE systems, information systems supporting the task of prescribing were introduced at a much slower pace. Such systems were virtually non-existent in clinical practice in the United States in the early 1990s (Lipton and Bird 1993), but efforts were made to expand DUR systems to provide physicians with the possibility of reviewing a patient's drug-use profile before writing a prescription and making suggestions about alternative drug therapy regimens and costs (Wertheimer and Kralewski 1993).

In the 1990s, while many hospitals, long-term care facilities, and government agencies conducted in-house DUR, most insurance plans subcontracted the DUR task to firms which process claims from participating pharmacies. A market study in the mid-1990s found an industry of DUR services consisted of about twenty companies, and affecting about 30 million people in their role to approve, deny, or change drug therapies for clients. Significant large drug utilization review databases were also maintained by the so-called prescription-benefits-management (PBM) companies which provide prescription drugs to HMOs and the employees of large organizations. Among other 'benefits' PBM companies were able to negotiate drug prices through bulk buying contracts, handled mail order pharmaceuticals for patients with chronic illness, and with their DUR and DUE systems could change prescribing behaviours of doctors (Kreling and Mott 1993; Thomas 1996). In this way substantial DUR information systems were developed in specialized prescription service companies in conjunction with other services, such as reimbursement claims processing, benefits consulting, mail order pharmacy services, and drug benefit management.

The kind of data maintained in the various DUR information systems and the use made of them varied significantly. The literature of the early 1990s suggests a controversy about the purposes DUR systems served, or ought to serve in the context of American health care. There were concerns that financial imperatives reduced DUR systems to mere cost containment tools, despite the potential of databanks on prescribed drugs in detecting and correcting prescribing problems, thus improving the effectiveness of drug therapy. The challenging task, as seen by many authors, was to exploit the potential of DUR to serve the double objective of achieving cost-effectiveness and improving quality of therapy (Lipton and Bird 1991; Wertheimer and Kralewski 1993).

With widespread implementation of on-line and retrospective DUR systems in the second part of the 1990s there have been mixed views about the extent of their use, and their utility (Armstrong et al. 2000; Moore, Gutermuth, and Pracht 2000). Most pharmacies and many doctors' practices were linked to databases providing information on patients' healthcare coverage, such as the copayment for prescriptions that varied by employer and insurer. They were also increasingly used to influence doctor's prescribing, by providing information for the design of educational interventions, incentives for change of prescribing behaviour, or awareness of general prescribing trends (Thomas 1996).

An important trend has been towards building on the availability of patient-specific data in DUR systems to implement the new concepts of 'disease management' from pharmacoeconomic research. Disease management takes a broader perspective than the quality and cost of medication and evaluates the appropriateness of drug therapy in the context of treating particular diseases. Thus, it is aimed at 'the creation of population-based integrated approaches to the provision of ongoing, cost effective, clinically efficacious care' (Armstrong et al. 2000: 542). Rather than focusing on drug-specific optimization of use and cost containment, DUR programmes started being seen as providing information for the consideration of the impact of drug therapy choices on the treatment of a disease, and the overall medical costs incurred (Elrodt et al. 1997).[7] This trend reinforced DUR systems as instruments for cost containment and quality of care improvement with new ideas from 'outcomes' research and 'pharmacoeconomics'. The criteria embedded in DUR and DUE had to be reconsidered (Armstrong et al. 2000) and the data captured in DUR databases had to expand to include details on diagnosis and patients' conditions (Thomas 1996). In effect, the prospects were created for DUR to play a more significant role in introducing new approaches to safeguard quality of care while containing overall care costs in the context of managed care.[8]

Such developments stem from a complex institutional setting in the American health care system. For the government, DUR systems were instruments to control cost and quality. For health care providers, such as physicians and hospitals, they were associated with concerns of quality of care, but also more business-like interests, such as safeguarding their clientele (employers) and satisfying their paymasters (insurers). For insurers, DUR systems were primarily instruments of cost containment, but were often associated with more sophisticated business strategies, such as managing their relations with health care providers, clients (employers, or patients), and suppliers of pharmaceutical products. For enterprises in prescription services, such as PBMs, the development of rich data bases on drug use was one of their core business services. For pharmaceutical companies DUR information had strategic importance for marketing purposes; it could be used to identify areas of drug innovation, and to launch direct links with consumers through or without established institutions, such as physicians and pharmacists.

In the market-driven setting of the US health care sector, a major driver in the development of DUR information systems has been their business potential. Not only were DUR services part of the industry of PBM, but DUR information resources had a market value on their own. In 1993/4 a number of large pharmaceutical companies acquired PBMs in order, mainly, to tap their DUR resources.[9] An impressive such merger was

---

[7] Disease management is thought to involve coordination of care across a health care delivery system, comprehensive knowledge base of a disease, clinical and administrative information systems to analyse medical practice patterns; and continuous quality improvement methods.

[8] Such an approach is 'evidence-based medicine', understood as a mix of current clinical research evidence with pathophysiological knowledge and patient preferences in doctors' decisions about care of individual patients, which is discussed later in this chapter (Elrodt et al. 1997).

[9] Examples other than MedCo's acquisition by Merck are the acquisitions of Diversified Pharmaceutical Services Inc. by Smith-Kline Beecham and PCS Health Systems by Eli Lilly and Co.

undertaken by Merck, the worldwide leader in prescription pharmaceuticals at that time, which acquired Medco Containment Services, a mail order pharmacy and PBM.

In an interview with the *Harvard Business Review* journal, Merck's CEO P. Roy Vagelos presented a clear, albeit idealized, view of the significance of Medco's information resources to his company:

> once the drug is on the market and has been prescribed to a patient, we must be sure that the patient is taking the right drug, that he or she has the appropriate information to take the drug properly, and that the drug will not interfere with other medications the patient is taking. We can ensure all this by capturing information as it comes through the pharmacy and then putting in into a central data bank that feeds the information back to the physician, the plan sponsor, and ultimately the labs, where it can be used to create new drugs. (Nichols 1994: 106)

Merck expected that through Medco they could achieve much more than owning a pharmacy network for promoting their own products. The main idea was to use prescription information to understand and influence prescribers' and patients' behaviour. Vagelos listed a number of ways that such information could be used by Merck to make mutually beneficial deals with the four actors he saw as the 'customers' of a pharmaceutical company in the American context: plan sponsors, doctors, pharmacists, and patients. With DUR information the possibility to reach the ultimate consumer without the professional intermediaries was there, opening unprecedented market opportunities.

To be sure, Merck's vision to directly link pharmaceutical production with drug 'consumers' was controversial, raising medical and social concerns such as on health risks and privacy implications (Kassler 1994). Nevertheless, in the market-driven health care system of the United States, Merck's vision was not only a legitimate business 'strategy' that could propel further DUR information systems development and new uses of DUR information. It was also a force of innovation in the institutional relationship among actors involved in drug utilization, that is a major force in the reform of the health care system more broadly.

DRUG UTILIZATION SYSTEMS IN EUROPE

Even though there are big differences among European states in the way they organize, fund, and distribute their health care services, their common fundamental difference from the health care context of the United States is their extensive compulsory population coverage.[10] Most European countries have some form of universal rights to health care, meaning the same rights to all citizens, although such rights may be limited to few services, e.g. access only to public hospitals. In terms of financial insurance arrangements, European countries fall into three groups: financed by a mixture of social and private insurance with mainly private providers (Netherlands); financed mainly through social insurance with mixed public and private providers (e.g. Germany and France); and financed mainly by taxation with mainly public providers (e.g. United Kingdom) (Abel-Smith et al. 1995).

[10] Covering over 85% of the population, except in the Netherlands.

In the institutional health care contexts of European countries, national authorities have had the capacity to conduct population-wide drug use surveillance and utilization studies, and indeed in many countries there are population-wide prescription databases. Examples of such systems are given by Alonso et al. (1993). They describe the large-scale systems existing in the early 1990s in four European countries, Czechoslovakia, Ireland, Spain, and Sweden—all countries with state-financed systems and mainly public health care providers, therefore with the organizational mechanisms to produce large-scale databases. The socialist Czechoslovakia began collecting data on drug consumption in 1952. Its computerized databases stored such data as wholesale drug deliveries to community and hospital pharmacies, as well as health data on the population, such as incidents of particular diseases and treatments applied. The Irish National Drugs Advisory Board set out two drug utilization studies: it maintained records of all drugs prescribed to occupants of specified beds in general medical hospitals and attendees for consultation with specified general practitioners, and monitored all patients for whom one or more specified drugs have been prescribed. Spain's drug utilization resources were developed through efforts to regulate the pharmaceutical market that was considered to run out of control in the early 1970s. Its drug utilization databank emerged from the data collected for prescription reimbursement. But, with time, this national databank came to contain much more information than prescription costs. In the early 1990s it contained basic information about the pharmaceutical products in the country; prescription data; pharmacological information on all drugs marketing in the country and their active ingredients; pharmacological and administrative information relating to the registration of the pharmaceutical products in use in the country. Finally, Sweden, one of the first European countries to develop databases with full prescription information, has created comprehensive drug utilization data, allowing the health authorities to follow sales of drugs over long periods of time and to do surveys of diagnoses and therapies.

Such rather static accounts of drug information systems operation in a country give an indication of the range of concerns and related solutions that historically came to prevail under more or less publicly funded and controlled, health care settings.[11] But health care has been anything but static in Europe in the past two decades, during which the historically established public sector governance of most national health care systems has been subject to extensive reform. It is, therefore, against a background of questioning, reconsidering, and revising health care

---

[11] Static descriptions of existing systems hide the negotiations among institutional actors involved in drug utilization processes. An example of such negotiations is given in a thorough empirical study conducted in Denmark by Nørgaard (1996). Adopting a social constructivist perspective, Nørgaard shows how the efforts for the development of a system of patient medication records were related with the concerns of pharmacists to safeguard their professional role, as they felt threatened by prospects of liberalization that would allow drugs to be sold over the counter in places other than pharmacies, and as technological innovation in pharmaceuticals limited their traditional dispensing role. Yet, the development and use of that innovation in pharmacies was a slow process that created reactions from pharmacists and other interested groups. A database of patient medication records proved a controversial innovation in the Danish context.

governance and service delivery mechanisms that drug utilization systems have to be understood.

Invariably, reforms in modern health care organizations are confronted by issues of accessibility, costs, and quality of services. While in the European context accessibility has been a fundamental principle and therefore less of an issue, quality of care and increasing costs have been at least as important and challenging as in the United States. The search for ways to 'manage' care led to the implementation of a range of organizational interventions (Mossialos, Kanavos, and Abel-Smith 1997). There has been a discernible trend to separate purchasers of services from providers, e.g. separating authorities and management structures for hospitals—providers of services—from the family practitioners—'purchasers' of hospital care for their patients. Many countries introduced overall budgets for health care expenditure and budget controls for particular services, e.g. pharmaceuticals or hospitals (Abel-Smith and Mossialos 1994). Also, many countries started prioritizing services by devising criteria of what is necessary care and, consequently, ruling out services thought to be less critical, such as *in vitro* fertilization, or that could be left to individual responsibility, such as dental care (Abel-Smith et al. 1995).

With regards to medical drugs, most European governments apply strong regulation to the pharmaceutical industry, controlling either the prices of their products or their profits. A relatively new system of control, initially introduced in Germany but later adopted in other countries too, has been the grouping of similar products and specifying a price which will be fully covered by the insurance. Moreover, most countries introduced positive and negative lists of drugs that doctors use in prescribing. The result of such regulation is that the number of brand-named products on the market varies substantially from country to country. Norway has only about 2,000 brand-named products, while Germany has over 23,000 products, the highest in Europe. Still, this is only a bit more than half the amount in the United States, which has 43,000 products (Abel-Smith et al. 1995).

In addition to issuing either negative or positive lists of drugs, during the 1980s and early 1990s European governments introduced measures to influence prescribing. They developed prescribing and dispensing profiles of doctors and pharmacists as a mechanism to identify cases of fraud, they encouraged doctors to prescribe drugs generically rather than by brand and provide incentives to pharmacists to substitute for expensive products (Abel-Smith 1992; Abel-Smith and Mossialos 1994).

But measures to control costs and improve efficiency often conflicted with public expectations for high quality health care. Attention shifted to the 'appropriateness' of health care interventions, and new measures were devised to reduce ineffective treatment. This presented requirements for new 'managed care' instruments, such as guidelines to doctors in order to assist them to take decisions informed by research evidence, and information systems reporting on clinical effectiveness of alternative medical interventions (Mossialos, Kanavos, and Abel-Smith 1997). Among them are drug utilization information systems. Indeed, this is the area where drug utilization information systems innovation was oriented in the late 1990s in the United

Kingdom, a country with a history of daring healthcare policy, which in the 1990s introduced and experimented with the 'internal market' reform model.

The Changing Institutional Setting of Health Care in the United Kingdom

The United Kingdom has a national health care system providing universal access to all its services and financed through state tax revenue. Hospital doctors are paid salaries by the government and primary care doctors receive capitation payments[12] from a public authority as independent contractors.

The beginning of this system goes back to the National Insurance Act of 1911, which provided free primary care—but not hospital treatment—to blue-collar workers. Still, by the beginning of the Second World War half of the adult population were not covered by the national system. In the United Kingdom, it was the middle and upper classes, not covered by the national system, that were mostly uninsured. Today's national health system (NHS) was conceived during the Second World War and was introduced in 1948, when the first Labour government after the war took office. The establishment of the publicly operated delivery system for universal coverage involved nationalization of all hospitals and a great deal of effort to win the confidence of the medical professions, mainly the British Medical Association. Doctors secured a powerful position in the operation of the system, and were given a substantial proportion of seats on hospital boards and executive councils.

In this publicly operated delivery of health services, priorities were developed by central government and then communicated through a hierarchical system of administration to local health authorities. In 1974 the NHS structure comprised fourteen Regional Planning Authorities, and, under them, about 200 District Health Authorities, responsible for providing hospital and community services. In parallel to the district authorities, another structure of Family Health Service Authorities were responsible for the administration of contracts with general practitioners, pharmacists, and dentists.

Nationally allocated public funds covered (and still do) about 95 per cent of the system's costs, the rest being covered from charges to patients. The extent to which this institutional setting of 'socialized' system has been effective is controversial (Morgan 1999). The NHS boasted one of the lowest per capita, and as a percentage of GDP, costs among industrialized countries.[13] Until the mid-1980s public opinion was positive, and a matter of pride for the British. But in the 1990s concern that the health care budget was insufficient for a good quality national health system became widespread. Waiting lists for hospital treatment became the most frequently discussed indicator of the 'crisis' of the NHS, a symbol of the problems facing the entire health care system.

---

[12] Capitation means the payment of a standard fee per person registered with a family doctor, or more generally with an organization providing a range of services.

[13] See e.g. how health expenditure increases in the UK between 1970 and 1993 compare with the European countries and the US in the OECD statistics quoted by Mossialos, Kanavos, and Abel-Smith (1997).

Concerns about the quality of care such a system can sustain at a time of rapid technological development and high patient expectations, combined with the Prime Minister Margaret Thatcher's passion for the market, led to the launching of substantial reforms in the early 1990s (DOH 1989). In 1991 a provider market was introduced, in which District Health Authorities purchased hospital services from public and private hospitals. Family doctors' practices were encouraged to become 'fundholders', that is to administer their own budget, including spending on prescriptions of drugs, and were given economic incentives for cutting costs. Thus, general practitioners operated as purchasers of services, such as out-patient consultations and diagnostic tests, some hospital in-patient services, and community services. Hospitals were allowed to become 'trusts', a status which gave them freedoms, such as in determining the level of pay of their staff (Abel-Smith et al. 1995). The government remained the primary financier of health care.

Further reforms were launched by the Labour government that took office in 1997.[14] It changed the 'internal market' that had sought to achieve efficiency by competition among providers, and introduced yet another governance logic, 'integrated care', intended to lead to more collaboration among health care actors (DOH 1997). The general practitioner fundholders were abolished, and larger groups of general practitioners and community nurses were created, with financial and clinical responsibilities for all health services to the population of their area. It maintained, though, the principle of the split between 'purchasing' general practitioners and 'provider' hospitals, with different decision-making entities for each of these health care services.[15]

In short, during the 1990s, the centralized publicly funded and delivered NHS in the United Kingdom—often called the 'command and control' approach—was repeatedly reorganized to improve efficiency and meet the expectations of the British public for a modern healthcare. The government has been reluctant to allow for substantial market competition, particularly regarding private insurers. Rather, it introduced 'managed care' mechanisms in NHS organizations, for example, professional management to run hospital 'trusts' and information systems to influence the behaviour of general practitioners with guidelines for and monitoring of 'good practice' (Flood 2000). Although controversial,[16] measures such as 'evidence-based medicine' (Evidence based medicine working group 1992; Davidoff, Haynes, and Sackett 1995; Rosenberg and Donald 1995; Sackett, Rosenberg, and Muir Guir 1996), which present practising doctors with the 'best evidence' on clinical effectiveness from research

[14] In the meantime, in 1996, an interim restructure merged District Health Authorities into 100 Health Authorities, directly overseen by eight branches of the NHS executive—an agency within the Department of Health.
[15] The organizational reforms in the UK health care sector have been associated with a plethora of initiatives for the development of supporting information systems. Many situated studies of organizational change and information systems innovation in this context demonstrate rationality tensions similar to those manifested in the prescriptions systems studied here (see e.g. M. R. Jones 1994; Bloomfield et al. 1997).
[16] Mechanisms such as evidence-based medicine are often seen with suspicion by the clinical professionals as methods restricting clinical judgement (Sweeney 1996), and ultimately reducing the power of medical professionals vis-à-vis managers.

reports to influence their decisions became a prominent feature of the NHS. And although the utilization of drugs is still regulated and influenced by guidelines,[17] practitioners' groups responsible for both financial and medical decisions have new requirements for prescription information systems that are used for managing their budgets as well as for choosing appropriate interventions for their patients.

Drug Prescription Systems in the United Kingdom

In the reforming NHS of the 1990s, information systems concerning aspects of drug utilization emerged in three distinct areas of activities: monitoring of prescription costs and rationalization of prescribing habits, pharmacovigilance research, and evaluation of outcomes of health care interventions. In the period covered by our study at the London School of Economics, up to 1995 (see Appendix), the only established large-scale information system on drugs was PACT (Prescribing Analysis and CosT), in the first of these three areas. However, amidst continuing institutional reform, several systems were under development in the other two areas. A brief general view of the United Kingdom's drug utilization infrastructure in the first half of the 1990s is as follows.

PACT was run by the Prescription Pricing Authority, which was (and still is) responsible for processing all prescriptions, authorizing payments, and providing information to prescribers, dispensers, and health authorities. It was first introduced in 1988 and its major objectives were to monitor prescribing trends and costs in primary care and to influence general practitioners' habits towards more cost-effective prescribing. PACT, based on information by dispensing agents, provided quarterly reports to general practitioners with information about their prescribing. Most of the information was presented in comparative form, using average data from similar practices as an index for comparison, while more detailed reports were available on request. However, few doctors requested detailed information from PACT (N. K. Jones 1993). In essence, the PACT reports provided a channel for the government to pass the message of cost containment to general practitioners and managers of the various health units, and to suggest ways of achieving this, showing, for example, the proportion of drugs prescribed generically.[18]

---

[17] Indicative of the restrictions on the market of pharmaceuticals in the UK is that, in the discussions of potential reforms in 1996, mail order pharmacy was considered inappropriate for the NHS (Mossialos, Kanavos, and Abel-Smith 1997).

[18] It is impossible to say whether and to what extent PACT contributed to cost containment. The overall cost of prescription drugs continued to increase throughout the 1990s, although it dropped slightly in 1989 and 1990, the first two years PACT was introduced. A significant shortcoming of using data from this system as an indicator of drug consumption in the country is that it contains only prescription data. Patients in the UK have to pay a flat rate per prescription—although there are extensive exemptions, and it is estimated that only about 20% of patients pay for their prescriptions. As prescription charges increased substantially, doctors increasingly issued private prescriptions to patients when the cost of the medicine was lower that the national health prescription charges. PACT, not capturing drugs sold over the pharmacists' counter, did not reflect accurately trends on prescribing (Heath 1994).

Information systems for pharmacovigilance purposes were less visible. PACT data were used in studies of adverse drug reactions, but such studies tend to require much more medical data, which were not collected routinely for the whole population. Relevant data were more likely to be found in the computers of general practitioners and hospitals, some of which fed into databases with patients' medical data. The extent of such data resources was limited, raising concerns that post-marketing surveillance of drugs did not follow a systematic path through population-wide data repositories (Fleming 1994). It tended to be narrowly focused both in terms of data used and criteria applied, and was, therefore, inadequate to address the potential risks from ever-more complex drug treatments.

The evaluation of outcomes of health care interventions was an emerging effort to form a broader, evidence-based view of the issues of quality and cost in health care. Reductions in ineffective treatment were seen as a valuable strategy in reducing health care costs, and 'outcomes management' research was intended to monitor what interventions are effective in terms of health outcome and to produce guidelines to change the behaviour of doctors accordingly (Wennberg 1992; Abel-Smith et al. 1995). Outcomes measurement research led to more complex models of pharmaceutical costs, e.g. by including the impact on reducing the length of stay in hospitals, and could identify over-prescribing as well as under-prescribing. Efforts to introduce such measurements started in 1993 at a central level, the Central Health Outcomes Unit in the Department of Health, with the development of information systems to integrate information on clinical trials, disease management, treatment outcomes, and evaluation of costs. Outcomes management information systems included drug use data as one form of intervention to be compared and evaluated against alternative treatments.

Meanwhile, the continuing reform interventions in the NHS were creating new potential for drug utilization studies and information systems. Two major developments since 1995 with implications for the development of new prescription information systems have been the formation of the National Prescribing Centre (NCP) in 1996 and the National Institute for Clinical Excellence (NICE) in 1999. The NCP is the organization in charge of the overall use of drugs in the NHS, with the stated aim to 'facilitate the promotion of high quality, cost-effective prescribing through a co-ordinated and prioritised programme of activities aimed at supporting all relevant professionals and senior managers in the new NHS'.[19] To that end, it has been building either new or onto existing information systems, such as PACT, to disseminate information on medicines to prescribers and NHS authorities and influence 'good practice' by adopting managed care methods such as evidence-based medicine. The NICE is an evaluation centre, intended to safeguard medical quality and cost-effectiveness through the appraisal of new and existing health technologies, the development of clinical guidelines, and clinical audit. As part of its role, it undertook responsibility for the promotion of information systems regarding drug prescription.

---

[19] <http://www.ncp.co.uk>, visited on 2 Nov. 2000.

216   *Insights from Case Studies*

Thus, by the end of the 1990s, a number of information systems concerning drug utilization became noticeable in the United Kingdom's 'new NHS'. PACT was further developed to allow for electronic access through the 'electronic PACT' and EPACT.net, and expanded its functionality, e.g. by covering nurse prescribing.[20] The 'Hospital Prescribing Information Project' began efforts to collect prescription data from hospitals (Jackson and Walker 1998) in a national database; a task considered particularly difficult, because prescriptions in hospitals have not been adequately standardized and a variety of computer systems are used in hospitals. A computerized decision support system for general practitioners, PRODIGY, widely promoted since 1998 as good practice in primary health care aims at directly influencing doctors' prescribing by offering recommendations for a number of conditions, checks for allergies, contraindications, and interactions.

It is too early to know the extent to which each of these systems will be used and grow, but it is clear that prescription systems have assumed significant, albeit contradictory, roles to play in the NHS actors' network. It is important to note that all major drug prescription information systems have been developed and run by national health authorities: the Prescription Pricing Authority, the Central Health Outcomes Unit, the National Prescribing Centre, the NICE. Nevertheless, even in an organizational setting still to a large extent governed by the 'command and control' approach, the establishment of these systems depends on many other health care actors. Pouloudi and Whitley (1997) identified a long list of stakeholders in these systems, actors on whose negotiations with the changing NHS the drug prescription systems circulated by the central authorities may be seen as allies or as enemies. Of them, the attitude and behaviour of health professionals (general practitioners and hospital doctors, nurses, pharmacists) is critical.

The drug prescription systems entered the health care system scene with the double script of cost control and quality improvement. The reforms required the provider organizations of the NHS to pursue the cost-containment objective without compromising quality. Doctors and hospital administrators had to search for cost efficiencies on their own initiative. The internal market system held promise for maintaining the accessibility and quality, while keeping control of the spending to play their role in the transformation towards a new institutional logic.

In the early 1990s general practitioners seemed to find little value in the services of PACT and were suspicious of evidence-based methods. They were part of a series of instruments, such as formularies and generic prescribing, introduced as gentle pushers towards a behaviour desired by the government for the realization of the 'new NHS'. They could not be ignored as irrelevant, though. In combination with more coercive actions—most importantly their fixed budget—they were indispensable instruments of the new conditions of practice. Ploughing through their double-sided functionality as tools for cost containment, but also offering potential for

[20] The Prescription Pricing Authority boasted 'the largest drug database of its kind in Europe [handling] 10 million prescriptions every week, or 520 million prescriptions per year' (<http://www.ppa.org.uk>, visited 20 Oct. 2000).

avoiding errors, and improving outcomes of medical interventions, doctors saw ways to use them as their own allies in the reforming system. They could be, as the authorities that circulated them suggested, tools that help them plan their budget, and make cost-effective choices for their own benefit. They could also use them in voicing their concerns. As intermediaries between health authorities and general practitioners, the PACT reports did not simply reinforce the latter's pressure for cost-effective prescribing. They were used by the former to express their concern that the reform is insensitive to the patients' needs. General practitioners complained that the comparisons of their patterns of prescribing with idealized average units without taking into account the specific characteristics of their patients were misguided (Harris 1994). In effect, PACT bore the marks of the cautionary, but in many ways dubious, efforts to restabilize the new governance of the health care system through consensus: it reminded and informed rather than coercing, but it also triggered lurking concern, such as whether maintaining accessibility and quality is possible with a fixed budget, and whether the autonomy of medical professional work is eroded by rationalization interventions.

The other actors involved in the process of drug production and use in the United Kingdom have had less opportunities to exploit the possibilities of drug prescription systems circulated by the central authorities. Moreover, in the context of the tightly regulated NHS there was limited scope for initiatives of other actors to develop drug utilization systems for their own purposes. With the data accumulating in the centre for the management of outcomes scientists could find new scope to weigh the efficacy of drugs against alternative interventions, although overall, an NHS under financial stress was not keen to devote resources for large-scale pharmacovigilance information systems. Pharmacists, in search for a new role,[21] considered that drug use monitoring may be an activity they should develop if the reforms move towards an American-style managed care (Touche 1996). A major chain of pharmacies made efforts to introduce patient medication smart cards and offer checking for drug-to-drug interactions. However, so far neither pharmacies nor the pharmaceutical industry have found much scope for innovative interventions in drug use management. The 'strategic' significance of drug utilization systems, in the form of various prescription information systems, in the United Kingdom lies in being a mechanism to control quality and costs of services in a government-regulated health care service.

Initiatives by the European Union

The European Union (EU) is a relatively new actor in the scene of health care policy of the region. Until the Maastricht Treaty in 1992, health care remained essentially a policy area for individual member states. But even after the legal formulations of the Maastricht Treaty, most member states show unwillingness to accept the EU's supranational authority on issues as critical as their health care systems (Redwood 1994). Moreover the EU lacks the institutional ability to play a substantial role vis-à-vis the

[21] See e.g. Calder 2000; Walker 2000.

member states' health care systems. One of its major weaknesses in this area is that matters related to health care are dealt with by a plethora of offices. In the European Commission separate Directorates deal with pharmaceuticals and medical services, health and safety affairs, medical research, and medical informatics.

Nevertheless, against the background of heterogeneous government practice, the EU has taken a number of initiatives for the harmonization of health care across its member states. In the area of drug use the EU has been influential through policies determining the liberalization of the pharmaceutical industry, the setting of health quality standards that influence developments by national governments, and the definition of data requirements, such as on comparable indicators, which member states have to supply. In order to be effective such initiatives involve highly political processes as they require agreement by the political authorities of member states, each of which pursues its own situated policies of health care reform to meet the challenges of cost containment and quality.

Drug utilization information has been of interest to the EU for epidemiological and pharmacovigilance purposes but also as an instrument for the harmonization and rationalization of member states' health care policy. Programmes aiming at the creation of data banks at European level and improving data transferability among states are abundant. However, many of them are limited to producing advance technology prototypes. Those that are implemented face the difficulty of data compatibility, plethora of meanings, and the willingness of national institutions to comply with supranational standards. The following examples demonstrate the kind of initiatives in this area and their limitations.

A report produced from the initiative of the Public Health and Consumer Affairs Committee of the European Parliament in 1993 recommended the establishment of an epidemiological investigation unit in the Social Affairs Directorate General with the goal of collecting and examining data from member states. While generally highly desirable, the major obstacle facing such a project was that data from the member countries was not compatible. Data incompatibility stems from a fundamental difference of medical practice: the medical record.

Indeed, the development of a common electronic medical record was the subject of another EU initiative, the GEHR project sponsored by the European Commission's R&D programme on Health Telematics Applications (Ingram 1995). The problem is that the medical record is a fundamental element of health care institutions. The design of a technological innovation in this area may produce powerful artefacts, but it hardly begins to challenge the medical records of the myriad health care organizations.

[22] Another example of efforts to create an infrastructure of drug use systems in Europe is the development of a databank on pharmaceutical prices in the European Union's Joint Research Centre in ISPRA, Italy. This 'ECPHIN' database has been designed to store information such as pharmaceutical prices, ingredients, packages, and national therapeutic classification of products. It is suggested that standardized data stored in the ECPHIN system will provide for the needs of national authorities, the industry, and research. Sceptics find the value of this database marginal because it does not provide data on consumption patterns.

The severe limitations of such technology innovations initiatives are amply demonstrated with the effort to implement a pre-commercial version of 'an intelligent, cost-minded prescription system of drugs', that will be possible to customize in different European countries, the OPADE project of Health Telematics.[22] OPADE was set up as a collaborative project involving partners from Britain, France, Italy, and Sweden and partially funded by the European Union with the ambitious aim to achieve optimization of drug prescription from a medical, patient compliance, and economical point of view (de Zegher et al. 1995).

Although OPADE focused on prescribing, its analysis went far beyond making drug therapy decisions on medical grounds only, taking into consideration prescription policy, patient compliance, and cost of therapy. The project attempted to capture a number of aspects of the drug utilization context in an overall 'Prescribing Optimization Model'. It perceived the prescribing process within a health care environment which is governed by legal norms, accommodates conventions and standards for the communication of its participants, operates under limitations of resources, and complies to specific quality of care requirements. It included the identification of policy affecting prescribing, such as resource allocation at the point of care and relevant regulations. Furthermore, prescribing was conceptualized as a 'chain', i.e. as a linear series of events which were referred to as 'value adding', in an attempt to study the health care environment as a domain managed by principles of demand and supply. Also, it recognized the needs and concerns of different categories of participants directly involved in the drug use process, and suggested a semantic analysis to capture the ways they affect prescribing.

The OPADE research team recognized the difference and the relative significance of a number of elements across European countries, such as different distribution of prescribing functions among different professional groups, different clinical practice, different ways that knowledge on drug therapies is developed and used, different management of prescribing and drug use, different auditing practices. The approach adopted by the project team in order to cope with this multiplicity of circumstances was to begin with a functional core of a system on the basis of the adopted prescribing optimization model, which after local analysis could be tailored to specific national environments. A mapping tool was developed for the interpretation of different drug coding and prescribing notation that are found in different prescribing settings (Venot et al. 1992).

The different national conditions presented particular difficulties for the achievement of the economic 'optimization' objective of OPADE. The project dealt with this issue by using theoretical models of methods intended to influence prescribing behaviour which reflected the American experience. Perhaps overwhelmed with the differences of administrative settings, the project adopted mainly an educational intervention approach for the achievement of cost-containment, by providing cost-related information and self-evaluation tools to prescribing doctors.

Despite its sound conceptual foundations, the OPADE was a technical exercise, rather than an effort to fulfil the requirements of the European health care environment. Most research partners were technology specialists and the project may have benefited the European software industry with the development of state of the art prototypes, but it never led to the implementation of information systems to support the task of prescribers or to collect drug utilization data. The existence of analytical models, technical experiments, and prototypes, and of course a competent IT industry, are valuable building blocks for the effective development of information systems should a need for their application mature. However, in a field as politically sensitive as health care, the real battle is the realization of the need for a rationalization such as OPADE was conceived to support. This battle was not won by the EU in the 1990s.

As in many other areas of social policy, the institutional actors of the EU (mainly the European Commission and the Parliament) are confronted with the well-established institutions of the member states. Health care reforms are a crucial subject of the internal political contest in all European countries. Interventions by outsiders, such as the supranational authorities of the EU, are considered by 'Euroskeptics' as threats to national sovereignty and are not particularly welcome. The scope for EU action in this area is restricted to some rather marginal harmonization legislation and technology innovation.

The latter is one area where the EU managed to establish a legitimate role (Cram 1997) becoming the major public sponsor of collaborative ICT R&D in the region. The OPADE is a typical project in a series of programmes which tend to benefit the ICT industry rather than the intended users.

THE ORIGINS OF DIVERSITY IN DRUG USE INFORMATION SYSTEMS

It does not come as a surprise to information systems scholars and practitioners that while technically it is possible to develop systems that store information about a broad range of aspects of drugs, including costs, medical efficacy, adverse effects, patients' details, and prescribing profiles of doctors, the systems in operation in the countries examined are partial and incomplete. Technically, in the 1990s, the DUR databases in the United States as well as PACT in the United Kingdom could store more data for pharmacovigilance purposes, but they did not. Prospective DUR and prescription support systems in hospitals and doctors' practices could inscribe economic, medical, as well as social criteria, and provide guidance on appropriate medication accordingly, but few such systems were in use until the late 1990s. Pharmacy systems could keep trace of the entire range of drugs taken by each individual of the population, thus protecting them from medical misuse and financial waste, but such systems did not become widespread. It is also hardly a surprise that innovative technologies, e.g. OPADE and prescription expert systems with remarkable 'artificial intelligence' capacity, did not reach implementation. Information systems research has amply shown that the actual uses of technology in the domain of health organizations, as elsewhere, are determined by the interests, capabilities, and concerns of their intended and actual users (Kaplan 1987; Forsythe 1992; Dunker 2000). At the very least, this study of drug use systems confirms the situatedness of ICT innovation, in defiance of universalist claims—both medical and managerial—on its value and the expected impact of ICT in the domain of health care.

Nevertheless, the mosaic of information systems outlined in this study raises the question about the sources of their variety and significance of their biases. If they are examined separately against their immediate organizational context, each information system, such as PACT or the DUR systems of a PBM in the United States, reveals a plethora of idiosyncratic elements and actor behaviours. But, if they are studied situated in their institutional health care context, the elements that shaped the development of particular systems on drug utilization are neither idiosyncratic nor uniquely relevant to the specific system and its immediate users. The argument that will be made here is that the drug utilization systems that were deployed in the 1990s and their limitations are a product of pervasive rationality tensions in the reforming modern health care systems of the countries concerned.

A health care system can be seen as an organizational field collectively enacting protective and corrective mechanisms for the preservation of health, according to perceptions of 'healthy' bodily and mental states that have historically come to prevail in a social context (Foucault 1973). In contemporary liberal democracies health care rests upon three sets of values: social fairness, economic optimization, and scientific effectiveness. Roughly, these translate into three main concerns: to secure universal access to health care services, to secure adequate economic resources and put in place efficient mechanisms for the delivery of services, and to achieve 'quality' outcomes according to medical possibilities.

In all industrialized countries the governance of health care involves three institutions that are historically entrusted guardians of each of these sets of values: national government-led public administration, management, and professional practice of medicine and pharmacy. This does not mean that each of these institutions is single-mindedly devoted to one of these values, 'uncontaminated' by the others. In many ways each of these institutions bears elements of the other two sets of values. Historical accounts of the formation of modern health care systems suggest that a great deal of the influence of medical professions in the shaping of the governance of health care systems had to do with their economic interests and political power rather than their scientific concerns (Elston 1991; Miller 1996; Reagan 1999; Flood 2000). Management governed, private health care insurance systems have been under social pressure to achieve some form of equity in the delivery of health care,[23] and the Netherlands' health care system is often quoted to demonstrate that this is feasible (Wagstaff, van Doorslaer, and Paci 1989; Morgan 1999). Also, in contemporary neo-liberal economies, governments adopt many of the features of private sector management. Increasingly they allow the private sector to enter areas which have traditionally been considered the responsibility of the state, such as health, pensions, and education, in order to overcome scarcity of investment and therefore open opportunities for policies of social fairness (Cavers 1998).

[23] See e.g. the discussion of the ethical and pragmatic dilemmas facing health care at times of 'compromises of justice forced by scarcity' (Cartwright 1998; Cavers 1998; Weale 1998).

Thus, the governance of health care involves a mix of institutions considered legitimate carriers of each of these three rationalities, but which are also sensitive to the other two concerns, either through their own interests or by coercion. In the last twenty years each of the three fundamental values of the modern health care context is being reaffirmed, challenging the institutional hold of the others. Health care systems have been faced with intensification of medical, biological, and pharmaceutical sciences and increasing output of innovation. There have been political pressures for fairness in social services such as health. And there has been increasing faith in market mechanisms as appropriate for the efficient production and distribution of goods and services—including health—as well as the realization of science and technology innovation. Consequently, established interrelations among the institutions of health care have been stretched and reforms to relieve the tensions have been pursued.

In a nutshell, the association suggested here between the diversity of drug utilization systems and the clash of rationalities of health care is as follows. The organizational field of health care is nationally entrenched, a historical formation of the socioeconomic institutions of a country's public life. While health care systems are confronted by common global pressures, such as increasing costs of medical and drug interventions, health care governance reforms are situated in national political processes. Supranational influences are negotiated locally and adapted by the national institutional actors of health care. Drug utilization information systems, which have for long been low profile entities with dubious identity as guardians of scientific integrity or cost efficiency, acquired prominent new roles, mobilized as allies to various actors of the reforming national health care networks. Thus, their characteristics—where they are, what they do, what impact they make—are the result of local negotiations of globally shared concerns and international pressures. Moreover, in the unfolding de-institutionalization and re-institutionalization of health care systems, drug utilization information systems mutate, as they draw from and reinforce the various compromises devised in the rationality clashes of the changing institutional setting.

The significance of the national situatedness of health care systems is obvious in the cases studied in this chapter. Each of the countries examined aspired to the three sets of values, but not quite in the same way. In their different regimes of organizing health care public administration, management, and professional norms were maintained and reformed by different patterns of vested interests and taken-for-granted beliefs. This point is supported by more general cross-country studies of health care systems: 'the patterns of health service organisations adopted in different countries are the result of the interaction between political, historical, cultural and socioeconomic factors. Ultimately, these reflect broader societal values and the relative weights assigned to different social objectives such as equity, efficiency or the merits of individual freedom versus collectivism.' (Abel-Smith et al. 1995: 23).

The national variation in health care governance and in the drug use systems that emerged under them is striking in comparing the United States and the United Kingdom in the 1990s. After a decade of pressures and efforts for reform, always in the name of the three rationalities, the health care systems of these countries continued to be exemplary ends of the range of health care organizing regimes in industrialized countries. And although in both countries drug use systems were mobilized under the same principles of 'managed care', promising to reach a satisfactory compromise between medical quality and cost containment, their differences remained conspicuous. In the United States there was a proliferation of drug utilization information systems, circulated by both government and market institutions and growing under loosely regulated competition. DUR acquired power as a mechanism of organizing for state health care and insurance companies as well as a business in its own right, transacted in the market. That bustling context generated innovation, promised efficiency and quality, but abandoned the pursuit of social fairness. In contrast, in the United Kingdom, large-scale prescription systems emerged gradually and spread quite cautiously, tightly controlled by nationwide institutions bearing political authority and, increasingly, managerial expertise. The so-called internal market reforms triggered innovation at the hospital level. Under an organizing regime striving to balance management and medical concerns various pharmacy systems included prospective and retrospective drug utilization functionality. But for fear that the principle of universal care might be compromised, little room was allowed for market actors to circulate drug utilization systems. Prescription systems never became a business, autonomously growing and fuelled by market opportunities. And although the British public became increasingly dissatisfied with the quality of health care services, the US health care system, which is reputedly capable of the highest quality care in the world, was never taken as a case to emulate.[24]

Despite the strong national character of health care governance, there are many cross-national and supra-national institutional influences. Global institutions, such as medical research and the canons of WHO, shape contemporary views about health and required health services in a modern society. Regional political institutions, such as the EU, legislate and encourage common, across countries, elements of governance. Governments themselves keep an eye on the organizational innovations in other countries health care systems. Health care professionals—a new category of professionals claiming a driving role in health care reforms—compare and generalize. Doctors, medical technicians, pharmacists develop common professional aspirations and capabilities through common information and training channels. The multinational pharmaceutical industry spreads common medicines and standards of what is high quality in drug therapy.

In the 1990s the most prevalent isomorphic effect exerted by the combination of such forces was the spread of the concepts and practice of 'managed care'. Managed care mechanisms have been applied in many health care systems, whether they followed an organizing model driven by competition—with government providing certain safety net services and a degree of regulation—or by government controlled 'markets'—which cautiously opened space for competition in the delivery of certain

---

[24] Indicative of the attitudes of medical professionals in the UK towards the American health care system, when at a DURG meeting I asked how PACT compares with retrospective DUR in the US the answer I received was that the systems developed in the US are irrelevant for the NHS.

services (Mossialos, Kanavos, and Abel-Smith 1997; Flood 2000). A common element of managed care has been the monitoring and review of the delivery of services and of family doctors' recommendations, including drug prescriptions. Interventions to medical practice, such as evidence-based disease management, that drug use information systems are mobilized to reinforce stem from the same set of principles.

As part of managed care, drug utilization information systems enter the translation of health care aligned with the rationality of management, modifying traditional public administration accountability and decision-making processes, but also challenging the taken-for-granted roles of medical professions in health care governance. The conflict between the rationalities of public administration and management is a pervasive issue, part of the ideological battles in national politics.[25] But the confrontation of the managerial rationality with the institutionalized authority of the medical professions is a distinct element of health care reform.

In the United Kingdom, this confrontation is manifested in conflicts between appointed management and doctors in hospitals, where traditional lines of decision making and accountability on medical grounds are intercepted by appointed managers. Doctors both in hospitals and community practice are asked to consider the economy aspects of their professional actions. Moreover, managed care interventions, such as evidence-based guidelines and mechanisms for monitoring their professional actions, have added new concerns to the domain of medical decision. They challenged the whole ethos of professional conduct, changing the domain of doctors' and nurses' judgement and influencing their medical decisions (Sweeney 1996).

In the United States, although the medical professions have traditionally been aligned more with the rationality of management rather than public administration, the political choice of managed care over government mandates in the 1990s opened new scope for monitoring and intervening in the decisions of prescribing doctors, and new ways of sharing responsibilities among doctors, pharmacists, and managers. The role of drug utilization information systems was contested. They were instruments of efficiency and innovation in the hands of cost minding and strategically thinking managers of insurance companies and pharmaceutical services firms (Nichols 1994; Thomas 1996; Elrodt et al. 1997), or guardians of medical quality and promoters of best medical outcomes (Lipton and Bird 1993; Armstrong et al. 2000) in the hands of doctors and dispensing chemists.

One might dismiss the concerns and resistances of doctors and pharmacists to adopt practices such as evidence-based methods, and the information systems they entail as a manifestation of their economic vested interest. However, even though

---

[25] For example, the internal market reform of the British NHS was consistent with the then Conservative government efforts to reduce the size of public administration and introduce market efficiency in public services, which formed the basis for 'public management'. As privatization of the NHS was not feasible politically, a main element of the reform of 1991 was the entrance of professional managers in the governance of hospitals and the NHS structures more generally. The political and economic significance of this change continued to be subject to controversy and debate in the national politics during the 1990s, but a public administration accommodating the rationality of management came to be accepted as the modern form of governance, and was left intact by the Labour government that took office in 1997.

economic interests are undoubtedly involved, the issues at stake are more complex. The scrutiny and continuous attempts to influence the decisions that have traditionally been the undisputed domain of judgement of scientifically trained medical experts through mechanisms conveying the logic of efficiency alters established forms of integrity of medical practice. The concerns go deeper than the economic status, or even the power of stakeholder groups. For example, Sweeney (1996) is concerned about change of the nature of medical consultation by doctors basing their decisions on the results of 'randomized controlled trials' captured in the databases and reports of evidence-based medicine. He senses that this change assaults the established bond of doctors with their patients: 'From the point of view of general practice the anxiety is that an overemphasis on the questions that can be asked and answered by EBM [evidence-based medicine] may run the risk of devaluing those questions that cannot be so expressed' (ibid. 76). Information systems claiming to guide the optimization of medical decisions raise questions about the meaning of 'the optimum', bringing to the fore conflicting rationalities, historically settled in taken-for-granted practices.

CONCLUDING REMARKS

There are two points worth noting at the end of this case study, on the origin of rationality tensions, and on the significance of diversity of information systems on drug use as an infrastructure of global modernity. First, tensions of rationality result from cross-country isomorphic influences challenging the historically formed national health care systems, but are also locally generated by the de-institutionalization processes within the nationally confined health care organizational fields. The diversity of partial drug use information systems arises from differences in the interrelationship of conflicting rationalities both across organizational fields and within an organizational field under conditions of de-institutionalization.

Second, the variety, partiality, and ambiguous identity of drug use information systems is a characteristic of contemporary large-scale information infrastructures, which cannot be rationalized in universal terms, or circumvented by good design. Bearing inscriptions of particular resolutions of rationality conflicts in health care systems, drug use information systems cannot be but inherently political entities, and therefore context and time specific. At the period of widespread questioning of the merits of the organizing regime of health care governance in the 1990s, drug use information systems proliferated, took a large variety of forms, entered institutional alliances, and formed infrastructures which, from a global perspective, are anarchic, and fragmented. The DUR in the United States and the prescription systems deployed in the United Kingdom's NHS are odd realizations of WHO's vision of DURG information systems. Despite efforts by international institutions for standardization,[26] the dynamics for the circulation of such systems create hybrids rather

---

[26] Taking a much longer time perspective, and a much more specific information system, the International Classification of Diseases (ICD), Bowker and Leigh Star (2000) trace the history of a

than standards. They exemplify, nevertheless, the kind of information infrastructure that should be realistically expected in the contemporary era of globalization. Not a universal interlinkage of compatible systems, but a mosaic of information banks and information processing rules, products of organizing regimes and continuously mutating.

successful universal standardization, in effect telling a story complementary to the one of the proliferation of drug use information systems. They examine how, against a background of political contingencies and technological possibilities, ICD (as well as a series of other universal classifications) emerged in the late 19th cent., providing fundamental tools for communication and control to the modern state. Interestingly, they also point out that the universality of the ICD not only has been achieved through political and 'scientific' processes that ignored the life and medical realities of developing countries, but that ICD continues to be insensitive to and of little use in the conditions of Africa. One could speculate that particular key drug use information systems may also acquire universal status, either by the dominance of one rationality over the others, or by a pragmatic alliance of the institutional actors with vested interests in each of them. Nevertheless, as Bowker and Leigh Star note, '[t]owers of Babel are perhaps the rule, not the exception' in information systems infrastructures (ibid. 131).

References

Abel-Smith, B. (1992). *Cost Containment and New Priorities in Health Care*. Aldershot: Avebury.
—— and Mossialos, E. (1994). 'Cost Containment and Health Care Reform—A Study of the European Union'. London, The European Institute, London School of Economics.
—— Figueras, J., Holland, W., McKee, M., and Mossialos, E. (1995). *Choices in Health Policy: An Agenda for the European Union*. Aldershot: Dartmouth.
Alonso, F. G., Scott, A. I., Stika, L., and Westerholm, B. (1993). 'Health Authorities and Drug Utilization Studies', in M. N. G. Dukes (ed.), *Drug Utilization Studies: Methods and Uses*. Copenhagen: WHO, 147–67.
Armstrong, E. P., Byrns, P. J., Foster, T. S., Stockwell-Morris, L., and Fulda, T. R. (2000). 'Drug Utilization Review: Mechanisms to Improve its Effectiveness and Broaden its Scope'. *Journal of the American Pharmaceutical Association*, 40(4): 538–45.
—— and Terry, A. K. (1992). 'Impact of Drug Use Evaluation upon Ambulatory Pharmacy Practice'. *Annals of Pharmacotherapy*, 26: 1546–52.
Bloomfield, B. P., Coombs, R., Owens, J., and Taylor, P. (1997). 'Doctors as Managers: Constructing Systems and Users in the National Health Service', in B. P. Bloomfield, R. Coombs, D. Knights, and D. Littler (eds.), *Information Technology and Organizations: Strategies, Networks, and Integration*. Oxford: Oxford University Press, 112–34.
Bowker, G. C., and Leigh Star, S. (2000). *Sorting Things Out: Classification and its Consequences*. Cambridge, Mass.: MIT Press.
Calder, G. (2000). 'Pharmaceutical Care in Minneapolis: Initial Impressions'. *Pharmaceutical Journal*, 264: 375–6.
Cartwright, W. (1998). 'Equal Access to Health Care', in T. Sorell (ed.), *Health Care, Ethics and Insurance*. London: Routledge, 165–80.
Cavers, D. (1998). 'More Private Health Insurance is Desirable and Inevitable', in T. Sorell (ed.), *Health Care, Ethics and Insurance*. London: Routledge, 151–64.
Cram, L. (1997). *Policy Making in the EU*. London: Routledge.
Dasta, J. F., Greer, M. L., and Speedies, S. M. (1992). 'Computers in Healthcare: Overview and Bibliography'. *Annals of Pharmacotherapy* 26: 109–17.

Davidoff, F., Haynes, B., and Sackett, D. (1995). 'Evidence Based Medicine'. *British Medical Journal*, 310: 1085–6.

de Zegher, I., Venot, A., Milstein, C., Sene, B., de Rosis, F., de Carolis, B., Pietri, P., and Dahlberg, B. (1995). 'OPADE: Optimization of Drug Prescription Using Advanced Informatics', in M. F. Laires, M. J. Ladeira, and J. P. Christensen (eds.), *Health in the New Communications Age*. Amsterdam: IOS, 151–60.

DOH (1989). 'Working for Patients'. London: HMSO.

——(1997). 'The New NHS: Modern. Dependable'. London: HMSO.

Dukes, M. N. G. (1993). 'Introduction', in M. N. G. Dukes, *Drug Utilization Studies*. Copenhagen: WHO, 1–4.

Dunker, E. (2000). 'How LINCs were Made: Alignment and Exclusion in American Medical Informatics'. *The Information Society*, 16(3): 187–99.

Economist, The (2000). 'Thirty-six Places to go'. *Economist*, 24 June: 62–7.

Elrodt, G., Cook, D. J., Lee, J., Cho, M., Hunt, D., and Weingarten, S. (1997). 'Evidence-Based Disease Management'. *Journal of the American Medical Association (JAMA)*, 278(20): 1687–92.

Elston, M. A. (1991). 'The Politics of Professional Power: Medicine in a Changing Health Service', in J. Gabe, M. Calnan, and M. Bury (eds.), *The Sociology of the Health Service*. London: Routledge, 58–88.

Evidence-based medicine working group (1992). 'Evidence Based Medicine: A New Approach to Teaching the Practice of Medicine'. *JAMA* 268: 2420–5.

Fish, C. A., Kirking, D. M., and Martin, J. B. (1992). 'Information Systems for Evaluating the Quality of Prescribing'. *Annals of Pharmacotherapy*, 26: 392–7.

Flanagan, M. E. (1994). 'Clinton's Health Plan: Pros and Cons for Pharmacy'. *American Pharmacy*, NS 34(1): 43–90.

Fleming, D. M. (1994). 'Practice Based Information Systems for Monitoring Medicines'. *Pharmaceutical Medicine*, 8: 161–76.

Flood, C. M. (2000). *International Health Care Reform: A Legal, Economic and Political Analysis*. London: Routledge.

Forsythe, D. E. (1992). 'Blaming the User. The Cultural Nature of Scientific Practice'. *Knowledge and Society: The Anthropology of Science and Technology*, 9: 95–111.

Foucault, M. (1973). *Birth of the Clinic*. London: Tavistock.

Glinn, J., Hubbard, N., and Pickup, J. F. (1993). 'Intervention Reporting on the South Western Region Computer System'. *Pharmaceutical Journal*, Sept.: 24–6.

Grasela, T. H., Walawander, C. A., Kennedy, D. L., and Jolson, H. M. (1993). 'Capability of Hospital Computer Systems in Performing Drug-Use Evaluations and Adverse Drug Event Monitoring'. *American Journal of Hospital Pharmacy*, 50: 1889–95.

Harris, C. M. (1994). 'Better Feedback on Prescribing for General Practitioners'. *British Medical Journal*, 309: 356.

Heath, I. (1994). 'The Creeping Privatization of NHS Prescribing'. *British Medical Journal*, 309 (10 Sept.): 623–4.

Ingram, D. (1995). 'GEHR: The Good European Health Record', in M. F. Laires, M. J. Ladeira, and J. P. Christensen (eds.), *Health in the New Communications Age*. Amsterdam: IOS Press, 66–74.

Jackson, C., and Walker, D. (1998). 'Hospital Prescribing Information—Can We Achieve an Effective National Database? A Preliminary Report on the National Prescribing Centre's Hospital Prescribing Information Project'. *Pharmaceutical Journal*, 261: 205–8.

Jones, J. (1991). 'A View from the Drug Utilization Review Management Organization Sector'. *Clinical Pharmacology & Therapeutics*, 50(5): 620–5.

Jones, M. R. (1994). 'Learning the Language of the Market: Information Systems Strategy Formation in a UK District Health Authority'. *Accounting Management and Information Technology*, 4(3): 119–47.

Jones, N. K. (1993). 'Assessing Patient Drug Compliance Using a Computer Drug Database'. *Healthcare Computing*: 429–33.

Kaplan, B. (1987). 'The Medical Computing "Lag": Perceptions of Barriers to the Application of Computers to Medicine'. *International Journal of Technology Assessment in Health Care*, 3: 123–36.

Kassler, J. (1994). *Bitter Medicine: Greed and Chaos in American Health Care*. New York: Birch Lane Press.

Kreling, D. H., and Mott, D. A. (1993). 'The Cost-Effectiveness of Drug Utilisation Review in an Outpatient Setting'. *PharmacoEconomics*, 4(6): 414–36.

Laporte, J. R., Baksaas, I., and Lunde, P. K. M. (1993). 'Drug Utilization Studies: General Background', in M. N. G. Dukes (ed.), *Drug Utilization Studies*. Copenhagen: WHO, European Series No. 45, 5–22.

Lee, J., and Morgan, S. (1993). 'Development of a Computerized System to Provide Audit of Pharmaceutical Activity'. *International Journal of Pharmacy Practice*, 2: 117–23.

Linnarson, R. (1993). 'Decision Support for Drug Prescription Integrated with Computer-Based Patient Records in Primary Care'. *Medical Informatics*, 18(2): 131–42.

Lipton, H. L., and Bird, J. A. (1991). 'Drug Utilization Review: State of the Art from an Academic Perspective'. *Clinical Pharmacology & Therapeutics*, 50(5): 616–19.

—— —— 1993). 'Drug Utilization Review in Ambulatory Settings: State of the Science and Directions for Outcomes Research'. *Medical Care*, 131(12): 1069–82.

Marmor, T. R. (1994). *Understanding Health Care Reform*. New Haven: Yale University Press.

Miller, I. (1996). *American Health Care Blues: Blue Cross, HMOs, and Pragmatic Reform since 1960*. New Brunswick, NJ: Transaction.

Moore, W. J., Gutermuth, K., and Pracht, E. E. (2000). 'Systemwide Effects of Medicaid Retrospective Drug Utilization Review Programs'. *Journal of Health, Politics, Policy and Law*, 25(4): 653–88.

Morgan, O. (1999). *A Cure for Change: Global Comparisons in Health Care*. London: Social Market Foundation.

Mossialos, E., Kanavos, P., and Abel-Smith, B. (1997). 'Will Managed Care Work in Europe?' *PharmacoEconomics*, 11(4): 297–305.

Nichols, N. A. (1994). 'Medicine, Management, and Mergers: An Interview with Merck's P. Roy Vagelos'. *Harvard Business Review*, Nov.–Dec.: 105–14.

Nørgaard, L. S. (1996). 'The Development of Patient Medication Records in Denmark: A Social Constructionist Perspective'. *The Department of Social Pharmacy*. Copenhagen, The Royal Danish School of Pharmacy.

O'Connell, H. M., Chance, S., and Bowman, L. (1994). 'Computerized Drug-Use Evaluation' *American Journal of Hospital Pharmacy*, 51: 363–7.

Pouloudi, A., and Whitley, E. (1997). 'Stakeholder Identification in Inter-organizational Systems Gaining Insights for Drug Use Management Systems'. *European Journal of Information Systems*, 6: 1–14.

Reagan, M. D. (1999). *The Accidental System: Health Care Policy in America*. Boulder, Colo.: Westview Press.

Redwood, H. (1994). 'Public Policy Trends in Drug Pricing and Reimbursement in the European Community'. *PharmacoEconomics*, 6(1): 3–10.

Rosenberg, W., and Donald, A. (1995). 'Evidence Based Medicine: An Approach to Clinical Problem Solving'. *BMJ* 310: 1122–6.

Sackett, D. L., Rosenberg, W., and Muir Guir, J. A. (1996). 'Evidence Based Medicine: What It Is and What It Isn't'. *BMJ* 312: 71–2.

Schulke, D. G. (1991). 'A Congressional Perspective on Inappropriate Drug Therapy and Drug Utilization Review'. *Clinical Pharmacology & Therapeutics*, 50(5): 606–11.

Stork, M. W., and Greene, R. J. (1993). 'Expert Systems in Pharmacy Practice'. *International Journal of Pharmacy Practice*, 2: 53–7.

Sultz, H. A., and Young, K. M. (1997). *Health Care USA: Understanding its Organization and Delivery*. Gaithersburg, Md.: Aspen Publishers.

Sweeney, K. (1996). 'Evidence and Uncertainty', in M. Marinker (ed.), *Sense and Sensibility in Health Care*. London: BMJ, 59–85.

Thomas, N. (1996). 'The Role of Pharmacoeconomics in Disease Management'. *Pharmaco-Economics*, 9(suppl. 1): 9–15.

Thompson, B. H., and Chantry-Price, A. E. (1993). 'Interfacing a MUMPS-based drug-prescribing scheme with other health service systems'. *Healthcare Computing*: 434–9.

Touche, D. A. (1996). 'Managing Medicines: Managing Care'. London, Royal Pharmaceutical Society of Great Britain.

Venot, A., Kostrewski, B., Milstein, C., Sene, B., Harding, N., Weeks, R., Pietri, P., and de Zegher, I. (1992). 'OPADE: Optimization of Drug Prescription Using Advanced Informatics, Necessary Input for a CDPS'. European Commission.

Wagstaff, A., van Doorslaer, E., and Paci, P. (1989) 'Equity in the Finance and Delivery of Health Care. Some Tentative Cross-Country Comparisons'. *Oxford Review of Health Policy*, 5(1): 89-112.

Walker, R. (2000). 'Pharmaceutical Public Health: The End of Pharmaceutical Care?' *Pharmaceutical Journal*, 264: 340–1.

Weale, A. (1998). 'Ethical Issues in Social Insurance for Health', in T. Sorell (ed.), *Health Care, Ethics and Insurance*. London: Routledge, 137–50.

Wennberg, J. E. (1992). 'Innovation and the Politics of Limits in a Changing Health Care Economy', in A. C. Gelijns (ed.), *Technology and Health Care in an Era of Limits*. Washington, DC: National Academy Press, 9–33.

Wertheimer, A., and Kralewski, J. (1993). 'DUR Programs: Current Trends and Future Directions'. *American Pharmacy*, NS 33(2): 37–42.

WHO (1977). 'The Selection of Essential Drugs', Copenhagen.

—— (2000). 'Health Care Financing Administration'. Copenhagen, WHO.

Zawistiwich, L. (1991). 'What the Government Wants'. *Clinical Pharmacology & Therapeutics*, 50(5): 603–5.

9

The Nature and Significance of Global Diversity for Information Systems

The cases studied in Chapters 5 to 8 provide evidence supporting the non-deterministic, non-essentialist view of ICT, uncovering how erratically information systems innovation unfolds in different organizational circumstances. They demonstrate the diversity of organizing regimes within which the meaning and potential value of information systems innovation is negotiated. In these cases information systems innovation often exposed rationality contradictions, surfacing either through direct conflict with the intended or perceived objectives of the innovation, or in tacit resistances that distort and annihilate the intended innovation. The cases show that the making and negotiation of the meaning of information systems innovation, as well as consequent action, are embedded in multiple contexts, which need to be taken into account in order to make sense of the technology translations attempted, and the conditions leading to their durability or reversion. Moreover, the case studies show some of the dynamics of contemporary globalization. Insights are gained on the processes involved in the tortuous globalization of the 'technologies of globalization'.

This concluding chapter elaborates on these points, linking theory and empirical evidence, and refining the socio-technical theoretical conception of the process of information systems innovation. But the study of information systems cannot afford to be concerned with theoretical elaboration alone. The institutional forces of ICT play an important role in the contemporary globalization process and information systems scholars have always felt an obligation to inform practice. For many, this has been an overwhelming concern and has led to a large body of normative and theoretically weak knowledge. A theoretical research tradition has gradually become visible in the field of information systems, but it remains important to spell out the implications of theoretical ideas on constructive action. Thus, I think it appropriate to close this book with reflections on the significance of understanding diversity not only as a theoretical concern in the study of information systems, but also for influencing responsible professional practice.

MANIFESTATIONS OF ALIENATION IN INFORMATION SYSTEMS INNOVATION

The concerns which enrolled ICT in the organizations studied in the previous chapters are familiar and ordinary for somebody with knowledge of the uses of ICT in organizations, and, one would be justified to think, uncontroversial. In Pemex generations of information systems projects were launched with the objectives of efficiency, accountability, informed planning, and management. In IKA, the enduring aspiration has been to use IT to design a modern, efficient social security service; a perfectly reasonable objective for an information-intensive service organization. In neither of these cases was ICT associated with highly contentious issues, such as job cuts. In the plan for the restructuring of the small manufacturing enterprises of Cyprus, computers were recommended as a necessary tool to enable them to address international competition. In the national arenas of 'community pharmacodynamics', ICT has, in the first place, been seen as means for gathering data on large populations, and disseminating the knowledge distilled from them to inform efficient and appropriate use of a powerful but expensive and inherently risky drug technology. Yet, the realization of these apparently uncontroversial objectives met a variety of obstacles.

One could observe at this point that discussion of obstacles, and indeed failures are not rare in information systems innovation literature (Sauer 1999). It is known that they not only plague leading-edge innovation—being what Sauer calls 'the price of progress' (p. 282)—but also frustrate ordinary information systems projects concerning core organizational functions, such as payroll (see e.g Myers 1994). Information systems projects frequently fail to fulfil the objectives set by the initial problematization, they are abandoned or deliver poor quality systems, or the innovation fails to engage the intended 'users'[1] The long established stream of research on failure has identified lists of factors responsible for these problems, such as technical competencies or lack of management commitment. More importantly for analytical purposes, research on failures has also explored the processes of failed projects, thus adding to the understanding of the sources and the dynamics of occurring difficulties, and turning attention to social processes in the organizational context of information systems innovation.

One of the most common problems highlighted by such research is user resistance (Markus 1983), an issue that seems also relevant to the cases studied here. Resistance, in the information systems literature, refers to intended users' behaviour of being either uncooperative during systems development or rejecting the new technology system in implementation or use. The classic response requires managers—of the business and the project—to fight back and see the innovation through. Peter Keen suggests that an implementation strategy should be able to respond to counter-implementation action by employees with a counter-counter-implementation strategy (Keen 1981). For the proponents of the industrial democracy socio-technical approach, such an attitude is insensitive to what resistance signifies. If managers were prepared to listen to the voices of resistance instead of working out counter-counter-implementation action to push forward with their initial plans, they would be able to see the point of view of those unconvinced by the merits of the innovation or feeling threatened by it. They would see aspects they had missed in the initial plans, and they would be able to adapt, compromise, and reach consensus on feasible and desirable to all action.

Understanding systems implementation as an inherently political process in terms of the more recent socio-technical theory implies a different attitude to resistance. In the

---

[1] This is what Lyytinen and Hirschheim (1987) categorize as correspondence failure, process failure, and interaction failure, accordingly.

more messy world of socially constructed technologies and organizational orders, encountering resistances, vested interests, and alternative interpretations of the meaning and significance of an innovation is not an exceptional turn of events, but the nature of the innovation process itself. Resistance is not an aspect of conservative human nature that has to be bent in order for innovation to progress, and it cannot always be avoided by well-meaning project managers. It is an intrinsic aspect of the social processes through which technology innovation is actually shaped. It is not surprising that management may not have control over the course of the innovation, that information systems implementation may not go according to initial plan, that systems projects may drift, and that the resulting technology and organizational ensembles may be different from what was initially intended. It betrays the influence of the technocratic management science illusion to expect that it is possible to manage information systems innovation towards a preconceived set of benefits (Knights, Noble, and Willmott 1997). Instead, information systems change should be thought of as contested by actors with diverse interests and power bases. The innovation process is most likely to act as a catalyst to bring into the open otherwise hidden latent conflicts.

Indeed several authors not only acknowledge that planned action and control of information systems processes is unrealistic, but they take a positive stance to the social and political nature of innovation. While control by technical/rational means may stifle or exacerbate the social friction inherent in innovation, incremental action and improvisation to address emergent issues of a 'drifting process' may steer information systems innovation effectively (Orlikowski 1996; Ciborra 1999). A creative drifting process, that adopts an attitude of care, hospitality, and cultivation, rather than controlling management measures, is suggested as the required approach for effective innovation (Ciborra 2000). From this perspective resistance, tensions, breakdowns, and misfits are part of an effective process of learning and building up new solutions.

The cases in this book point to problems on a different scale, though. They suggest that, in certain contexts, obstacles and frictions may become chronic and pervasive, and the drifting may not be accompanied by learning. ICT may remain marginalized, a dormant actor, with its promised potential unappreciated and unfulfilled, or it may secure its presence and grow without fulfilling desirable objectives, even adding inefficiencies to the organization. The small enterprises in Cyprus, IKA, and to a large extent Pemex, demonstrate such long-lasting difficulties in achieving positive outcomes from information systems innovation.[2]

---

[2] In the literature on the nature of information systems innovation, debating the merits and shortcomings of particular approaches for successful systems innovation, case studies usually focus on a single innovation project or translation. Even cases that indicate severe problems of an innovation translation may be isolated incidents of failure. The brief background information most case descriptions provide on the organizational context often suggests that there is already a functioning infrastructure of information systems (see e.g. Knights, Noble, and Willmott 1997). In other cases, later publications indicate that the problems of a particular project were subsequently addressed, or a failed project was subsequently superseded by further successful initiatives (see e.g. the story of computerization of the DHSS in the late 1970s and early 1980s in the UK described in Avgerou 1989). High costs and potential organizational damage of individual projects notwithstanding, such failures are incidents in the continuous innovation efforts organizations have been pursuing since the advent of computers, and may well be part of the learning process. The problem raised here is that there are environments where such learning does not occur, and failure—of one type or another—is endemic.

More specifically, in the small manufacturers of Cyprus, the central problematization failed to convince, and the mobilization of ICT was minimal. It was not a matter of resistance to technology, and computers had in fact a presence in the administration of most firms. Simply they were not entrusted to play a significant enough role and neither raised expectations for significant benefits nor posed a threat. With the gradual reversal of the industrial translation experiment, computers remained low-profile actors for mundane administrative tasks. Without resistance, but with no interest in exploiting their potential either, computers stayed in the background, perhaps waiting for future opportunities.

In IKA there was no particular difficulty in conceiving a strategic role for computers. Ever since the 1970s successive administrations considered ICT an agent necessary for the transformation of the dysfunctional bureaucratic organization into a modern service organization. Successive strategies were worked out to align the technologies of the day with chosen organizational designs. When they faltered they were abandoned and allowed to drift, in a negative sense though. They were starved of resources and interest. Consequently, new innovation aspirations took the place of the unfulfilled hopes of the earlier information systems strategies and projects. At no point in time was ICT explicitly resisted. No strikes by the civil servants took place, no protesting public crowded at the doors of IKA,[3] On the contrary, there has been a constant stream of positive expressions on technology innovation. Again and again politicians, journalists, the learned of the Greek society and the management of the bureaucracy declared their dismay that IKA was late in implementing 'modern' ICT—being, at various points of time, on-line systems, distributed computing, and network technology. The vast majority of IKA's civil servants remained silent, of course. And when I asked them, they did not blame computers, 'but . . .'. While the 'but' continues to be fought in multiple battles, at the macro political level as well as in the daily life of civil servants and the Greeks who depend on IKA's services for their living, the dysfunctional ICT is there to stay. To be accepted, it had to be stripped of its alleged rationalizing potency, adapted to the dysfunctional environment, becoming blatantly dysfunctional itself. ICT's imaginary role has never been enacted. Its actual enactment has so far been a caricature of its envisaged character.

In Pemex too there was no great difficulty in conceiving a role for ICT and launching information systems projects. Computers proliferated, appropriated by many men of power, who were keen to do 'their job' effectively, and of course to safeguard their control over their own part of the corporation. They were not against computers, in fact they wanted them for themselves, and they mobilized resources to construct their own information systems and to organize their own information systems centres. It was the successive integrated systems projects, launched by the modernizing forces of the headquarters, that they found suspicious and threatening and that they eroded in various ways. Until the last administration, which was headed by an executive convinced of the merits of a modern integrated systems infrastructure,

---

[3] The gross problems caused by computerization, such as the damage of the records on pension entitlements, were accepted with stoic patience by all affected. This is a stark contrast with, for example, the case of the problematic SOCRATE reservation system in the French railways studied by Mitev (1996).

even the top echelons of the company were ambivalent about the value they would get from integrated information systems. And as the meaning and the logistics of modernization were contested, the technologies that were intended to contribute to turning the corporation to an efficient business continued to spread. The fact that for more than twenty years little of their imaginary potential was realized hardly posed an obstacle to their proliferation.

IKA and Pemex were not irrational to persevere with ICT innovation despite the poor outcomes of successive projects. In the contemporary institutional context organizations have no other 'option' but to persevere with continuous information systems innovation. But these cases make it clear that the irreversible diffusion of ICT may be quite ineffectual for the interests of these organizations and their intended beneficiaries. In IKA, and to a lesser extent in Pemex, successive generations of ICT were developed and used without contributing to the solution expected by the concerns that mobilized them. ICT adapted opportunistically to the existing organizational context, consequently itself reflecting the behaviour of the organizational context.

Not all adaptations are dysfunctional, of course. The case of drug utilization systems shows that ICT may adapt to the circumstances of an organization, shedding part of its expected potential, but still contributing to the dynamics of organizational change. It is shaped in the course of the translation that mobilized it. In the United Kingdom, prescription systems cautiously anticipating and adapting to the changing organizing regime in the NHS, appear to be able to grow with friction, but not in alienation from their social context.

Still, it is interesting to contrast all these cases with the growth of DUR systems in the United States, where ICT has been playing multiple strategic roles as an ally to various actors in the drug use processes. Questions regarding the weaknesses of the US health care organizing regime notwithstanding, this is a case that many information systems scholars would single out as a successful exploitation of the strategic potential of the technologies of globalization.

To sum up the discussion in this section so far, two types of problematic states are manifested in the cases studied in this book. The first—not an unknown issue in the information systems literature[4]—is that in certain contexts there is indifference to the potential benefits of ICT and a reluctance or inability to engage in the processes of technology-mediated globalization. The second, much less recognized and, I believe, more insidious, is that ICT may grow as an autonomous institutional network amidst alienated organizational actors. Cases such as IKA suggest the risk that in certain contexts ICT may acquire its own power as a symbol and carrier of modernity and consolidate its own functions, while growing disjoint from both the declared rational objectives that justify its development and the social preoccupations of its immediate context. This is a state of autonomization of ICT that entails the alienation of the agents in the organizational context to the institutionalized ICT.[5] ICT may keep

---

[4] See e.g. the country classifications of Palvia and Palvia (1996), suggesting that one of the most important issues regarding information systems in developing countries is lack of awareness of the value of ICT. This issue is targeted by international institutions, such as the World Bank and development aid organizations, with awareness campaigns.

growing in an organization and spreading widely in a society, partly by its own local dynamics—such as the professionals inside the organization and in the local consultancy market—and partly by international forces—such as the international ICT market and disembedded global ideas on its potential and crucial necessity. Meanwhile, the organizational enactment does not change by accommodating the ICT network; it proceeds by shouldering, in whatever way its actors are accustomed to, the additional dysfunctionalities of the self-perpetuating ICT network. This kind of drifting differs from the state of drifting described by Ciborra (2000). Little cultivation takes place, no situated choices of innovation are made. Information systems innovation is self-perpetuated, fuelled by imported images of modernity.

MULTIPLE SUBSTANTIVE RATIONALITIES CONFRONTING THE ALLIANCE OF INFORMATION SYSTEMS AND MANAGERIALISM

The theoretical approach and the empirical studies in this book can be followed further to probe into the question why such problems occur. Why has there not been much cultivation of ICT in IKA, and the Cypriot enterprises? Why did alienation happen in IKA? Why did Pemex face chronic difficulties in deploying efficient information systems and why has it been unable to achieve strategic gains from such powerful technologies? Why are some environments, such as the health care systems of the United Kingdom cautious with ICT and others hyperactive?

Here, the search for an answer to these questions has built on the concept of ICT as institution: as a global heterogeneous network loaded with and conveying particular visions of organizational action. More specifically, it was argued in Chapters 1 and 2 that ICT is tightly linked with management, an institution in its own right, that sets up a particular under-socialized organizing rationality.

Several voices in the literature of information systems have drawn upon debates and critical analyses in the literature of management. There has been concern about the dominant positivistic epistemology, which seeks to generalize on the basis of measurable factors, missing out the complexity of social processes in organizations (Mumford et al. 1985; Nissen, Klein, and Hirschheim 1991). More relevant to the analytical approach followed in this book, a stream of studies has been critical of the technical/rationalistic assumptions of management theory and practice that have been adopted in the field of information systems (Knights and Morgan 1991; Knights, Noble, and Willmott 1997). Several authors stressed the significance of aspects of power and subjectivity that are ignored or suppressed in the managerialist discourse that guides information systems innovation. A number of authors voiced concern about the instrumental role of management (Engeldorp Gastelaars, Magala, and Preub 1990; Alvesson and Willmott 1992; Alvesson and Deetz 2000) and of information systems within the prevailing managerial ideology (Lyytinen 1992).

---

[5] This point was made in Chap. 1, drawing from Castoriadis's analysis of political institutions (Castoriadis 1987).

Such critiques observe that most of the knowledge accumulated in the field of information systems concerns the instrumental use of ICT. Information systems studies tend to provide guidance—whether theoretical, analytical, or methodical—on how to use a powerful technology, no matter for what purpose. The field is therefore preoccupied with issues of means—of formal rationality—ignoring questions of substantive rationality. This echoes a critical view of management: 'the sciences of management have accomplished a colonisation of the life-world in which debate over the norms is bracketed or suppressed in favour of an exclusive concern with the development of more effective strategies for achieving the existing, unquestioned objectives—the most prevalent and taken-for-granted of these being "profitable growth"(Alvesson and Willmott 1990: 52).

In contrast to such an instrumental managerialist perspective, analyses adopting critical—and increasingly postmodern—theoretical perspectives have raised questions of political and ethical choice (Walsham 1993; Hirschheim, Klein, and Lyytinen 1996; Bowker and Leigh Star 2000). In early critical studies some researchers adopted a Marxist stance, seeking to align information systems with the interests of trade unions as instruments for the emancipation of workers (Sandberg 1985). Most prevalent in the critical studies of management and information systems has been the influence of the critical social theory of Habermas (see e.g. Alvesson and Willmott 1990; Lyytinen 1992). Such research aspires to complement the economic instrumental rationality of mainstream management with the 'communicative rationality' of pursuing 'mutual understanding and consensus among participants grounded in critical evaluation of unconstrained argumentation' (Alvesson and Willmott 1990: 59) and with the aim of 'emancipation'.

It should be noted that most critical analyses refer to the context of 'late-capitalistic, affluent society' (ibid. 61), and most specifically to Northern European industrial democracies.[6] They assume that there is no intrinsic conflict between the economic rationality of management and organizing action serving the substantive value of 'deep and lasting social and personal fulfilment'(ibid.). The extent to which such emancipatory aspirations are possible in late capitalism, and whether Habermas's theory of communicative action offers appropriate means to achieve them is an open debate. My critical arguments in this book are different. The empirical cases highlighted the existence of contexts where the economic rationality is confronted by other substantive rationalities, which have not received much attention in the management and information systems literature. Thus, I argue for a relativist perspective that recognizes the substantive rational underpinnings of different organizing regimes.

If we understand rationality in a substantive sense to refer to socially constructed, institutionally sedimented beliefs of what matters for the agents involved in organizing enactments and why, information systems innovation, bound to the economic

---

[6] Information systems publications with a critical tendency draw empirical evidence almost exclusively from advanced industrialized contexts. See e.g. Baskerville et al. 1994; Orlikowski et al. 1996. Notable exceptions are Walsham (1993) and some papers focusing on issues relevant to developing countries at the IFIP WG 9.4 conferences (such as Bidarkar, Madon, and Sahay 2000).

rationality of modern management, is an attempt to enforce a particular rationality over others in the organizational reform. Rationality contradictions are an inherent aspect of organizations, which, however, in periods of stability are effectively kept under control through institutionalization.[7] In other words, stable regimes of truth are formed, entailing certain values, of certain social structures, and of certain missions and certain ways of attaining them as the dominant mode of rationality. At times of reform such stabilizing effects of institutions are disturbed and institutional confrontations emerge: the nation state vs. the free market; locally meaningful tacit regimes of truth vs. modern technology-based information systems; family associated, craft-based economic activity vs. technically organized market competition; technical scientific rationality and professional responsibility vs. economic rationalization.

In the small enterprises of Cyprus a main clash occurred at the individual level, as the life conditions of the entrepreneurs were challenged by the required rational economic behaviour of the industrial restructuring experiment. Several other clashes of rationality are discernible in the case. Notable is the clash between the role of the state implicit in the industrial model intended to promote international competition and the role of the Cypriot government. The delay of the government to launch the initiatives prescribed by the transformation model, its slow action to embrace and entrust ICT and marshal information resources indicate a more pervasive reluctance to substitute the hand of the free market for the protective hand of the state.

Nevertheless, it was the entrepreneurs that were meant to be the protagonists in the flexible specialization reform and it seems to me it is their action—or lack of— that was crucial in this case and merits more careful study. They were unable to appreciate the rationalizing benefits of ICT—efficiency in organizing production, infrastructure for a new basis of collaboration and competition in the local market, necessary means for entering international markets. This is not a matter of lack of awareness, information about the potential of ICT, and training. The firms' owners kept a distance from the formal rationality of management because they could not trust ICT and professional managers as allies that could lead them to more fulfilling life conditions. The problematization that sought to entrust the survival of enterprises to a network of foreign customers, foreign competitors, the invisible hand of the market, professional management, ICT and a new (still unknown) type of government agency were not convincing. To be sure the firms owners were aware of the looming risk of declining local demand and bankruptcy. But they continued to place their trust on the familiar network they had improvised to overcome the earlier catastrophe of the war: the local customers, the family, the government, the local

---

[7] The contradictions of substantive rationality that are of interest here are a consequence of structural contradictions, and not contradictions of logic often manifested as unintended consequences of rational action, discussed by Giddens (1984). Giddens argues that structural contradiction—defined as opposition of structural principles, such that each depends upon the other and yet negates the other—is a constitutive aspect of modern societies. He points out the contradictory form of the capitalist state that involves both private appropriation and 'socialized production', e.g. public services such as transport and health care. Giddens's analysis points out that the particular conciliations of substantive rationalities harboured in modern societies are maintained through contradictory institutional mechanisms.

competitors whose limitations and tactics they knew, their craft of furniture making that they could organize utilizing their own capability.

The fact that ICT entered the organizational field of furniture manufacturing as the carrier of efficiency and a constituent part of formal management and was rejected for that reason, is significant not only for the failure of the attempted reform but also for the future networking of the local furniture manufacturing and ICT. The long-term limitations are not so much the consequences of a lost opportunity but the stifling of the imagination as far as the potential of this technology is concerned. There was no cultivation of the newcomer technologies, no strategic vision for partnership with the technology and through the technology with the global economic sectors. As I discussed in Chapter 7, there may well be other processes under way through which ICT and reform may enter the organizational field of these firms. In the near future, ICT may enter by means of the formal education of the successors to the entrepreneurs who resisted it in the 1980s and 1990s. It may take a more flexible form, such as Internet and email, and decouple itself from formal management. Meanwhile management too may become more acceptable, through local professional networks and local improvisations. But if a favourable situation is created by some combination of social forces, the rationalities at stake will be very different from those in the case discussed. The point is that in the particular *milieu* of the small firm owners in the 1980s and 1990s ICT was not considered a credible and reliable ally in their struggle to improve the chances for the survival of their business.

In the case of IKA a different set of clashing rationalities are discernible amidst the political and socio-economic processes in Greece in the last two decades of the twentieth century. From being the means to handle massive bureaucratic operations—indeed having become as awkward as the surrounding organization—ICT was expected to play a different role, to serve the modernization aspirations of the Greek society. My analysis in Chapter 6 sought to explain that, as far as the transformation of IKA is concerned, 'modernization' conveyed different rationalities at different periods of the two decades examined in the case study. The potential modernizing effects of ICT innovation have been repeatedly suppressed by forces maintaining the traditional role of state administration as a political employer.

In the information projects of the early 1980s there was an orientation for political intervention that aspired—in rhetoric and in strategic plans, but also in the imagination of large numbers of Greeks—to eliminate the political and social problems at the root of public sector dysfunctionality. As, under broader pressures, the socialist reformist rationality of the government of that period was in essence abandoned, commitment to the reform of IKA fell short of what was required, and the clash of missions that had been the root of the dysfunctionalities intensified rather than being eliminated. In that process, the managerial rationality was largely irrelevant and information systems innovation lost its *raison d'être*. In the second instance—the initiatives of technology-driven operational change of the 1990s—an ideological direction towards management in running business and state administration alike was more visible in the country. But there continued to be a great degree of ambivalence in the Greek society regarding modernization. Conflicts of rationality in the broader context continued to be responsible for the delays and setbacks of the ICT-induced organizational transformation of IKA. Due to mistrust towards the modernizing rationality ICT was assimilated into the bureaucracy, which consequently deprived the organization of effective means to act as an institution of a modern economy, thus perpetuating the mistrust towards modern institutions.

In Pemex, ICT was entangled in the struggle between modernization in the sense of economic liberalization and established organizational practices legitimated through the company's historical mission for national development. The case shows that inasmuch as the developmental mission continues to be a valid concern for key actors, such as politicians, Mexican citizens, and even the top echelons of management in Pemex, information systems innovation cannot bring the strategic business benefits generally associated with them. ICT is mobilized in an ambiguous and controversial translation. Consider, for example, the position of managers in the production plants of Pemex away from the headquarters in Mexico City. Despite all the market orientation of Pemex since the late 1980s, they continued to see the company as more than a profit-making organization. Pemex was a company with a mission for the production of oil or gas and petrochemicals, oilmen's livelihood, and indirectly, but always validly, the development of the more outlying Mexican communities, Those men had local political power, they knew how to work with local workers to carry through hard engineering tasks. How could their visions, actions, and sense of what is 'rational' be catered for by the integrated information systems? Their own strategic visions were remote from the information systems strategies that were deployed in translating Pemex to a free market actor.

These three cases may give the impression that clashes of rationality in information systems innovation are a 'problem' of traditional societies, where modern institutions confront pre-modern ones. The fourth case examined in this book suggests otherwise. Contradictory rationalities do not occur only where the modern meets the traditional. Modern societies have not become single-dimensional in terms of the values they foster. Information systems innovation is implicated in surfacing conflicts associated with the rationality contradictions of modern society. The study of drug utilization systems in different countries manifests three rationalities complementing—and contradicting—each other in the different institutionalized arrangements of national health care contexts.

In an abstract schematic form, the first sees health care as a public service. Public accountability of professional actors and a fair share of services to citizens are two of its driving principles. Drug utilization systems are useful resources for monitoring the fair and correct availability of a powerful medical technology, keeping prescribers and dispensers accountable, keeping control of an expensive technology under conditions of scarce economic resources. The second sees health care as the domain of professional practice of medical and pharmacy sciences. Scientifically competent professionals exercise their judgement about the best medical interventions for the benefit of their patients, pragmatically under economic constraints. Drug utilization systems can play an important role as means of research, monitoring the effects of medical drugs on a large population. Also they can inscribe and distribute the latest research results to all practising doctors, nurses, and chemists. Moreover they can inform them about the economic options or restrictions. The third rationality is based on the premiss that health care is a service that can be efficiently delivered through market forces. A plethora of activities—devising insurance arrangements, delivering medical professional services, producing and distributing pharmaceutical products—are linked in complex networks to make available an ever-increasing range of powerful drugs. Drug utilization systems can be mobilized to perform many different roles according to this rationality: to spot market opportunities for the production and distribution of new drugs, to make optimal decisions for choosing which drug to use, to make mutually beneficial alliances between those who pay for the drugs and those who produce or distribute them, as well as to support research and inform the decisions of practising doctors and pharmacists.

In conditions of pervasive uneasiness about health care services in both Europe and the United States the inherent limitations and contradictions of these three rationalities are experienced in very different ways, as their historically achieved balance is de-institutionalized and new combinations are attempted. Some contexts have been more conducive to innovation in drug utilization information systems infrastructures. But this is a clear case where more—or 'more strategic'—innovation is not considered a priori better in a substantive sense of what is valued in the context concerned. Few health policy experts and medical professionals in the United Kingdom feel that the creativity in the arena of the American DUR systems is appropriate for the reforming NHS. The penetration of managerial rationality is subject to local institutional conditions too: managed care has different meanings in different countries, partly reflecting different combinations of the three rationalities outlined above. Thus, a main difference between the drug utilization case with the other three in this book is that innovation in the drug utilization information area in the countries examined is pursued with more confidence to the situatedness of health care service, rather than by mimesis of what is considered universally advanced.

To sum up, the cases studied here indicate that the diversity of organizational settings harbours multiple rationalities, and that information systems innovation brings to the fore various rationality contradictions. They also show that information systems innovation in close alignment with management is so biased towards economic rationality and the dominant perception of rational economic behaviour that it is often unable to perceive, let alone to address, the rationality contradictions manifested in the context where it takes place.

THE LAYERED AND OVERLAPPING CONTEXTS OF GLOBALIZATION

If, as my studies suggest, the diversity observed in situated analyses of information systems innovation stems from context-specific substantive rationalities, which through power relations have been sedimented in specific organizing regimes, the delineation of the contexts that gave rise to and sustain these rationalities acquires crucial significance. It is insufficient to account only for the internal processes that led to and shaped an information systems innovation case, because such an account misses important influences stemming from outside the organization. To begin with, an information systems innovation process cannot be adequately understood without opening the researcher's and the practitioner's scope beyond the microcosm of the immediate technology-user's interaction with an organization. But how to take the vast 'outside' into account? Unlike the localized 'inside', the 'outside' is as large as global and as multifaceted as the current literature of globalization discussed in Chapter 4 indicates. It cannot be studied ethnographically, while any general theoretical conceptualizations run the risk of being too abstract, too thin, or deterministic.

In Part I, I suggested two overlapping structures of context: institutional and geographic. The institutional structure of context builds on the perception that clusters of 'outsiders'—such as an organization's industry, the information systems industry, the government, the financial system—form an institutional field that exerts influences on an organization's information systems innovation process. Because many organizations are engaged in multifaceted activities and have multiple different institutional interactions, it may be more appropriate to consider information systems processes situated at the intersection of multiple institutional fields, rather than in a single, excessively complex organizational field.[8] The geographic structure of context points to the study of processes across boundaries of geographic regions and across layers of geographically deployed institutions. An organization's location can be seen as nested in national, regional, and globally extending contexts, each being a source of distinct influences.[9] Combining the institutional and geographic structures of context, information systems innovation is situated at the intersection of institutional fields spanning a variable number of geographic contexts. In this scheme it is important to recognize also the existence of disembedded institutions, the most important of which in information systems innovation are ICT and management. Such institutions comprise action whose rationality and legitimacy are constructed through opportunistic links to specific geographical locations and maintained by ultra-mobile social actors.

The context of information systems innovation in IKA is relatively simple. Being part of the Greek public administration, IKA's information systems projects were directly dependent on the actions, decisions, and norms of a network of public or semi-public organizations: the supervising ministries, the inter-organizational computer centre KHYKY. But these are only the institutions with a formal organizational presence. Confining analysis to the influences of these organizations traces only the movements of the puppets, unable to follow the institutions that compel the movements: Greek politics, the economy, family. As I argued in Chapter 6, it is impossible to explain how the IKA/KHYKY employees managed to turn generations of

[8] Situating an organization in more than one organizational field can account for contradictory influences on information systems innovation, overcoming the oversimplifying notion of isomorphism.
[9] I have not considered 'virtual' organizations in this book, but they too are subject to geographic influences, inasmuch as they involve material elements, such as people and transactions of physical commodities, and are subject to geographically delineated institutions, such as national or international law.

computer-based information systems to grossly dysfunctional operations without taking into account how their employment was shaped through history by the combination of these institutions of Greek society. By the same token it is not possible to have a realistic view of the feasibility of new innovation initiatives to serve modernization objectives without assessing the meaning of modernization in the political, economic, and cultural institutions of the country, and the conflicts it raises in the Greek society.

But even in an organization rigidly nested in such an entrenched organizational field, the forces shaping information systems innovation are not confined to the national institutional arena. Three sources of influence are clear in IKA's computerization story.[10]

(1) The social security institutions of the European countries, whose operations and information systems infrastructures set a measure of what the operations of a 'modern' social security should be like, and what technology can do.

(2) The European Union, which reinforced the modernizing political forces, repeatedly adding their concerns about the inefficiency of Greek public sector organizations. It also coerced with legal conditions—such as setting limits to public sector expenditure in order to accept Greece in the European monetary union—and intervened with funding of public management reform and computerization programmes.

(3) The international ICT professional practice. Local professionals follow disembedded best practice norms, and in the 1990s foreign consultancy firms were called to play a leading role in IKA's computerization projects.

In the contradictions, ambiguities, and anxieties formed by the meeting of these three powerful extra-national institutions within the national organizational field sketched above, the organizational reform of IKA and its information systems innovation process remained precarious at the end of the period of the case study.

Pemex, too, demonstrates the formation of an information systems innovation context by the interaction of national and international institutions. Moreover, as was discussed at length in Chapter 5, this case study shows how the intersection of multiple local and broader contexts changed over time. Between the first efforts to overcome bureaucratic inefficiencies with computers and the implementation of integrated information systems in the 1990s the context of information systems innovation changed dramatically. What was mainly an indigenous struggle of engineers, bureaucrats, trade unions, and politicians, with technology transfer from abroad and the mimetic influences of international computer applications became an arena of Mexican, foreign national, international, and disembedded political, economic, and professional institutions. In the 1990s information systems innovation can be understood as contested at the intersection of two institutional fields. The

---

[10] It is possible to trace more indirect international institutional influences, such as those of the global economy on the Greek economy, or of the international media on the views of the Greek society of what is 'modern'. How far an analysis goes in considering institutional influences is of course a matter of an analyst's judgement. The accounts of the more immediate actors in the innovation process—in this case IKA's employees and directors, and Greek studies on public sector reform—provide a good indication of the forces more directly implicated.

first comprises institutions nurtured by the country's history: the government, the oilmen's trade unions, the local consumers of oil products, the local intelligentsia and elite classes contesting powerful positions in the country's economy, the country's felt obligation for the development of its 'poor'. The second is a combination of institutions crossing national borders: the international oil industry, the international banks and financial institutions to which Pemex is indebted, the US market, the international ICT software market and consultancy industry, the local modernizing forces of business management professionals and information systems professionals. The latter put forward clear challenges and visions for action. The former exerted mostly apologetic, defensive, and tacit reaction.

In the attempted flexible specialization reform of the manufacturing industry of Cyprus, information systems innovation was proposed and attempted at several locations: the small producer firms, the consortia, the government agencies. Each of them operated in particular local circumstances. For example, the network of actors directly involved in determining the functionality of the systems was different in each case. In the small firms, they comprised the entrepreneurs, their administrators, and external ICT vendors. In the consortia, the main actors were the professional managers, producer firm owners, and ICT vendors. In the government agencies, they were the civil servants and professional ICT experts and vendors. Nevertheless, they shared significant common contextual influences. The Cypriot socio economic institutions can be seen as a major common, nationally bounded organizational field. Among others, it comprised the island's furniture manufacturing industry and its customers, the government, the families, the financial system, the education system that produced professional skills as well as substantive values. Collectively, it reproduced a network of relations of power, and maintained particular substantive rationalities as a local regime of truth that conditioned perceptions of value of business, the roles of government, the entrepreneur, the manager. But it attached little value to ICT-mediated forms of management practice.

Another institutional field is discernible by tracing the institutions that came together to initiate the flexible specialization translation effort. It comprised the international free market economy, the European Union demanding the lifting of the protective economic regime of the island to accept it as a member, the international academic systems masterminding and keen to test industrial development models, the UN agencies interested to assist Cyprus's economic development. Also, it involved the institutions of international ICT, and the international management practice determining what technologies and information processes a modern company should possess. The institutions that exerted the flexible specialization reform influences were foreign regional (such as the EU), global (such as the UN), the international economy, the academia of economics, and global disembedded, such as the standards of ICT and management, the creation of which is more difficult to pinpoint to concrete organizational actors.

The study of drug utilization systems leads us more directly to consider the context of information systems innovation as an organizational field. The immediate organizational setting of most such systems is not a single organization but a cluster of organizations and institutions making a health care system. At first glance drug utilization systems demonstrate how different the context of a category of systems can be from one country to another. Nevertheless, it would be a mistake to underestimate the extra-national institutional forces. For example, regulations and legislation from international centres such as the WHO and the EU have been important in determining what should be monitored in the use of drugs, and what degrees of freedom the pharmaceutical industry has to influence the marketing and use of their products. The emergence of managed care as a legitimate way to weigh considerations of medical efficacy and cost, and the concomitant development of a new category of health management professionals has been a major source of ideas for information systems monitoring and controlling the prescribing of drugs. Finally, medical and pharmacy sciences are major disembedded institutions, claiming universal knowledge regarding diseases, health and therapy, albeit, as argued in Chapter 8, the way these sciences are put into professional practice undergoes further institutionalization by national health care systems.

To summarize, the argument here is that the contradictory rationalities implicated in these case studies can make sense by considering the innovation efforts as situated at the context formed under multiple institutional influences. Imposing universal a-contextual assumptions of rational decisions and actions regarding information systems innovation condemns any case that does not fit the assumptions as irrational. It confuses and frustrates efforts to mobilize the powerful ICT in locally meaningful information systems translations, thus perpetuating a grossly uneven state of globalization. On the other hand, focusing too narrowly on the 'event in its setting' is myopic, unable to see where the forces shaping the local translations stem from. The challenge for information systems research and practice is to develop the ability to identify what makes innovation in the current diversity of organizational circumstances so unevenly effective.

FACING UP TO THE DIVERSITY OF GLOBALIZATION: IMPLICATIONS FOR INFORMATION SYSTEMS INNOVATION

In this book I analysed cases where the rationalizing role of the technologies of globalization was frustrated. I pointed out that information systems innovation practice, being institutionalized in alliance with modern management, is unable to detect and cope with the rationality conflicts often emerging at the intersection of multiple contexts that globalization creates. By so doing I sought to develop an analytical perspective capable of accounting for the pragmatics of information systems innovation, rather than to propose a preferred state of affairs. I assumed no particular quality of social order—whether democracy, emancipation, or economic development—as universally desirable. My analysis has been driven by suspicion of the homogenizing tendencies of globalization and concern about the destruction— not always 'creative'[11]—such a tendency triggers in various contexts.

---

[11] Here I have in mind Schumpeter's notion of creative destruction (Schumpeter 1934), which acknowledges that waves of technology innovation cause widespread havoc, but implies that ultimately the result is a boost to economic growth.

I must stress that exposing the dilemmas that faced the Cypriot entrepreneurs and their inability to accommodate and appropriate ICT does not imply the position that their resistance and inaction was endowed by wisdom. Observing the historical reasons for the inability of the public servants in IKA to be hospitable to ICT and their failure to appropriate it in a strategy fulfilling the declared mission of the social security institution does not imply the demeaning of the significance of the contradiction confronting the Greek society, namely its striving to participate in the global socio-economic order without effective modern public sector institutions. Highlighting the contradictions of the mission of Pemex as a historical cause anni-hilating ICT-driven rationalization is not meant to be a justification of dysfunctional bureaucratic organizing. Tracing the roots of the caution or hyperactivity in the way ICT is applied in areas riddled by unreconciled rationalities, such as in drug utilization innovation, does not imply indifference to the role ICT plays in the drug therapy.

I am aware that exposing the ineffectiveness of ICT to contribute to the realization of an optimistic vision of globalization without proposing an alternative universal ideal or solution to the problems revealed, risks being seen as too negative to be of any use. The last section addresses such criticisms and spells out consequences of the theoretical stance formed in this book for research and practice. First, I return to the issue of relativism that was repeatedly raised in Part I, to explain that highlighting the diversity of rationalities involved in the dynamics of globalizing the technologies of globalization does not imply a nihilistic attitude towards this process. Lastly, I draw the implications of recognizing diversity, as understood in this book to be a matter of different substantive rationalities, for professional practice.

Relativism in the Global Context

Inasmuch as the dominant discourse in contemporary globalization is economic globalism, homogenization is a widespread perception associated with the technolo-gies implicated in globalization processes. There are two interrelated aspects of homogenization associated with information systems innovation: perceived outcomes and professional interventions. The information systems literature has contributed to the homogenization perception with general associations of technical potential and their economic 'impact'. Information systems professionals are trained to con-sider their professional interventions primarily as enablers of efficiency, competitive advantage, or the emergence of organizational forms suitable for the new global economy, such as the 'knowledge organization'. As a professional field, information systems has devoted most of its attention to developing universalist know-how and competencies, closely associated with an economistic, under-socialized view of organizations and management. To the extent information systems professionals are sensitized to the social consequences of information systems interventions, they tend to aspire to universal ideals such as emancipation or employee empowerment.

But, globalism is an impoverished view of globalization, and universal social ideals are often insensitive to the substantive values and situated concerns of various communities.[12] Information systems research and practice have not developed the

---

[12] A good example of this is the friction among different countries regarding privacy law and copyright law.

capacity to comprehend the complexity of negotiations of the role of ICT in different organizational contexts. At present, the homogenizing orientation of the information systems academic field and profession contributes to a grossly uneven socio-economic order. As part of the institutional forces of ICT, information systems academics and professionals share responsibility for the failure of the technologies of globalization to produce positive economic effects for those who need it more desperately, that is, organizations of non-advanced industrialized Western contexts.

The most significant intellectual break from the homogenizing approach of information systems research and practice is made in research that is based on the premiss of the situated nature of human action. Such research, and concomitant direction for professional practice, marks a departure from the technology deterministic, undersocialized economistic attitude of mainstream information systems of the 1980s and 1990s. It enriches the perception of information systems by revealing processes of improvisation, power conflicts, and local meaning making. In short, it provides a way to address information systems innovation without a preconceived general view of what benefits an organization stands to achieve from information systems innovation and how. Yet, it should not be assumed that information systems researchers have no preconceived views about ICT and the conduct of information systems innovation processes. On the contrary, they should be understood as interested parties in a heavily political domain of human action. The difference from the universalist approach is that the situated study of information allows for the perception of local social structures and processes implicated in the making and remaking of human and technology ensembles.

Still, as I argued in the previous section, plunging into the diverse information systems innovation settings exposes the dynamics of their microcosm, but it does not necessarily reveal their meaning. And while the predisposition to respect otherness and celebrate diversity as a condition of globalization is undoubtedly morally valid and pragmatically promising, it leaves crucial questions on the enactment of the technologies of globalization untouched. For, unless information systems research contributes to the understanding of the roots and the significance of the peculiarities of the situated ICT innovation, information systems 'experts' are ad hoc arbiters of apparently idiosyncratic power struggles. Striving to address local power dynamics they remain spectators of the prolonged frustration of the globalization of ICTs.

The research I presented in this book suggests that understanding the dynamics of the diffusion of the technologies that are capable of shrinking time and space requires analytical decompression of the time and space of innovation instances. It requires understanding of the history of events that gave rise to the problematization to which an information systems innovation is a response. Moreover it requires linking the local actions for the formation of an ensemble of machines, techniques, and users with larger processes in their environment.

What could such research be aiming to achieve? What is a valid role for information systems research vis-à-vis globalization? A frequently heard self-criticism of information systems research is that is has not been able to predict the major stages of the revolutionary advent of ICTs and has not been able to put forward a vision of the ICT-mediated future to guide innovative action. But an expectation that theory can predict the course of innovation and guide it towards a preconceived desirable state assumes a deterministic view of history and instrumental view of technology which is theoretically untenable and empirically unjustified. Information systems research can neither predict the future of globalization, nor design it.

Instead, information systems research can contribute as a reflexive participant of the globalization process, by observing and explaining the action, preferences, and resistances of the various actors encountered at the intersection of multiple institutions. This view converges with Bauman's concept of the social scientist as a translator of cultural traditions. In what he calls the postmodern challenge of the exposure of 'plural forms of life and plural versions of truth' (Bauman 1988: 140), Bauman argues convincingly against knowledge legislating what is right. Instead, the problem that needs to be addressed is communication across traditions. As information systems research exposes subjugated rationalities and challenges to entrenched regimes of truth, the communication Bauman refers to may not be realistically addressed by the notion of Habermas's 'ideal communicative action'. A better metaphor is Latour's perception of the social sciences as aiming at the revealing of 'objections' to the representations which guide social action (Latour 2000). This should be understood to include not only the loud voices of opposition, but also the reluctances and fears which, although most often hidden and latent, ultimately may be powerful enough to distort even benign initiatives triggered by the forces of globalization. Information systems research has a significant role to play in understanding the origins of the ideologies/rationalities carried out by the institutional forces meeting at the point that constitutes the circumstances of an innovation instance, the information systems project.

Information Systems Innovation Praxis

The main conclusion from the study of diversity confronting information systems innovation regarding professional practice is that the role of the 'expert' that develops the means to achieve desirable ends is unrealistic, for two reasons. First, the desirability of the ends is not determinable either theoretically or as the result of methodical planning. Theoretical claims for universally desirable gains associated with information systems, such as productivity or competitive advantage, are expressions of currently dominant, but not necessarily universally equally meaningful, values. Moreover, innovation in arenas of interaction of multiple institutional fields stirs up the quest for the new, challenges organizing regimes that keep in balance structural contradictions, and cannot be pre-empted by universally desirable objectives or preconceived plans. Second, ICT is not an instrument to fulfil the mythical 'user requirements', in whatever way they have been determined, it is an institutional force contesting for its own development and more often than not conveying what requirements users should have.

Building on the notion of autonomy, a more valid concept for the practice of information systems innovation is as praxis in the sense of the 'doing in which the other or others are intended as autonomous beings considered as the agents of the development of their own autonomy' (Castoriadis 1987: 77). Autonomy, Castoriadis explains, points to the relation of the agency with the institutions of society. In this sense, autonomy refers to a structurational relationship between agents and institutions: the autonomous agent is instituting society and is instituted by society.

As I argued in Chapters 1 and 2, information systems 'experts' are formed in and through an institution; they are embedded in a partly rational and partly symbolic professional domain. As agents in the praxis of information systems innovation they are not just free rational individuals but carriers of a number of assumptions about ICT and the way to go about developing and using ICT applications. And this is where, I think, the concept of autonomy is crucial. Being autonomous means that experts are engaged in the information systems innovations with certain assumptions and prior knowledge, but still capable of engaging with 'others' to address a situation by acknowledging its particularities: the relevant substantive rationalities, the pragmatics of the local regime of truth. Rather than treating the innovation context as an 'empty vessel' to be filled by their institutionalized knowledge,[13] information systems intermediaries need to be able to interact with 'others', learn, negotiate, and develop the institutionalized knowledge.

So far, the professionalization of information systems has not fostered the development of such a capacity of autonomy in its agents, the various categories of information systems experts. At present information systems professionals tend to be inflexible agents, unable to act autonomously in situations such as those discussed in the case studies of this book and to enrich the socialized professional information systems knowledge. Without such autonomy they perpetuate the alienation of the ICT institution from the 'others' whose rationality differs from their standardized knowledge.

The question that needs to be asked, therefore, is what lessons can be derived from this research on the current impediments for this kind of autonomous professional action. I will first discuss briefly the limiting effects of the legacy of methodical action for the construction of ICT artefacts that has been a contentious issue since the information systems discipline emerged as a field distinct from computer engineering. I will then turn to highlight what I presented in this book as an important limitation that has received too little attention in the information systems literature: the way information systems has been instituted as a discipline by unquestionably adopting the managerialist rationality.

Seeing professional information systems practice as praxis does not deny the validity of the role of the methodical construction of artefacts, where technique, abstraction, purposeful and skilful problem-solving activity are dominant modes of action. Such action can be thought of as bracketed enactment, contained in the socially constituted contexts discussed above. Whether in close proximity with 'users' (Kyng 1998), self-regulated as in the open source community of software programmers (Raymond 1999), or industrially organized as in the software industry (Cusumano

---

[13] The metaphor of the 'empty vessel' is used in Suchman (2000), drawing from Brigitte Jordan's work.

and Selby 1995), the continuous production of ICT artefacts is a constituent component of the institution of ICT. Each of the professional categories of analysts, programmers, designers has their own mix of technical/rational skills, legitimation conventions, and tacit capacities to compensate for the limitations of their techniques and see tasks through in an inherently unstructured domain of action. Nevertheless, some cautionary remarks on these 'technical' tasks are appropriate here. As indeed is well known in the information systems literature, technical know-how alone is not capable of determining information systems innovation. Technical experts should not imagine that their partial knowledge is capable of determining desirable futures for the 'others' involved in the innovation process, and that their partially rational techniques are capable of mobilizing translations to that end. The other side of this position, that enlightened designers can build emancipating technologies for users by certain ways of staging of the innovation process, for example via participatory design, is often naively misguided, not recognizing the autonomy of the 'other'. Participation of intended users who are suspicious of the innovation intentions, uninterested, complacent, or unconvinced of their ability to make a difference by actively pursuing their interests can easily add to demoralization or become manipulative.

Finally, the close association of information systems professional practice with management has created a homogenizing tendency and stifled ability to address the circumstances of the diverse organizing regimes of the global condition. In other words, it has limited unduly the praxis of information systems in the sense defined above. A narrow perception regarding organizing activities that best serve the economic imperatives has resulted in an inflexible body of knowledge on the mobilization of ICT.

The decoupling of information systems from the dominant institution of management requires the development of an alternative set of capabilities, oriented towards comprehending the multiple dimensions of the unfolding phenomena of globalization. The preconceived under-socialized perception of globalization restricted to the spread of some of the mechanisms of the free market economy that emerged in the advanced Western industrialized societies is inadequate to that end. Contextualist situated analysis has been proposed here as a cognitive platform for professional participation in the praxis of information systems innovation. Information systems education needs to change accordingly, creating skills for a professional engagement with diverse substantive rationalities.

A crucial question however is whether such institutional change is feasible. In principle, institutions do change by their reflexive agents. But one has to consider the vested interests and the power gained by information systems professionals through their alliance with such a powerful institution as management. To a large extent this is a manifestation of the major political issue of globalization itself: there are too powerful vested interests promoting globalization as globalism. In the West at least the economistic rationality of management makes information systems an exciting specialist area fuelled by the rational myth of pushing the frontiers of wealth creation and power gains.

Yet, to consider it utopian that the institution of information systems can reorient itself towards a more reflexive practice guided by a pluralistic perception of globalization betrays the continuing influence of the under-socialized view. Hints about the possibility of change can be drawn from the optimistic literature of globalization, which shows confidence that society is capable of avoiding succumbing to globalism. Closer to home, the information systems field itself has intellectual resources to challenge the dominant tendencies in its institutionalized practice. Being at the frontier of the globalization process by virtue of the technical knowledge for the deployment of its most central mechanism may turn out to be a more powerful professional position than following the legacy of management, another powerful institution. In facing up to the diversity of globalization, the challenge for the information systems field, as research and practice, is to develop the capacity to respond to the plurality of the human condition. The risk entailed in failing to do so is becoming intermediaries in the perpetuation of a grossly uneven world.

References

Alvesson, M., and Deetz, S. (2000). *Doing Critical Management Research*. London: Sage.
—— and Willmott, H. (1990). 'Critical Theory and the Sciences of Management', in Ph. v. Engeldorp Gastelaars, Sl. Magala, and O. Preub (eds.), *Critical Theory and the Science of Management*. Rotterdam: Universitaire Pers Rotterdam, 23–74.
—— —— (eds.) (1992). *Critical Management Studies*. London: Sage.
Avgerou, C. (1989). 'Information Systems in Social Administration: Factors Affecting their Success'. Ph. D. thesis, Information Systems Department, London School of Economics.
Baskerville, R., Smithson, S., Ngwenyama, O., and DeGross, J. I. (eds.) (1994). *Transforming Organizations with Information Technology*. Amsterdam: North-Holland.
Bauman, Z. (1988). *Legislators and Interpreters*. Cambridge: Polity Press.
Bidarkar, S., Madon, S., and Sahay, S. (2000). Indigenous information systems and empowerment of slum dwellers in Bangalore, in S. Sahay (ed), The proceedings of the IFIP WG 9.4 conference Information Flows, Local Improvisations and Work Practices, Cape Town, 23–26 May.
Bowker, G. C., and Leigh Star, S. (2000). *Sorting Things Out: Classification and its Consequences*. Cambridge, Mass.: MIT Press.
Castoriadis, C. (1987). *The Imaginary Institution of Society*. Cambridge: Polity Press.
Ciborra, C. U. (1999). 'A Theory of Information Systems Based on Improvisation', in W. L. Currie and B. Galliers (eds.), *Rethinking Management Information Systems*. Oxford: Oxford University Press, 136–55.
—— (2000). 'A Critical Review of the Literature on the Management of Corporate Information Infrastructure', in C. U. Ciborra and associates, *From Control to Drift*. Oxford: Oxford University Press, 15–40.
Cusumano, M. A., and Selby, R. W. (1995). *Microsoft Secrets: How the World's Most Powerful Software Company Creates Technology, Shapes Markets, and Manages People*. New York: Free Press.
Engeldorp Gastelaars, Ph. v., Magala, Sl. and Preub, O. (eds.) (1990). *Critical Theory and the Science of Management*. Rotterdam: Universitaire Pers Rotterdam.

Giddens, A. (1984). *The Constitution of Society: Outline of the Theory of Structuration.* Cambridge: Polity Press.

Hirschheim, R., Klein, H. K., and Lyytinen, K. (1996). 'Exploring the Intellectual Structures of Information Systems Development: A Social Action Theoretical Analysis'. *Accounting, Management & Information Technology,* 6(1/2): 1–63.

Keen, P. G. W. (1981). 'Information Systems and Organizational Change'. *Communications of the ACM* 24(1): 24–33.

Knights, D., and Morgan, G. (1991). 'Corporate Strategy, Organizations, and Subjectivity: A Critique'. *Organization Studies,* 12: 251–73.

—— Noble, F., and Willmott, H. (1997). '"We should be total slaves to the business": Aligning Information Technology Strategy—Issues and Evidence', in B. P. Bloomfield, R. Coombs, D. Knights, and D. Littler (eds.), *Information Technology and Organizations.* Oxford: Oxford University Press, 13–35.

Kyng, M. (1998). 'Users and Computers: A Contextual Approach to Design of Computer Artifacts'. *Scandinavian Journal of Information Systems,* 10(1–2): 7–44.

Latour, B. (2000). 'When Things Strike Back—A Possible Contribution of "Science Studies" to the Social Sciences'. *British Journal of Sociology,* 51(1): 107–23.

Lyytinen, K. (1992). 'Information Systems and Critical Theory', in M. Alversson and H. Willmott (eds.), *Critical Management Studies.* London: Sage, 159–80.

—— and Hirschheim, R. (1987). 'Information Systems Failures; A Survey and Classification of the Empirical Literature'. *Oxford Surveys in Information Technology,* 4: 257–309.

Markus, M. L. (1983). 'Power, Politics and MIS Implementation'. *Communications of the ACM* 26(6): 430–45.

Mitev, N. (1996). Social, organisational and political aspects of information systems failure: the computerised reservation system at French railways. 4th European Conference on Information Systems, Lisbon.

Mumford, E., Hirschheim, R., Fitzgerald, G., and Wood-Harper, A.T. (eds.) (1985). *Research Methods in Information Systems.* Amsterdam: North-Holland.

Myers, M. D. (1994). 'A Disaster for Everyone to See: An Interpretive Analysis of a Failed IS project'. *Accounting, Management and Information Technologies,* 4(4): 185–201.

Nissen, H.-E., Klein, H. K., and Hirschheim, R. (eds.) (1991). *Information Systems Research: Contemporary Approaches & Emergent Traditions.* Amsterdam: North-Holland.

Orlikowski, W. J. (1996). 'Improvising Organizational Transformation Over Time: A Situated Change Perspective'. *Information Systems Research,* 7(1): 63–92.

—— Walsham, G., Jones, M. R., and DeGross, J. I. (eds.) (1996). *Information Technology and Changes in Organizational Work.* London: Chapman & Hall.

Palvia, P. C., and Palvia, S. C. (1996). 'Understanding the Global Information Technology Environment: Representative World Issues', in P. C. Palvia, S. C. Palvia, and E. M. Roche, *Global Information Technology and Systems Management: Key Issues and Trends.* Nashua, NH: Ivy League, 3–30.

Raymond, E. S. (1999). *The Cathedral & the Bazaar.* Sebastopol, Calif.: O'Reilly.

Sandberg, Å. (1985). 'Socio-technical Design, Trade-Union Strategies and Action Research', in E. Mumford, R. Hirschheim, G. Fitzgerald, and A. T. Wood-Harper, *Research Methods in Information Systems.* Amsterdam: North-Holland, 79–92.

Sauer, C. (1999). 'Deciding the Future for IS Failures: Not the Choice You Might Think', in B. Galliers and W. L. Currie (eds.), *Rethinking Management Information Systems.* Oxford: Oxford University Press, 279–309.

Schumpeter, J. A. (1934). *The Theory of Economic Development*. Cambridge, Mass.: Harvard University Press.

Suchman, L. (2000). Practice-based design of information systems: notes from the hyper-developed world, in S. Sahay (ed), The proceedings of the IFIP WG 9.4 conference Information Flows, Local Improvisations, and Work Practices, Cape Town, 23–26 May.

Walsham, G. (1993). *Interpreting Information Systems in Organizations*. Chichester: John Wiley.

Appendix: Research Methodology

The case studies in this book have been constructed with varying combinations of primary and secondary data sources. The methods employed include the study of documentation available in the organizations involved in each case, relevant published material, interviews, and observations. Of central significance for my understanding of each case study have been the interviews with actors of the cases and observations at their sites, as these gave me the 'feeling' of the institutional aspects of each case. The extent to which these methods were used varies from hundreds of interviews and months of observation in the study of IKA to a few interviews and system demonstrations in the study of information systems for medical drug use.

In the case study of Chapter 5 the story of Pemex was traced through interviews with managers and IT specialists in Pemex, by documentation available in the company, and by searching secondary sources. The first substantial study was conducted in 1993, one year after the most significant transformation undertaken by the organization since its initial formation. At that time, an appointment to produce a 'diagnostic report' on the IS function in Pemex Gas, one of the new subsidiaries of the corporation, provided me with extensive material on the recent history of Pemex, its IS development efforts, and its culture. Data gathering lasted two weeks and involved group and individual interviews with the sub-directors and their management teams in all five divisions of Pemex Gas headquarters; the IT managers in the central IT department of the company and the five IT units of the company's sub-divisions; the management team in a production site outside the headquarters; the management team of an IT centre of another production site; the IT manager of the corporate headquarters of Pemex.

Interview sessions began with clarifying the objective of the study, and inviting the description of facts and opinions regarding the following areas: the organizational tasks and perceived mission pursued by each division of the company, their information systems and further information requirements, and how they were going about meeting such requirements. With the exception of one sub-director who was laconic and rather uncooperative, the study was generally welcome by the sub-directors. Introductory team sessions lasted at least two hours and were followed by subsequent interviews with employees that were identified as additional significant informants. A facilitator and interpreter prepared and mediated the interview sessions when there were language difficulties. Invariably, interviewees gave a historical account of the recent creation of their divisions or offices in order to provide the background that made their descriptions and views meaningful. Also, interviewees were reflexive, offering explanations about the subject of their description and their opinions, elaborating on the values and cultural aspects they considered significant either in the past or current affairs of the company. The validity of my understanding of the company's organizational aspects and IS issues was subsequently confirmed with a meeting where a colleague and I presented an outline of the main, although still not analysed, findings to a group of informants from all the sub-directions and centres.

Since that initial study the history of events was extended and updated through various sources. For the early part of the history of the successive administration, reform efforts, and computerization projects of the company, I relied mainly on the thorough research of a doctoral dissertation (Volkow, forthcoming) exploring the contextual nature of IS development.

Additional sources included interviews with directors and IT managers in the corporate headquarters and another subsidiary company, Pemex Refinery, as well as IT service contractors involved in Pemex projects. I had two additional data collection sessions with visits to Pemex in 1996 and 1999, during which the history of the company was updated. At those visits I held interviews with the directors responsible for planning and information resources and IT managers in Pemex Gas, and Pemex Exploration and Production, with IT managers in Pemex companies, and with IS services contractors.

For the case study in Chapter 6, I traced the story of IKA with four studies over a period of fifteen years. The first and most substantial study took place in 1983, with the opportunity of participating in an OECD-sponsored project that attempted to design effective task descriptions for the various units of the organization and to redistribute its human resources accordingly. My task in that project was to assess the existing information systems infrastructure of the organization and to make recommendations on further developments as required by the reorganization project. That first study lasted three months and involved data collection on the organization's formal and informal work processes, its computer services and systems development efforts. With enthusiastic support of the Director-General the project had unlimited access to the organization's documentation and staff. There was an air of optimism at the headquarters at that time, as many expected that chronic problems were about to be resolved. Most interviewees were keen to explain 'the way IKA works', its problematic computer services, earlier efforts for 'change', their concerns that this latest project might 'change nothing'. The study produced a large amount of material on the history of organizational change efforts in IKA, and the state of its information systems. I never got as far as making recommendations for information systems requirements, though. The Director-General was replaced by the Minister of Social Security; his modernization efforts had challenged deep-rooted traditions of civil service and caused a great deal of concern to influential political circles. The new Director-General, a traditionalist with no wish to upset the status quo in civil service structures, did not make the formal application required by the OECD for the continuation of the project following the completion of the first diagnostic phase.

The second study of IKA, in 1986, lasted nine days and involved interviews with IT managers in order to collect information on the organization's continuing information systems development efforts. There was no organizational reform effort under way in IKA at that time, but an ambitious computerization strategy was under way and some people at the headquarters believed it could have a significant impact on the efficiency and accountability of the organization. The third study, in 1993, focused on the launching of another IT strategy formulation effort, this time by employing subcontractors. It was again a time of optimism regarding information systems, as the organization was attempting to overcome its severely limited IS competence through outsourcing. Over a period of five months I followed the details of the outsourcing experience, the relationship between IKA and subcontractors and the resulting 'information systems master plan'. Finally, the latest information was gathered in 1997 and 1998, catching up with the continuing experience of IKA with outsourcing, not only of IS development, but operational reform as well.

The case study presented in Chapter 7, on the organizational restructuring of the furniture manufacturing sector in Cyprus according to the principles of flexible specialization draws heavily from the empirical material of a doctoral research (Chrysohos, 1999) conducted mostly in the period of 1993–6. In addition I visited Cyprus twice, in 1996 and 2000, and collected data through interviews with entrepreneurs, consortia managers, service providers, and government officials. This case involved an extensive study of documents and interviews in agencies that participated in the formulation and the implementation of the flexible specialization strategy of Cyprus. The empirical research effort was directed towards reconstructing the history and following up the formation, operations, and subsequent decline of flexible specialization agencies in the furniture manufacturing sector of Cyprus. Also, through interviews and study of relevant literature the research effort aimed at understanding the life circumstances of the entrepreneurs, their perceptions of business opportunities in the changing socio-economic context of Cyprus, and their perceptions of ICT.

The case study on drug utilization information systems in Chapter 8 owes its origin to a research project requested and funded by a large pharmaceutical corporation. That project examined the prospects of setting up in Europe the kind of large-scale drug utilization systems that have been developed in the United States. A confidentiality agreement prevents me from disclosing the identity of the corporation. However, this does not affect in any other way the presentation of the insights gained from the research that was conducted in that research. A research team was set up at the London School of Economics to make the comparison between the drug utilization systems in the United States and in Europe, and to examine how Europe can develop similar resources to those of the United States. Relevant data and understanding of the issues discussed in the case study continued after the completion of that research. The first data collection involved a combination of sources and methods. Data on the US systems were collected primarily from secondary sources, mainly publications and some unpublished industry reports. Data on information systems supporting various functions of drug use management in the context of Europe were collected both from secondary sources and through a series of interviews, system demonstrations, and participation in professional discussion groups on drug utilization.

In particular the history, functionality, and role (intended role in one case, as the system was still under development) of the two systems discussed in Chapter 8, OPADE and PACT, were traced with visits to the sites hosting them. Interviews were conducted with a core set of questions about the circumstances of the genesis of the development of systems, the information they collected, the output they produced, and their direct and indirect users. However, the interviews allowed for 'drifting' to issues that emerged as important to the perception of either the interviewer or the interviewee. In this way the data collection grew and took directions which were unforeseen at the outset of the research on this area. For example, in trying to trace the history and potential of the OPADE system development project, it emerged that the prospects of that system being fully operational were poor, because the data the system was intended to process were available in few European countries only. The research team, therefore, devoted interview time with the systems developers to understand their perceptions and experience of the particularities of drug data availability in different country contexts.

References

Chrysohos, N. (1999). 'Information Systems and Organizational Change: The Case of Flexible Specialisation in Cyprus'. Ph.D. thesis, Information Systems Department, London School of Economics.

Volkow, N.(forthcoming). 'Interaction between Organizational Change and IT Innovation: The Case Study of Petroleos Mexicanos'. Ph.D. thesis, Information Systems Department, London School of Economics.

Author Index

Author Index

General Index